THE KHMER ROUGE ACCOUNTABILITY PROCESS

EDITED BY
JOHN D. CIORCIARI
AND ANNE HEINDEL

WITH A FOREWORD BY
YOUK CHHANG

Documentation Series
No. 14 – Documentation
Center of Cambodia

ស្វែងរកការពិត ដើម្បីការចងចាំនិងយុត្តិធម៌

Searching for the Truth: Memory & Justice

មជ្ឈមណ្ឌលឯកសារកម្ពុជា

Documentation Center of Cambodia (DC-Cam)
P.O. Box 1110, 66 Sihanouk Boulevard, Phnom Penh, Cambodia
Tel.: + 855 (23) 211-875
Fax.: + 855 (23) 210-358
E-mail: dccam@online.com.kh
Website: www.dccam.org | www.cambodiatribunal.org

On Trial: The Khmer Rouge Accountability Process/ John D. Ciorciari and Anne Heindel
   1. Cambodia—Law—Human Rights
   2. Cambodia—Politics and Government
   3. Cambodia—History

Funding for this project was generously provided by the U.S. Agency for International Development (USAID) and Swedish International Development Agency (Sida).

The views expressed in this book are the points of view of the authors only.

Copyright © 2009 by the Documentation Center of Cambodia.
All rights reserved. No part of this book may be reproduced or utilized in any form or by any means, electronic or mechanical, including photocopying, recording, or any information storage and retrieval system, without permission in writing from the publisher.

Cover and Book Design
Artistic concept and photo selection © 2009 by Youk Chhang
Graphic design and layout © 2009 by Yvonne Wong

ISBN: 9789995060176

Printed in Cambodia

*This book is dedicated to the victims of Democratic Kampuchea
and to promoting a legal accountability process that will honor their memory and
provide their families with justice.*

Prosecutor, defense lawyer, and judge in traditional Khmer legal attire, painted by an unknown artist in the late 19th century.
The judge's crown inspired the folio image that appears above the page numbers throughout this book. Photo by Phat Piset.
Source: Ministry of Justice, Royal Government of Cambodia

Table of Contents

5	Acknowledgements
6	List of Acronyms and Key Terms
9	Foreword by Youk Chhang
13	Introduction by John D. Ciorciari
33	1. History and Politics Behind the Khmer Rouge Trials, *John D. Ciorciari*
85	2. Overview of the Extraordinary Chambers, *Anne Heindel*
125	3. Jurisprudence of the Extraordinary Chambers, *Anne Heindel*
172	4. Court Administration at the ECCC, *John A. Hall*
214	5. Including the Survivors in the Tribunal Process, *Sarah Thomas and Terith Chy*
294	6. The ECCC's Role in Reconciliation, *John D. Ciorciari and Sok-Kheang Ly*
348	About the Authors

ACKNOWLEDGEMENTS

This book examines the Extraordinary Chambers in the Courts of Cambodia (ECCC), often called the "Khmer Rouge Tribunal." We decided to prepare the book on the third anniversary of the ECCC's creation, because the tribunal was originally established with a three-year mandate and funding. We use this opportunity to take stock of the progress at the tribunal and to offer recommendations that we hope will be helpful as the process continues. We begin with an overview of the tribunal's history and features. We then assess its progress to date, focusing on its jurisprudence, administration, and engagement of survivors of the Pol Pot years. Finally, we comment on its role in the broader process of reconciliation. This volume is part of our longstanding effort at the Documentation Center of Cambodia (DC-Cam) to promote historical memory and justice in a country that has only begun to emerge from the torment of the Khmer Rouge tragedy.

In the course of preparing this volume, we benefitted from the opportunity to interact regularly with officials from the ECCC, the Royal Government of Cambodia, the Tuol Sleng Genocide Museum, supporting international states and organizations, non-governmental groups, and many ordinary survivors of Democratic Kampuchea. We are also grateful to a number of scholars and officials for their comments and insights. Dara Vanthan and Kosal Path provided useful guidance on issues in Chapters 1 and 2, and Joanna Geneve contributed to Chapter 3. Comments and insights from Tracey Gurd, Heather Ryan, Panhavuth Long, Douglas Gillison, Robbie Corey-Boulet, and Erika Kinetz helped prepare Chapter 4. George Cooper generously reviewed Chapter 5, and Craig Etcheson provided expert comments on Chapter 6. Elizabeth Do, Rehan Abeyratne and Spencer Cryder also helped edit the manuscript. Yvonne Wong designed the book and was invaluable in preparing it for publication. Any remaining errors are ours.

Lastly, we owe thanks to the Swedish International Development Agency and the U.S. Agency for International Development, which provided generous grants to make this project and many other activities at DC-Cam possible. We hope that the finished product justifies the generosity of our donors and the scholars and experts who assisted us. Above all, we hope it honors the victims and survivors of the Khmer Rouge tragedy.

John D. Ciorciari and Anne Heindel
September 2009

ASEAN	Association of Southeast Asian Nations
CGDK	Coalition Government of Democratic Kampuchea
CPK	Communist Party of Kampuchea
CPP	Cambodian People's Party
DC-Cam	Documentation Center of Cambodia
DK	Democratic Kampuchea
ECCC	Extraordinary Chambers in the Courts of Cambodia, also referred to as the "Khmer Rouge Tribunal"
ECCC Law	The law governing the ECCC, as promulgated by the Cambodian government in 2004, a precursor of which was promulgated in 2001 (the "2001 ECCC Law")
ECHR	European Court of Human Rights
Framework Agreement	The agreement reached between the United Nations and Royal Government of Cambodia regarding the parties' cooperation in connection with the Khmer Rouge Tribunal
FUNCINPEC	National United Front for an Independent, Neutral, Peaceful, and Cooperative Cambodia
HR	Human resources
HRM	Human resource management
ICC	International Criminal Court
ICCPR	International Covenant on Civil and Political Rights
ICTR	International Criminal Tribunal for Rwanda
ICTY	International Criminal Tribunal for the Former Yugoslavia
JCE	Joint criminal enterprise
KPRP	Kampuchean People's Revolutionary Party
NGO	Non-governmental organization
OA	Office of Administration (ECCC)
OAPR	Office of Audit and Performance Review (United Nations)
OCIJ	Office of the Co-Investigating Judges (ECCC)
OCP	Office of the Co-Prosecutors (ECCC)
OIOS	Office of Internal Oversight Services (United Nations)
OSJI	Open Society Justice Initiative
PRK	People's Republic of Kampuchea
PTC	Pre-Trial Chamber (ECCC)
RGC	Royal Government of Cambodia
SCSL	Special Court for Sierra Leone
SOL	Statute of Limitations
TRC	Truth and Reconciliation Commission
UN	United Nations
UNAKRT	United Nations Assistance to the Khmer Rouge Tribunal
UNDP	United Nations Development Program
UNTAC	United Nations Transitional Authority in Cambodia
VU	Victims Unit (ECCC)
WESU	Witnesses and Experts Support Unit (ECCC)

ON TRIAL: THE KHMER ROUGE ACCOUNTABILITY PROCESS

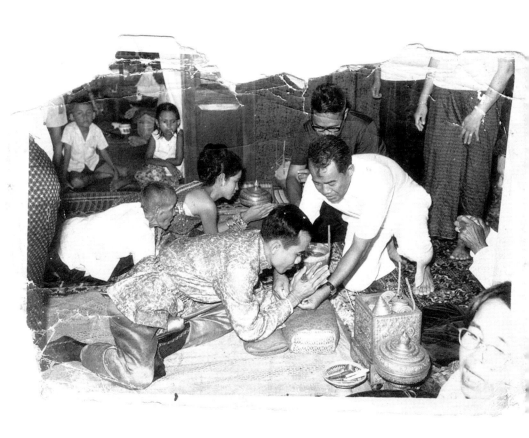

Wedding photograph of Youk Chhang's late sister, Keo Tithsorye (mentioned in the Foreword) and her husband Ong Sutharak, 1969. Chhang is the boy in the far left corner. The girl to the far right is his cousin, Keo Savary, who died of starvation during the Khmer Rouge period. The man in a white uniform is Chhang's neighbor, Chey En, a police commissioner in Kampong Cham province later executed by the Khmers Rouges. His wife, beside him, was also executed by DK cadres. The elderly woman behind the couple is Chhang's great grandmother, who passed away of old age. The man behind Chey En dressed in a dark gray uniform and wearing glasses is Chhang's uncle, Sakou Saphon, who was executed by the Khmer Rouge.
Source: Youk Chhang's Family Collection

FOREWORD

BY YOUK CHHANG

In 1975, my family was evacuated from our homes in Phnom Penh and sent to the countryside to be re-educated by the radical new Khmer Rouge regime. Like millions of others, we suffered terrible cruelty and deprivation. One day, my sister's husband found a cucumber that some Khmer Rouge cadres had discarded in the commune kitchen. He tried to take the cucumber to his family, but Khmer Rouge cadres caught him and beat him brutally. Left weak and unable to eat or drink, he died days later from his injuries and starvation. After his death, my sister became very ill and was unable to nurse her infant son. She begged other nursing women for breast milk to feed her son, but he passed away. The Khmer Rouge later killed my sister after they wrongfully accused her of stealing rice and cut open her stomach to prove it.

Thirty years later, my family is divided over whether putting Khmer Rouge leaders on trial will bring justice for the death of my sister and other family members. After the Democratic Kampuchea period, the chief of a village where some of my family members disappeared pedaled his bicycle to Phnom Penh to apologize to our family. He brought us bananas and meat as a sort of restitution. No one in the family accepted his apology except my mother, who said it was enough. Her attitude is a very Buddhist one, and his act put her heart to rest. She never wanted me to return to Cambodia and work toward a legal accounting for the crimes committed during Democratic Kampuchea, and she never understood why I did not remain in the United States. Over time, my mother has come to see the tribunal as a good thing, but she believes it will only be effective with the support of the international community.

My niece Theavy is the daughter of my deceased sister. She has a different view. She was only five or six years old when her parents died. She then watched her sister Thevin become gravely ill, screaming in pain until she passed away. Theavy eventually escaped to a refugee camp in Thailand and has lived most of her life in the United States. She once wrote me saying, "I don't believe that justice is enough for what had happened to my family. No justice in the world will bring my family back." She has never wanted to return or even visit surviving family members in Cambodia, believing that the reality of Cambodia today would be just an illusion to her.

I believe the tribunal is important and that we need prosecution before we can ever reach the point of true forgiveness. Justice has already been obtained to some degree: it was meted out at the local level in the 1980s, when people took the law into their own hands and killed many of the worst Khmer Rouge perpetrators. Successful trials will not so much bring justice to the victims as give people a perception that justice is possible in the future.

The larger Cambodian family, both at home and abroad, is also divided over the trials. This is because genocide has always been a political act, and always will be. After 30 years, people have largely moved beyond the need for personal revenge. They are concerned about how the trials will affect their futures and the future of their country, but they view justice from very different political perspectives.

SURVIVORS IN CAMBODIA

Survivors generally fall into two camps. The first includes survivors who support the tribunal. Most of them have never been out of the country and have decided that at least some of their future lies with the ruling Cambodian People's Party (CPP). They see the CPP as the party that liberated Cambodia from the Khmers Rouges and fought to bring the guerillas to heel in the 1990s when the international community was ignoring Cambodia. As evidence of their party's intent to broker honest trials, they point to the ranking CPP government officials who are former Khmers Rouges and have publicly stated their willingness to appear before the tribunal. They also note the inability of the United Nations (UN) to bring the Khmers Rouges to the ballot box in the 1992-93 national elections, thereby failing to institute the rule of law in Cambodia. This group distrusts the international community, and finds the UN at least partly at fault for the country's culture of impunity.

The second camp contains many people who returned from the Thai border camps in the 1990s. They are generally opposed to the government, and believe that national problems like poverty and corruption are linked directly to the CPP. They feel the trials will only serve to polish the ruling party's image. So, they are calling for more international control of the proceedings and would like to see certain CPP officials brought to trial, hoping to drag the current government into the fray.

CAMBODIAN EXPATRIATES

Cambodian survivors abroad are often highly politicized, and their views about the tribunal are also divided. Some support the government and are very vocal in their support of the tribunal. Some have even returned to Cambodia and become engaged in the accountability process, partly to improve their economic opportunities by gaining the favor of the ruling party.

Three other groups of expatriates oppose the trials. The first comprises the supporters of former King Norodom Sihanouk, who worry that he might be brought before the Extraordinary Chambers. (Some supporters of the king who live in Cambodia have similar fears). Like the king, they argue that the money dedicated to the trials would be better spent on alleviating poverty in Cambodia. A second group disfavoring the trials is made up of people opposed to the CPP for political reasons; some were able to obtain visas to third countries after the fall of Democratic Kampuchea by adopting a strong anti-communist stance, which they retain to this day (during the 1980s the CPP was closely associated with the Vietnamese Communist Party). The last is a small group of emigrants who were Khmer Rouge officers or cadres; they are simply afraid their former lives might be revealed.

THE NEXT GENERATION

While they are not highly politicized, the children of Democratic Kampuchea's survivors are a burgeoning part of the population, and their beliefs and expectations must be taken into account. This group is somewhat more cohesive and well as more nationalistic than their parents' generation. Most of them find it difficult to believe that Cambodians could have killed each other; thus, they feel that foreigners must have caused the genocide in their country. Some of them are curious to learn what happened but don't have what could be termed as a "political agenda." Others are much more interested in finding justice for the victims and look at the genocide in black and white terms: the Khmer Rouge were always bad and always will be. Both groups of young Cambodians, however, seem far better able to hold dialogues with each other than older adult survivors.

OPPORTUNITIES FOR THE ECCC

This book examines the background to the Extraordinary Chambers in the Courts of Cambodia (ECCC), offers opinions about its first three years of operations, and provides recommendations. The tribunal faces many challenges. Perhaps the most burning question is whether the government of Cambodia and the United Nations—both of which have indirectly supported the Khmer Rouge in the past (the government by granting amnesties in return for peace during the 1990s and the United Nations by allowing the Khmers Rouges to hold their seat at the United Nations for ten years)—can find a solution that helps each of the disparate parties find hope for the future through the tribunal.

Both the Royal Government of Cambodia and UN have arguments for doing what they did, but in the eyes of the survivors and the generation of Cambodians under the age of 25, they have much to account for. Ironically, the tribunal presents a great opportunity for both to gain trust and respect in Cambodia. If the government is perceived as open and fair, the resulting public trust would allow it to move forward with its policy agenda. Similar actions on the part of the UN would produce both popular and government support for its activities in Cambodia. Such a visible success would also allow it to further its agenda of preventing, intervening, or prosecuting genocides in other parts of the world.

A very important way in which the ECCC gain people's trust is by engaging the public in a transparent and even-handed manner. Whether or not all these diverse parties like the results is less important than whether their concerns were taken into account in the first place: whether someone listened to them and took them seriously.

For example, when King-Father Norodom Sihanouk calls officials from the UN side to come and talk, they should go. The royalists would be encouraged and everyone else would see that all sides of the story are being heard. If evidence indicates that some of today's CPP leaders should be indicted, then they should be. This will show Cambodia and the world that justice is for all, not merely those in power. Whatever the response of the ECCC, it should be open and public. Cambodia has had enough justice administered behind closed doors.

It is essential that the ECCC provide some answers to all of these groups about who is accountable and why. The tribunal must leave the Cambodian people with a judgment, something concrete they can take away and debate, and something they feel was done in fairness to all. After all, it is primarily for them that the trials are being held.

INTRODUCTION

BY JOHN D. CIORCIARI

This is a book about the Extraordinary Chambers in the Courts of Cambodia (ECCC), better known as the Khmer Rouge Tribunal. The ECCC is a hybrid or "mixed" criminal tribunal, established and operated by officials of the United Nations (UN) and Royal Cambodian Government. It is housed in a revamped military building complex on the western edge of Phnom Penh. Since opening its doors in July 2006, the ECCC has been entrusted with a monumental task. Its job is to put selected former Khmer Rouge officials on trial for grave crimes committed between April 1975 and January 1979, when Pol Pot and other members of the shadowy Communist Party of Kampuchea ruled the country, renamed it "Democratic Kampuchea" (DK), and implemented an infernal reign of terror.

When the ECCC was established, international donors and the Cambodian government provided it with three years of funding and a mandate to proceed with the accountability process. Much has happened at the tribunal since 2006. Investigations have been undertaken, arrests have been made, and one of the five defendants in custody is now standing trial. Surveys consistently show that a large majority of Cambodians support the Khmer Rouge trials. Thousands of survivors have participated in the process by filing complaints, becoming parties to the proceedings, or visiting the tribunal. Alongside these accomplishments, however, the ECCC has faced serious challenges. The process has taken more time and more funding than originally envisioned, and the tribunal has been criticized frequently for administrative deficiencies and other shortcomings.

On the occasion of the ECCC's third anniversary, this book takes stock of the tribunal's evolution and progress and offers recommendations on how best to proceed going forward. The chapters of this volume examine some of the forces that drove the tribunal's creation, analyze its basic legal and institutional features, assess its progress in a variety of areas, recommend improvements, and discuss its potential to contribute to reconciliation in Cambodia.

WHY THE ECCC IS IMPORTANT

The ECCC has profound moral, legal, and political significance. Its activities represent the latest stage in a long, tortuous process of dealing with the Khmer Rouge legacy. The crimes of the Khmer Rouge regime are not simply shards from the country's shattered past. They continue to haunt survivors today and contribute to unhealthy divides in Cambodian society and politics. After three decades of waiting, the ECCC gives Cambodians an opportunity to pursue a measure of justice, learn more about how and why so many innocent people suffered, and hopefully achieve a degree of closure and healing that will facilitate reconciliation.

The atrocities committed in Democratic Kampuchea are certainly not the only past wrongs casting shadows over modern Cambodian society. They were embedded within decades of conflict that involved abuses by many domestic and foreign actors. Nevertheless, the Pol Pot era was the most savage and shocking act in that tragedy. Nothing will erase survivors' pain, but to the ECCC's many supporters, the Khmer Rouge trials represent an indispensable stand against impunity that can help Cambodians come to terms with the past and move on with their lives.

CHALLENGING IMPUNITY

The single greatest reason for holding the Khmer Rouge trials is to deliver a measure of justice to a society that has suffered impunity for far too long. The world has long been aware that the Pol Pot regime committed abuses on a staggering scale. The Documentation Center of Cambodia (DC-Cam), Tuol Sleng Archives, and other institutions and scholars have amassed vast collections of documents, films, and photos showing the extent of the atrocities. Survivors have detailed their experiences in myriad memoirs, interviews, diaries, and artistic products. DC-Cam and others, including ECCC investigators, continue to collect evidence of the history of Democratic Kampuchea.

Moreover, the Cambodian countryside is still littered with the remains of Khmer Rouge brutality. DC-Cam has identified roughly 20,000 mass graves and almost 200 former Khmer Rouge detention centers across the country, many with rusty remains of torture devices. These remains provide daily reminders to Cambodians of the agony that they or their family members suffered during the Pol Pot period.

Both the sheer number of Khmer Rouge atrocities and the stories of individual victims issue powerful pleas for justice. Most scholars believe that roughly 1.5 to 2 million people perished during the Khmer Rouge era—roughly one quarter of the population. In fact, the piles of human remains are so vast, and survivors' accounts so abundant, that the world may never have an accurate estimate of the carnage. Of course, the Khmer Rouge tragedy can never be reduced to mere statistics. Each life lost was a father or mother, sister or brother, son or daughter, husband or wife, friend or companion.

Documents and abundant witness testimony tell of unimaginable suffering and cruelty. Khmer Rouge cadres sometimes required villagers to watch as their loved ones faced firing squads for arbitrary or trivial offenses, such as stealing rice or vegetables to avoid starvation. Some pregnant women, accused of ill-defined "anti-revolutionary" behavior, were strung up and disemboweled for all to see. One expectant mother even asked DK officials to abort her child so that she would not be arrested and killed for the "offense" of becoming pregnant without permission. In makeshift prisons, Khmer Rouge interrogators tested baseless accusations of espionage or subversion by strapping their victims to metal bed frames, burning them with embers, and ripping off their fingernails. Without ever facing trials, many thousands of prisoners were taken to mass burial pits, where Khmer Rouge executioners were often instructed to kill them with axe-handles or other agricultural equipment. This, DK officials argued, would avoid wasting precious bullets better saved for killing Vietnamese on the battlefield.

Those who lived through the period also suffered grave mistreatment. Sick and elderly Cambodians endured endless hours of forced labor, occasionally unearthing the corpses and bones of their lost loved ones as they toiled in the field. Most ordinary people slaved away, furtively eating bugs and bark to stay alive, wondering if they would ever see their families again. The regime denied them even the most basic rights of religious worship, free expression, and intimacy. Children were indoctrinated at commune gatherings to disavow their parents and devote their lives only to *Angkar* (the "Organization.") Indoctrinated to kill, those young cadres were criminal perpetrators, but in many respects they were victims of the regime as well. The scars of the DK era run deep.

Until quite recently, even the most senior surviving architects of Democratic Kampuchea walked about freely. Some lived in comfortable villas while their victims wrestled with the demons of the past. The ECCC provides a long-overdue opportunity to challenge that abhorrent legacy of impunity, which is a crucial step toward building a stronger overall rule of law. Three decades after the fall of the Pol Pot regime, no senior Khmer Rouge official has ever been convicted of wrongdoing by a credible court. That may soon change. Since commencing operations in 2006, tribunal officials have taken a crucial first step against impunity by detaining five former Khmer Rouge officials and charging them with criminal offenses.

The trial of one DK official is already well underway. The defendant is Duch, the former chief of the infamous "S-21" security office in Phnom Penh, where thousands of victims were interrogated and tortured on the site of the former Tuol Sleng Secondary School. Four other surviving Khmer Rouge senior leaders are also in custody: Nuon Chea, Ieng Sary, Khieu Samphan, and Ieng Thirith. All four were high-level members of the Communist Party of Kampuchea and occupied important posts in the DK regime.

The clock is ticking. Several senior Khmer Rouge leaders have died in the past decade—

including Party Secretary Pol Pot, Defense Minister Son Sen, Central Committee member Ta Mok (also known as "the Butcher"), Education Minister Yun Yat, and Zone Commander Ke Pauk. Many second-tier perpetrators of Khmer Rouge terror also lived out their final years in relative comfort without facing so much as a slap on the wrist. All five current charged persons are advanced in years, and some or all could pass away or lose their mental capacity before their trials are complete. Allowing all Khmer Rouge leaders to pass freely from the scene would be an affront to the millions of innocent victims whose lives they tore asunder.

DELIVERING JUSTICE

For the ECCC to succeed, one thing is clear: it has to deliver a significant measure of justice in the eyes of Cambodians and the international community. Justice is a complex concept, especially in the wake of such wide-ranging atrocities. Conducting a process and producing outcomes that satisfy diverse audiences' notions of justice will be no easy endeavor. Issuing a few guilty verdicts is certainly not enough. As the authors of this book will argue, the ECCC needs to address retributive, restorative, and procedural aspects of justice.

Justice means many different things to Cambodians and international observers of the trials. Notions of *retributive justice* provide much of the foundation for criminal law. The moral logic behind legal retribution is simple: an offender committed a social harm and must be condemned and punished by the state. The ECCC's success will certainly be judged in part by its ability to issue moral condemnation and mete out punishment where it is due. However, retribution is only one aspect of justice. Victims may derive satisfaction from seeing Khmer Rouge leaders shamed and punished, but even life sentences will hardly make victims whole.

As this book will discuss, one of the key issues relating to retribution will be the scope of the prosecution. Trying only a handful of leaders means that many mid-level Khmer Rouge officers will go free. So will low-level cadres, who committed an overwhelming majority of the physical abuses that continue to haunt survivors to this day. The United Nations and Cambodian government agreed to prosecute only "senior leaders" and others deemed "most responsible" for the atrocities of Democratic Kampuchea. Like other tribunals, the ECCC has been accused of "selective justice." The tribunal will not be able to erase all of the impunity that lingers after the DK era, but it needs to do its best to identify and successfully prosecute key architects of Khmer Rouge terror.

One problem with focusing on criminal trials and retribution is that even guilty verdicts provide little *restorative justice*. Throwing a thuggish Khmer Rouge leader in prison does not compensate victims or "restore" their well-being before the crimes in question. Providing restorative justice in a country as badly ravaged as Cambodia is a tall order, but taking some significant steps to address victims' needs is vital. Victims should, after all, be the primary beneficiaries of the accountability process.

Restorative justice has historically been a weakness of international tribunals, and it represents a special challenge for the ECCC. Money is never a substitute for lost loved ones of serious human rights abuses. Even if money could provide meaningful solace to victims, the ECCC and other tribunals lack the resources to issue much beyond token financial compensation. As subsequent chapters will discuss, the ECCC has taken an innovative approach to restorative justice. It established a mechanism for victims to participate as civil parties, which has enabled them to play a direct role alongside the prosecutors in the trial against Duch. (As Chapter 5 will discuss, that civil party mechanism is now in some jeopardy.) The ECCC has also envisioned providing victims with restorative awards in the form of "collective or moral reparations," such as memorials to honor the deceased or centers that provide basic health or educational services to survivors. The success of the ECCC's restorative efforts will go a long way toward determining public perceptions of the tribunal.

A third imperative feature of the ECCC process is *procedural justice*, which means holding fair trials. To some observers, it is doubtlessly enervating to watch Khmer Rouge defendants receive basic due process rights that the DK regime so cruelly denied to millions. Most people harbor few doubts that the suspects now in custody are guilty of serious wrongdoing, even if their exact crimes remain unspecified. Some observers would probably consider justice done if former Khmer Rouge leaders were simply lined up against a wall and shot. In the aftermath of any widespread human rights abuses, the thirst for retribution is a powerful and understandable impulse. This is true even in Cambodia, where religious and cultural norms and the passage of time have softened public vindictiveness to some degree.

Nevertheless, defendants' rights must be respected if the ECCC is to be a model for justice and not a kangaroo court. Every international tribunal since Nuremberg has been lambasted by critics as offering only "victor's justice" or "show trials." These critiques are not entirely unfounded—tribunals inevitably do reflect the political realities in which they are created. The best way to reduce the force of such critiques is to promote transparency and fairness. The Nuremberg Tribunal set an important precedent in this regard by acquitting a few Nazi defendants for lack of evidence. Other international tribunals—including those for the former Yugoslavia and Rwanda—have also issued some acquittals. As discussed throughout this book, the ECCC is bound by a complex set of substantive laws, procedural rules, and rules of evidence that are designed to promote fairness. If the ECCC is to set an example of justice, it must stick to them.

Fair trials require that convictions be based on sound legal proof, and even the most odious defendants must be able to mount defenses. Guilty verdicts cannot be foregone conclusions. There is extensive potential evidence available against Khmer Rouge leaders—including official DK documents, witness testimony, and physical remains—but proving individual defendants responsible for particular offenses is not as simple as it may seem. Where particular crimes cannot be proven, defendants have to be acquitted.

Treating Khmer Rouge defendants in this way may be morally or politically tough to swallow, but the ECCC will only fulfill its mandate with an even-handed administration of justice. The ECCC cannot provide a complete sense of retribution or restoration to Cambodians, but it does have control over running a fair process. In addition to setting an example of fairness and transparency, sticking to due process principles can facilitate a useful transfer of knowledge between Cambodian and international officials that helps to strengthen Cambodia's beleaguered and notoriously corrupt judicial system. One tragic legacy of Democratic Kampuchea is that few intellectuals survived the Pol Pot era, leaving the country with a dearth of lawyers and other professionals. Without a critical mass of well-trained judges and lawyers, it is difficult if not impossible to build a strong legal system. The potential for knowledge transfer has been a key justification for the establishment of hybrid tribunals, in Cambodia and in other war-torn states.

The retributive, restorative, and procedural aspects of justice are not mutually exclusive, even if they are sometimes in tension or suggest different ways of using limited resources. Retribution can challenge the culture of impunity and provide moral condemnation of offenders. Proponents of the trials hope they will also deter future criminal behavior and help to uphold the rule of law. Restorative justice can help to repair social and economic damage and thus facilitate reconciliation. Setting an example of procedural fairness can pave the way toward a more robust rule of law, addressing the future as well as the past. In Cambodia, like other societies plagued by mass human rights atrocities, all of these aspects of justice are crucial. The ECCC's challenge is to optimize them under conditions in which time and money are limited and in which the demands for justice would be difficult for any tribunal to deliver.

PERFORMING A TRUTH-TELLING FUNCTION

To many observers, the ECCC also holds the promise to perform an even wider range of functions than running fair trials and issuing verdicts of guilt or innocence. The tribunal can also serve as an invaluable truth-telling mechanism in a country where public education about the Khmer Rouge tragedy has been sorely lacking. Essentially all survivors of the Pol

Pot era know that mass human rights abuses occurred between 1975 and 1979, but few know the full extent of the atrocities. Even fewer have a good sense of why Khmer Rouge leaders and cadres inflicted such agony on their own people. In thousands of interviews with DC-Cam, victims often show more interest in seeking an explanation than in seeking revenge. To cope with the past, those who bear the scars of Khmer Rouge rule and lost loved ones want to know why.

In addition to benefiting survivors of Democratic Kampuchea, public dissemination of facts about the Pol Pot period can help their children by showing the need for a just and orderly society and the perils of a breakdown in the rule of law. Most of Cambodia's current citizens were born after the Khmers Rouges were thrown from power. They have no first-hand experience of the extraordinary suffering of their parents' generation. Some young Cambodians hear about the terror from relatives and teachers, but for many others, the period is a darkly shrouded mystery. Without an understanding of the Pol Pot era, many youths have difficulty understanding the psychological, emotional, and social challenges that their elders face.

For years, Cambodian schools offered little if any instruction about the Khmer Rouge period. Only recently has the Ministry of Education approved the first textbook on the topic for use in the national public school curriculum. Published by DC-Cam, the book is entitled *A History of Democratic Kampuchea (1975-1979)* and has been introduced into 1,321 secondary schools around the country. The ECCC can serve as one credible source of history about the regime, alongside the accounts given in textbooks, museums, and other media. Court reports, media coverage, public visits, and outreach by ECCC officials can all help provide answers. The court cannot be the only source of historical truth, however. NGOs, academic institutions, and official agencies also bear the burden of providing much better public education about the Pol Pot period and other aspects of modern Cambodian history. Only if they are armed with knowledge of the past can young Cambodians make sense of their country's troubled history, achieve a greater degree of closure than they have to date, and prepare themselves to prevent human rights abuses in the future.

SETTING AN INTERNATIONAL EXAMPLE

The ECCC has importance well beyond Cambodia's borders. It is one of the most recent embodiments of an expanding international effort to hold venal regimes accountable for their abuses and promote greater respect for human rights. Since the era of Nuremberg, key members of the international community have worked to devise international proceedings to address the limitations of domestic criminal proceedings in post-conflict societies. During the 1990s, the United Nations established *ad hoc* international tribunals for the former Yugoslavia and Rwanda and later a permanent International Criminal Court in The Hague.

The tribunals for the former Yugoslavia and Rwanda have been criticized on a number of grounds, including their cost and their relative distance—geographic and otherwise—from the victimized societies. The ECCC is one of the few examples of an alternative "mixed tribunal" model that involves shared duties between the United Nations and the government of the affected state. Proponents of the model believe mixed tribunals will better enfranchise victims, facilitate transfer of expertise, and deliver justice at a lower cost in countries that need money for many other uses. Opponents of the hybrid court model fear that partnering with suspect governments could water down the trials' legal and procedural integrity, undermine the UN's reputation, and reduce the likelihood of credible justice. Some also fear that holding trials locally could reopen old wounds and backfire in the quest for reconciliation. The ECCC's performance will be a crucial test for the mixed tribunal model.

AFFECTING CAMBODIAN POLITICS

The ECCC's mandate is a legal one, but it has great political relevance in Cambodia as well. In 1979, when the Pol Pot regime was overthrown, a new Vietnamese-backed government took over in Phnom Penh. The party governing the new "People's Republic of Kampuchea" was the Kampuchean People's Revolutionary Party (KPRP), which had been established in 1951 during the struggle against French colonialism. Although it shared much of the same lineage as Pol Pot's Communist Party of Kampuchea, the KPRP distanced itself from Khmer Rouge policies and based its claim to power and legitimacy largely on having saved the country from the DK regime. In 1991, the KPRP renamed itself the Cambodian People's Party (CPP). After UN-sponsored elections in 1993, the CPP shared power for several years with the rival royalist party FUNCINPEC (the National United Front for an Independent, Neutral, Peaceful, and Cooperative Cambodia). The CPP gained the upper hand after a series of violent clashes with FUNCINPEC in July 1997 and has since emerged as the dominant party in Cambodian politics. To win public support, the CPP and its long-time leader, Hun Sen, have often emphasized their historical role in ousting the DK regime and defeating the Khmer Rouge insurgency.

Members of other Cambodian political parties—including FUNCINPEC and the opposition Sam Rainsy Party and Human Rights Party—have attacked that claim and accused the CPP of worsening rather than improving respect for human rights in Cambodia. Some foreign governments and human rights organizations have said the same. The Khmer Rouge trials could indeed have some impact on public perceptions of the CPP. If they proceed well, the CPP will probably reap a modest political benefit. If the trials are botched, they may have an opposite effect. A shoddy process would likely contribute to public and international donor frustration with government—and particularly judicial—corruption in Cambodia. The trials are unlikely to become an existential issue in national politics, as they are sometimes portrayed in the foreign press, but they could generate significant diplomatic and domestic political disruptions. They clearly have importance well beyond the courtroom.

OVERALL: A HERCULEAN SET OF TASKS

The goals above are a tremendous amount to ask of a single tribunal. One of the ECCC's greatest challenges is to manage public expectations about what it can realistically accomplish. Even if the tribunal is wildly successful, a series of criminal trials cannot cure all of the ills of a society struggling to overcome mass atrocities. It cannot replace lost loved ones, and it cannot rectify all of the political and economic problems that flow from the Khmer Rouge reign of terror. It cannot alone transform Cambodian governance, put an end to criminality and corruption, bring about a major improvement in contemporary human rights in Cambodia, or address a host of other developmental needs.

The tribunal's importance lies more in its ability to serve as a catalyst and bellwether for change in Cambodia. It can be a highly visible step toward a more promising future by challenging impunity, setting an example of a just trial, sharing information about the Pol Pot period, and drawing attention to victims' needs. The ECCC can also focus renewed domestic and international attention on issues of governance and human rights and increase the prospects for future progress. If it performs all of these functions ably, the ECCC will have done a great service indeed.

OVERVIEW OF THIS BOOK

The chapters of this book examine the ECCC's origins, basic features, performance, and prospects. We begin by discussing how the ECCC came to be established and analyze the particular form that it took. We then critique its operations during its first three years of operation, looking at three aspects of its work—its judicial findings, its institutional management, and its outreach to victims. Finally, we examine how the ECCC can best deliver credible justice and contribute to genuine reconciliation in Cambodia going forward.

THE ROUGH ROAD TO JUSTICE

To understand the ECCC's strengths, shortcomings, and progress to date, some background is essential. This book therefore begins with a review of the history and politics behind the ECCC's establishment. As I discuss in Chapter 1, there have been countless calls for justice in Cambodia since the demise of Democratic Kampuchea. Victims, human rights advocates, domestic political parties, and foreign governments have all pressed for accountability to varying degrees. Nevertheless, the tribunal's creation was a slow, painful process. The ECCC did not open its doors until almost three decades after the fall of the Khmer Rouge regime.

The delay in the tribunal's creation owed primarily to power politics. The Khmer Rouge movement was forged in the crucible of Cold War conflict, and subsequent treatment of Khmer Rouge members has always been embedded in broader domestic and international competition for influence in Cambodia. Despite heroic efforts by some individuals and non-governmental groups, calls for Khmer Rouge accountability were buried beneath broader political and strategic considerations during the latter stages of the Cold War. A serious international push for accountability began only after the negotiated withdrawal of Vietnamese troops from Cambodia, eighteen months of United Nations administration, and UN-sponsored elections brought a measure of peace to the country and marginalized the Khmers Rouges as a political and military force.

Beginning in 1997, the United Nations and Cambodian government began a decade-long diplomatic dance to establish a tribunal. Disputes flared over the "balance of influence" between UN and Cambodian officials on the tribunal, the scope of the tribunal's jurisdiction, the defendants to be charged, and the laws and procedures to be applied. Finally, in 2003, more than a quarter century after the collapse of the Khmer Rouge regime, the United Nations and Royal Cambodian Government hammered out an agreement (the "Framework Agreement") to establish the ECCC. The following year, the Cambodian National Assembly passed a law—also blessed by the United Nations—to govern the tribunal proceedings (the "ECCC Law"). Between 2004 and 2007, further negotiations continued as the parties decided upon the funding for the tribunal, established a physical site for the trials, staffed the court, and devised various procedural rules to govern the proceedings.

The Framework Agreement was a product of grueling political battles and frequent compromises between the Cambodian government and United Nations. Some of the key sticking points related to the tribunal's temporal, personal, and subject-matter jurisdiction. It would be empowered to try only certain former Khmer Rouge officials for certain crimes committed during the specific period of Khmer Rouge rule. Another key bone of contention related to the balance of influence on the court. Unlike other tribunals, which had been dominated by international civil servants, the ECCC was designed in a manner than ensured a narrow preponderance of Cambodian personnel. The Framework Agreement and subsequent ECCC Law drew sharp criticism from many Western observers, who argued that it conceded too much authority to the Hun Sen government and compromised on considerations of integrity and justice.

All international criminal tribunals reflect political realities and carry important political implications. The ECCC is certainly no exception. For better or worse, the tribunal's jurisdictional limits and organizational structure were deemed necessary to achieve buy-in from the relevant parties. Nevertheless, as I discuss at the end of Chapter 1, the legacy of tough negotiations and political compromises has left residual discomfort and distrust. Much of the political friction that surfaced during the UN-Cambodian negotiations continues to haunt the ECCC proceedings. In particular, the tribunal's jurisdiction and the appropriate balance of influence remain key subjects of debate, as Cambodian and UN officials continue to argue over whether to undertake additional prosecutions and spar over ways to improve the tribunal's management.

THE TRIBUNAL TAKES SHAPE

The Framework Agreement and ECCC Law set out the substantive laws that would govern the proceedings and established many aspects of the tribunal's organization. In Chapter 2, Anne Heindel discusses the tribunal's legal and institutional features. She also discusses a number of administrative and procedural issues that were not specifically addressed in the Framework Agreement or ECCC Law.

She begins by reviewing the ECCC's jurisdiction and examining the substantive criminal laws governing the proceedings. In addition to deciding what time period to cover and who to prosecute, the architects of the ECCC had to define the tribunal's subject-matter jurisdiction. This meant deciding which of the many possible crimes of the DK regime to prosecute. Cambodian and UN officials drew from both local and international law and ultimately settled on eight crimes, including genocide, war crimes, crimes against humanity, torture, homicide, religious persecution, and a few lesser-known, previously untried international offenses.

The legal definitions in 1975-79 of some of these crimes are not obvious. Justice requires that Khmer Rouge defendants be tried only for crimes that existed at the time of the acts in question, and both international criminal law and Cambodian law were in flux during the 1970s. As Heindel describes, the ECCC Law left open some important questions about the precise "elements" (i.e., the specific acts and criminal intent) that prosecutors must prove to secure convictions for particular offenses. It also left open some complex legal issues surrounding the "forms" of criminal responsibility. In cases of mass human rights abuses, holding high-ranking leaders accountable usually requires proving that they issued orders, engaged in conspiracy, or otherwise bore indirect responsibility for the crimes of their colleagues or subordinates. The ECCC's legal formulation of direct and indirect criminal responsibility could have a major practical impact on the trials.

Equally important are the laws and rules established to safeguard the rights of defendants. As argued above, the ECCC can only be deemed a success if it enables defendants to mount defenses and adheres to common notions of procedural justice. Heindel touches upon the legal defenses made available to Khmer Rouge defendants under the ECCC Law and other relevant sources of law.

In the latter part of the chapter, Heindel describes the structure and composition of the ECCC and examines the tribunal's rules of evidence and procedure. These were the subjects of extensive negotiation as the tribunal began to take shape following the passage of the ECCC Law. It was not until 2007 that UN and Cambodian officials agreed to a set of Internal Rules (which were later amended) to govern administrative and procedural aspects of the trials. As Heindel explains, creating a new judicial institution has required addressing a host of complicated questions, and a significant number of issues have yet to be resolved.

ASSESSING THE ECCC'S PERFORMANCE TO DATE

When the ECCC finally took shape and commenced operations in 2006, it was given an unofficial three-year mandate and a corresponding budget to tackle Khmer Rouge impunity by putting some surviving DK officials on trial. Over its first three years, the ECCC has validated both the hopes of its proponents and the fears of its critics. To its supporters, the ECCC has taken major steps toward justice. To some critics, the tribunal has been a farce and a failure. As the authors of this book will discuss, the truth lies somewhere in between.

Conducting effective criminal trials is no easy task, especially when the scale of the crimes committed is so vast. The challenge is even greater in a new institution using multiple languages, serving diverse donors, and implementing rules and procedures based on a complex blend of local and international legal traditions. Since 2006, notable progress has been made. An administrative apparatus has taken shape, and Internal Rules have been adopted to govern the ECCC's procedure. Investigations have been conducted, five key suspects are in custody, numerous pre-trial proceedings have transpired, and the trial against Duch has begun. ECCC judges have issued numerous decisions on important aspects of law and procedure. Viewed in this light, the ECCC has exceeded many observers' expectations.

Nevertheless, the accountability process is far from complete, and the ECCC has hit frequent bumps in the road. A number of disputes, problems, and scandals have arisen. These have impeded the tribunal's efficiency, sometimes undermining its perceived legitimacy and occasionally jeopardizing its existence. Many of the challenges at the ECCC have involved tension between Cambodian and international officials, and tough compromises have been necessary throughout the process to keep the tribunal functioning.

Although some of the ECCC's legal decisions have been subject to valid critiques, the tribunal's most severe critics have tended to focus on its administrative deficiencies. The tribunal has often moved slowly, and some analysts have expressed frustration at the pace and cost of criminal investigations. It is now clear that the tribunal will consume much more time and money than originally envisioned to complete its mission. To many critics, the ECCC has also failed to provide adequate outreach to victims, despite the welcome establishment of a Victims' Unit to aid that process. Even more damning are allegations that some ECCC officials have mismanaged the institution and allowed or facilitated corruption. Some observers, including prominent human rights advocates, have even advocated shutting down the ECCC. Chapters 3-5 evaluate various aspects of the ECCC and provide assessments of its progress to date.

THE ECCC'S LEGAL JUDGMENTS

Heindel begins in Chapter 3 by reviewing and critiquing the tribunal's judicial performance since it commenced operations. Since mid-2007, the Pre-Trial Chamber, a unit composed of three Cambodian and two international judges, has conducted a number of public hearings and issued a number of important decisions.

Many have related to procedural rights and the lawfulness of the ECCC's detention of the defendants. A number of the charged persons have filed appeals against the Co-Investigating Judges' detention orders, arguing that they are either too sick to be in detention or unfit to stand trial. Duch has sought release on the grounds that his rights were violated by a lengthy pre-trial detention by the Phnom Penh Military Court—which began in 1999 and extended well beyond the three-year maximum in Cambodian law. Ieng Sary has argued that he should be immune from prosecution and released from detention due to the principle of "double jeopardy"—he was convicted *in absentia* of genocide in a brief trial in 1979. Ieng also argues for his release based on the amnesty and pardon he received when he defected to the government in 1996.

The Pre-Trial Chamber has rejected all of the foregoing appeals. It has also had to grapple with other diverse issues. These have included the rights of civil parties to participate in the process, the forms of criminal responsibility that will be accepted at trial, the scope of the defendants' right to translation of case file documents, and the possibility of charging additional suspects. Heindel reviews the Pre-Trial and Trial Chambers' decisions, examining both the quality of the ECCC's legal reasoning and the appropriateness of its judicial findings.

THE TRIBUNAL'S INSTITUTIONAL MANAGEMENT

The ECCC is not only a court of law—it is also a complex bureaucratic organization subject to various forms of political oversight and influence. The ECCC cannot perform its mandated judicial and public outreach functions without running an effective institution. The ECCC faces steep challenges that all international and hybrid tribunals have faced—how to set up a sophisticated bureaucracy from scratch, manage complex donor relations, assemble a diverse staff, manage linguistic and logistical headaches, and tackle tough criminal cases.

In Chapter 4, John Hall analyzes and critiques the administration of the ECCC to date. He discusses both the tribunal's internal management and the roles that the Cambodian government, United Nations, and major donor states have played in overseeing the process. As he discusses, the ECCC has enjoyed some notable success but has also faced significant administrative challenges. Foremost among these challenges have been problems related to human resource management and alleged corruption in the tribunal.

The human resources issue has been addressed more effectively than the issue of alleged corruption. In 2007, an audit conducted for the UN Development Program generally supported allegations of kick-backs, illegal hiring practices, and other malfeasance. A few ECCC employees later issued corroborating claims. The episode sparked a significant crisis, provoking recriminations between the United Nations and Cambodian government and prompting some donors to suspend financial contributions. The ECCC has since issued new guidelines and created an anti-corruption commission and an "Independent Counsellor" to receive complaints, but as Hall discusses, concerns about corruption have not evaporated. Most donors and external observers perceive the measures taken to date as inadequate, but at times key donors have sent mixed signals, providing funds without insisting on sufficient safeguards. The corruption issue presents one of the most serious threats to keeping the Khmer Rouge trials on track.

Another concern about the ECCC's operations surrounds the financial cost of the process. One reason for a mixed tribunal structure is that it was expected to be much cheaper (if not quicker) than the *ad hoc* international tribunals for the former Yugoslavia and Rwanda. Supporters of the ECCC note that it has indeed consumed fewer resources. Moreover, they argue, the funds provided for the tribunal would not necessarily be furnished to Cambodia for other ends. Pressure is nonetheless mounting from critics, who argue that the ECCC is proving wasteful and that money could be more productively used for development projects given all of Cambodia's needs.

The ECCC began with an agreed budget of roughly $56 million, of which the international community contributed the lion's share. That budget was intended to cover the entire trial process for a period of three years. However, by early 2008, the ECCC estimated a need for a further $114 million to complete its work. Most donors were not enthusiastic, especially in the wake of corruption allegations. Some donors withheld funds while ECCC officials—especially on the Cambodian side—threatened that without further infusions, operations would grind to a halt. After a bit of diplomatic brinkmanship, compromise came. The ECCC shaved its budget request by a significant margin, asking for an additional $44 million through 2009, and Japan and other key donors filled most of that shortfall. Still, the tribunal's price tag is a hefty one, especially compared to the meager $3.5 million annual budget for the rest of the Cambodian judiciary.

ECCC officials now estimate that the expected indictments and trials of four charged persons will not take place until 2011, making further funding requests likely. Should the ECCC decide to prosecute additional defendants, the price tag will further rise. Donors have taken some measures to improve financial oversight, but as Hall discusses, budgetary tugs-of-war will likely continue.

The ECCC's human resource and budgetary challenges have also affected other aspects of administration. Hall notes that translation has been a particular problem at the tribunal, which has three official languages—Khmer, English, and French. Outreach to the public has also been an area of relative weakness, and Hall concludes by highlighting recent controversy in that area.

THE ECCC'S OUTREACH TO SURVIVORS

In Chapter 5, Sarah Thomas and Terith Chy address a third key aspect of the tribunal's operations: its outreach to victims and other survivors of the DK era. Robust survivor participation is essential if the ECCC is to be successful. The Khmer Rouge trials are not just an antiseptic legal exercise; they represent an effort to help millions of Cambodians heal and to advance principles of justice and human rights in a society that has seen too little of both. The ECCC can fulfill those missions only if Cambodians are able to follow, understand, and meaningfully participate in the process.

Thomas and Chy discuss the evolution of survivor participation in international and hybrid international tribunals. They contend that limited access to survivors has severely compromised the effectiveness of the tribunals for the former Yugoslavia and Rwanda and contrast those tribunals with the Special Court of Sierra Leone, which has made considerable advances in connecting the local community to the proceedings.

Thomas and Chy then proceed to describe and critique the framework for survivor participation at the ECCC. They unpack the various ways in which survivors who qualify as "victims" have been participating directly in the trial of Duch—by issuing formal complaints, serving as witnesses, or joining the proceedings as civil parties. They also discuss indirect ways of participating through educational sessions, visits to the court proceedings, and village discussion forums. Thomas and Chy delve into the many challenges that the ECCC faces in responding to the needs of millions of Cambodian survivors. These include the legal complexities of including civil parties, the difficulty of managing voluminous victim complaints and coordinating NGO activities in the field, and the need for strong outreach and witness protection programs.

Finally, Thomas and Chy review the success and impact of survivor participation efforts to date. They draw on field research to argue that the initiative has been successful in many respects, despite outreach shortcomings and inadequate funds and staff for the new Victims Unit. They argue that the civil party scheme has ample room for improvement, but they criticize recent proposals to eliminate or severely limit civil party participation in the trials, which would disenfranchise victims and forfeit their valuable contribution to the accountability process. The authors conclude by offering offer a series of recommendations to strengthen the various aspects of survivor participation going forward.

THE ECCC'S ROLE IN RECONCILIATION

Survivor participation relates to the important question of whether and how the ECCC can help to foster reconciliation in Cambodia. As a criminal tribunal, the ECCC is set up primarily to deliver justice by putting selected Khmer Rouge defendants on trial. Criminal trials are not ideally designed to provide a complete historical account of the Khmer Rouge tragedy, because their mission is to focus on facts relevant to the particular defendants standing trial. For that reason, some conflict-torn societies have used Truth and Reconciliation Commissions instead of criminal courts to promote transitions toward more peaceful futures.

In the final chapter of this volume, Sok-Kheang Ly and I examine the ECCC's role in reconciliation. We begin by putting the tribunal in context, noting that the ECCC is part of a broader process of healing that is taking place on both societal and personal levels.Cambodians pursued various forms of reconciliation long before the tribunal was created. Those efforts have helped survivors and their families begin to rebuild and have contributed to improved social stability after decades of armed conflict. However, they have fallen short in two key areas: they have not delivered a sense of justice, and they have not provided an adequate public understanding of the history of Democratic Kampuchea. It is in these respects that we believe the ECCC has a constructive role to play.

Criminal trials are not always conducive to reconciliation, but we contend that the ECCC can play a positive role in the particular context of contemporary Cambodia. It can do so by providing Cambodians with a sense of justice and an enhanced understanding of the truth about Democratic Kampuchea. Of course, even perfectly run cases with well-reasoned verdicts will ring hollow if the public is not able to follow and understand the process. Educating the public is admittedly a great deal to request from a tribunal already entrusted with a complex set of criminal cases. The ECCC cannot take on too many tasks without losing its moorings. However, it is not acting alone; government agencies, international organizations, non-governmental organizations, religious groups, and ordinary citizens are also providing services to the public in connection with the trials. The ECCC simply needs to be an effective spearhead for connecting Cambodians to the trials.

Lastly, we review findings, based on extensive field research by DC-Cam and other organizations, to shed light on how Cambodians have viewed the process thus far. Those findings suggest that Cambodians remain broadly supportive of the ECCC and that most—though not all—perceive the trials as conducive to personal and societal reconciliation. These are among the most critical findings of this book. Public perceptions do not comprise the only scorecard for the ECCC's success, but they are vitally important, because the trials should be held above all for the benefit of ordinary survivors and their families.

A unit of soldiers who defected from Democratic Kampuchea to join the resistance at a military base near the Vietnam-Cambodia border, 1978.
Source: Documentation Center of Cambodia Archives/Vietnamese News Agency (VNA)

Platoon Commander Pen Sa Men (second from right) in the eastern zone of Democratic Kampuchea, 1978. Pen Sa Men organized a revolt against Democratic Kampuchea and led a unit that provided intelligence to the resistance before he was captured and executed by the Khmers Rouges. *Source: Documentation Center of Cambodia Archives/Vietnamese News Agency (VNA)*

Sok Tha, a Khmer Rouge cadre who defected into the Kampuchean United Front for National Salvation, 1978.
Photo by Nguyen Dinh
Source: Documentation Center of Cambodia Archives/Vietnamese News Agency (VNA)

1. HISTORY & POLITICS BEHIND THE KHMER ROUGE TRIALS

JOHN D. CIORCIARI

To understand how the ECCC was designed and how it has functioned during its first three years, some historical and political background is imperative. The Khmer Rouge trials have been one of the most hotly contested issues in Cambodian law and politics for more than a decade. They have featured prominently in Cambodia's relations with major Western nations, which continue to provide much of the aid on which the country depends. They have also been the subject of intense haggling among domestic political parties. The importance of the trials in Cambodian public life is both a product of genuine moral convictions by many victims and outside observers and the result of a complex, troubled history that has given both foreign and domestic actors powerful stakes in the outcome of the process. The history and politics behind the creation of the Extraordinary Chambers in the Courts of Cambodia (ECCC) do not always paint a flattering picture of the parties involved in the discussion.

In this chapter, I begin by briefly reviewing the origins, evolution, and consequences of the Khmer Rouge movement. That history helps explain why the accountability process is more than a simple, straightforward quest for justice: it is also a powerful vehicle whereby nations, parties, and individuals pursue political and other gains. It also helps explain why an accountability process was so slow to come to fruition. Second, I examine how the push for justice rebounded in the post-Cold War period and discuss the tense negotiations that led, painstakingly, to the passage of a law establishing the ECCC in 2004. Third, I evaluate the results of those negotiations and explore how political factors at the local and international levels contributed to the ECCC's ultimate form, composition, and mandate. Finally, I conclude by drawing attention to the continuing political tensions surrounding the tribunal. Politics are usually not the pretty side of international legal processes, but they exert tremendous influence, and the Cambodian case is no exception.

THE KHMER ROUGE MOVEMENT AND CAMBODIA'S TORMENTED COLD WAR HISTORY

The Khmer Rouge trials are part of an effort to come to grips with the darkest chapter in Cambodia's modern history, a history that has been plagued by frequent violence and discord. The difficulty in forging agreement on the ECCC owes largely to the wide range of domestic and international actors with profound interests in the proceedings and axes to grind. The section below sets the stage for a discussion of the tribunal negotiations by reviewing the evolution and effects of the Khmer Rouge movement during the Cold War period.

WAR, TURMOIL, AND THE ORIGINS OF KHMER ROUGE RULE

The Khmer Rouge movement is a descendant of the broader Indochinese communist movement. That movement was born in Vietnam during the French colonial period and flourished during and after the Second World War, first to fight Japanese imperialism and then to resist the re-imposition of French rule. Soon after a bitter war of independence erupted in 1946, groups of left-wing Khmer rebels began fighting alongside their Vietnamese and Lao comrades. By 1951, Cambodian communists formed the Kampuchean People's Revolutionary Party as a national branch of the Vietnamese-led Indochinese Communist Party.[1] The war gradually swung in favor of the communist forces, culminating with the defeat of the French Expeditionary Forces at Dien Bien Phu in 1954.

Even before that battle ended, a concert of powers—including Cambodia, Laos, Vietnam, China, the USSR, France, and the United Kingdom—met in Switzerland to hammer out a political settlement for Indochina. The resulting Geneva Accords drew a line across Vietnam at the 17th parallel, giving the communist Viet Minh control of the North and granting authority in the South to a conservative French-backed regime.[2] (The latter would receive increasing support from the United States, which refused to recognize the validity of the settlement.)

The Geneva Accords declared Cambodia and Laos to be "neutral" in the context of the escalating Cold War rivalry that gripped the region. In practice, "neutralization" meant at least a temporary diminution of foreign support for communist or right-wing forces operating in Cambodia. The accords thus helped solidify the position of Prince Norodom Sihanouk, who constructed a new royalist regime called the *Sangkhum Reastr Niuym* ("People's Socialist Community") and successfully co-opted some of his principal political challengers on both the left and right.

To some radical Khmer communists, including future leaders of the Pol Pot regime, the Geneva Accords represented a deep betrayal by their Vietnamese comrades, by the Soviet Union, and to a lesser extent by China. Khmer radicals saw the settlement as a self-serving pact whereby weak-willed leaders in Hanoi and Moscow locked in limited gains and avoided further struggle against the dreaded Western imperialists. In their eyes the Cambodian communists—who had shed blood in the common fight against the French—were left out in the cold.[3]

By the early 1960s, a radical new Khmer communist movement began to take shape under the leadership of Pol Pot, Nuon Chea, and others. Based primarily in destitute outlying areas of Cambodia, these rebels formed the Communist Party of Kampuchea (CPK) and began to mount resistance against Sihanouk's *Sangkhum* regime.[4] The Prince dubbed these rebels the *Khmers Rouges* (red Khmers), distinguishing them from right-wing republican *Khmers Bleus* (blue Khmers) and royalist *Khmers Blancs* (white Khmers). Those groups came to represent the three principal pillars in Cambodian political life for nearly two decades.

By the mid-1960s, Sihanouk was playing an increasingly difficult balancing game to preserve relative neutrality and avoid unwanted embroilment in the escalating war in neighboring Vietnam. In response to mounting pressure from Hanoi and Beijing, he began allowing Vietnamese communists to establish bases on Cambodian soil. However, he simultaneously authorized lethal force to subdue local communist uprisings. The Samlaut Rebellion, which began in 1967, was a key turning point. Thousands of peasants took to the hills and forests around the northwestern city of Battambang in response to repressive military measures. The government's draconian response drove new recruits into the arms of the increasingly radical and nationalistic Khmer Rouge movement.[5]

The royalist regime also faced mounting pressure from the right. Conservative republican groups—some of which were supported by the U.S. Central Intelligence Agency—challenged the government from bases in Thailand and South Vietnam. Some members of the government also resented Sihanouk's decision to allow Vietnamese troops to operate in the country.[6] As Vietnamese bases proliferated and Khmer Rouge activity increased, the U.S. government began a secret bombing campaign over Cambodia in the spring of 1969. By March 1970, Sihanouk had lost control. While the Prince was out of the country, Marshal Lon Nol staged a coup, imposed military rule, and declared a new "Khmer Republic." Sihanouk relocated to Beijing to form an opposition government-in-exile.

Although the Lon Nol regime initially pursued a policy of espoused neutrality, the country soon descended into a grueling five-year civil war that became deeply intertwined with the war in Vietnam. Repressive military rule and popular frustration at the exile of Sihanouk contributed to an expansion of the Khmer Rouge movement. In addition, a massive U.S. aerial campaign against Vietnamese sanctuaries and Khmer Rouge targets resulted in widespread collateral damage, further alienating many members of the rural peasantry.[7]

As the war dragged on, public support for the Lon Nol regime steadily declined due to rampant corruption, cruelty, and general mismanagement. Although the regime enjoyed considerable U.S. support, China and Vietnam funneled guns and grains to the Cambodian revolutionaries. The tide of the conflict gradually shifted until Khmer Rouge forces finally punched through a ring of right-wing military defenses and captured Phnom Penh in April 1975.

Cambodia's pre-1975 history helps to explain some of the features of the brutal regime that the Khmers Rouges established after taking power. Years of domestic upheaval and repression, coupled with embroilment in broader regional conflicts, had helped to forge a peasant-based movement that was intensely class-conscious, xenophobic, and utterly ruthless. This history is also directly relevant to an understanding of the Khmer Rouge accountability process. As discussed below, some of the key advocates for the tribunal in the post-Cold War era—including the U.S. government—have been keen to avoid a process that would focus public attention and judicial review on the events of the 1960s and early 1970s.

THE POL POT YEARS

After years of embroilment in conflict, Cambodians entered an even more terrifying period with the onset of Khmer Rouge rule. Khmer Rouge revolutionaries first took power during the tumultuous spring of 1975, toppling the Lon Nol regime just as Vietnamese communist forces tightened the noose on Saigon. After years of civil war and deprivation, Khmer Rouge rebels streamed out of the countryside wearing only the simple cotton garments of the peasantry, traditional checkered headscarves, and shoes made from used-up tires. When they captured Phnom Penh on April 17, city dwellers initially rejoiced in the possibility of peace.

That dream died quickly. Within hours, zealous young Khmer Rouge cadres began to hunt down and execute members of the *ancien regime* without even the faintest pretense of trials. Before most city dwellers knew what was happening, Khmer Rouge forces began a sudden and wholesale evacuation of Phnom Penh. They expelled or killed foreigners, screened out intellectuals and other perceived political enemies, and pushed almost two million civilians of all ages onto long dirt roads, carrying their belongings on their backs and knowing almost nothing about their destinations.[8]

The early purges and evacuation of Phnom Penh were initial steps in a radical and catastrophic program organized by the inner circle of the CPK. The leaders of the newly-renamed state of Democratic Kampuchea (DK) launched a merciless campaign to create an authentically Khmer, self-sufficient agrarian state on an "ultra-Maoist" ideological model. Khmer Rouge leaders blamed both traditional Cambodian culture and foreign influence for the country's weakness and the indignities it had suffered from expanding Siamese and Vietnamese empires, French colonial overlords, and Cold War chess-masters in Moscow and Washington.

The architects of Khmer Rouge policy sought to expunge all such foreign and traditional influence and to return to "Year Zero"—a blank slate on which the country could build a new history. Money was abolished, books were burned, and the regime brutally repressed any form of resistance to its rule. Purging and dispersing the urban population—with its merchants, ethnic minorities, military officers, and bureaucrats—was a key to the Khmer Rouge plan of reconstituting Cambodian society. The DK regime sent these "New People" to remote rural cooperatives to mingle with impoverished "Base People," whom the Khmer Rouge perceived as more amenable to indoctrination.

As the DK regime walled itself off from most of the outside world, an opaque curtain fell over the country. Nevertheless, it soon became clear from journalistic and refugee reports that human rights abuses were unfolding on a massive scale. Families were separated, and civilians of all backgrounds suffered harsh forced labor conditions and "re-education." Ethnic and religious minorities were persecuted, and anyone suspected of espionage or sympathy for foreign powers faced a harrowing fate. Even the slightest infractions of arbitrary Khmer Rouge dictates often led to beating, imprisonment, torture, and death.[9]

As ill-conceived Khmer Rouge domestic policies took hold, the economy went into free-fall. Starvation and illness began to claim countless lives alongside routine executions. However, internal calamity did not deter DK leaders from conducting a dangerously antagonistic and provocative foreign policy. Almost immediately after the fall of Saigon in April 1975, Khmer Rouge forces clashed with their former Vietnamese comrades over disputed territories along their shared border. Khmer Rouge soldiers even seized an American ship, the *Mayaguez*, a provocative move that risked drawing U.S. forces back into the fray. (In the event, the U.S. military chose to conduct only a limited rescue effort and recovered the ship quickly.) By 1977, the conflict with Vietnam intensified along Cambodia's eastern frontier.[10]

An anemic economy and rising conflict with Vietnam only fed the flames of Khmer Rouge paranoia and brutality. The regime constructed a massive internal security apparatus centered on the notorious Office S-21 (since converted into the Tuol Sleng Genocide Museum) and the "Killing Fields" of Choeung Ek.[11] Khmer Rouge officials at all levels perceived enemies lurking behind every shadow and sent droves of suspects to their deaths without even hints of a trial. In some cases, the DK regime focused on particular ethnic or religious minorities for abuse.[12] However, members of the majority Buddhist Khmer population found themselves in harm's way with comparable frequency, as DK officials targeted a wide array of "enemies" and "no-good elements" on political and other grounds. Atrocities continued until the final hours of the Khmer Rouge regime, before Vietnamese armed forces invaded the country in the final days of 1978 and captured Phnom Penh in early January 1979.

The two other major domestic political forces in Cambodia—right-wing republican forces and monarchists—did not fare well in Democratic Kampuchea. Hours after Khmer Rouge tanks rolled into Phnom Penh, young cadres began hunting down and executing former officials of the Lon Nol regime. As the Khmer Rouge evacuated the teeming city of Phnom Penh, they established checkpoints to weed out former officials of the Khmer Republic. Some Lon Nol allies escaped into Thailand or elsewhere, but those who stayed in the country were among the prime targets for interrogation, torture, and killing.

The Khmer Rouge leadership also sought to weaken the monarchy. The royal family and Sihanouk himself enjoyed a broad popular following, especially in rural villages where the Khmers Rouges also enjoyed support. To neutralize Sihanouk, who initially opposed DK rule from his outpost in Beijing, the Khmer Rouge leadership invited him back to Cambodia and effectively put him under house arrest. Years later, one of the most sensitive questions raised in the establishment of a tribunal would be the role that Sihanouk played. Was he simply a witness to the terror, or did his acts amount to a form of complicity? Few issues have ignited more passion in the course of subsequent negotiations for a Khmer Rouge tribunal.

In foreign affairs, although Khmer Rouge officials espoused a militant commitment to self-sufficiency, the country's inherent vulnerability and weak economic and military constitution forced the DK leadership to look quickly for an external lifeline. China—in the throes of its own domestic upheaval surrounding the death of Mao and the downfall of the "Gang of Four"—became the principal sponsor of the new DK regime. Chinese grain, machinery, and technical training became critical support structures as Khmer Rouge officials sought to rebuild and refashion the state, root out perceived enemies, and prosecute a mounting conflict against Vietnam.[13]

In many respects, China also provided an ideological model for the Khmer Rouge inner circle. The regime certainly bore prominent Stalinist features, such as a bone-crushing internal security apparatus and a highly centralized bureaucratic and party structure, but the nature and organization of Khmer Rouge agricultural communes and many of the rhetorical features of the regime bore a more striking resemblance to China under the Cultural Revolution. The DK leadership explicitly drew a connection to China by expressing its desire to achieve a "super great leap forward."[14] Pol Pot also pointedly chose to unveil himself as leader and his regime as the Communist Party of Kampuchea during a September 1977 visit to China—a favor to his comrades in Beijing.[15]

Like other foreign interventions in Cambodia, China's material support and ideological inspiration for the Khmer Rouge regime would affect the course of subsequent efforts to hold the Pol Pot regime accountable for its offenses. By bankrolling such an odious regime, Chinese leaders risked being subjected to international opprobrium themselves.

A VIETNAM-BACKED REGIME AND THE 1979 TRIBUNAL

In late 1978, amid escalating conflict on both sides of the Viet-Cambodian border, Khmer rebels and Vietnamese armed forces swept into Democratic Kampuchea. In early January 1979, the invading forces ousted the Khmer Rouge regime, secured Phnom Penh, and occupied most of the country. Heng Samrin, the head of the Cambodian resistance, became the head of the new People's Republic of Kampuchea (PRK), which rested on the foundation of a powerful 180,000-member contingent from the People's Army of Vietnam and a steady stream of aid from Moscow.

The invasion and installation of the PRK regime contributed to a crisis between China and Vietnam. Relations between those two countries had chilled rapidly after the U.S. withdrawal from Saigon eliminated their need to cooperate against a common foe. As their ties worsened, Vietnam moved closer into the Soviet orbit, adding to the sense of intra-communist rivalry. For China, the invasion of Cambodia was the final straw. Chinese forces attacked Vietnam in February 1979, launching a brief but angry war to "teach Vietnam a lesson" for defying Beijing, allying with the USSR, and invading a Chinese ally.[16]

Inside Cambodia, the correlation of forces changed quickly after the invasion. Most beleaguered survivors of the DK regime welcomed the new government, even if they resented the presence of Vietnamese troops. With the aid of Chinese advisors, the Khmer Rouge leadership fled to the western part of the country and took refuge, mostly in the dense jungles of the Cardammon mountain range near the Thai border. In the ensuing months, a significant number of former Khmer Rouge cadres fell victim to vengeance killings. Those who remained alive generally adopted low profiles or moved to new villages, hoping to escape retribution.

In August 1979, to solidify its domestic credentials and deal with the problem of Khmer Rouge impunity, the new PRK government set up a "People's Revolutionary Tribunal." The PRK Ministry of Justice conducted trials *in absentia* of Pol Pot, the former DK Prime Minister, and Ieng Sary, the former DK Deputy Prime Minister in charge of foreign affairs. The 1979 trials were the first judicial attempts to promote justice and reconciliation in Cambodia after the Khmer Rouge tragedy, and they marked the first effort to hold individuals accountable for the crime of genocide since the creation of the 1948 Genocide Convention.

Although few domestic or international observers doubted that the "Pol Pot clique" was guilty of grave abuses, the trial had a limited effect for a few reasons. It had serious procedural flaws that gutted it of international legitimacy. The tribunal failed to respect the defendants' right to be presumed innocent. Even the tribunal's long-winded title came close to announcing their guilt: "The People's Revolutionary Tribunal Held in Phnom Penh for the Trial of the Genocide Crime of the Pol Pot-Ieng Sary Clique."[17] The judge presiding over the trial, Keo Chenda, revealed his belief that the defendants were guilty before the trials began, saying at a press conference: "Trying the Pol Pot-Ieng Sary clique for the crime of genocide will on the one hand expose all the criminal acts that they have committed and mobilize the Kampuchean people more actively to defend and build up the people's power, and on the other hand show the peoples of the whole world the true face of the criminals who are posing as the representatives of the people of Kampuchea."[18]

Pol Pot and Ieng Sary were tried without appearing in court, and there was no communication between the absent defendants and their appointed attorneys. Defense counsel was not permitted to cross-examine witnesses. Finally, the defense mounted a feeble line of argument, suggesting that defendants' role in the atrocities was mitigated by the fact that they were mere accomplices to crimes ultimately conspired and executed by China. The trial lasted just five days, and the "Pol Pot-Ieng Sary clique" was found guilty of genocide and sentenced to death.[19]

Cold War politics also undermined the trial's effects. In an era when China and the United States had aligned loosely against Moscow, many international organizations and foreign governments viewed the PRK regime as a pawn of the Soviet Union and its chief regional ally, Vietnam. Many outsiders thus viewed the proceedings as "show trials" orchestrated by the Kremlin to justify Vietnam's occupation of Cambodia and hegemony over Indochina. Although Chinese support of the Khmer Rouge regime was clear, the tribunal's pointed references to a Chinese master plan of genocide fueled impressions that the trials were nakedly political in nature. As noted above, the 1979 trials of Pol Pot and Ieng Sary followed shortly after China's ill-fated invasion of Vietnam in the spring of 1979.

KHMER ROUGE PAWNS IN THE "SECOND COLD WAR"

In the context of Cold War rivalry, the guilty verdicts against Pol Pot and Ieng Sary had limited practical impact. They were issued at a time when the convicted defendants still controlled much of the country's territory and could not be apprehended. Khmer Rouge leaders remained well beyond the reach of the new Cambodian regime, surrounded by a small army of AK-47-wielding guerilals and waging guerilla war from the jungle. Far from being squeezed into submission by the international community, Khmer Rouge forces were given quiet support by anti-Soviet governments in China, the member states of the Association of Southeast Asian Nations (ASEAN), and the West.

Under the cover of the jungle and with direct or indirect support from many foreign governments, Khmer Rouge forces were able to regroup and wage asymmetrical warfare against the vastly superior PRK and Vietnamese conventional forces. They continued to terrorize vulnerable villages and vie for control of significant swathes of the countryside.

Although the Khmers Rouges had few admirers in the international community, their capacity and willingness to fight made them convenient instruments for external powers bent on "bleeding Vietnam white." An elaborate proxy war unfolded, with the Soviet Union and Vietnam defending the PRK regime against a determined Khmer Rouge insurgency fueled by foreign states. Foremost among these were China and Thailand. China provided an estimated $100 million of military and other aid per year, while the Thai military—fearful of an encroaching Vietnamese hegemon on their doorstep—provided sanctuaries and ferried aid to the Khmer Rouge guerillas. The United States and other Western powers offered substantial albeit less direct support, as did some ASEAN members.

To isolate the PRK politically, the Western powers and ASEAN states organized a "Coalition Government of Democratic Kampuchea" (CGDK) nominally headed by Sihanouk and including the remnants of the old right-wing republican forces. Western and ASEAN governments led a campaign to present the Cambodian struggle as an issue of foreign (Vietnamese) conquest and occupation. They met with widespread success outside the Soviet bloc. For largely self-interested reasons, the governments of most developing countries framed the issue as a violation of a weak state's sovereignty rather than the liberation of a brutalized population. By an overwhelming international vote in 1982, the CGDK retained the Cambodian seat at the United Nations (UN) General Assembly.

The construction of the CGDK—which had Sihanouk as its President, republican Son Sann as Prime Minister, and former DK head of state Khieu Samphan as Vice President—was an effort by outside powers to develop a credible alternative to PRK rule. It was also a way to whitewash the fact that without the Khmers Rouges, the resistance would have lost its ability to fight. Like the *mujihadin* in Afghanistan or right-wing paramilitaries in Central America, the CGDK included ugly bedfellows used by the United States, China, and their allies to bash Soviet-sponsored regimes and drain the overstretched USSR. In that context, Pol Pot and his colleagues became useful pawns and "cannon fodder" in a larger regional and geopolitical game. Little serious thought was given to putting them on trial for the abuses they had committed just years before. Rather, key states held their noses and used the United Nations to provide an indirect kind of political cover for the Khmer Rouge-led insurgency.

Although strategic considerations trumped concerns about justice in the major political capitals, some private actors did continue to promote Khmer Rouge accountability. In 1981, human rights advocate Gregory Stanton founded the Cambodian Genocide Project at Yale University to study the abuses of the late 1970s and promote justice. In 1986, human rights investigator David Hawk and international lawyer Hurst Hannum presented a model prosecution brief to the International Court of Justice entitled "The Case Against the Standing Committee of the Communist Party of Kampuchea."[20] Hawk also established a Cambodian Documentation Commission to compile information about the DK period. The work of scholars, journalists including Dith Pran and Sidney Schanberg, and films such as *The Killing Fields* (1984) also drew considerable public attention to the terror that had transpired in Democratic Kampuchea.

USING KHMER ROUGE KILLERS TO BUILD THE PEACE

The efforts described above planted the seeds for a broader international campaign to hold Khmer Rouge leaders responsible for their abuses, but little changed on the ground. Conflict continued between the Khmers Rouges and PRK forces throughout the mid-1980s. The situation began to change only gradually after 1985, when Mikhail Gorbachev's policies of *glasnost* and *perestroika* foreshadowed a possible rapprochement between the USSR and its principal adversaries. Without a steady stream of Soviet support, Vietnam would be hard-pressed to survive a crippling regime of international sanctions and maintain large forces on Cambodian soil.

By 1987, shifting relations among the great powers and their regional allies began to "unlock" the conflict. The Indonesian government brokered a series of informal talks in which the relevant parties began to explore a possible peace settlement in Indochina. In the context of those negotiations, the Khmers Rouges again appeared politically indispensable. Governments in China, some Southeast Asian states, and to a lesser extent the United States believed it would be difficult to drive the Vietnamese out of Cambodia and establish a "friendly" regime in Phnom Penh without the leverage that Khmer Rouge guerillas brought to the table. It would also be exceedingly difficult to guarantee the peace if the Khmers Rouges were excluded from the ultimate bargain. Without a clear stake in the settlement, grizzled Khmer Rouge veterans would simply keep on fighting, with or without external support.

In April 1989—while the Iron Curtain began to collapse and Soviet aid to Vietnam began a steep downward descent—officials in Hanoi and Phnom Penh announced plans for the withdrawal of Vietnamese forces in September. That announcement raised the real possibility of renewed civil war between the Khmers Rouges and a vulnerable PRK regime that had lost its crutch. In July 1989, UN Secretary General Javier Peréz de Cuéllar convened a series of peace talks in Paris to hammer out a compromise for Cambodia's future. Around the table were representatives from the PRK, the three branches of the CGDK (including the Khmers Rouges), and 18 other states. China in particular insisted on giving a seat to the Khmers Rouges. Other states also saw the Khmers Rouges as abhorrent but indispensable partners in building the peace.

Although the initial peace talks in Paris failed to deliver a comprehensive settlement, they kick-started a diplomatic process led by the permanent five members of the Security Council—the United States, United Kingdom, France, China, and the USSR. Eventually those talks produced general agreement on the Paris Peace Accords, signed in October 1991. The Accords established a UN Transitional Authority for Cambodia (UNTAC) that would monitor a cease-fire among the parties and conduct free and fair elections to produce a successor government in Phnom Penh. UNTAC's mandate did not call for an accountability process against the Khmers Rouges or any other party. Its objectives were to build a sustainable peace and to facilitate the country's political reconstitution.

DEMISE OF THE KHMER ROUGE MOVEMENT AND A NEW PUSH FOR ACCOUNTABILITY

The Paris Peace Accords and the UNTAC mission represented important turning points in Cambodia's modern history and in the fate of the Khmer Rouge movement. Over the following several years, the movement gradually came apart at the seams. Internationally, a major new push for accountability was afoot. These developments provided some of the enabling conditions for a Khmer Rouge accountability process.

UNTAC AND THE POLITICAL MARGINALIZATION OF THE KHMERS ROUGES

In 1992 and 1993, UNTAC officials administered most of Cambodia's public affairs, as well as international processes like refugee repatriation and the demobilization of militants in the border areas. Almost immediately, the Khmers Rouges began to break their end of the bargain and violate the cease-fire agreement. Negotiations between UN and Khmer Rouge officials fell apart in mid-1992, and thereafter "blue-helmet" UN peacekeepers had to fend off Khmer Rouge attacks and defend vulnerable Cambodian villages from Khmer Rouge pillage and plunder. Khmer Rouge malfeasance sapped their already meager public appeal and reinforced their status as international pariahs.

By May 1993, when the UN successfully sponsored national elections, the Khmers Rouges boycotted the affair and added to their own political marginalization. In that sense, the UNTAC mission contributed to the ultimate resolution of the Khmer Rouge problem and helped pave

So Vanna alias So Phim (center, in black) and Khmer Rouge troops visiting a unit of volunteer Vietnamese communist fighters, 1973. The photo was taken shortly before the allied guerillas launched an attack on the Krabao military base in Kampong Cham province as part of the civil war against the Khmer Republic government led by Marshal Lon Nol. So Phim later became the Secretary of the CPK for the Eastern Zone of Democratic Kampuchea. He committed suicide on June 3, 1978.
Source: Documentation Center of Cambodia Archives/VNA

Chroy Chang-Va Bridge, opposite the French Embassy, after its destruction by Khmer Rouge forces during the civil war, 1970.
Source: Documentation Center of Cambodia Archives/The Lon Nol Dossier

Khmer Rouge soldiers slain by Khmer Republic troops in fighting near the French Embassy in Phnom Penh, 1970
Source: *Documentation Center of Cambodia Archives/The Lon Nol Dossier*

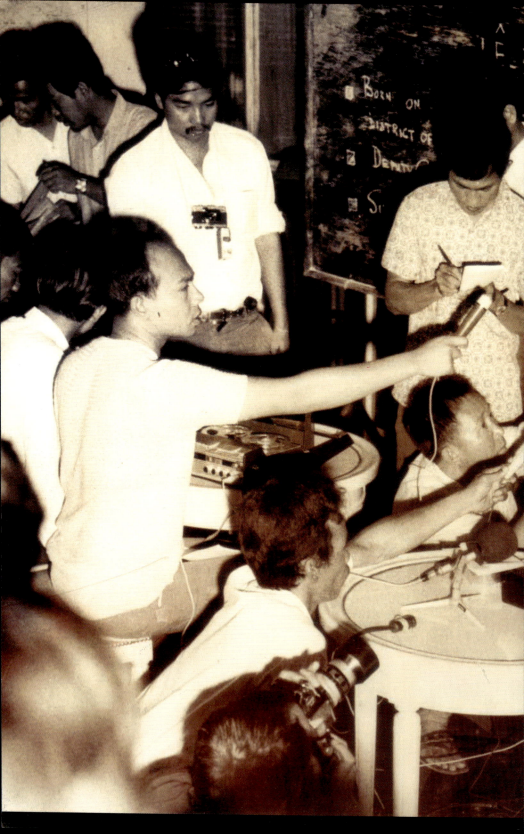

Press Conference with Lon Nol's spokesperson, Am Rong, whose name was pronounced *I'm Wrong* by Western reporters at the time, 1970. His assistant Chhang Song, standing to the right with a logo on his left sleeve, was later appointed Minister of Information of the Khmer Republic.
Source: Documentation Center of Cambodia Archives/The Lon Nol Dossier

Soldiers of the Kampuchean United Front for National Salvation taking over Phnom Penh, January 1979. Allied Vietnamese armed forces and members of the Front ousted the Khmers Rouges and established the People's Republic of Kampuchea. Photo by Ding Fong.

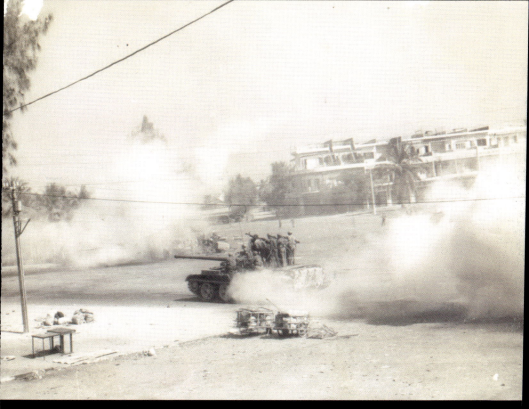

Constructed as the National Theater in 1950, the Khmers Rouges used this building as an Assembly Hall where they adopted their resolution to form Democratic Kampuchea in 1976. In 1979, the same building was used for the People's Revolutionary Tribunal's genocide trial against Pol Pot and Ieng Sary. The entrance sign reads "People's Assembly of Kampuchea." *Source: Documentation Center of Cambodia Archives*

Keo Chenda, President of the People's Revolutionary Tribunal (center, behind placard), August 1979.
Source: Documentation Center of Cambodia Archives

Proceedings at the People's Revolutionary Tribunal, August 1979.
Source: Documentation Center of Cambodia Archives

Courtroom of the People's Revolutionary Tribunal, August 1979.
Source: Documentation Center of Cambodia Archives

the way for an eventual accountability process. In 1994, the Cambodian National Assembly formally outlawed the Khmer Rouge organization. From a political standpoint, the Khmers Rouges were clearly losing ground.

However, the elections did not resolve other political tensions in the country. Intense political jockeying took place before and throughout the UNTAC period. In 1990, leaders of the PRK regime had changed the country's official name to the State of Cambodia. Their leader was a young Prime Minister Hun Sen, who had defected from the Khmer Rouge ranks during the DK period and joined the resistance in southern Vietnam. Under Hun Sen, Cambodia steered way from socialist economic tenets and sought foreign investment, but the evaporation of Soviet and Vietnamese aid left the economy in dire straits. Liberalization of the economy also exacerbated economic inequalities, spurring some popular indignation and perhaps contributing to the prolongation of civil war.

The most formidable political challenge to Hun Sen was a revived royalist party called FUNCINPEC, led by Sihanouk's son, Prince Norodom Ranariddh. Frustration at the harsh conditions of daily life under the PRK and the regime's heavy-handed security practices helped Ranariddh accumulate considerable support among both rural and urban constituencies. FUNCINPEC also enjoyed the backing of many Western and ASEAN governments.

In the May 1993 elections, FUNCINPEC and Hun Sen's Cambodian People's Party (CPP)—the successor to the governing party of the PRK—finished in almost a dead heat. After some negotiation, Ranariddh and Hun Sen agreed to serve as Co-Prime Ministers in a newly refashioned constitutional monarchy, with Sihanouk as King and official head of state. A new constitution was adopted several months later, and the country was again re-named to become the Kingdom of Cambodia. Continuing rivalries within Cambodian politics would profoundly affect subsequent efforts for Khmer Rouge accountability.

A NEW SURGE FOR INTERNATIONAL CRIMINAL JUSTICE

The idea for putting Khmer Rouge officials on trial re-emerged in this context, as a fragile political settlement in Phnom Penh and the establishment of a tentative peace raised the possibility of pursuing justice at some point in the not-too-distant future. Much of the pressure for accountability came from the outside. In Southeast Asia and elsewhere, the end of the Cold War created new perceived opportunities for pursuing international criminal justice.

Liberal Western democracies—which have been the principal drivers behind international criminal law since the era of Nuremberg—had more political opportunity to press for their notions of justice. A Soviet veto no longer hovered over the UN Security Council table, as Russia temporarily groped for aid and turned toward internal reconstruction. The more "unipolar" order gave Western powers (and above all the United States) much greater capacity to advance their values, norms, and interests, enabling the rapid development of international humanitarian and human rights law and instruments. In addition, Western states were more prepared to prioritize human rights law than they had been during the Cold War, when they frequently subordinated such concerns to the geo-strategic struggle against the Soviets.

Beginning in 1993, a number of international and mixed criminal courts were created to deal with instances of mass human rights abuses. The UN tribunals for the former Yugoslavia and Rwanda (the ICTY and ICTR, respectively) were the first of this genre. They attracted enormous resources and attention as models for ensuring accountability and promoting human rights in the new global order. The push for justice in Cambodia would become part of that post-Cold War trend, but the ECCC would eventually possess unique features reflecting the different political circumstances of its creation.

The political momentum for accountability in Cambodia increased in 1994, when American policy shifted. Before and during the UNTAC years, the U.S. government had acquiesced in the inclusion of the Khmers Rouges as part of the Cambodian settlement. With the elections over, officials in Washington turned their eye toward justice. The U.S. Congress passed the Cambodian Genocide Justice Act, established a special Office of Cambodian Genocide Investigation at the State Department, and provided funds for the collection of documentary and other potential evidence against Khmer Rouge officials.[21]

With support from the State Department, Yale University's Cambodian Genocide Program established the Documentation Center of Cambodia (DC-Cam) as a field office and began to lay the groundwork for possible trials.[22] DC-Cam soon accumulated voluminous information about Khmer Rouge atrocities through interviews, mapping studies, and documents received from the Cambodian government and private sources. Among other things, the materials amassed by DC-Cam included numerous original documents from the DK regime, such as minutes of meetings, confessions, biographies of party cadres, and correspondence among Khmer Rouge officials.[23] These materials have been indispensable to the ECCC, constituting the bulk of the documentary evidence used at the tribunal.

THE KHMER ROUGE MOVEMENT BEGINS TO CRUMBLE

Despite progress in documenting DK atrocities, conditions on the ground were still not ripe for an accountability process in the mid-1990s. The Khmers Rouges were marginalized politically, but neither UNTAC nor the Cambodian government had engineered their military defeat. With the former leaders of Democratic Kampuchea at large in the jungle, criminal trials were understandably a secondary concern for Cambodia's leaders. The first problem was to bring the insurgency to heel.

In 1994 and 1995, Khmer Rouge guerillas continued launching their annual dry-season offenses, but without continued foreign support and large new waves of recruits, the Khmer Rouge insurgency began to weaken. Both the CPP and FUNCINPEC sought to secure political defections from senior Khmer Rouge figures by offering them land, money, choice military or government positions, and protection from prosecution. Both CPP and FUNCINPEC officials justified their actions as the necessary steps toward reconciliation. They also argued—correctly—that "buying out" some senior Khmer Rouge figures would splinter the movement. However, peace and reconciliation were not the parties' only incentives. Khmer Rouge defectors could be useful allies in tipping the correlation of political and military forces between the two rival parties.

The pivotal moment came in August 1996, when Hun Sen brokered a deal with Ieng Sary. Under the deal, which Ranariddh approved, Ieng defected to the government, bringing with him about 3,000 guerillas from a total Khmer Rouge fighting force estimated at 7,500. In exchange, King Sihanouk issued a formal pardon to Ieng for the death sentence handed down during the 1979 tribunal. Sihanouk also granted Ieng amnesty from prosecution under the 1994 law prohibiting Khmer Rouge membership. This deal would later produce tension in the negotiations to create the ECCC.

The government's deal with Ieng Sary was controversial and unpopular among many members of both political parties. However, it appeared to be effective in breaking the back of the Khmer Rouge movement. In 1997, Khmer Rouge solidarity came undone. Both the CPP and FUNCINPEC began talks with former DK Defense Minister Son Sen, but Pol Pot did not respond kindly on hearing the news. Son Sen and his family were brutally murdered in June 1997. Shortly afterward, Khmer Rouge cadres arrested Pol Pot and three of his comrades for the killing. In July, Pol Pot was found guilty after a short outdoor hearing in the jungle town of Anlong Veng. That "People's Tribunal" sentenced him to life in a makeshift Khmer Rouge prison, and he died the following year, reportedly of natural causes.

THE UNITED NATIONS ENGAGES

The fragmentation of the Khmer Rouge movement enabled the international community to push for Khmer Rouge accountability more assertively in 1997. In April of that year, the UN Commission on Human Rights opened the door for talks with the Cambodian government by requesting that the UN Secretary-General examine Cambodian requests to bring past human rights violators to justice.[24] Two months later, Co-Prime Ministers Hun Sen and Prince Ranariddh formally requested UN help in promoting Khmer Rouge accountability.[25]

Relations between the United Nations and Cambodian government quickly came under strain, however. Throughout the mid-1990s, tension had simmered between Hun Sen and Ranariddh, with the former gradually gaining an upper hand. As the 1998 national elections approached, that rivalry intensified. Among other things, both CPP and FUNCINPEC officials sought to attract Khmer Rouge defectors on terms that would benefit their respective political parties.[26] In July 1997, tensions came to head when Hun Sen accused Ranariddh of illegal dealings with the Khmers Rouges and other offenses. The CPP proceeded to orchestrate what most international observers have called a coup. In bloody street fighting, troops loyal to Hun Sen defeated their royalist opponents, and an uncertain number of FUNCINPEC officials were executed. Ranariddh was marginalized to a considerable degree, and CPP elements in the armed forces solidified their control of most areas of the country.[27]

The events of July 1997 exacerbated an already sour relationship between the CPP leadership and the foreign governments most interested in holding Khmer Rouge trials. The U.S. Congress cut off all bilateral aid to the Cambodian government shortly after the episode. Even neighboring Southeast Asian states, which were usually disinclined to intervene in one another's domestic political affairs, expressed concern and delayed Cambodia's scheduled entry into ASEAN. Calls mounted in Western capitals for Hun Sen to be condemned for human rights abuses. In 1998, U.S. Congressman Dana Rohrabacher (R-CA) took a bolder step, introducing a successful House resolution that advocated bringing international criminal charges against Hun Sen, not just "a handful of geriatric Khmer Rouge leaders."[28]

It was in this politically charged context that the United Nations became more deeply engaged in planning for a tribunal. In the spring of 1998, UN Secretary-General Kofi Annan decided to assemble and dispatch a small "group of experts" to Cambodia to study the possibility of bringing Khmer Rouge leaders to justice. The members of that group included Australian Ninian Stephen, Mauritian Rajsoomer Lallah, and American Steven Ratner, and they arrived in Phnom Penh in November with a three-fold mandate. Their job was to evaluate the evidence against surviving Khmer Rouge officials; assess the practical feasibility of bringing them to trial; and analyze various ways that a tribunal could be organized.

Meanwhile, political and military conditions were changing rapidly on the ground. The Hun Sen government consolidated its position through a decisive victory in the July 1998 national elections. At the same time, the strength of the Khmer Rouge insurgency continued to deteriorate, creating a greater opportunity to apprehend potential suspects and conduct trials.

MORE KHMER ROUGE DEFECTORS

In December 1998, the Khmer Rouge movement suffered a major blow when former DK leaders Khieu Samphan and Nuon Chea announced their defections to the government. To some outside observers, this provided an ideal time to redouble efforts to form a tribunal. However, Hun Sen shifted away from his previous support of criminal trials and instead emphasized the need for "national reconciliation." He argued that Khieu Samphan and Nuon Chea should be welcomed "with bouquets of flowers, not with prisons and handcuffs." He argued that Cambodia "should dig a hole and bury the past and look ahead to the 21st century with a clean slate."[29]

Opposition parties and international critics attacked Hun Sen's remarks and accused the CPP of negotiating with the United Nations in bad faith. Less than two years earlier, he had requested UN assistance in setting up a tribunal. Hun Sen was not interested in justice, they claimed; he had merely used the threat of international trials to scare Khmer Rouge leaders into defecting. That, critics argued, would enable the CPP to claim credit for eradicating the Khmers Rouges and add to the party's ill-gotten political dominance.

The growing dispute reflected a genuine difference in emphasis between the various parties involved. To Hun Sen and the CPP, reconciliation required breaking apart the Khmer Rouge insurgency, bringing its leaders to heel, and securing their political allegiance (or at least their pledge to disband and disarm). A tribunal—or planning for a tribunal—was useful primarily in achieving those objectives. Where the interests of justice and pacification collided, Hun Sen favored the latter. To most of the UN officials involved, the two processes—weakening the Khmer Rouge movement and holding trials—were closely related and not necessarily sequential. Justice was necessary to achieve real reconciliation, they reasoned, and bringing Khmer Rouge crimes to light would contribute to the movement's dissolution.

There were also clear political undertones to the dispute. To the CPP, reconciliation implied peace and stability in Cambodia under its leadership. To many international (and especially Western) officials involved in the process, reconciliation meant developing a more liberal and tolerant multiparty democracy. Many saw the CPP's pre-eminence as more of an obstacle than an asset in meeting that objective. Thus, they tended to be less concerned than the Hun Sen government about the possibility that trials could be politically destabilizing. Tensions between the CPP and some key states and offices within the United Nations ran deep, contributing to mutual suspicion and creating a political challenge to the establishment of a tribunal.

NEGOTIATIONS FOR THE TRIBUNAL

From the outset, key officials from the Cambodian government and United Nations had very different views of how to organize the tribunal. Although neither side was monolithic, Cambodian officials tended to favor a smaller number of trials and a greater relative role for the local judicial system. UN officials generally favored a preponderantly international process with a more open-ended universe of defendants. Subsequent negotiations focused primarily on reconciling those positions.

Many key questions needed to be addressed, including the laws and procedures to apply, the scope of the tribunal's jurisdiction, its funding, its location, and the composition of its personnel. The preferences of the Cambodian government and United Nations diverged on essentially all of these major points. As discussed below, the U.S. government also came to play a crucial role as an unofficial third party to the negotiations, often siding with the United Nations but sometimes taking positions more favorable to Cambodia. Periodic U.S. intervention would become one of the keys to achieving the ultimate agreement on the ECCC.

DIFFERENT APPROACHES TO ACCOUNTABILITY

The most basic issue to be decided was the form of the tribunal. Most key members of the UN staff and key Western governments began with the notion that a tribunal would resemble the ICTY or ICTR. Thus, in the spring of 1998, the U.S. government had proposed that the UN Security Council issue a resolution creating an "International Criminal Tribunal for Cambodia" in The Hague.[30] Cambodian officials tended to favor a preponderantly domestic tribunal with some international support. Hun Sen tried to discourage the formation of an international tribunal, both by appealing to the norm of sovereignty and by arguing that any such body would also need to investigate foreign countries' roles in supporting the Khmers Rouges after 1979.[31]

The debate magnified with the completion of the UN experts' report. In February 1999, shortly before the planned release of the report, a copy was leaked to the Cambodian government. The experts argued that a *prima facie* case existed against members of the Khmer Rouge regime for genocide and crimes against humanity. They also concluded that criminal trials would be workable. However, they recommended that the UN Security Council pass a resolution to establish an *ad hoc* international tribunal like the ICTY or ICTR. They recommended against using Cambodia's courts, contending that the domestic system lacked the trained personnel, infrastructure, and culture of respect for human rights to manage the trials reliably.[32]

Hun Sen immediately struck back. Before the official release of the report, he dispatched a testy letter to Kofi Annan. He challenged the UN experts' conclusion about an international tribunal and asserted that:

> If improperly and heedlessly conducted, the trials of Khmer Rouge leaders would panic other former Khmer Rouge officers and rank and file, who have already surrendered, into turning back to the jungle and renewing the guerrilla war in Cambodia.[33]

He added that Cambodia was considering a Truth and Reconciliation Commission along South African lines as a possible model for accountability, a suggestion that U.S. Secretary of State Madeline Albright promptly and publicly rejected.[34] The U.S. government favored a tribunal.

Just days after Hun Sen's letter arrived, the last pillar of the Khmer Rouge leadership fell when government forces arrested Ta Mok, the infamous one-legged military officer and DK Central Committee member known by many as "the Butcher." Mok was taken from his hideout near the Thai border and thrown in prison in Phnom Penh. With a key suspect in custody, trials were finally a real practical possibility. Politics were the primary remaining obstacle.

Tense exchanges ensued between the Cambodian government and United Nations. Hun Sen announced publicly that he intended to try Mok in a domestic court.[35] Cambodian officials also accused the United Nations and major Western backers of the tribunal—such as the United States and France—of hypocrisy. Foreign Minister Hor Nam Hong met Annan and complained that the United Nations had responded to the government's 1997 request for help only the following year, when the insurgency was nearly vanquished.[36] The underlying accusation was clear: the United Nations and powerful Western states were riding in on a white horse, demanding justice and claiming the moral high ground only after the CPP had done most of the dirty work to defeat Khmer Rouge insurgents.

In a late March meeting with Ambassador Thomas Hammarberg, the UN Special Representative for Human Rights, Hun Sen was even more assertive. He announced that there would be no international trials and that any international intervention in its domestic affairs would be a violation of national sovereignty. Any outside legal experts would have to be invited by the court, but they would be relegated to observer status. Hor Nam Hong put the case bluntly:

> The international community talks about finding justice for the Cambodian people. Cambodia agrees to find justice for Cambodians and for humanity. But what has the international community been doing vis-à-vis the Khmer Rouge lately? Once the genocidal Khmer Rouge regime was toppled, the so-called international community continued to support the Khmer Rouge. The so-called international community forced Cambodia to accept the Khmer Rouge as partners in the Paris Peace talks... It said nothing about responsibility of the Khmer Rouge, let alone prosecution of them. But now that Cambodia has achieved peace and reconciliation, they call for an international tribunal. Can we

trust them?³⁷

Hammarberg and other UN officials were undeterred in their demand that justice be delivered according to international standards. Cambodian courts were simply not up to the task, they argued. However, the government's stinging critique suggested that it would not follow UN guidance gently.

EDGING TOWARD A HYBRID TRIBUNAL

Establishing a tribunal via UN Security Council resolution would be difficult, because China and Russia expressed opposition to any course of action that would impose trials on Cambodia. Indeed, Hun Sen argued that a purely international tribunal in Cambodia was a practical impossibility, because China opposed the idea and would veto such a proposal at the UN Security Council.³⁸ China's veto threat meant that the UN Security Council could not impose an international court on Cambodia: it would have to compromise. In that sense, China's position strengthened the hand of the CPP.

To deal with the impasse, members of the international community began to consider another possible model: the idea of a hybrid or "mixed" tribunal. In April 1999, U.S. Senator John Kerry met with Hun Sen to discuss the idea of including both Cambodian and international judges and personnel. No mixed tribunal had ever been established, but Kerry and some other U.S. officials saw a shared process as a way to break the negotiating deadlock and promote accountability.³⁹ The UN leadership took no official position on the form of a tribunal, leaving the door open to compromise.

Meanwhile, pressure increased on the Cambodian government to hold trials meeting international standards. Part of that pressure came from the CPP's domestic opposition, particularly the more liberal Sam Rainsy Party.⁴⁰ Pressure also came from foreign-funded NGOs and Western governments and media. Human rights groups and Western governments argued, like the UN experts, that Cambodian courts could not deliver credible trials due to endemic corruption and mismanagement. Many Cambodians agreed—including elites as well as the general public—adding to the political push for robust international participation. The notion of a hybrid tribunal gave Hun Sen an option short of international control, and his previous hard-line position began to soften.

In a step toward compromise, Hun Sen informed Kofi Annan in late April that he planned to try Mok and others in domestic courts but that "foreign judges and prosecutors would be allowed to take part fully," rather than merely observing the process, to ensure that the trials met "international standards of due process."⁴¹ Meetings between Hun Sen and Hammarberg explored the mixed tribunal option more fully in the months that followed.

Conditions on the ground also continued to increase the practical possibility of trials. In May, government forces also arrested Duch, the former head of Office S-21, the hub of the gruesome DK internal security system. He and Mok waited in jail cells in Phnom Penh while the next phase of negotiations got underway to determine their fate and the fates of some of their Khmer Rouge colleagues. In the summer of 1999, the UN Office of Legal Affairs convened a team to consider options on behalf of the United Nations, and Hun Sen appointed a special Khmer Rouge Tribunal Task Force for a similar purpose.

In July 1999, the UN Secretariat issued a proposal that would establish a hybrid tribunal with majority international participation. The concept of a hybrid court also gained at least implicit support from a broad array of countries in the UN Commission on Human Rights and other forums. Many observers saw the hybrid tribunal concept as a necessary compromise but also an improvement over the ICTY model. The ICTY and ICTR had provided valuable legal judgments and precedents, but by 1999, they had cost the international community enormous sums of money and had begun to draw complaints from donor governments. Critics also accused the large ICTY and ICTR bureaucracies of moving at a snail's pace and consuming too many resources.

The locations of the ICTY (in The Netherlands) and ICTR (in Tanzania) drew fire as well. Distance made it difficult for the victimized populations in the Balkans and Rwanda to follow the complex and lengthy proceedings. Distance also reduced opportunities for UN personnel to interact with local officials, jurists, attorneys, and the public in the affected countries. Some critics accused the international tribunals of delivering victors' justice to satisfy Western elite audiences and interests. Limited on-the-ground contact with the affected communities and Western domination of the proceedings sometimes made that charge difficult to dispel.

Problems with the *ad hoc* tribunals encouraged the international community to consider other options. In 1998, over 60 countries signed the Rome Statute to establish the International Criminal Court in The Hague. However, that body would only be empowered to hear cases relating to future crimes, and it possessed some of the same shortcomings as the ICTY and ICTR. Thus, the mixed tribunal concept that came to be known as the "Cambodia model" had some appeal.

DIGGING INTO THE DETAILS OF A MIXED TRIBUNAL

In August 1999, the United Nations and Cambodian government entered a second phase of negotiations, drilling deeper into the possible features of a mixed tribunal. A UN delegation traveled to Phnom Penh to meet with Senior Minister Sok An and other members of the Khmer Rouge Tribunal Task Force. The following month, the Cambodian group visited Kofi Annan in

New York and U.S. officials in Washington. The parties thus began to hammer out the more specific details of what would eventually become the ECCC.

Most of the key bones of contention were already well known by August 1999. One related to the "balance of influence" on the tribunal. Which side would have a majority of judges or personnel? How would those personnel be picked? Whose law would govern? A second set of contentious issues concerned jurisdiction. Who would stand trial, and for what offenses? Differences in opinion were manifest in the competing draft laws that the UN and Cambodian delegations presented to establish a tribunal.

DETERMINING THE "BALANCE OF INFLUENCE"

One of the most contentious issues was to decide upon the balance of foreign and international influence at the tribunal. At the heart of this debate was mutual mistrust between the governing CPP and the predominantly Western UN officials and member states involved in the talks. CPP officials feared that a UN-dominated process could be used by foreign powers and opposition domestic political parties to undermine the CPP's standing.

On the other side, many Western and UN officials and domestic opposition parties believed that the CPP lacked both the competence and commitment to human rights needed to conduct fair trials and deliver credible justice. Many also feared that CPP corruption and political meddling would gut the trials of legitimacy. Further, the CPP's opponents believed that it would use the tribunal process to build its public appeal in Cambodia and defuse pressures to govern more effectively and democratically.

The negotiators first had to determine which side would have "home-field advantage." Would trials be held in an entirely separate judicial body governed by international law—the UN's favored option—or in normal domestic courts, as the Cambodian team preferred? In October 1999, the U.S. government again intervened with a proposed compromise to break the impasse. New Ambassador to Cambodia Kent Wiedemann and U.S. Ambassador for War Crimes David Scheffer floated the idea of establishing special chambers within the Cambodian court system. (This is the origin of the tribunal's official name: the "Extraordinary Chambers.") The Cambodian government accepted that formula, partly because the label of "special" or "extraordinary" chambers was more compatible with its notion of sovereignty. The UN team did not immediately agree but gradually came to acquiesce in the compromise.[42]

A second aspect of the balance of influence was the relative number of judges and personnel that each side would have. Hun Sen rejected the July 1999 UN proposal for a predominantly international court, arguing that Cambodians should be in the majority.[43] Wiedemann suggested a "supermajority" provision to work through the stalemate. Cambodian judges would constitute the majority, but at least one international judge would be required for any judicial decision. The Cambodian team agreed. The UN negotiators were less prepared to accept the proposal, arguing that its acceptability would depend on how judges were appointed.

The UN team argued that all judges and prosecutors should be appointed by the Secretary-General to ensure that international standards were met and reduce the scope for political interference. Human rights groups, fearful that the CPP would "stack the court" with obedient party members, took the same position. The Cambodian government favored having all judges appointed by the Supreme Council of Magistracy, the body responsible for judicial appointments under Cambodian law, though it anticipated that the UN Secretary-General would nominate international judges for approval. Again, Hun Sen invoked sovereignty as a shield. This issue remained unresolved during the early rounds of negotiation.

JURISDICTIONAL BOUNDS

Another contentious set of issues revolved around the proposed tribunal's jurisdiction. First, who would be tried? The tribunal's *personal jurisdiction* would become a major sticking point. All parties agreed to focus on a limited universe of defendants—trying all levels of surviving Khmer Rouge cadres would be logistically impossible, quite possibly destabilizing, and arguably unjust. However, UN and Cambodian views differed in important ways. UN officials argued that the criminal proceedings should include both senior leaders of the Khmer Rouge and those believed to be most responsible for the atrocities. The UN Group of Experts had suggested that 20 to 30 defendants would be appropriate.

The Cambodian government vehemently objected. Hun Sen and his negotiating team argued that the prosecutions should be highly selective and focused on just four or five senior Khmer Rouge leaders. Casting a wider net, they argued, would invite social unrest and possibly renewed civil war. In 1999, the CPP was still very much in the midst of a "reconciliation" program aimed at coaxing remaining Khmer Rouge fighters out of the jungle by offering formal or informal amnesties and giving some defectors positions in the government. Hun Sen announced publicly in late 1999 that he intended to try only "four or five of the people responsible."[44]

Critics argued that Hun Sen also sought to limit the number of potential defendants out of self-interest. Until defecting to Vietnam in 1977, he served as a military cadre in the Khmer Rouge armed forces. The same is true of other high-ranking CPP members, such as Heng Samrin and Chea Sim. A wide prosecutorial net could conceivably catch former cadres of their levels. At the very least, allowing prosecutors to go after a large number of defendants could reveal some of the CPP's dirty laundry. Any trial of a current government official could reduce the CPP's popularity and perceived legitimacy by focusing attention on the deals it cut with Khmer Rouge officials during its campaign for defections and reconciliation.

Haggling over the tribunal's personal jurisdiction also ignited debate on the 1996 pardon of Ieng Sary. The UN team insisted that amnesties and pardons were invalid in cases of crimes against humanity. The Cambodian government pushed back, arguing that it could not overturn a constitutionally sanctioned act by the King and again warning of the possibility of renewed civil strife if the tribunal did not select its defendants carefully.

It was easier to reach agreement on the tribunal's *temporal jurisdiction*—the period of history that it would address when hearing criminal cases. After some negotiation, UN and Cambodian officials agreed that the tribunal would hear cases for alleged crimes only between April 17, 1975 and January 6, 1979. That limit was justified as appropriate given the tribunal's focus on Khmer Rouge atrocities, but it also served clear political ends. Some outside powers, and the United States in particular, sought to avoid consideration of crimes during the Cambodian civil war of 1970-75, because attention would certainly be drawn to the abuses of the U.S.-backed Lon Nol regime and the carpet bombing of Cambodia by American B-52s.

The Cambodian government was equally concerned about stretching the tribunal's jurisdiction beyond January 1979, wishing to avoid a focus on crimes committed during the Third Indochina War.[45] Focusing prosecution only on the DK period made it much more likely that only Khmer Rouge officials—and not CPP or foreign leaders or troops—would be tried. That limitation did not please everyone, but it was a virtual imperative in building political support for the Extraordinary Chambers, both at home and abroad.

The *subject-matter jurisdiction* of the Extraordinary Chambers was also less controversial. UN and Cambodian officials largely agreed on the most important crimes to be charged and the need to draw from both international and domestic law. They agreed to hold trials for three well-known international crimes: genocide, crimes against humanity, and grave breaches of the 1949 Geneva Conventions (better known as "war crimes.") The ECCC would also be empowered to try suspects for the domestic crimes of homicide, torture and religious persecution under the 1956 Cambodian Penal Code. Lastly, the tribunal would be able to hear cases for the destruction of cultural property and attacks against diplomatic personnel. These offenses are described in more detail in Chapter 2.

COMPETING BLUEPRINTS

To dig in its position, the Cambodian government's Khmer Rouge Tribunal Task Force sent a draft law to the National Assembly in early 2000, copying UN Secretary-General Kofi Annan.

The draft law raised many eyebrows at UN headquarters in New York. It envisioned a tribunal with a Cambodian majority of judges and Cambodian and international Co-Prosecutors and Co-Investigating Judges. It included only vague provisions on judicial appointments and the touchy issue of amnesties and pardons. It also left unclear how disputes between Co-Prosecutors and Co-Investigating Judges would be resolved, which UN officials feared would leave the CCP with an effective veto over indictments. Annan responded quickly with a number of demands. He insisted on an international majority of judges, an exclusion of amnesties and pardons, and a foreign prosecutor.

With the two sides locking horns, the U.S. government again intervened and secured a compromise. Senator John Kerry proposed creating a five-judge panel (with three Cambodians) that would adjudicate disputes between Co-Prosecutors and Co-Investigating Judges and decide based on a super-majority vote. UN Legal Counsel Hans Corell and his negotiating team remained skeptical of a hybrid tribunal with majority Cambodian participation. However, under pressure from the UN Secretary-General and U.S. government to forge an agreement, they returned to Phnom Penh.

In July 2000, Corell offered a significant concession, describing the tribunal as "a Cambodian court with the participation of international judges and prosecutors." At roughly the same time, however, the UN team unveiled a plan of its own in the form of a draft Framework Agreement that would govern UN and Cambodian conduct in the creation and operation of the tribunal. The draft Framework Agreement included some key provisions on sticky issues. For example, it gave the United Nations authority to appoint international judges, as well as the international Co-Prosecutor and two new officials: a deputy international prosecutor and a deputy director of administration. UN negotiators insisted that the Cambodian law establishing the tribunal could not differ materially from the draft Framework Agreement.

The UN team's presentation of the draft Framework Agreement catalyzed another series of protracted negotiations, but the Cambodian side gave little ground. In January 2001, the Cambodian National Assembly approved a law (the "2001 ECCC Law") establishing the ECCC. Opposition leader Sam Rainsy withdrew his support for the tribunal, arguing that it would merely be a CPP-led show trial, but the government pressed ahead. In August, King Sihanouk signed the law.

The differences between the 2001 ECCC Law and the draft Framework Agreement were substantial; the two documents brought tensions between the UN and Cambodian sides into plain public view. The United Nations insisted that international support—whether in the form of staff, money, or political support—would come only when an acceptable Framework

Agreement was in force. This, of course, meant an agreement more in line with UN preferences. The Cambodian government resisted, again invoking the veil of sovereignty and threatening to conduct the trials on its own if the UN team did not agree to abide by the terms of the 2001 ECCC Law.

THE UN TEAM WALKS OUT...AND RETURNS

Frustrated with what they saw as Cambodian intransigence, the UN team abandoned the negotiations and headed home in early 2002. Many human rights organizations supported the move, arguing that any deal giving the CPP such a strong role would lead to a tribunal plagued by corruption, procedural irregularity, and blatant political influence. It was better to have no trials, they argued, than to hold a flawed process that would not deliver credible justice. A number of Western governments—especially in Scandinavia—voiced private or public support for the pull-out on similar grounds.

However, several other key UN member states condemned the cessation of talks. The United States was probably the most important engine for re-engagement, but Japan, France, India, Russia, and others echoed the view that abandoning talks would mean missing any chance for justice and acquiescing in impunity. Some high-ranking UN officials also pushed for re-engagement, including the Secretary-General's Special Representative for Human Rights in Cambodia, Peter Leuprecht.

In a resolution sponsored by Japan and France in late 2002, the UN General Assembly authorized the Secretary-General to renew the ECCC negotiations and encouraged the UN team to return to Phnom Penh and conclude a deal on the tribunal. Most western European governments abstained from that vote, but the resolution passed. Soon afterward, the UN team was effectively ordered to return to the negotiating table. Hans Corell and his team were displeased with the resolution, which forced their hand and reduced their subsequent bargaining leverage by making it clear that the powers behind them were ready to make a deal.[46]

THE 2003 FRAMEWORK AGREEMENT

Negotiations recommenced in early 2003 but made little progress. The UN team reissued demands for a majority of international judges and an independent prosecutor nominated by UN officials. The Cambodian government declined and insisted on strict adherence to the 2001 ECCC Law. Driven by public and private appeals from powerful UN member states—including Australia, Japan, the United States, and France—the UN negotiators returned for a final round of talks several months later. The draft Framework Agreement followed the 2001 ECCC Law in most respects and thus represented a victory of sorts for the Cambodian government. However, it did include a few key changes. Perhaps most notably, it contained language indicating that the government would not request amnesties or pardons for alleged crimes under the ECCC's jurisdiction.

Many human rights advocates criticized the draft Framework Agreement as a defeat for international standards of justice, fairness, and due process. Mike Jendrzejczyk of Human Rights Watch argued that it embodied "the lowest standards yet for a tribunal with U.N. participation." He argued that "with Cambodia's judiciary at the center of the tribunal, the agreement ensures that it will be politics and not law that dominate the tribunal's work."[47]

Kofi Annan expressed a similar view, albeit more diplomatically, in a 2003 report to the UN General Assembly shortly before the two sides signed the Framework Agreement. He wrote:

> [T]here are continued problems related to the rule of law and the functioning of the judiciary in Cambodia resulting from interference by the executive with the independence of the judiciary. I would very much have preferred that the draft agreement provide for both of the Extraordinary Chambers to be composed of a majority of international judges... given the precarious state of the judiciary in Cambodia.[48]

Annan also issued an explicit threat that "any deviation by the government from its obligations could lead to the United Nations withdrawing its cooperation and assistance from the process."[49] That threat has remained intact, albeit with varying levels of credibility, to this day. Nevertheless, gritting their teeth, the UN team signed the Framework Agreement with the Cambodian government in June 2003.

REVISING THE LAW GOVERNING THE ECCC

The next step would be for the Cambodian government to amend the 2001 ECCC Law to bring it into conformity with the Framework Agreement. That process was delayed for over a year after the 2003 Cambodian general elections resulted in political paralysis. The CPP won comfortably but lacked enough seats in the National Assembly to convene the legislature. Both the opposition FUNCINPEC and Sam Rainsy Parties refused to join a CPP-led coalition, and deadlock ensued. The CPP used honey and vinegar to try to pry legislators away from the opposition parties but met with little success. Without a functioning legislature, Cambodia could not pass an updated version of the 2001 ECCC Law. Justice was again on hold.

Hun Sen insisted that he would make passage of the revised ECCC Law and formal adoption of the Framework Agreement top priorities as soon as the legislature reconvened. Eventually, FUNCINPEC and the CPP struck a deal in the summer of 2004 and formed a coalition. In October, the National Assembly adopted the Framework Agreement and passed an amended

ECCC Law (the "ECCC Law").

THE RESULTS OF THE NEGOTIATIONS: THE AMENDED ECCC LAW

The amended ECCC law finally put the Khmer Rouge trials in sight. It reflected compromises and concessions by both sides. However, the form of the tribunal it created aligned more closely with the preferences of the Cambodian government.

THE BALANCE OF INFLUENCE

First, the Cambodian team was able to secure majority participation at the ECCC. Its judges would constitute the majority in each of the ECCC's three judicial bodies. The Pre-Trial Chamber, which adjudicates disputes preceding the onset of criminal trials, includes three Cambodian and two international judges. The same ratio applies in the Trial Chamber, which hears the criminal cases. A panel of four Cambodian and three international judges will hear appeals. This contrasts with the hybrid courts in Sierra Leone and East Timor, where international judges comprised majorities. Moreover, under the terms of the Framework Agreement and ECCC Law, Cambodia's Supreme Council of Magistracy appoints all Cambodian judges and selects among international judges nominated by the UN Secretary-General.[50] This adds to the Cambodian government's influence on the bench.

One key provision limits the possible scope of Cambodian judicial dominance. All chambers require a super-majority decision, meaning that there must be an affirmative vote of at least four judges at the Pre-Trial or Trial Chamber and an affirmative vote of at least five judges at the Supreme Court Chamber to reach a decision. The super-majority provision effectively grants the international judges a veto and represents a significant institutional safeguard for the UN side. However, it also means that international judges cannot dictate outcomes by convincing a single "swing judge" on the Cambodian side.

The Cambodian government also secured control over several of the most important administrative posts at the Extraordinary Chambers. Unlike other mixed tribunals, which have had an international Registrar to manage administrative operations, the ECCC has a Cambodian Director of the Office of Administration and an international Deputy Director. The Chief of Public Affairs is also a Cambodian appointee, giving the government a commanding role in public communication from the tribunal.

Prosecutorial duties are more evenly split between Cambodian and international Co-Prosecutors. Defense teams also comprise Cambodian and international attorneys, and the ECCC has a Defense Support Section led by an international appointee. (A much more detailed account of the ECCC's structural features and rules of procedure is provided in Chapter 2.)

JURISDICTIONAL COMPROMISE

The scope of the tribunal's personal jurisdiction was less clearly defined in the amended ECCC Law. As noted above, the CPP placed great priority on limiting the tribunal's jurisdiction to a small number of the most high-ranking or otherwise influential Khmer Rouge defendants. The result of negotiations reflected that emphasis. The Framework Agreement and ECCC Law permit the Extraordinary Chambers to try only "senior leaders" of the Khmer Rouge regime and others who were "most responsible for serious violations of Cambodian and international law" during a very specific timeframe of April 17, 1975 to January 6, 1979.

The amended ECCC Law did not establish a concrete number of defendants, allowing the Cambodian government and UN officials to interpret the provision on personal jurisdiction differently. The Cambodian team read the provision narrowly and suggested that the universe of defendants would be small, amount perhaps to five or six people. UN officials did not agree to that reading of the law, envisioning a somewhat larger number of possible defendants. The absence of agreement of a specific number helped achieve political buy-in from both sides, but it essentially deferred an important question that remains a source of dispute at the ECCC today.

PAYING FOR JUSTICE

Finally, the Cambodian government got a relatively good deal from a financial standpoint. After the passage of the amended ECCC Law, UN and Cambodian negotiators agreed on a proposed budget for the ECCC over a three-year period of operations. The estimated tab for the tribunal was $56 million. International donors would pay $43 million, and Cambodia would contribute $13 million. Ultimately, the Cambodian government paid for only a fraction of its allotted share, with international donors contributing the rest. (International donors have also contributed a large majority of the additional funds later requested by the ECCC.)

UNDERSTANDING THE OUTCOME

Overall, it is fair to characterize the outcome of the negotiations as a qualified victory for the Cambodian government, especially when comparing the ECCC to other hybrid tribunals, in which the United Nations has exercised a much more decisive upper hand. The Cambodian government's negotiating successes owed largely to political forces that gave it significant bargaining leverage. Since the era of Nuremberg, most international criminal tribunals have been constructed immediately after conflicts, while a weak host country government stumbles to gain its balance and extends its hand to international institutions for support. That occurred in the former Yugoslavia, Rwanda, Sierra Leone, and East Timor. When a transitional government has dire need for cash and arms to solidify its position, it has little leverage to dictate the terms of transitional justice.

The Cambodian case was different. Unlike the cases above, the Khmer Rouge tribunal was designed years after war, during a period when the CPP had achieved dominance in Cambodia's domestic political system and was not deeply dependent on Western cash or kudos to survive. The Cambodian government no longer needed UN or other foreign troops to quell a festering insurgency. The most likely defendants were under its watch or control. Although Cambodia enjoyed large volumes of international aid, the CPP had fortified its domestic position during a period of strident criticism from the West. Thus, CPP leaders arguably saw only modest need for the stamp of international approval that an international or hybrid tribunal would afford. Cambodian negotiators could credibly threaten to walk away from the table and manage the trials themselves.

The Cambodian government also benefitted from divisions within the UN Security Council. China was long opposed to the tribunal and called the Khmer Rouge matter an "internal affair." Officials in Beijing promised to veto any proposal that came to the Security Council without Cambodia's support, giving the Cambodian government an important form of insurance. China's opposition was based partly on its long-standing normative commitment to strong state sovereignty, but it was also a way to avoid embarrassment given the nexus between Khmer Rouge and Maoist ideology and China's crucial role in backstopping the DK regime. Moreover, Chinese leaders were not eager to see a Western-led tribunal on their doorstep, fearful that such a process would draw attention to China's own human rights record.

Regionally, the Cambodian government faced little pressure to arrange the tribunal in accordance with UN wishes. Its ASEAN neighbors harbored no love for the Khmers Rouges but generally invoked the norm of "non-interference" and took a hands-off approach to the tribunal. Thailand and a few others were less than enthused about a process that could shed light on their own past support for the Khmer Rouge insurgency, but the greater concerns were forward-looking. No Southeast Asian government was eager to alienate the CPP or China by taking sides with the United Nations. Many shared China's concern about introducing a precedent of international tribunals to adjudicate human rights violations in the region. Governments in Myanmar, Laos, and Vietnam—often castigated by human rights groups—had particular reasons to fear that they could be next in line. This helps to explain why even officials in Hanoi, once the bitterest of foes to the Khmers Rouges, stayed quietly on the sidelines of the tribunal debate.[51]

International pressure on the CPP came primarily from the West, as it has in the run-up to most internationalized tribunals. Western donors certainly were not without influence.

They accounted for a large share of Cambodia's sizable foreign aid, both bilaterally and via their roles as board members at multilateral agencies like the World Bank and Asian Development Bank. Western states were also major sources of export revenue, tourism, and private investment. Without these important levers, the United Nations may not have secured agreement for a hybrid tribunal at all. Yet Western donors were not all-powerful in Cambodia, which also had increasing sources of aid and trade in Asia.

Western ambivalence about running a mixed tribunal with the Cambodian government also reduced the leverage—or at least bargaining effectiveness—of the UN team. Without a clear set of marching orders and consistent political backing, the UN negotiators arguably lost some of their credibility. They also had to proceed somewhat tentatively given the expressed objection of many Western officials and human rights groups to making compromises with the CPP. Moreover, unilateral U.S. interventions early in the talks were effective in breaking key impasses but created uncertainty about where the real bargaining authority lay. Finally, Kofi Annan's decision to send his negotiators back to Phnom Penh in early 2003 shortly after they had walked out of the talks doubtlessly undercut their leverage in subsequent negotiations.

THE LEGACY OF THE NEGOTIATIONS

The complex domestic and international politics surrounding the ascent and demise of the Khmer Rouge movement contributed to long delays in justice and tough, sometimes bitter wrangling over the establishment of a tribunal. The eventual agreement to create the ECCC reflected shared aspirations for justice, but it also reflected political calculations and compromises. The cold pragmatism sometimes needed to make the ECCC a reality sat uncomfortably beside the lofty ideals of justice that the institution was designed to fulfill. This tension continues to affect the ECCC and perceptions of the accountability process today.

Although polls show broad public support for the ECCC in Cambodia, the tribunal has won much less overwhelming support among international observers. Critics of the ECCC point to key compromises and limitations of the tribunal as evidence that politics won out over principles. Above all, critics contend that the tribunal leaves too much power in the hands of the CPP, which many human rights activists and domestic opposition figures—and some foreign governments—view as venal (or at least ineffective). Critics worry that the ECCC is designed in a way that allows Hun Sen and his colleagues to manage the proceedings to suit their own interests rather than the interests of victims.

Opponents of the CPP fear that whenever politics and principles of justice diverge, the Cambodian leadership will prioritize political gain, bullying judges into politically motivated verdicts and corrupting the process. This, critics charge, could fatally damage the credibility of the proceedings, tarnish the reputation of the United Nations, and undermine the broader advancement of international criminal justice.

On the other side of the debate are supporters of the ECCC. They generally acknowledge the risks of the mixed tribunal structure adopted but argue that Cambodian participation is important as a way of promoting reconciliation and connecting victims to the process. Supporters also express confidence that civil society and public engagement can help prevent corruption or undue political influence. Moreover, supporters view the compromises leading up to the tribunal's establishment as necessary steps toward achieving the best possible accountability process. Allowing the ECCC to fail, they argue, would be tantamount to giving up on justice—an outcome even worse than imperfect trials. Genocide scholar Gregory Stanton, who was among the first Western advocates for Khmer Rouge trials, has argued that in a case like Cambodia, "perfection is the enemy of justice."[52]

There are strong arguments on both sides. Pro-tribunal voices have generally come out on top, but critics of the tribunal remain vocal even as the trials proceed. Continuing spats between the Cambodian government and the United Nations during the ECCC's first three years of operations only reinforce the perception that politics are intruding excessively into the search for justice. Indeed, some of the key disputes between UN and Cambodian officials during the negotiations to establish the ECCC continue to resurface. The most salient recent example is the dispute between the Cambodian and international Co-Prosecutors on whether to extend the prosecution beyond the five suspects currently in custody. (That dispute, which led to a split decision by the Pre-Trial Chamber along national/international lines in August 2009, is discussed more fully in Chapter 3.) The same basic arguments that Cambodian and UN negotiators used when debating the scope of the tribunal's personal jurisdiction are back. The intensity of debates about the ECCC's basic legitimacy has only increased with allegations of corruption against Cambodian court officials (as discussed in Chapter 4).

The ambivalence among rights groups and some foreign governments has lent a sense of uncertainty to the ECCC process, which has often seemed to be on the verge of falling off of its tracks. This is the same sense that surrounded the long negotiations leading to its creation. As the next chapter will discuss in greater detail, the ECCC's relative instability as a judicial body is not only attributable to episodic flare-ups among its donors and observers. The institution itself reflects and embodies those continuing tensions.

[1] The close "fraternal" relationship between the Vietnamese and Cambodian communist movements, in which Vietnam considered itself the older sibling, would later become a source of resentment to some Khmer Rouge leaders and contribute to the nationalistic character of the DK regime. *See generally* BEN KIERNAN, HOW POL POT CAME TO POWER: COLONIALSM, NATIONALISM, AND COMMUNISM IN CAMBODIA, 1930-1975 (2ND ED. 2004); STEVE HEDER, CAMBODIAN COMMUNISM AND THE VIETNAMESE MODEL: IMITATION AND INDIEPENDENCE, 1930-1975 (2004).

[2] Agreement on the Cessation of Hostilities in Viet-Nam, July 20, 1954, Fr.-Viet Minh.

[3] NAYAN CHANDA, BROTHER ENEMY: THE WAR AFTER THE WAR 58-59 (1986).

[4] *See* DAVID P. CHANDLER, THE TRAGEDY OF CAMBODIAN HISTORY: POLITICS, WAR AND REVOLTION SINCE 1945, at 107-15, 125-30 (1991).

[5] *See* BEN KIERNAN, THE SAMLAUT REBELLION, 1967-70: THE ORIGINS OF CAMBODIA'S LIBERATION MOVEMENT (Monash University Centre of Southeast Asian Studies Working Papers No. 4 and 5, ca. 1975).

[6] CRAIG ETCHESON, AFTER THE KILLING FIELDS: LESSONS FROM THE CAMBODIAN GENOCIDE 6 (2005).

[7] *See* WILLIAM SHAWCROSS, SIDESHOW: KISSINGER, NIXON, AND THE DESTRUCTION OF CAMBODIA 236-58 (1979); KIERNAN, *supra* note 1, at 228-357.

[8] For two early accounts of the evacuation of Phnom Penh, *see* FRANÇOIS PONCHAUD, CAMBODIA YEAR ZERO (1978); BERNARD HAMEL, DE SANG ET DE LARMES: LA GRANDE DÉPORATION DU CAMBODGE (1977).

[9] Numerous histories of Democratic Kampuchea have been written. Some of the leading academic treatments of the period include CHANDLER, *supra note 4*, at 236-72; BEN KIERNAN, THE POL POT REGIME: RACE, POWER, AND GENOCIDE IN CAMBODIA UNDER THE KHMER ROUGE, 1975-79 (1996); CRAIG ETCHESON, THE RISE AND DEMISE OF DEMOCRATIC KAMPUCHEA (1984); MICHAEL VICKERY, CAMBODIA, 1975-1982 (1984). A leading journalistic account is ELIZABETH BECKER, WHEN THE WAR WAS OVER: CAMBODIA UNDER THE KHMER ROUGE REVOLUTION (1986).

[10] Stephen P. Heder, *The Kampuchean-Vietnamese Conflict*, *in* THE THIRD INDOCHINA CONFLICT 21-62 (David W.P. Elliott, ed., 1981).

[11] *See* DAVID P. CHANDLER, VOICES FROM S-21: TERROR AND HISTORY IN POL POT'S SECRET PRISON (1999).

[12] *See* KIERNAN, *supra* note 9, at 251-309

[13] On the Sino-DK relationship, *see* ROBERT S. ROSS, THE INDOCHINA TANGLE: CHINA'S VIETNAM POLICY, 1975-1979, at 155-67 (1988); KIERNAN, *supra* note 9, at 357-85; Sophie Richardson, China, Cambodia, and the Five Principles of Peaceful Co-existence: Principles and Foreign Policy (2005) (Ph.D. dissertation, University of Virginia); John D. Ciorciari, Unmanageable Lackeys: The Asymmetrical Alliance between China and the Pol Pot Regime, unpublished manuscript (on file with the author). The photo on the cover of this book shows a high-level delegation from the Politburo of the Chinese Communist Party visiting Democratic Kampuchea on November 5, 1978. Heading the delegation were Wang Dongxing and Yu Qiuli, both trusted associates of the late Mao Zedong. Both were leftists who resented Vietnam's budding alliance with the USSR and sought to support the DK regime in their effort to bleed Vietnam. During this trip, Pol Pot requested that China send troops to Cambodia, and Wang carried that request back to Beijing, but China ultimately rejected that request. *See* ANDREW SCOBELL, CHINA'S USE OF MILITARY FORCE 129-30 (2002).

[14] POL POT PLANS THE FUTURE: CONFIDENTIAL LEADERSHIP DOCUMENTS FROM DEMOCRATIC KAMPUCHEA, 1976-1977, at 11 (David Chandler, Ben Kiernan, and Chantou Boua, eds. and trans., 1988). *See also* Karl D. Jackson, *The Ideology of Total Revolution*, in CAMBODIA 1975-1978: RENDEZVOUS WITH DEATH 37-78 (Karl D. Jackson, ed., 1989).

[15] CHANDA, *supra* note 3, at 98-102.

[16] KING C. CHEN, CHINA'S WAR WITH VIETNAM, 1979: ISSUES, DECISIONS, AND IMPLICATIONS 92 (1987).

[17] Decree Law No. 1: Establishment of People's Revolutionary Tribunal at Phnom Penh to Try the Pol Pot-Ieng Sary Clique for the Crime of Genocide (July 15, 1979), *reprinted in* PRK RESEARCH AND PUBLICATION OFFICE, TRIBUNAL FOR THE PROSECUTION OF THE GENOCIDAL POL POT-IENG SARY CLIQUE 305 (1979).

[18] Keo Chanda, Minister of Information, Press, and Culture, Chair of Legal Affairs Committee, press conference of July 28, 1979, *cited in* GENOCIDE IN CAMBODIA: DOCUMENTS FROM THE TRIAL OF POL POT AND IENG SARY 47 (Howard J. DeNike et al., eds., 2000).

[19] For brief accounts of the trial, see EVAN GOTTESMAN, CAMBODIA AFTER THE KHMER ROUGE: INSIDE THE POLITICS OF NATION-BUILDING 60-66 (2002); ETCHESON, supra note 6, at 14-17.

[20] Hurst Hannum and David Hawk, The Case Against the Standing Committee of the Communist Party of Kampuchea, Draft ICJ Memorial (1986).

[21] Cambodian Genocide Justice Act, 22 U.S.C. 2656, Part D, §§ 571-74.

[22] DC-Cam became an independent Cambodian NGO in January 1997 and operates with the support of the Cambodian government and funding from a wide range of international sources. For a brief history of DC-Cam and its cooperation with Yale University's Cambodian Genocide Program, see ETCHESON, supra note 6, at 53-76; Letter from the Cambodian Council of Ministers to DC-Cam (Feb. 18, 1999), available at www.dccam.org/Abouts/History/DC-Cam_Permission_in_Eng.htm; Documentation Center of Cambodia, History and Description of DC-Cam, available at www.dccam.org/Abouts/History/Histories.htm.

[23] For a detailed review of the types of materials held by DC-Cam and their possible contribution to the Khmer Rouge trials, see John D. Ciorciari with Youk Chhang, Documenting the Crimes of Democratic Kampuchea, in BRINGING THE KHMER ROUGE TO JUSTICE: PROSECUTING MASS VIOLENCE BEFORE THE CAMBODIAN COURTS 224-34 (Jaya Ramji and Beth Van Schaack, eds., 2005).

[24] See U.N.C.H.R. Res. 1997/49 (XVIII), E/CN.4/1997/L.80 (Apr. 11, 1997).

[25] Letter dated June 21, 1997 from the First and Second Prime Ministers of Cambodia to the UN Secretary-General, in U.N. Doc. A/51/930-S/1997/488 (June 24, 1997).

[26] DAVID W. ROBERTS, POLITICAL TRANSITION IN CAMBODIA 1991-99: POWER, ELITISM AND DEMOCRACY 140-44 (2001). The competition for Khmer Rouge allegiance between FUNCINPEC and the CPP also appears to have contributed to the splintering of the Khmer Rouge movement. Seth Mydans, The Khmer Rouge Implosion, N.Y. TIMES, June 16, 1997.

[27] For one description of this complex and controversial series of events, see SORPONG PEOU, INTERVENTION & CHANGE IN CAMBODIA: TOWARDS DEMOCRACY? 290-310 (2000).

[28] See House Resolution 533, 105th Congress, 2nd Session (1998). The quoted text comes from Rohrabacher's oral defense of the resolution on the House floor in October 1998. Jesse Helms introduced the resolution in the Senate. See NGO Letter to Congress on Cambodia, INDOCHINA INTERCHANGE 9:1 (Jan. 1999).

[29] Seth Mydans, Cambodian Leader Resists Punishing Top Khmer Rouge, N.Y. TIMES, Dec. 29, 1998.

[30] David Scheffer, The Extraordinary Chambers in the Courts of Cambodia, in INTERNATIONAL CRIMINAL LAW 222-23 (M. Cherif Bassiouni, ed., 3rd ed. 2008).

[31] Hun Sen included that suggestion in a letter to Kofi Annan. Hun Sen War Crimes Court Would Try U.S., SYDNEY MORNING HERALD, Jan. 22, 1999.

[32] See Report of the Group of Experts for Cambodia, established pursuant to G.A. Res. 52/135, U.N. GAOR, 53rd Sess., Annex, ¶ 110, U.N. Doc. A/53/850, S/1999/231 (Mar. 16, 1999).

[33] Letter from Prime Minister Hun Sen to UN Secretary-General Kofi Annan (Mar. 3, 1999), available at www.camnet.com.kh/ocm/government7.htm.

[34] Keith B. Richburg, U.S. Wants Tribunal for Top Khmer Rouge, WASH. POST, Mar. 4, 1999.

[35] Premier Says Khmer Rouge Leaders Will Be Tried in the Country, BBC SUMMARY OF WORLD BROADCASTS, Mar. 15, 1999.

[36] See Elizabeth Becker, Cambodia Spurns U.N. Plan for Khmer Rouge Tribunal, N.Y. TIMES, Mar. 13, 1999.

[37] See Thomas Hammarberg, How the Khmer Rouge Tribunal Was Agreed: Discussions between the Cambodian Government and the UN, SEARCHING FOR THE TRUTH (2001).

[38] China reportedly used a variety of carrots and sticks to discourage the CPP from proceeding with the tribunal. TOM FAWTHROP AND HELEN

Jarvis, Getting Away with Genocide? Elusive Justice and the Khmer Rouge Tribunal 234 (2004).

[39] Scheffer, *supra* note 30, at 226.

[40] *Rejection of International Khmer Rouge Trial Frustrates Opposition*, Deutsche Presse-Agentur, Mar. 15, 1999.

[41] Letter from the Cambodian Prime Minister to the UN Secretary-General (Apr. 28, 1999).

[42] Scheffer, *supra* note 30, at 229-30.

[43] Kay Johnson, UN-Cambodia Split on Khmer Trial, Straits Times (Singapore), Aug. 27, 1999; Philip Shenon, *U.N. Plans Joint War Crimes Tribunal for Khmer Rouge*, N.Y. Times, Aug. 12, 1999.

[44] *Only a Few Khmer Rouge to Face Trial: Hun Sen*, UN Wire, Dec. 23, 1999.

[45] Opposition leader Sam Rainsy stated publicly that any tribunal considering the period after 1979 would surely implicate Hun Sen. *Cambodian Opposition Leader Says Wider Tribunal Would Implicate PM*, Deutsche Presse-Agentur, Jan. 19, 1999.

[46] Fawthorp and Jarvis, *supra* note 38, at 202-03.

[47] Human Rights Watch, *UN: Khmer Rouge Tribunal Flawed*, commentary dated Apr. 30, 2003.

[48] Report of the Secretary-General on Khmer Rouge Trials, presented to the U.N. to the General Assembly, 57th Sess., Agenda item 109(b), U.N. Doc. A/57/769 (Mar. 31, 2003).

[49] *Id.*

[50] Law on the Establishment of Extraordinary Chambers in the Courts of Cambodia for the Prosecution of Crimes Committed During the Period of Democratic Kampuchea, as amended and promulgated on Oct. 27, 2004, NS/RKM/1004/006, art. 11 new; Agreement between the United Nations and the Royal Government of Cambodia Concerning the Prosecution under Cambodian Law of Crimes Committed During the Period of Democratic Kampuchea (June 6, 2003), art. 3.

[51] For more on the international political factors that helped shape the tribunal, see Etcheson, *supra* note 6, at 151-62; John D. Ciorciari, *Great-Power Posturing and the Khmer Rouge Tribunal*, Searching for the Truth (Fall 2002).

[52] Gregory H. Stanton, *Perfection Is the Enemy of Justice: A Response to Amnesty International and Human Rights Watch's Criticisms of the Agreement Between the Cambodian Government and the U.N. to Establish the Khmer Rouge Tribunal*, paper published online by Genocide Watch (May 19, 2003), *available at* www.genocidewatch.org/aboutgenocide/stantonperfectionjustice.htm.

2. OVERVIEW OF THE EXTRAORDINARY CHAMBERS

ANNE HEINDEL

The ECCC is the first legal institution of its kind. No other court established to prosecute mass crimes has the same hybrid structure, civil law orientation, or distant temporal jurisdiction. As a consequence, although the ECCC greatly benefits from the prior experience of international criminal tribunals, it also must address many new questions and answer them through practice.

This chapter provides an overview of the core documents that guide this process: the Framework Agreement, ECCC Law, and Internal Rules adopted by the Extraordinary Chambers, which govern many procedural aspects of the tribunal. Unique features of the ECCC's legal character, structure, and subject matter jurisdiction are discussed, and notable challenges and unanswered questions are highlighted. Finally, some of the key actors who are involved in shaping the character and jurisprudence of this Court are introduced.

A UNIQUE HYBRID COURT

Unlike the International Criminal Tribunals for the Former Yugoslavia (ICTY) and Rwanda (ICTR) or the Special Court for Sierra Leone (SCSL), the ECCC was not established by the United Nations or by an international agreement. Instead, the ECCC was established by a domestic Cambodian law pursuant to a 2003 framework agreement between the United Nations and the Royal Government of Cambodia setting out the "legal basis and the principles and modalities for... [their] cooperation." This Framework Agreement was approved by the Cambodian legislature and implemented by it through a 2004 law (the "ECCC Law"). According to the Framework Agreement, the ECCC has been created "with international assistance...within the existing court structure of Cambodia for the prosecution of crimes committed during the

Child survivors of S-21 Norng Chanphal and Norng Chanly after their rescue, January 10, 1979. They were the last prisoners sent to S-21, arriving with their mother on January 1, 1979.
Source: Documentation Center of Cambodia Archives/HTV (Ho Chi Minh Television)

period of Democratic Kampuchea."

Although the ECCC is formally part of the Cambodian court system, it also has some features of an international court. For this reason, Cambodian Deputy Prime Minister Sok An has characterized it as "a national court with international characteristics." He has noted that it is "a mixed or hybrid tribunal—firmly located in the national courts but involving both national and international law; national and international judges, prosecutors, staff; and national and international financing."[1] The ECCC's Pre-Trial Chamber (PTC) has said that the Court is "a special internationalized tribunal" because it is "an independent entity within the Cambodian court structure."[2] Nevertheless, no ECCC Chamber has clearly defined or directly ruled on the Court's legal status to date.

The legal characterization of the ECCC as either a national or an international court—or something in between—matters because it could impact a number of issues that have arisen before the Court. These include the extent of the ECCC's responsibility to remedy violations of Kang Guek Eav (Duch)'s human rights while he was detained without trial for eight years by the Cambodian Military Court, and the impact on ECCC jurisdiction of Ieng Sary's 1996 amnesty and pardon. These topics are addressed in Chapter 3.

The ECCC is not the first hybrid court, but it has many features that make it unique. For example, it is the only court with distinct national and international "sides" that have separate hiring and reporting structures. Moreover, it is the only one to have "co-" national/international prosecutors, to provide a substantial role for (co-)investigating judges, or to provide an opportunity for victims to act as civil parties. The ECCC is also the only internationalized court with the jurisdiction to prosecute international crimes committed in the 1970s. The ECCC's unique temporal jurisdiction falls after the Nuremberg trials—the post-WWII origins of international criminal prosecutions for serious crimes—and before international criminal law's rapid development in the 1990s with the establishment of the ICTY and ICTR. It will therefore be the first internationalized court to determine which principles of law existed during that period. Finally, the ECCC is the only internationalized court that is mandated to follow domestic criminal procedural rules—rules governing, for example, the conduct of the proceedings and the role of each party to those proceedings. As discussed below, circumstances and practicalities have nevertheless led the Court to develop its own internal rules, with some controversy as to their legal primacy.

THE ECCC'S JURISDICTION

The Khmers Rouges took control of increasingly large sections of Cambodia after the 1970 overthrow of Prince Sihanouk by General Lon Nol. Nevertheless, the official Democratic Kampuchea era is considered to have begun only after Phnom Penh fell to the Khmers Rouges on April 17, 1975. The entire population of the capital and other cities was forced to evacuate to and labor in the countryside, often on starvation rations; individuals and whole families associated with the former regime or foreign powers, intellectuals, and minority groups were killed; and eventually even Khmer Rouge cadres were purged. By the end of its three years, eight months, and twenty days in power, the DK leadership's plans to eradicate all foreign influences and develop a self-sufficient agrarian economy had resulted in the death of nearly a third of the population.[3] In December 1978 Vietnamese troops and Khmer Rouge defectors fought their way through Cambodia. Although armed conflict continued for over 10 years and the Khmers Rouges continued to exist until 1999, the DK period is considered to end on January 6, 1979, the final day before the Vietnamese-led forces took control of Phnom Penh.

The ECCC's jurisdiction is narrowly focused on the responsibility of the senior DK leadership and those most responsible for serious crimes committed between April 17, 1975 and January 6, 1979. For that reason, it will not have the capacity to reach all acts that contributed to or resulted from Khmer Rouge crimes, nor the lower-level persons who physically committed the atrocities. The Court's subject-matter jurisdiction is discussed below; its temporal and personal jurisdiction is discussed in more detail in Chapter 1.

SUBJECT-MATTER JURISDICTION

Subject-matter jurisdiction refers to the crimes a court may adjudicate. Like the statutes creating international and hybrid tribunals, the ECCC Law gives the Court the mandate to prosecute only a few serious international and national crimes, discussed below. Importantly, even though the Court has explicit jurisdiction over enumerated crimes, the Chambers will nevertheless be required to determine the legal status and elements of each during the temporal jurisdiction of the Court.

THE *NULLUM CRIMEN* PRINCIPLE: INTERNATIONAL LAW CHALLENGES

The principle of *nullum crimen sine lege*, a Latin term meaning "no crime without law," prohibits the retroactive application of criminal laws. As a consequence, acts that are not criminalized under either domestic or international law at the time they are committed may not be prosecuted. Not only must the act have been criminalized, but also the proscription must have been sufficiently accessible to the accused person. This means that the definition of the crime must have been specific enough to make it foreseeable to the accused person that his or her actions would entail criminal responsibility. The prohibited act need not have been criminalized in precisely the same terms in which it is prosecuted as long as the underlying conduct is the same.

The Framework Agreement, ECCC Law, and Internal Rules do not reference the *nullum crimen* prohibition. Nevertheless, it is one of the fundamental principles of legality and is included in numerous international instruments, including the International Covenant on Civil and Political Rights, to which Cambodia is a party. This principle's implications for the prosecution of the Khmers Rouges were also explicitly considered by the UN Commission of Experts that recommended creation of a tribunal for this purpose.

As discussed above, because the ECCC is the first internationalized court with a temporal jurisdiction falling between World War II and the rapid development of international criminal law after the Cold War, it will face unique challenges—and opportunities—to authoritatively define the existence and scope of international crimes during that period. The Chambers cannot merely assume that each substantive crime and mode of liability placed in the Court's jurisdiction by the 2004 ECCC Law complies with the *nullum crimen* principle, but must consider this principle in each case and define the charged crimes accordingly.

THE *NULLUM CRIMEN* PRINCIPLE: NATIONAL LAW CHALLENGES

ECCC Law Article 3 gives the Court jurisdiction over a few crimes in the Cambodian Penal Law of 1956. Because the 1956 Law provides that these crimes are subject to a ten-year statute of limitations (SOL), the ECCC Law also extends the SOL by thirty years. This extension raises *nullum crimen sine lege* questions. If the 1956 Law's SOL began running in 1979, the time available for prosecution would have lapsed in 1989 unless it was "tolled"—suspended because of the Khmers Rouges' complete destruction of the Cambodian justice system. If the ECCC finds that the SOL was not tolled, it will need to determine if the extension of the SOL in the ECCC Law violates the *nullum crimen* principle. If it does, the Chambers will need to determine if there are overriding reasons for nevertheless prosecuting violations of this law.

THE SUBSTANTIVE CRIMINAL LAW APPLIED BY THE ECCC

The ECCC Law empowers the Court to hear charges pertaining to five international offenses (genocide, crimes against humanity, grave breaches, destruction of cultural property, and crimes against diplomatically protected persons) and three offenses under the 1956 Cambodian Penal Code (homicide, torture, and religious persecution).

Every crime, international and domestic, has material and mental elements. A crime's material element or *actus reus* is a prohibited physical act, such as killing or otherwise harming someone. An accused person must contribute to this physical act with intent and knowledge. This is the crime's mental element or *mens rea*. Certain international crimes also have contextual elements that distinguish them from ordinary domestic offenses. For example, an unlawful killing can only amount to a "war crime" if it takes place in the context of an armed conflict. The Co-Prosecutors must prove each element of a crime in order to secure a conviction.

GENOCIDE

ECCC Law Article 4 gives the Extraordinary Chambers jurisdiction to try accused persons for genocide "as defined in the Convention on the Prevention and Punishment of the Crime of Genocide of 1948." However, as is discussed below, the definition in the ECCC Law is not identical to the definition in the Convention. No genocide charges have been brought against any of the charged persons. It is the author's understanding that the Co-Prosecutors have sought to bring genocide charges against some of the charged persons, but the Co-Investigating Judges have not yet determined that there is sufficient evidence to do so.

THE MATERIAL ELEMENT

Acts of genocide may include the following: killing members of the group; causing serious bodily or mental harm to members of the group; deliberately inflicting on the group conditions of life calculated to bring about its physical destruction, in whole or in part; imposing measures intended to prevent births within the group; or forcibly transferring children from one group to another group. An accused person must have contributed to the commission of at least one of these acts to be convicted of genocide by the ECCC.

THE MENTAL ELEMENT

The ECCC Law states that an act of genocide must be committed "with the intent to destroy, in whole or in part, a national, ethnical, racial, or religious group[.]" The 1948 Convention concludes this phrase with the words "as such."[4] The ICTY has said that the "as such" requirement means that "[t]he evidence must establish that it is the group that has been targeted, and not merely specific individuals within that group."[5]

Significantly, only national, ethnical, racial, and religious groups are protected by the Convention and the ECCC Law. It is extremely unlikely that the ECCC will find that any other protected groups fall within the definition of genocide as it existed from 1975-79 despite more recent efforts by some activists and scholars to include social, political, and economic groups. As a consequence, most crimes committed by the Khmer Rouge will not be prosecuted as genocide because they were intended to destroy political enemies. If genocide charges are brought against any accused persons, those charges will likely be for acts intended to destroy groups such as Buddhist monks, ethnic Vietnamese, and Cham Muslims.

The special intent requirement distinguishes the crime of genocide from all other crimes. To prosecute genocide, it must be proved that in contributing to one of the prohibited acts the accused person intended (or in a few cases acted with knowledge of the direct perpetrator's intent) to destroy the protected group. Nevertheless, the intent to destroy need not be the sole or even primary motive for contributing to this crime.

Intent to destroy "in whole" has been defined as the intent to bring about the destruction of the entire group, wherever its members are located, while intent to destroy "in part" has been found to include, for example, intent to destroy within a limited geographical area. According to ICTY jurisprudence, the targeted community must amount to a substantial part of the overall protected group, meaning that its loss would threaten the viability of the group as a whole.

CRIMES AGAINST HUMANITY

Article 5 of the ECCC Law gives the Extraordinary Chambers jurisdiction to try accused persons for crimes against humanity. The ECCC Law defines crimes against humanity as acts "committed as part of a widespread or systematic attack directed against any civilian population, on national, political, ethnical, racial or religious grounds." This definition is almost identical to the one in the ICTR Statute.

Like genocide, crimes against humanity often involve mass killing and other violent attacks against an identifiable group. However, because crimes against humanity do not require proof of a perpetrator's "intent to destroy" a protected group, they are usually easier to prove. Moreover, crimes against humanity include crimes committed for political reasons—which makes them applicable to many of the alleged offenses of the Democratic Kampuchea era. All five of the persons currently detained are charged with crimes against humanity.

THE PHYSICAL ELEMENT – PROHIBITED ACTS

The ECCC Law provides a non-exhaustive list of acts that, when other required elements are met, may constitute crimes against humanity. In theory, even one act may be sufficient for a conviction. Because these acts are not defined in the ECCC Law, the ECCC judges will be required to define them. The definitions below are derived from the International Criminal Court (ICC)'s Elements of Crimes. However, the principle of *nullum crimen sine lege* will require the judges to define the acts in accordance with the law as it existed during the temporal jurisdiction of the Court.

- *Murder* – killing one or more persons.

- *Extermination* – killing one or more persons as part of a mass killing of members of a civilian population, such as by inflicting conditions of life calculated to bring about the population's destruction.

- *Enslavement* – exercising powers attaching to the right ownership over persons, such as by purchasing, selling, lending, or bartering them or imposing a similar deprivation of liberty.

- *Deportation* – movement without lawful grounds of persons lawfully present in an area to another location by expulsion or other coercive acts.

- *Imprisonment* – detaining persons in a grave manner that the defendant knew violated fundamental rules of international law.

- *Torture* – inflicting severe physical or mental pain or suffering not inherent or incidental to lawful sanctions on persons in the custody or under the control of the perpetrator.

- *Rape* – penetration of any part of the body of a person with a sexual organ, or of the anal or genital opening by any object or any other part of the body. Committing such act by force, threat of force, or coercion; taking advantage of a coercive environment; or committing it against a person incapable of consent.

- *Persecution on political, racial, and religious grounds* – severely depriving persons of fundamental rights by reason of the identity of a group or targeting the group or collectivity as such.

- *Other Inhuman Acts* – inflicting great suffering or serious injury to body or to mental or physical health through an inhumane act of a character similar to the acts described above.

THE CONTEXT ELEMENT

To amount to a crime against humanity, the prohibited acts discussed above must be committed "as part of a widespread or systematic attack directed against any civilian population, on national, political, ethnical, racial or religious grounds." This contextual element distinguishes crimes against humanity from ordinary domestic crimes.

1. AS PART OF AN "ATTACK"

The ICTY and ICTR have found that an "attack" may include any mistreatment of a civilian population and need not meet the threshold of an armed conflict. Nevertheless, the Nuremberg Charter required a nexus between crimes against humanity and another crime within that court's jurisdiction—namely crimes against peace or war crimes. The ICTY has found that this requirement was particular to the Nuremberg Tribunal's jurisdiction and was not a customary international law requirement at least as of the 1990s. However, no court has yet specifically considered whether this nexus was an element of crimes against humanity in the late 1970s. For this reason, there is a possibility that the ECCC judges will determine that during the Court's temporal jurisdiction crimes against humanity could only be committed in connection with an armed conflict.

The prohibited physical act must be committed "as part of" the attack. According to ICTR/Y jurisprudence, the act may take place at a different time or place than the attack as long as it is related to the attack by its nature or consequences and is not isolated or random.

The ICC Statute uniquely defines "attack" as "a course of conduct involving the multiple commission of [prohibited] acts...against any civilian population, pursuant to or in furtherance of a State or organizational policy to commit such attack." None of the other international courts requires proof of the existence of a policy, suggesting that it is not a requirement under customary law.

2. "WIDESPREAD OR SYSTEMATIC"

The "widespread or systematic" requirement is disjunctive, meaning that it is only necessary to prove either that an attack was widespread, or that it was systematic. Moreover, it applies only to the attack; the accused person's acts do not need to be shown to be widespread or systematic.

The ICTY and ICTR have focused on the scale of abuses and number of victims in determining whether an attack is widespread. The ICTY has said that a crime may be considered widespread either by the "cumulative effect of a series of inhumane acts or the singular effect of an inhumane act of extraordinary magnitude."[6]

ICTY/R jurisprudence identifies an attack as systematic when there is evidence of an organized nature to the violent acts. The ICTY Appeals Chamber has held that, while evidence of a policy or plan may be useful in proving that an attack is systematic, it is not a required element of the crime.

3. "DIRECTED AGAINST ANY CIVILIAN POPULATION"

The attack must be "directed against any civilian population." ICTY/R jurisprudence says that this means that the civilian population must be the primary object of the attack. The "civilian population" includes members of armed forces who are no longer taking direct part in hostilities. Moreover, although the population must be primarily civilian, the presence of non-civilians does not deprive the population of its civilian nature.

4. PROTECTED GROUP REQUIREMENT

The ECCC Law includes a protected group requirement. As a consequence, at the ECCC, an

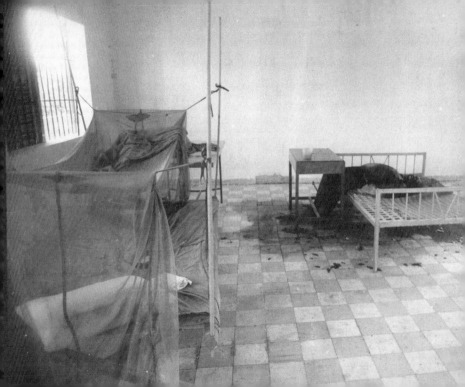

Office S-21, the Khmer Rouge central security office on the site of the former Tuol Sleng Secondary School for girls, shortly after the

attack must have been committed against a national, political, ethnic, racial, or religious group in order to constitute a crime against humanity. The ICTR is the only international court with a statute including similar language. Notably, the ICTR has found that this language does not require that a defendant possess discriminatory *intent* toward one of these five protected groups. Instead, it views this language as defining the character of the *attacks* over which the court has jurisdiction. The Extraordinary Chambers may choose to interpret the ECCC Law in a similar fashion.

THE MENTAL ELEMENT—KNOWING OF THE "WIDESPREAD OR SYSTEMATIC" NATURE OF THE ATTACK

The ECCC Law does not explicitly include a *mens rea* requirement for crimes against humanity. International courts have found that to commit crimes against humanity, an accused person must know that his or her acts form part of a larger attack. Isolated criminal acts committed without the understanding that they are part of a broader attack do not constitute crimes against humanity. Nevertheless, an accused person need not know the details of the attack or share its motive. Indeed, crimes against humanity can be committed for entirely personal reasons.

"WAR CRIMES" – GRAVE BREACHES OF THE GENEVA CONVENTIONS

War crimes are violations of international humanitarian law that give rise not only to state responsibility, but also to individual criminal responsibility. Significantly, the ECCC does not have jurisdiction to prosecute all war crimes, but only the enumerated grave breaches of the four 1949 Geneva Conventions.

THE CONTEXT ELEMENT

To convict for a grave breach, it must be shown that the alleged crime took place during and was connected to an international armed conflict. This is because, with the exception of the protections provided in Common Article 3, the 1949 Geneva Conventions apply only to international armed conflicts. Because the Conventions' grave breach articles do not list Article 3 violations, grave breaches by definition only establish criminal responsibility for violations committed during international armed conflicts. Some scholars and jurists have argued that violations of Article 3 could also constitute grave breaches of the Geneva Conventions. However, this is controversial and was not the majority view as of 1975-79.

In the *Duch* indictment, the Co-Investigating Judges found that an armed conflict existed between Cambodia and Vietnam during the entire period of the Court's temporal jurisdiction—1975-79. However, it is quite possible that the Trial Chamber will not accept this characterization and will determine that the conflict with Vietnam did not become an armed conflict until sometime in 1977, precluding prosecution for grave breaches for acts committed beforehand.

THE PHYSICAL ELEMENT

To satisfy the physical element of grave breaches, an accused person must have committed one of the enumerated acts against persons or property protected by the Geneva Conventions.

Protected property is any property that is not a lawful military target, including cultural property. Protected persons are persons not taking part in active hostilities, such as prisoners of war and civilians in the hands of a party to a conflict of which they are not nationals.

The definitions of grave breaches below are derived from the ICC's Elements of Crimes; however the principle of *nullum crimen sine lege* will require the judges to define the acts in accordance with the law as it existed during the temporal jurisdiction of the Court.

- *Willful killing* – killing persons protected by the Geneva Conventions.

- *Torture or inhumane treatment* – inflicting physical or mental pain or suffering on persons protected by the Geneva Conventions that is severe or for such purposes as obtaining information or a confession, punishment, intimidation or coercion or for any reason based on discrimination of any kind.

- *Willfully causing great suffering or serious injury* – causing great physical or mental pain or suffering to, or serious injury to the body or health of, persons protected by the Geneva Conventions.

- *Destruction and serious damage to property* – extensive destruction of property protected by the Geneva Conventions that is not justified by military necessity and is carried out wantonly.

- *Compulsory service for a hostile power* – compelling by act or threat protected persons to take part in military operations against their own country or military forces or in the service of a hostile power.

- *Willful denial of a fair trial* – depriving protected persons a fair and regular trial by denying judicial guarantees as defined in particular in the Third and Fourth Geneva Conventions.

- *Unlawful deportation or transfer or unlawful confinement of a civilian* – confining protected persons or deporting or transferring them to another State or location.

Vietnamese soldiers with child survivors of S-21, January 10, 1979. From left to right: Sochaet, Makara (named by a Vietnamese soldier after the Khmer word for the month of January, when the Khmer Rouge were ousted), Norng Chanphal, and Norng Chanly.
Source: Documentation Center of Cambodia Archives/HTV

Cambodian soldiers coming to rescue S-21 child survivors, 1979. At the far right is commander Khang Sarin, who became Minister of Interior of the People's Republic of Kampuchea. With help from Vietnamese officials, the PRK Ministry of Interior obtained and preserved many of the official documents that fleeing Khmer Rouge officials left behind. These documents are now part of the DC-Cam

- *Taking civilian hostages* – seizing, detaining, or holding civilian hostages in connection with threats that the hostages will be further detained, injured, or killed, and using the hostages to compel a State or other natural or legal person(s) to act or refrain from acting as an explicit or implicit condition for the safety or the release of such person or persons.

THE MENTAL ELEMENT

To secure convictions for grave breaches of the Geneva Conventions, the Co-Prosecutors must demonstrate that an accused person was aware of the victim's protected status and the factual circumstances establishing the existence of the international armed conflict. Moreover, the harm must be inflicted "willfully," meaning intentionally or in reckless disregard of the consequences.

DESTRUCTION OF CULTURAL PROPERTY

Article 7 of the ECCC Law gives the Extraordinary Chambers the power to hear cases involving the destruction of cultural property as set out in the 1954 Hague Convention for the Protection of Cultural Property in the Event of Armed Conflict (the "Convention on Cultural Property"). However, this convention does not itself define the elements of a crime or establish individual criminal responsibility for violations of its provisions. As a consequence, the ECCC Co-Prosecutors may be reluctant to pursue charges on the basis of this convention, and they have not done so as of yet.

Nevertheless, cultural property has long been protected by international law, including under the more general heading of "civilian" property. For that reason, it is possible that some or all of the prohibited acts against cultural property in the 1954 Hague Convention may have been subject to individual criminal responsibility during the temporal jurisdiction of the Court.

For example, as discussed above, the grave breach provisions of the Geneva Conventions of 1949 criminalize extensive destruction and appropriation of property during a time of international armed conflict. Harm to cultural property thus could be prosecuted as a grave breach if the ECCC Co-Prosecutors are able to establish the elements discussed above. Moreover, the Court may find that one or more of the acts prohibited by the Convention on Cultural Property was a crime under customary international law during the Court's jurisdiction.

CRIMES AGAINST INTERNATIONALLY PROTECTED PERSONS

Article 8 of the ECCC Law gives the Extraordinary Chambers the power to hear cases involving crimes against internationally protected persons, citing the Vienna Convention of 1961 on Diplomatic Relations (the Vienna Convention). The Vienna Convention protects the inviolability of certain protected persons and their residences and the premises of a foreign mission. However, the Convention neither establishes individual criminal responsibility nor requires states to prosecute the acts it prohibits. Therefore, although the prohibited acts may have been crimes under customary international law during the temporal jurisdiction of the Court, the ECCC Co-Prosecutors may be reluctant to pursue charges on the basis of this convention. Significantly, they have not done so as of yet.

DOMESTIC CRIMES

Article 3 of the ECCC Law gives the ECCC the jurisdiction to hear cases involving the crimes of homicide, torture, and religious persecution in the 1956 Cambodian Penal Code.

The inclusion of domestic offenses in the ECCC Law allows the prosecution to charge an accused person with both international and domestic offenses with different elements, making it more likely that they will be able to secure a conviction. For example, even if the Co-Prosecutors are unable to establish that someone is responsible for murder committed as part of an attack against the civilian population (a crime against humanity of murder), they may still be able to prove that he or she is responsible for murder under the domestic code.

Domestic charges may also be important in other ways. For example, prosecution for domestic charges shows that Khmer Rouge leaders not only violated international law, but also Cambodian law. This may make the proceedings more meaningful to Cambodians. As noted by the Co-Prosecutors in their appeal of the *Duch* closing order, some commentators "have argued that charging national crimes will foster a sense of 'ownership' of the judicial proceedings for the Cambodian judiciary and the population as a whole."

In the *Duch* closing order, the Co-Investigating Judges determined that acts identified by their investigation could constitute national crimes. Nevertheless, they did not charge Duch on this basis, finding that "these acts must be accorded the highest available legal classification, in this case: Crimes against Humanity or Grave Breaches of the Geneva Conventions of 1949."[7] This finding was appealed by the Co-Prosecutors and rejected by the Pre-Trial Chamber, which found that the CIJs had not provided any reasoning for their conclusion that international crimes are of a higher classification than domestic crimes. After finding that the domestic crimes have different legal elements than international crimes and are not subsumed by them, the Pre-Trial Chamber amended the closing order to add the charges of murder and torture. The *Duch* team has now raised objections before the Trial Chamber to these charges, including that the *nullum crimen sine lege* principle is violated due to the ten-year statute of limitations in the 1956 Code.

MODES OF LIABILITY: DIRECT AND SUPERIOR RESPONSIBILITY

When charging someone with substantive crimes listed in the ECCC Law, the Co-Prosecutors must also explain in what way he or she contributed to the crime: the mode of liability. Modes of liability refer to the various ways by which an individual can participate in the commission of a crime, either directly or indirectly. This is a crucial concept—particularly in mass-atrocity trials targeting leadership figures who may never have personally killed or tortured anyone. The Co-Prosecutors' challenge is to show that senior Khmer Rouge figures contributed to crimes in some other way, such as by creating criminal policies or plans executed by others.

At the ECCC, accused persons may be charged with either direct responsibility or their failure to exercise responsibility as a superior. Article 29 of the ECCC Law provides that direct responsibility attaches whenever an accused person "planned, instigated, ordered, aided and abetted, or committed" a crime over which the Court has jurisdiction. The statutes establishing the ICC, ICTY and ICTR contain similar modes of liability and the ECCC will likely look to their jurisprudence to flesh out the elements of each.

MODES OF LIABILITY FOR GENOCIDE

ECCC Law Article 4 provides that persons may be held responsible for attempts and conspiracy to commit acts of genocide, and for participation in acts of genocide. The 1948 Convention includes a list of punishable modes of liability for genocide: attempt, conspiracy, direct commission, incitement, and complicity. The ECCC Law omits incitement and complicity and adds the mode of "participation." It is likely that Article 29 modes will be found to apply to all crimes within the Court's jurisdiction, including genocide, allowing prosecution of genocide on the basis of the modes listed in both Article 4 and Article 29.

JOINT CRIMINAL ENTERPRISE

The main controversy that the ECCC will have to address regarding modes of liability has already arisen in pre-trial proceedings: whether an accused person can be charged with "committing" crimes through their active participation in a common criminal plan, also known as a "joint criminal enterprise" or JCE.[8] The status of JCE liability as of 1975 has never before been addressed. In the *Tadić* case, the ICTY determined that JCE has existed under customary international law as of 1992. In so doing, they relied primarily on post-WWII, pre-1975 international and domestic precedent. However, their reasoning remains controversial.

No ECCC Chamber has yet decided whether or not JCE liability can be charged. When the applicability of JCE is decided on the merits, it is likely that the ECCC will find that some form of common plan liability existed during the Court's temporal jurisdiction; however, it may determine that the scope of liability under this mode of responsibility was narrower in 1975-1979 than that which the ICTY found to exist as of the 1990s.

SUPERIOR RESPONSIBILITY

In addition to direct responsibility, Article 29 of the ECCC Law allows accused persons to be held responsible as a superior for the crimes of their subordinates if they "had effective command and control or authority and control over the subordinate…knew or had reason to know that the subordinate was about to commit such acts or had done so, and…failed to take the necessary and reasonable measures to prevent such acts or punish the perpetrators." The ICTY, ICTR, and ICC Statutes all provide for liability for superior responsibility. However, the application of this doctrine to civilian (as opposed to military) hierarchies as of 1975 is not entirely clear and likely will be litigated.

The line between direct and superior responsibility often blurs. The Extraordinary Chambers could find that DK leaders planned and ordered crimes in the field, participated in a criminal plan of which these crimes were a foreseeable consequence, and also knew about offenses by their subordinates and failed to act. International courts have not considered direct and superior responsibility to be mutually exclusive, and the Co-Prosecutors have charged the accused persons with multiple modes of liability. If an accused person is found responsible for both direct and superior responsibility for the same crime, the most recent jurisprudence from international courts suggests that they should be convicted on the basis of direct responsibility and their superior responsibility taken into account as an aggravating factor at sentencing.

AVAILABLE DEFENSES

"Defenses" are available grounds for excluding criminal responsibility. Some defenses, such as an alibi, are complete in the sense that they protect a defendant from criminal responsibility altogether. Others are recognized as mitigating factors at sentencing. The Framework Agreement and ECCC Law do not specifically provide for any defenses, but that does not prevent accused persons from raising them. Below is a discussion of those defenses most likely to be raised before the ECCC.

SUPERIOR ORDERS

The only defense explicitly mentioned in the core ECCC documents is excluded. The ECCC Law states, "The fact that a Suspect acted pursuant to an order of the Government of Democratic Kampuchea or of a superior shall not relieve the Suspect of individual responsibility." Superior orders have been excluded as a defense at least since the Nuremberg trials; however, they have been accepted as a mitigating factor in sentencing. Although this possibility is not mentioned in the ECCC Law, nothing would prohibit the Court from following this practice.

OFFICIAL CAPACITY

The defense of official capacity provides immunity from prosecution—both during and after an individual's tenure in office—in foreign national courts for acts committed as part of one's official functions. This defense has been rejected by international courts—including for heads of state—since Nuremberg. Notably, the ICTY and ICTR Statutes also reject this defense as a reason to mitigate punishment. The ICC not only rejects the defense of official capacity but also asserts the right to exercise jurisdiction over persons who have personal immunities because of their official status. Because the charged persons before the ECCC are not currently protected by any personal immunity and are not being charged by a foreign national court, they will not be able to use their former government positions as a defense to prosecution.

DURESS

The question of duress has arisen indirectly in the S-21 case. Duch, the former prison chairman, has suggested that at least one motivation for his work at the torture center was fear for his own life and that of his family. However, like the defense of superior orders, duress has not been accepted by international courts as a complete defense to charges of crimes against humanity and serious war crimes. For example, in the ICTY *Erdemovic* case where a Bosnian Serb soldier was found to have taken part in a massacre or be killed himself, this was only taken into account in the mitigation of his sentence.

The ICC's Rome Statute, which provides the most detailed definitions of defenses among international court documents, does not exclude a duress defense to serious crimes, but defines it in Article 31(1)(d) as:

> resulting from a threat of imminent death or of continuing or imminent serious bodily harm against that person or another person, and the person acts necessarily and reasonably to avoid this threat, provided that the person does not intend to cause a greater harm than the one sought to be avoided.

Thus, consistent with ICTY/ICTR jurisprudence, under this definition the need to protect oneself and one's family would never be a complete defense to participation in the murder of hundreds of people.

MENTAL INCAPACITY

Defenses related to persons' lack of capacity to appreciate the nature of their conduct are also recognized by national and international law. The ICC definition excludes criminal responsibility when "[t]he person suffers from a mental disease or defect that destroys that person's capacity to appreciate the unlawfulness or nature of his or her conduct, or capacity to control his or her conduct to conform to the requirements of law[.]" However, any mental incapacity must have existed at the time the crime took place. Therefore, for example, suggestions that Ieng Thirith may be suffering from diminished mental capacity as she faces trial cannot be a defense to actions she took thirty years ago, but would instead be considered in relation to her fitness to stand trial.

CONCLUSIONS ON SUBSTANTIVE LAW

The ECCC faces a number of important questions in applying the substantive law over which it has jurisdiction. One is the scope of various modes of liability as of 1975, including whether the doctrine of superior responsibility applied to civilian leaders at that time and the appropriate contours of joint criminal enterprise.

A second question is if the Co-Prosecutors will charge any accused person with crimes against cultural property or crimes against internationally protected persons, since both are defined with reference to sources of law that do not specifically set out the elements of a crime or establish individual responsibility. It appears extremely unlikely that anyone will be charged with these offenses.

There are also uncertainties with regard to the definition of crimes against humanity in the ECCC Law. The two main questions are likely to be if crimes against humanity had to be committed in the context of an armed conflict during the temporal jurisdiction of the Court, and if the *chapeau's* reference to protected groups requires that the accused person acted with discriminatory intent, or merely that the attack was discriminatory.

If genocide is eventually charged, it will encompass only crimes committed against groups protected by the Genocide Convention, such as the Cham Muslims, ethnic Vietnamese, and Buddhist monks. The "intent to destroy" these groups will be extremely difficult to prove due to the fact that mass crimes were committed not only against protected groups but against the Cambodian population as a whole.

The Co-Prosecutors will face challenges in establishing that Khmer Rouge defendants committed crimes in the context of an international armed conflict. In the *Duch* case they have argued that an international armed conflict existed between Cambodia and Vietnam for all of the DK period and particularly beginning in 1977 and 1978. The Co-Investigating Judges have accepted this argument. If the Trial Chamber also accepts it, there will be greater scope for grave breach convictions. Should the Court determine that border clashes with Vietnam did not begin until 1977 or that crimes were unrelated to the armed conflict with Vietnam, less conduct will be subject to this characterization.

Proving the domestic crimes of homicide, torture, and religious persecution, taken from the 1956 Cambodian Penal Code, would appear to pose fewer difficulties for the Co-Prosecutors. However, the domestic statute of limitations for these crimes may be found to invoke the principle of *nullum crimen sine lege*.

Although no defenses are explicitly recognized by the ECCC Law or Internal Rules, it is possible that some may be raised, in particular if additional prosecutions are launched against less senior leaders. However, available defenses to serious crimes are very limited and even if accepted would likely only be taken into account as a mitigating factor at sentencing.

STRUCTURE AND COMPOSITION OF THE ECCC

This section introduces the structure and composition of the ECCC's four primary organs: three judicial chambers (Pre-Trial, Trial, and Supreme Court), the Office of Co-Investigating Judges, the Office of the Co-Prosecutors, and the Office of Administration. It concludes with brief biographies of Duch, who is currently on trial, and the four charged persons who are expected to be tried together in the second case: Nuon Chea, Ieng Sary, Khieu Samphan, and Ieng Thirith.

JUDICIAL CHAMBERS

Each of the three ECCC judicial chambers includes both Cambodian and international judges. As discussed in Chapter 1, unlike other hybrid courts, each of these chambers has a majority of national judges and votes by a "supermajority," meaning that the vote of at least one international judge is required for any decision. Thus far, it appears that the supermajority requirement may be encouraging the judges to work together and reach decisions by consensus.

The ECCC Law provides that ECCC judges shall be appointed from currently practicing judges and appointed in accordance with existing judicial appointment procedures. Judges are required to have high moral character, a spirit of impartiality and integrity, and criminal or international law experience. Both national and international judges are appointed by the Cambodian Supreme Council of Magistracy. In the case of the international judges, the

UN Secretary-General selects candidates and submits a list to the Supreme Council for its approval.

The Pre-Trial Chamber is made up of five judges—three national and two international.[9] Pursuant to the ECCC Law, the Pre-Trial Chamber's only responsibility is to decide disagreements between the Co-Prosecutors or between the Co-Investigating Judges. However, as discussed below, with the adoption of the Internal Rules, the Pre-Trial Chamber's jurisdiction was expanded to include, most importantly, appeals against orders of the Co-Investigating Judges.

Like the Pre-Trial Chamber, the Trial Chamber is made up of five judges—three national and two international.[10] It presides over the conduct of trial proceedings and pronounces judgment against accused persons. Its decisions in the *Duch* case are starting to fill in gaps in the Internal Rules on questions such as the scope of civil party participation and the admissibility of various types of evidence.

The Supreme Court Chamber is made up of seven judges—four national and three international.[11] It is the chamber of last instance and hears appeals from decisions and judgments of the Trial Chamber.

Some non-governmental organizations have criticized the selection of national judges, both with regard to the judges' professional qualifications and their independence from the government. Because most educated people including lawyers and judges were wiped out or fled during the DK era, Cambodia is still recovering from a severe "brain drain." Connected with this, personal connections have played a large role in determining judicial appointments and continue to do so, including at the ECCC.

In early January 2008, Nuon Chea sought to disqualify Pre-Trial Judge Ney Thol under Internal Rule 34(2) for associations that might "objectively give[] rise to the appearance of bias." The Defense argued that Judge Ney's position as an officer of the Royal Cambodian Armed Forces and his involvement in political cases that show an "apparent willingness to inappropriately employ his judicial power at the behest of the [governing] Cambodian People's Party" (CPP) create an appearance of bias.[12] The Pre-Trial Chamber quickly dismissed the motion, finding that because Judge Ney sits in his personal capacity and has sworn to act impartially, a reasonably informed observer would not apprehend bias. The Pre-Trial Chamber's decision has been criticized for not taking into account the social and political context of Cambodia, and therefore in effect requiring evidence of actual bias. It is likely that additional judicial bias challenges will be raised before the Trial Chamber.

THE CO-PROSECUTORS AND CO-INVESTIGATING JUDGES

The ECCC Law creates an office of two Co-Prosecutors—one national and one international—who together conduct preliminary investigations. Unique among special internationalized courts, the ECCC Law retains the civil law preference for giving investigative judges the primary investigatory role and the power to decide which persons to send to trial and for what crimes.

The Supreme Council of the Magistracy appoints both the national and international Co-Prosecutors and Co-Investigating Judges, with the international head of each office first nominated by the UN Secretary General. The Co-Prosecutors are to be appointed "in accordance with the existing procedures for selecting prosecutors who have high moral character and integrity and who are experienced in the conduct of investigations and prosecutions of criminal cases."[13] Like the other ECCC judges, the Co-Investigating Judges must be appointed from among currently practicing judges or additionally appointed judges with "a high moral character, a spirit of impartiality and integrity, and experience."[14]

The political necessity to have two Co-Prosecutors and two Co-Investigating Judges has engendered concerns about the potential repercussions on the Court's efficiency. Thus far, it appears that the Co-Prosecutors have worked well together in spite of their disagreement over whether or not to charge more suspects. Due to the secrecy of the judicial investigation, it is difficult to determine if continued delays in charging the remaining four persons (now anticipated to take place in 2010) are the consequence of the national and international Co-Investigating Judges' different viewpoints or work styles, or are due to other factors.

In August 2007 the government announced that Co-Investigative Judge You Bun Leng would be transferred to head the Cambodian Appeals Court. International observers, including the UN Secretary General's Special Representative for Human Rights in Cambodia and Special Rapporteur on the Independence of Judges and Lawyers, argued that the transfer would result in delays and cast doubt on judicial independence in Cambodia because the decision was made by the executive branch and not by the body with the constitutional authority to assign judges. Ultimately, although Judge You received the appointment he did not leave the ECCC. Instead, he continued on as national Co-Investigating Judge and was given reduced responsibilities in his second job at the Appeals Court.

THE OFFICE OF ADMINISTRATION

The Office of Administration (OA) is the umbrella organ responsible for all general administrative functions at the ECCC:

- the *Personnel Section* hires and trains Court personnel;

- the *Budget and Finance Section* handles the Court's fiscal matters;

- the *Public Affairs Section* supports the Court's legal organs by serving as the official channel for internal and external ECCC communications;

- the *Court Management Section* maintains a database of all case files and preserves and stores evidence;

- the *Security and Safety Section* protects the staff and the ECCC premise;

- the *Witnesses/Experts Support Unit* develops and implements procedures for protecting victims and witnesses;

- the *Detention Unit* monitors the conditions of detention; and

- *General Services* provides requirements such as supplies, equipment, facilities, and transportation.

Pursuant to the Internal Rules, the OA was given the authority to create an autonomous Defense Support Section (DSS) to support defense counsel teams, and a Victims Unit (VU) to inform victims of Democratic Kampuchea about their right to participation at the ECCC and to assist them in exercising that right. The VU is discussed further in Chapter 5.

The OA is headed by a Cambodian Director and an international Deputy Director. The Director of the Office is responsible for the OA's "overall management," except with respect to "matters that are subject to United Nations rules and procedures."[15] The Director's responsibilities include hiring Cambodian staff and requesting their appointment by the Cambodian government. The Deputy Director is responsible for the administration of all UN components of the Court, including recruitment and administration of all international staff.

In fulfilling these responsibilities, the Director and the Deputy Director are required to "cooperate in order to ensure an effective and efficient functioning of the administration."[16] Despite what have been reportedly cordial and constructive working relationships between the Director (on permanent leave) and acting Director and both the former and current Deputy Directors, the split authority in managing the budget, hiring, and staff reporting between the two "sides" of the Court has created management problems that are discussed in Chapter 4.

THE CHARGED PERSONS

At the time of writing, there are four charged persons who are still being investigated, and one accused (indicted) person who is on trial. All five are in custody and each has the representation of at least one national lawyer and one foreign lawyer. They also have the assistance of a legal consultant and a case manager. In August 2009, the international Co-Prosecutor was given permission by the Pre-Trial Chamber to forward two additional introductory submissions to the Co-Investigating Judges requesting the judicial investigation of additional suspects. The Pre-Trial Chamber decision and the dispute between the two Co-Prosecutors that led to it are discussed in Chapter 3. The five persons currently charged by the Court are:

- *Kaing Guek Eav* (known as "Duch") was Chairman of the S-21 prison in Phnom Penh, where an estimated 14,000 persons perceived to be enemies of the DK were tortured and killed. He is the only person who has been indicted by the Co-Investigating Judges. His trial formally began in February 2009 and is expected to continue throughout 2009. He is being represented by Mr. Kar Savuth, who has practiced criminal law since 1982, and Mr. François Roux (France), who has defended four genocide cases at the ICTR and has recently been appointed defense chief of the Special Tribunal for Lebanon.

- *Nuon Chea* (known as "Brother Number Two") was Deputy Secretary of the Communist Party of Kampuchea and a member of the CPK Central and Standing Committees. He is believed to have played an important role in directing and implementing DK's criminal policies and was allegedly in charge of the regime's detention centers, including S-21. Nuon Chea is being defended by Mr. Son Arun, who has specialized in defending persons in Cambodia charged with serious crimes, and Mr. Michiel Pestman and Mr. Victor Koppe (Netherlands), both of whom have practiced before the SCSL.

- *Ieng Sary*, husband of Ieng Thirith, was Deputy Prime Minister and Minister for Foreign Affairs and a member of the CPK Central and Standing Committees. He is believed to have played an important role in directing and implementing DK's criminal policies. He is also believed to have either encouraged or failed to prevent the transfer of large numbers of Foreign Ministry personnel to S-21. He is being defended by Mr. Ang Udom, a criminal defense lawyer and head of the Legal Unit at the Cambodian NGO Center for Social Development, and Mr. Michael Karnavas (United States), who has defended several clients before the ICTY.

- *Ieng Thirith*, wife of Ieng Sary and sister-in-law of Pol Pot, was Minister of Social Affairs and Action and a candidate member of the CPK Central Committee. In this capacity, she is believed to have contributed to the implementation of criminal DK policies. She was sent to investigate and report on health issues in the Northwest Zone and is therefore believed to have been aware that DK policies were contributing to starvation. She is also believed to have either encouraged or failed to prevent the arrest and killing of ministry staff. She is being defended by Mr. Phat Pouv Seang, a criminal lawyer and professor at the University of Law and Economics, and Ms. Diana Ellis QC (United Kingdom), a criminal lawyer who has practiced before the ICTR.

- *Khieu Samphan* was Democratic Kampuchea head of state and a member of the CPK Central Committee. In this role, he is believed to have contributed to criminal DK policies. He is being defended by Dr. Sa Sovan, previously a senior legal adviser of the Cambodian National Assembly and an expert within the Ministry of Justice, and Mr. Jacques Vergès (France), infamous for his long career defending clients charged with crimes related to terrorism and crimes against humanity and his attacks on the legitimacy of the courts in which they are tried.

THE ECCC'S RULES OF EVIDENCE AND PROCEDURE

Unlike the core documents of the ICTY, ICTR, and SCSL, the ECCC Law does not authorize its judges to adopt or amend the Court's rules of evidence and procedure—rules that provide detailed information about topics including the organization of the Court, the scope of each office's authority and how it interacts with others, how suspects are investigated and arrested, the rights of charged persons, and how proceedings before each Chamber are conducted. As originally conceived, the ECCC was intended to apply domestic Cambodian rules of criminal procedure and to draw on international rules as needed. Article 12(1) of the Framework Agreement provides:

> The Procedure shall be in accordance with Cambodian law. Where Cambodian law does not deal with a particular matter, or where there is uncertainty regarding the interpretation or application of a relevant rule of Cambodian law, or where there is a question regarding the consistency of such a rule with international standards, guidance may also be sought in procedural rules established at the international level.

Consistent with this, the ECCC Law allows the judges to consult international law when necessary to fill in the gaps between domestic Cambodian law and international standards.

Until the Code of Criminal Procedure was adopted in August 2007, Cambodia lacked a comprehensive criminal procedural code for the Extraordinary Chambers to consult. For that reason, the ECCC judges almost immediately began drafting rules of procedure and evidence specifically tailored to ECCC proceedings. After almost a year of difficult negotiations between the national and international judges, particularly over the role of foreign defense counsel, the

Internal Rules were adopted by judicial plenary in June 2007. In the preamble to the Internal Rules, the judges state that the rules were drafted in order to

> consolidate applicable Cambodian procedure for proceedings before the ECCC, and ... to adopt additional rules where these existing procedures do not deal with a particular matter, or if there is uncertainty regarding their interpretation or application, or if there is a question regarding their consistency with international standards.

Although the judges acted without statutory authority in adopting the Internal Rules, the Pre-Trial Chamber has affirmed that the Internal Rules have primacy over the Cambodian Code of Criminal Procedure:

> The Internal Rules...form a self-contained regime of procedural law related to the unique circumstances of the ECCC, made and agreed upon by the plenary of the ECCC. They do not stand in opposition to the Cambodian Criminal Procedure Code ... but the focus of the ECCC differs substantially enough from the normal operations of Cambodian criminal courts to warrant a specialized system. Therefore, the Internal Rules constitute the primary instrument to which reference should be made in determining procedures before the ECCC where there is a difference between the procedures in the Internal Rules and the CPC.[17]

With regard to when the Cambodian Criminal Procedure Code is applicable, the PTC said that it "should only be applied where a question arises which is not addressed by the Internal Rules."[18] This is consistent with Internal Rule 2, which says that when a question arises that is not addressed by the Internal Rules, decisions should be made in accordance with Framework Agreement Article 12(1), quoted above.

RULES OF PROCEDURE

THE PRE-TRIAL AND INVESTIGATION PHASE

Under the ECCC Internal Rules, the pre-trial period encompasses two phases: a preliminary investigation led by the Co-Prosecutors and an ensuing judicial investigation led by the Co-Investigating Judges. The rules for the pre-trial and investigation phases govern the conduct of Co-Prosecutors, investigators, judicial police, and Co-Investigating Judges while protecting the rights of suspects during custody and interrogation.

The investigation and prosecution of crimes at the ECCC may only be initiated by the Co-Prosecutors, who can initiate a preliminary investigation on their own discretion or on the basis of a written complaint by a person or organization with knowledge of a crime. During their preliminary investigation, the Co-Prosecutors determine if evidence points to the commission of a crime within the jurisdiction of the Court and identify suspects and potential witnesses. If the Co-Prosecutors have reason to believe that crimes within the Court's jurisdiction have been committed, they open a judicial investigation by sending an introductory submission and the case file to the Co-Investigating Judges. The introductory submission includes the names of the persons to be investigated, a summary of the facts, the type of offenses alleged, and the relevant provisions under which the offenses would be charged. Due to the delay in adopting the Court's Internal Rules, the ECCC Co-Prosecutors had a full year to investigate the first five charged persons and were able provide the Co-Investigating Judges with a large amount of evidence together with their initial submission.

The Co-Investigating Judges' investigation is limited to the facts set out in the introductory submission or in any supplementary submission filed by the Co-Prosecutors. If new facts come to the attention of the Co-Investigating Judges, they shall not investigate them but must inform the Co-Prosecutors, who may file a supplementary submission including the new facts.

The judicial investigation is not conducted in public and all persons involved are required to maintain its confidentiality. Nevertheless, the Co-Investigating Judges are authorized to issue information they deem essential to keep the public informed and to rectify any false or misleading information. Disagreements between the Co-Investigating Judges and the Defense teams over the appropriate scope of confidentiality are discussed in Chapter 3.

During the investigation the Co-Investigating Judges may charge and provisionally detain any suspect against whom there is clear and consistent evidence of criminal responsibility for crimes included in the Co-Prosecutors' submissions. The requirements for provisional detention are discussed in Chapter 3. Charged persons may only be interviewed in the presence of their lawyer unless they waive that right. Once the judicial investigation is complete, the Co-Prosecutors are notified to prepare their final submission. The investigation is concluded once the Co-Investigating Judges issue a closing order either indicting a charged person and placing the matter before the Trial Chamber or dismissing the case. In drafting the closing order, the Co-Investigating Judges are not bound by the Co-Prosecutors' submissions. The Co-Prosecutors, but not the accused person, may appeal against the closing order.

The Co-Prosecutors decided to appeal against the closing order in the S-21 case on two grounds: the Co-Investigating Judges' failure to include in the indictment the mode of liability of joint criminal enterprise (JCE) and charges based on the 1956 Cambodian Penal Code.

The Pre-Trial Chamber did not add JCE, but decided to add crimes under national law to the indictment after finding that Co-Investigating Judges had not provided sufficient reasoning as to why they had been excluded.

As discussed in Chapter 1, the decision to create offices with two Co-Prosecutors and two Co-Investigating Judges was a compromise among the UN and Cambodian negotiators. In making this compromise, the drafters envisioned that disputes might arise between national and international counterparts—as one has between the Co-Prosecutors over who and how many persons to investigate. Possible disputes between the Co-Investigating Judges could involve the conduct of investigations or whether or not to arrest, detain, or indict particular charged persons. To address this problem, the ECCC Law includes a dispute resolution mechanism allowing one of the Co-Prosecutors or Co-Investigating Judges to file a notice of dispute with the Pre-Trial Chamber, which must reach an agreement by a super-majority vote of four out of five judges. If the PTC judges fail to attain a super-majority vote, the request of the moving party will proceed.

In the ECCC Law, the Pre-Trial Chamber's authority is limited to arbitrating disputes between the Co-Prosecutors and between the Co-Investigating Judges. However, the Internal Rules expand the Pre-Trial Chamber's jurisdiction to include deciding appeals against orders of the Co-Investigating Judges and deciding applications to annul investigative actions, among other responsibilities.

Pre-Trial Chamber decisions are not appealable; however, the extent to which its appellate decisions bind the Trial Chamber is not discussed in the Internal Rules and has not yet been addressed by the Trial Chamber. Pursuant to Internal Rule 89, at the initial trial hearing the Trial Chamber hears preliminary objections concerning the jurisdiction of the Chamber, issues requiring the termination of prosecution, and the nullity of procedural acts made after the indictment is filed. If not raised at the initial hearing, these objections are inadmissible. These objections may include issues already addressed by the PTC, suggesting that re-litigation before the Trial Chamber is possible in some circumstances. Indeed, the Pre-Trial Chamber has noted that questions raised on appeal that are also explicitly within the jurisdiction of the Trial Chamber can "be raised and addressed fully at later stages of the proceedings[.]"[19] For example, describing the Pre-Trial Chamber's decision not to amend the *Duch* closing order to include joint criminal enterprise as a non-binding "preliminary ruling," the Co-Prosecutors have requested that the Trial Chamber act under Rule 98(2) to "change the legal characterization" of the crimes and include this mode of liability.[20]

If the same challenges are argued both before the Pre-Trial Chamber and the Trial Chamber, then it will slow down the proceedings. However, if the parties are not able to raise core legal issues before the Trial and Supreme Court Chambers, this may be seen to compromise fair trial rights. The Pre-Trial Chamber has recognized the potential overlap and has exercised its jurisdiction narrowly. For example, in response to the *Duch* Defense team's request for a remedy for his illegal detention by the Cambodian Military Court, the Pre-Trial Chamber determined, "It would not be appropriate for the Pre-Trial Chamber to make the statements requested when another judicial body may well become seized of this case for trial and will have to make its own decisions on the basis of the evidence and the submissions made before it."[21]

THE TRIAL PHASE

The Trial Chamber becomes seized by an indictment from the Co-Investigating Judges or the Pre-Trial Chamber. Unlike pre-trial proceedings, trial proceedings are presumptively public.

During trial, both parties present their case before the Trial Chamber, a panel of five judges. The Judges, and then the parties, may question the accused person. The judges may also hear from civil parties, witnesses, and experts they consider useful. The accused person, Co-Prosecutors, and civil parties may call witnesses and experts approved by the Trial Chamber. The Trial Chamber may also order additional investigation at any time. Due to the perception that the proceedings are taking too long in the *Duch* trial, the Trial Chamber has decided to limit time for questioning of witnesses other than Duch. At the time of this writing, the prosecution has thirty minutes, the defense has forty minutes, and all civil party groups together have forty minutes.

As with the Pre-Trial Chamber, decisions by the Trial Chamber require an affirmative vote of at least four judges—a super-majority. The judgment—which is issued and announced at a public hearing—must be based on facts set out in the indictment; however, the Trial Chamber may change the legal characterization of the crime as long as no new constitutive elements are introduced.

APPEAL PHASE

The Supreme Court Chamber is the only body to which decisions and judgments of the Trial Chamber may be appealed, and its decisions are final. Like the other chambers, a final decision from the Supreme Court requires a super-majority vote.

The Supreme Court decides appeals on two grounds: (1) an error on a question of law invalidating a judgment or decision, and (2) an error of fact that has occasioned a miscarriage of justice. In making decisions, the Supreme Court may both examine evidence and call new evidence.

Internal Rule 104 allows interlocutory appeal regarding decisions that have the effect of terminating the proceedings, decisions on detention and bail, decisions on protective measures, decisions on interference with the administration of justice, and decisions declaring a civil party application inadmissible. All other decisions must be appealed at the same time as an appeal against the Trial Chamber judgment. The grounds for interlocutory appeal in Internal Rule 104 appear to be more limited than those recognized at international criminal tribunals, primarily because the Internal Rules do not provide the Trial Chamber authority to grant discretionary leave. For example, at the ICC, the Trial Chamber may grant leave to appeal when decisions "significantly affect the fair and expeditious conduct of the proceedings or the outcome of the trial."[22] It seems likely that there will be defense challenges on this basis.

In its judgment on the merits, the Supreme Court Chamber may change the Trial Chamber's legal characterization of the crimes but may not include new constitutive elements. When only the accused appeals, the Supreme Court Chamber may acquit, but cannot increase an accused's sentence. Also, the Chamber may only amend the judgment for an accused's benefit. On the other hand, where the Co-Prosecutors appeal a conviction, the Supreme Court may amend the sentence. Notably, if the accused was acquitted at trial, the Chamber may only modify findings of the Trial Chamber that it considers to be erroneous; it may not modify the disposition. This is unlike the ICTY, ICTR, SCSL, and ICC, which all allow reversal of acquittal on appeal. Nevertheless, it appears consistent with the newly adopted Cambodian Code of Criminal Procedure. Also consistent with Cambodian law, the Supreme Court Chamber does not have the authority to send a case back to the Trial Chamber for reconsideration.

RULES OF EVIDENCE

ADMISSIBILITY OF EVIDENCE GENERALLY

The ECCC Internal Rules set out very few rules of evidence, leaving a number of questions open for determination by the Trial Chamber. The rules of evidence applied by most civil law jurisdictions and international courts are similarly brief.

Internal Rule 87(1) states in part, "Unless provided otherwise in [the Internal Rules], all evidence is admissible." Rule 87(4) gives the Trial Chamber authority to admit "any new evidence which it deems conductive to ascertaining the truth." Only evidence obtained by Court interviewers through "inducement, physical coercion or threats thereof" is expressly excluded by Rule 21(3). Additionally, Rule 87(3) allows a Chamber to reject a request for

Former S-21 child survivors, Norng Chanphal, 39 years old, with his two daughters, six-year old Norng Chen Ammara (in pink) and 13-year-old Norng Chen Kimty (in yellow), at Tuol Sleng Genocide Museum, 2009. Photo by Heng Sinith.
Source: Documentation Center of Cambodia Archives

evidence that is:

(a) irrelevant or repetitious;

(b) impossible to obtain within a reasonable time;

(c) unsuitable to prove the facts it purports to prove;

(d) not allowed under the law; or

(e) intended to prolong proceedings or is frivolous.

The Co-Prosecutors have argued that the ECCC's admissibility rules allow the Court to consider any relevant evidence and are more flexible than the rules of most international courts, which require evidence to be both relevant and probative including some indicia of reliability.[23] The ICTY and ICTR Rules 89(C) are identical to each other and state, "A Chamber may admit any relevant evidence which it deems to have probative value." Article 69(3) of the Rome Statute gives the ICC Chambers "the authority to request the submission of all evidence that it considers necessary for the determination of the truth." Nevertheless, Rome Statute Article 69(4) states that, in ruling on the relevance or admissibility of any evidence, the ICC Chambers must take into account "the probative value of the evidence and any prejudice that such evidence may cause to a fair trial or to a fair evaluation of the testimony of a witness."

In contrast, Rule 89(C) of the procedural rules of the SCSL states without qualification that "[a] Chamber may admit any relevant evidence." The SCSL Appeals Chamber has said that this rule is "designed to avoid sterile legal debate over admissibility[.]"[24] Therefore, at the Special Court, all relevant evidence is admissible, with the question of probative value and reliability considered subsequently in determining the weight of all the evidence.[25]

As discussed above, the ECCC Pre-Trial Chamber has said that the Cambodian Code of Criminal Procedure may be applied when a question is not addressed by the Internal Rules. Article 321 of that Code states in part, "Unless it is provided otherwise by law, in criminal cases all evidence is admissible. The court has to consider the value of the evidence submitted for its examination, following the judge's intimate conviction." This would seem to require consideration of probative value at the admissibility stage. However, in the *Duch* case, the Trial Chamber more closely follows the SCSL approach:

> In order to be used as evidence, material on the case file must ... satisfy minimum standards of relevance and reliability necessary for it to be produced before the Chamber. Once produced before the Chamber, the probative value of this evidence, and hence the weight to be accorded to it, will then be assessed.[26]

It therefore appears that the ECCC Trial Chamber will not consider probative value as an admissibility requirement.

ADMISSIBILITY OF PRIOR STATEMENTS

One specific evidentiary question that will arise many times is the admissibility of an accused person's prior statements, as all five of the charged persons in custody have at one time granted interviews or issued public statements discussing the Khmer Rouge period. The Internal Rules explicitly recognize the admissibility of confessions, and courts generally admit self-incriminating statements when they are satisfied that they were made voluntarily. However, such statements are excluded if made in violation of the right to be free from compelled self-incrimination.

The Trial Chamber's determination of voluntariness will in part depend on to whom the statement was made. The right against self-incrimination is intended to protect suspects from overzealous law enforcement officials and thus is only implicated when the statements offered are made to investigating authorities, as opposed to statements made to others, such as the media. As mentioned above, the Internal Rules only specifically exclude coerced statements obtained by Court interviewers, not those obtained by other authorities.

The question of "voluntariness" has already become an issue in the S-21 case, as Duch has claimed that UN officials "tricked" him into confessing to crimes when they interviewed him over the course of several days in 1999. He has told the Trial Chamber that he only submitted to questioning because he was told that the interviewer had a "UN mandate," and that he was never informed of his right to silence or that the interview might be used against him in legal proceedings. Although his confession was not made to judicial officials and was not taken in anticipation of judicial proceedings, the Trial Chamber decided to exclude it under Internal Rule 87(3)(b), finding that it would take too much time to conduct the necessary supplementary investigation to assess his statement's validity. In making this decision, the Chamber noted that the interview was repetitious with many others already part of the record.[27]

ADMISSIBILITY OF EVIDENCE OBTAINED BY TORTURE

Ieng Thirith has requested the exclusion of "confessions" exacted under torture at S-21 prison by Khmer Rouge authorities from her case file and from consideration by the Co-Investigating Judges, arguing that pursuant to Cambodian and international law evidence obtained through torture may not be used as a basis for further investigation or for determining the final charges against her. Article 15 of the Convention Against Torture and Other Cruel, Inhuman or Degrading Treatment or Punishment generally prohibits the use as evidence in proceedings of "any statement which is established to have been made as a result of torture[.]" The Special Rapporteur on torture and other cruel, inhuman or degrading treatment or punishment has said that there are two rationales behind this ban: to exclude inherently unreliable information as a source of evidence and to remove an important incentive for the use of torture.

Notably, Article 15 of the Torture Convention includes one exception, allowing information obtained by torture to be used "against a person accused of torture as evidence that the statement was made." The Co-Prosecutors argue that the S-21 confessions fall within this exception because they are not being used against torture victims, but against persons who are alleged to be the superiors of or to have acted in concert with the torturers. Moreover, they argue that the exclusionary rule must be considered in the context of its overall purpose and that the use of information from "peripheral or background statements" in the confessions to prosecute torturers upholds those principles. They believe that the confessions provide an important and unique source of evidence about the hierarchy and policies of the Communist Party of Kampuchea that possess a degree of reliability because these issues were not the focus of the interrogations. During trial, Duch said that the confessions were "probably 40 percent true" and contain detailed information about "all levels of the party and of all administrative units."[28] The Co-Investigating Judges have dismissed Ieng Thirith's motion, and she is likely to appeal.

PRESENTATION OF EVIDENCE

The Chamber may decide guilt or innocence only based on "evidence that has been put before the Chamber and subjected to examination." Rule 87(3) provides that evidence in the case file is considered put before the Chamber "if its content has been summarized or read out in court." However, due to the lengthy amount of time this practice has been consuming in the *Duch* trial, the Trial Chamber Judges are proposing an amendment to the rule that would allow a document to be "appropriately identified in court."[29] It has also been suggested that a new Internal Rule 87(6) be added to allow the Chamber to consider a fact in the indictment proved when it is not contested by either the Co-Prosecutors or the Defense.

CONCLUSIONS ON PROCEDURAL LAW

Many of the procedural questions left open by the ECCC Law have now been answered with the creation and adoption of the Court's Internal Rules. The Pre-Trial Chamber has found that these Internal Rules should be looked to first, and only when they are incomplete should the new Cambodian Code of Criminal Procedure be referenced. Although additional challenges against the primacy of the Internal Rules are to be expected, it is likely that the Trial and Supreme Court Chambers will agree with the determination of the Pre-Trial Chamber on this question.

Some important procedural questions still open for judicial decision include the scope of the parties' authority to raise issues litigated before the Pre-Trial Chamber again before the Trial Chamber, the appropriate scope of confidentiality of the judicial investigation (discussed in Chapter 3), and the appropriate scope of interlocutory appeals.

The Internal Rules provide very few rules of evidence. The Trial Chamber has said that to be admissible as evidence, information need only be relevant and include some indicia of reliability, with probative value to be considered subsequently. Specific evidentiary questions that have arisen early in proceedings include the admissibility of prior inculpatory statements and "confessions" made under torture at S-21. Because Duch is essentially pleading guilty, he has not raised numerous evidentiary challenges; many more will arise if and when the four remaining charged persons and additional suspects are indicted and sent to trial.

CONCLUSIONS

As noted at the beginning of this chapter, the ECCC is an entirely new kind of hybrid institution. All international courts have had rocky starts due to the enumerable financial and logistical challenges of launching a tribunal tasked with prosecuting mass crimes. The ECCC's unique structural features, evolving procedure, and distant temporal jurisdiction have further complicated this process, leading to the legal and legitimacy challenges discussed in the following chapters.

---

[1] Sok An, Deputy Prime Minister and Minister in Charge of the Office of the Council of Ministers Chairman of the Royal Government Task Force for the Khmer Rouge Trials, Closing Remarks for the International Conference, Dealing with a Past Holocaust and National Reconciliation: Learning from Experiences, Aug. 28-29, 2006, Phnom Penh, Cambodia, *available at* www.eccc.gov.kh/english/cabinet/speeches/3/ dealing_with_a_past_holocaust.pdf.

[2] Decision on Appeal Against Provisional Detention Order of Kaing Guek Eav alias "Duch," Case No. 001/18-07-2007-ECCC/OCIJ (PTC01), ¶ 19 (Pre-Trial Chamber, Dec. 3, 2007).

[3] *See* KHAMBOLY DY, A HISTORY OF DEMOCRATIC KAMPUCHEA (1975-1979), at 3, n.1 (2007) (referencing the various estimates of the number of people who died during the DK era).

[4] These words are transposed to "such as" in the English and Khmer translations of the ECCC Law (but not the French); however, that is likely an unintended transposition error.

[5] Prosecutor v. Sikirica et al., Case No. IT-95-8-T, Judgment on Defence Motions to Acquit, ¶ 89 (Trial Chamber, Sept. 3, 2001).

[6] *See* Prosecutor v. Blagojevic & Jokic, Case No. IT-02-60-T, Judgment, ¶ 545 (Trial Chamber, Jan. 17, 2005).

[7] Closing Order Indicting Kaing Guek Eav *alias* Duch, Case No. 001/18-07-2007-ECCC/OCIJ, ¶ 152 (Co-Investigating Judges, Aug. 8, 2008).

[8] Joint criminal enterprise is discussed in more detail in Chapter 3.

[9] The three national Pre-Trial Chamber judges are Prak Kimsan, Ney Thol, and Huot Vuthy. The international judges are Rowan Downing (Australia) and Katinka Lahuis (Netherlands).

o Mr. Prak does not hold a law degree, but has been a Supreme Court judge since 1994 and is a member of the Cambodian Council of Jurists of the Council of Ministers.

o Mr. Ney is a general in the Cambodian armed forces, president of the Military Court, and a former member of the ruling Cambodia Peoples Party's Central Committee.

o Mr. Huot is a prosecutor in Kampong Cham province and was formerly a deputy prosecutor in Kandal province.

o Mr. Downing has been a judge of the Court of Appeal and Supreme Court of Vanuatu. He also has background in the laws of war.

o Ms. Lahuis is a justice in the criminal section in the Court of Appeal of Leeuwarden.

[10] The three nationals on the Trial Chamber are Nil Nonn, Thou Mony, and Ya Sokhan. The international judges are Silvia Cartwright (New Zealand), and Jean-Marc Lavergne (France).

o Mr. Nil is president of the Trial Chamber. Since 1993 he has been president of the Battambang provincial court.

o Mr. Thou has been a judge on Cambodia's Appeals Court since 1998.

o Mr. Ya has been a judge on the Banteay Meanchey provincial court since 1993.

o Dame Silvia Cartwright was the first woman to serve on her country's High Court and was a member of the UN Committee on the Elimination of all Forms of Discrimination against Women.

o Mr. Lavergne has served as a judge since 1988, most recently serving as vice-president of the High Civil Court of Mans.

[11] The four national judges on the Supreme Court Chamber are Kong Srim, Som Sereyvuth, Sin Rith, and Ya Narin. The three internationals are Motoo Noguchi (Japan), Agnieszka Klonowiecka-Milart (Poland), and Chandra Nihal Jayasinghe (Sri Lanka).

o Mr Kong has been a deputy general prosecutor at an appellate court in Kandal province since 2000.

o Mr. Som does not hold a law degree but has been a Supreme Court judge since 1988.

o Mr. Sin is a judge in Pursat province.

o Mr. Ya is a judge in Rattanakiri province.

o Mr. Noguchi is a professor and a senior attorney with the Japanese Ministry of Foreign Affairs and has served as a public prosecutor.

o Ms. Klonowiecka-Milart has extensive experience adjudicating international crimes in Kosovo, where she served as the senior international judge with the UN mission and now sits on the Supreme Court.

o Mr. Jayasinghe is a senior presiding judge of the Supreme Court of Sri Lanka and previously served as the president of the Sri Lankan Court of Appeal.

[12] Urgent Application for Disqualification of Judge Ney Thol, Case No. 002/19-09-2007-ECCC/PTC, ¶ 1 (Pre-Trial Chamber, Jan. 28, 2008).

[13] The national Co-Prosecutor is Ms. Chea Leang, who in June 2009 was named general prosecutor of the Cambodian Supreme Court. Prior to that she worked in the Ministry of Justice and then was appointed a prosecutor in the Appeals Court in 2002. International

Co-Prosecutor Robert Petit (Canada) stepped down on September 1, 2009, for unspecified "personal reasons" after three years in office. Prior to coming to the ECCC Mr. Petit worked as a prosecutor at several international and hybrid courts: the ICTR, the UN Mission in Kosovo, the Special Panels for Serious Crimes in East Timor, and the SCSL. At the time of publication his replacement had yet been named.

[14] The national Co-Investigating Judge is You Bun Leng. He has served on the Cambodian Appeals Court since 1993 and was appointed its head in 2007. The International Co-Investigating Judge is Marcel Lemonde (France). Judge Lemonde most recently served in the penal chamber of the Paris Court of Appeals. He has also served as an investigating judge and was President of the French Association of investigating judges from 1984-1987.

[15] Law on the Establishment of Extraordinary Chambers in the Courts of Cambodia for the Prosecution of Crimes Committed During the Period of Democratic Kampuchea, as amended and promulgated on Oct. 27, 2004, NS/RKM/1004/006, art. 31 new.

[16] Agreement between the United Nations and the Royal Government of Cambodia Concerning the Prosecution under Cambodian Law of Crimes Committed During the Period of Democratic Kampuchea (June 6, 2003), art. 8(4).

[17] Decision on Nuon Chea's Appeal Against Order Refusing Request for Annulment, Case No. 002/19-09-2007-ECCC/OCIJ (PTC06), ¶ 14 (Pre-Trial Chamber, Aug. 26, 2008).

[18] *Id.* ¶ 15.

[19] Decision on Appeal against Provisional Detention Order of Ieng Sary, Case No. 002/19-09-2007-ECCC/OCIJ (PTC03), ¶ 23 (Pre-Trial Chamber, Oct. 17, 2008).

[20] Co-Prosecutor's Request for the Application of Joint Criminal Enterprise, Case No. 001/18-07/2007-ECCC/TC, ¶¶ 10-18 (Pre-Trial Chamber, June 8, 2009).

[21] Decision on Appeal Against Provisional Detention Order of Kaing Guek Eav *alias* "Duch," Case No. 001/18-07-2007-ECCC/OCIJ (PTC01), ¶ 63 (Pre-Trial Chamber, Dec. 3, 2007).

[22] *See, e.g.,* Rome Statute of the International Criminal Court, art. 82(1)(d), U.N. Doc. A/CONF.183/9 (1998).

[23] Co-Prosecutors' Response to Ieng Thirith's Defence Request for Exclusion of Evidence Obtained by Torture dated Feb. 11, 2009, Case No. 002/19-09-2007-ECCC/OCIJ, ¶¶ 15-16 (Office of the Co-Investigating Judges, Apr. 30, 2009).

[24] Prosecutor v. Norman et al., Fofana — Appeal Against Decision Refusing Bail, Case No. SCSL-04-14-AR65, ¶ 26 (Appeals Chamber, Mar. 11, 2005).

[25] Only when admitting "information"—defined as "assertions of fact (but not opinion) made in documents or electronic communications"—as an alternative proof of facts does the court require a finding that the evidence is not only relevant, but also possesses "sufficient indicia of reliability" and "would not prejudice unfairly the Defense." *See* Prosecutor vs. Sesay et al., Case No. SCSL-04-15-T, Decision on Prosecution Notice Under Rule 92bis and 89 to Admit the Statement of TF1-150, ¶ 17 (Trial Chamber, July 20, 2006).

[26] Prosecutor v. Kaing Guek Eav *alias* "Duch," Case No. 001/18-07-2007/ECCC/TC, Decision on Admissibility of Material on the Case File As Evidence, ¶ 7 (Trial Chamber, May 26, 2009).

[27] *Id.* ¶¶ 18-20.

[28] Prosecutor v. Kaing Guek Eav *alias* "Duch," Case No. 001/18-07-2007/ECCC/TC, Transcript of Proceedings at 22 (Trial Chamber, Apr. 7, 2009). *See also* Douglas Gillison, *Ieng Thirith: S-21 Confessions "Torture-Tainted,"* CAMBODIA DAILY, Apr. 7, 2009; Bethany Lindsay, *Duch Admits to Draining Live Victims' Blood*, CAMBODIA DAILY, June 17, 2009 (quoting Duch as "estimating that, at best, the confessions were '50 percent truth...Pol Pot at one point did not even believe that the confessions were of true information'").

[29] Laura MacDonald, *War with Vietnam and Conflicts Within the ECCC*, CAMBODIA TRIBUNAL MONITOR BLOG, June 10, 2009, *available at* www.cambodiatribunal.org/images/CTM/ctm_blog_6-10-2009.pdf.

3. JURISPRUDENCE OF THE EXTRAORDINARY CHAMBERS

ANNE HEINDEL

The Extraordinary Chambers have now been in existence for three years and began their first trial in February 2009. Most ECCC jurisprudence thus far is from pre-trial proceedings, in particular issues related to provisional detention. This chapter will review, in the context of international precedent, the major topics that have arisen before the Court, including jurisdictional challenges, fairness challenges, substantive challenges, and the dispute between the Co-Prosecutors as to whether or not to seek additional judicial investigations.

As will be shown, to address challenging legal questions in the absence of direct guidance from the ECCC Law or Cambodian legal precedents, the Court has generally adhered to case law from international tribunals with jurisdiction over persons accused of similarly grave crimes. Only in one area—the scope of civil party participation—is there no direct international precedent for the ECCC to follow, requiring it to forge its own path and establish new law that for good or ill will in turn guide the decisions of future courts.

PROVISIONAL DETENTION

The charged persons—Duch, Ieng Sary, Nuon Chea, Khieu Samphan, and Ieng Thirith—will soon have been held in detention for two years. Of these five, only Duch has been indicted and is currently on trial. The remaining four are in provisional detention—detention prior to a decision by the Co-Investigating Judges (CIJs) that there is sufficient evidence to charge them with crimes within the jurisdiction of the Court and send them to trial.

Issues related to detention, including its legality and necessity, therefore make up the bulk of the ECCC's case law at this point in time. Nevertheless, in challenging their pre-trial detention, the Charged Persons have raised significant questions relating to their fair trial rights and the jurisdiction of the Court. Moreover, even at the pre-trial stage, civil parties have strongly asserted a broad right to participate in proceedings. Because Pre-Trial Chamber (PTC) decisions are not formally binding on the Trial Chamber and are procedurally limited to discrete pre-trial topics, many of these larger issues will arise again before the Trial and Supreme Court Chambers. These early decisions foreshadow some of the important legal challenges the Court will soon be addressing on the merits.

REQUIREMENTS FOR PROVISIONAL DETENTION

ECCC Internal Rule 63 sets out the conditions under which the Co-Investigating Judges may order the provisional detention of a Charged Person:

> a) there is a well founded reason to believe that the person may have committed the crime or crimes specified in the Introductory or Supplementary Submission; and
>
> b) The Co-Investigating Judges consider Provisional Detention to be a necessary measure to:
>
>> i) prevent the Charged Person from exerting pressure on any witnesses or Victims, or prevent any collusion between the Charged Person and accomplices of crimes falling within the jurisdiction of the ECCC;
>>
>> ii) preserve evidence or prevent the destruction of evidence;
>>
>> iii) ensure the presence of the Charged Person during the proceedings;
>>
>> iv) protect the security of the Charged Person; or
>>
>> v) preserve public order.

Thus, in order for the ECCC to detain a Charged Person, there must be both a "well founded reason to believe" that he or she has committed the charged crimes and evidence that his or her detention is "necessary." The five grounds for finding detention necessary are disjunctive, meaning that the existence of any one alone provides a sufficient basis for keeping a charged person in custody. In 2007, the Co-Investigative Judges found that provisional detention was appropriate for all five persons currently charged by the Court; in 2008 they extended their detention by one more year. The Pre-Trial Chamber has upheld all these detention orders.

Human rights bodies such as the European Court of Human Rights (ECHR), the Inter-American Commission and Court of Human Rights, and the UN Human Rights Committee have determined that pre-trial detention should only be allowed on an exceptional basis.[1] The International Criminal Tribunals for the Former Yugoslavia and Rwanda (ICTY and ICTR) and the Special Court for Sierra Leone (SCSL) have justified their more restrictive pre-trial detention policies by highlighting the gravity of the crimes charged and their inability to ensure the return of an accused released to his or her home jurisdiction.[2] Although the Cambodian government would appear to have little difficulty ensuring the return of the charged persons should they be released, the ECCC has thus far been following the approach of these tribunals.

In determining the appropriateness of pre-trial detention, international courts look at the individual circumstances of each accused and balance the factors weighing both for and against release.[3] Notably, once the ICTY began having a more cooperative relationship with the states of the former Yugoslavia, it increasingly released accused on bail pending trial. The International Criminal Court (ICC) has recently ordered the first provisional release of an accused, while deferring implementation until an agreement on cooperation is reached with a potential host state. On the other hand, neither the ICTR nor the SCSL has granted provisional release to any accused.

Because the factors considered are highly speculative and subjective in their application, it is not difficult for the ECCC to meet international standards and also to find that detention is "necessary."[4] Although it is never publicly acknowledged, it seems likely that there is an underlying reticence to release the charged persons due to the horrific nature of the crimes with which they are charged and the many years that they have lived in impunity. If, as many fear, some of them die of old age before reaching judgment, their provisional detention may be the only "justice" victims receive after 30 long years.

WELL FOUNDED REASON TO BELIEVE

In determining if there is a "well founded reason to believe" that a detained person has committed charged crimes, the ECCC Pre-Trial Chamber (PTC) has followed international jurisprudence in requiring a showing of "facts or information…which would satisfy an objective observer that the person concerned may have committed the offence."[5] This test has been easiest to meet for Duch, who has confessed to many criminal acts. With regard to Nuon Chea, the PTC has highlighted his own statements, as well as many statements by Duch implicating Nuon.

The *Ieng Thirith* Defense has argued that little actual evidence tying her to the crimes charged has been placed in the case file. The Pre-Trial Chamber, however, has found that documents and witness testmony showing she that chaired meetings where she explained DK policies, that she denounced people on a regular basis who were then arrested and tortured, and that she had knowledge of the desperate living conditions peopled faced at the time, among other evidence, is enough to meet the "well founded reason to believe" threshold. Nevertheless, the Chamber has noted with regard to both her and Khieu Samphan's orders of detention that "it would have been preferable for the Co-Investigating Judges to give more details about the evidence... support[ing] their conclusion."[6]

The *Ieng Sary* Defense has argued that even if evidence of a "well founded reason to believe" exists, a higher level of evidence is required after a year in detention. The Pre-Trial Chamber disagreed, determining that once "well founded reasons" are established, unless they are undermined by exculpatory evidence, the requirements of Internal Rule 63(3) are met throughout pre-trial proceedings.[7]

PREVENT PRESSURE ON WITNESSES, PREVENT COLLUSION, AND PRESERVE EVIDENCE

The likelihood that the accused, if released, will put pressure on witnesses or victims, interfere with victims and witnesses, collude, and destroy evidence, has also been considered by human rights bodies and international criminal courts. Generally, they have found that such arguments become less compelling over time as evidence has been gathered by the court and witnesses have been examined.[8] Moreover, they seek some actual evidence of a threat.[9]

In considering these factors, the ECCC Co-Investigating Judges and Pre-Trial Chamber appear to have relied to a great extent on presumptions and long-ago utterances rather than concrete evidence of present danger. For example, in the *Duch* case, the Pre-Trial Chamber said that "[i]n the particular context of the events that happened at [the central Khmer Rouge security office known as] S-21, the mere presence of the Charged Person in society can exert pressure on witnesses and prevent them from testifying."[10] It also noted that during the Democratic Kampuchea (DK) period, Duch warned a Khmer Rouge cadre that if he spoke to anyone about S-21, Duch "would report him to Ieng Sary to have him killed."[11]

For all the accused, the Pre-Trial Chamber has emphasized their knowledge of the names of witnesses from the case file, and (except Duch), both their former and continuing influence and thus ability to organize pressure on witnesses. With regard to Ieng Thirith, the PTC highlighted the fact that there are very few witnesses still alive who can testify to her role in the regime. It also noted that she had displayed hostility to people who have suggested that she is responsible for crimes during the DK period. It therefore found that this was a reason justifying her provisional detention.

With regard to Ieng Sary, the PTC has highlighted alleged reprimands he made to Duch in 1983 for not destroying S-21 documents. Notably, however, the PTC has said that despite Ieng's past statements and continuing influence, it had "not found evidence of any past actions and/or behavior of the Charged Person which in themselves would display a concrete risk that he might use that influence to interfere with witnesses and victims."[12]

ENSURE THE PRESENCE OF THE ACCUSED

Like the ECCC, human rights bodies and international criminal courts consider the gravity of the crime charged and potential length of sentence in determining the likelihood that an accused will appear for trial.[13] Human rights bodies have emphasized that the risk of an accused absconding cannot be guaged solely on the basis of the gravity of the crimes and the potential sentence; however, international courts seem to place more emphasis on these factors.[14] In addition, international bodies consider "the charater of the person, his home, his occupation and his assets[,]" as well as "his stakes and attachment in the society to which he [is] seeking to be released."[15]

Even though Duch eventually surrendered to authorities in 1999, the Pre-Trial Chamber has highlighted the fact that he hid his identity for the previous twenty years. For Ieng Sary and Ieng Thirth, the Court has noted that they have a residence near the Thai border, have travelled there regularly, have access to funds for expensive travel and medical treatment, and have friends in high places. The Chamber has discounted their argument that because they are of advanced age they have less motive or ability to flee.

PROTECT SECURITY OF CHARGED PERSON

In considering the effect of release on the security of Duch, the PTC has found that, because he has confessed to crimes, he has become more well known and there is greater potential for him to be the target of revenge by his victims' families and from cadre against whom he may offer evidence. Threats against Duch made at his first public hearing were then used by the Pre-Trial Chamber to explain why Nuon Chea and Ieng Sary, who are also allegedly connected to S-21 crimes, might also be threatened once that link becomes known to the public. With regard to Khieu Samphan, in addition to emotional statements of victims made to the press and to his Defense counsel at a Court press conference, the Pre-Trial Chamber highlighted an attack against him when he returned to Phnom Penh in 1991 and his own prior expression of concern for his safety at a public forum in 2000.[16]

PROTECT PUBLIC ORDER

Human rights bodies and the SCSL have considered the impact on public order of releasing an accused. Human rights bodies in particular have emphasized that it is not appropriate merely to consider the possible effect on public order of the gravity of the offense. Instead, there must be some actual evidence of a threat to public order.[17] Likewise, the ECCC Pre-Trial Chamber has said that public order must be actually threatened for detention on this basis to be legitimate.

The Co-Investigating Judges and the Pre-Trial and Trial Chambers have found that there is a risk of public disorder if the charged persons are released. The most specific threats identified have been the emotional statements issued to the press by two victims and the emotional reactions of a couple civil parties to Khieu's defense counsel at a Court press conference.[18] However, these reactions appear to be the exception and not the rule. Otherwise, all Pre-Trial Chamber decisions repeat the same general factors, such as the number of Cambodians suffering from post-traumatic stress disorder, ongoing public interest in the proceedings, and the likelihood that trials will raise new anxieties for survivors. For example, in the *Nuon* detention order decision, Pre-Trial Chamber stated:

> [T]he passage of time has not diminished the impact of the…regime on society… [T]he commencement of judicial activities before the ECCC 'may pose a fresh risk to the Cambodian society'…[and] may 'lead to the resurfacing of anxieties and a rise in the negative social consequences that may accompany them.'[19]

This abundance of caution regarding the potential fragility of Cambodian society is, however, not in evidence in a recent decision by the Trial Chamber regarding the security of civil parties. Supporting the finding of the Co-Investigating Judges that a majority of civil party requests for protective measures are not warranted in the *Duch* case, the Trial Chamber highlighted "the length of time that has elapsed since the commission of alleged crimes within the jurisdiction of the Court to which the witnesses and victims in question could be called to testify" and the fact that the Witness and Expert Support Unit "came to a different view [than the Co-Prosecutors] regarding both the generalized risks for the security of potential witnesses and victims, as well as the current danger."[20]

ALTERNATIVE FORMS OF DETENTION

Charged persons have asked for alternative forms of detention amounting to house arrest. In particular, Ieng Sary has asked repeatedly for hospital or house arrest due to his poor health. The Internal Rules do not provide for any alternative forms of detention and say nothing about release on the basis of health concerns. The Pre-Trial Chamber has rejected these requests thus far, finding that these alternatives could not be imposed in a way that would guarantee that the objectives of provisional detention are met. It also noted that there would be higher risks for personal safety, especially on occasions when travel to the Court is required for public hearings.

Like the ECCC, none of the international criminal tribunals explicitly allow provisional release on the basis of health concerns. However, in practice they have allowed release in three circumstances: when medical treatment is unavailable at the detention unit or in the

Pol Pot, July 1975.
Source: *Documentation Center of Cambodia Archives*

Ieng Sary (center, in black) and Ieng Thirith (left) with a visiting Chinese delegation, November 5, 1978.
Source: Documentation Center of Cambodia Archives

host country, on humanitarian grounds when an accused's condition is so grave that it is incompatible with any form of detention, and when an accused is found unfit to stand trial.[21]

When accused have been released for the purpose of receiving necessary medical treatment, release has been made conditional on the restriction of their liberty to the medical facility providing treatment, and on their return to the court's detention unit immediately after the completion of treatment.[22] Accused have been released to their family home on the basis of medical concerns only in a few cases when they have been found to suffer from inoperable and incurable cancer with a prognosis of at most a few months to live.[23]

With regard to Ieng Sary, the Pre-Trial Chamber has said, "There is no evidence of an immediate need for long-term hospitalisation and the ECCC Detention Facility is properly equipped to provide medical assistance as required."[24] If Ieng Sary's condition is not untreatable and imminently terminal, there is no obligation under international precedent to release him from the ECCC detention unit and place him under house arrest on the sole basis of his health concerns. Nevertheless, no international tribunals have tried accused of similarly advanced years as Ieng and the other charged persons. It is possible that due to the continuing fragility of their health the PTC may at some point be required to consider whether a different standard should be applied to elderly detainees who, even if not facing immediately life threatening illness, may be in a slow decline that is aggravated by their detention.

LENGTH OF DETENTION

The 2004 law establishing the ECCC (the "ECCC Law") requires the ECCC to follow "international standards of justice, fairness and due process of law, as set out in Articles 14 and 15 of the 1966 International Covenant on Civil and Political Rights." These include the right to trial "without undue delay." The ECCC Internal Rules allow provisional detention pursuant to charges of genocide and crimes against humanity for one year with the possibility of two one-year extensions. All five charged persons are now approaching the end of their second year of detention at the Court.

The Pre-Trial Chamber has found that "the nexus between the length of time a defendant spends in detention and the diligence displayed in the conduct of investigations is a relevant factor…when considering continuation of detention or release."[25] Human rights bodies and international criminal courts have found that even if the conditions for continued pre-trial detention have been met, an accused's right to trial within a reasonable time may be violated if proceedings are unduly delayed. Like international courts and human rights bodies,[26] in considering whether there has been undue delay in the proceedings the ECCC Pre-Trial Chamber looks at the complexity of the case, delay attributable to the conduct of the accused,

Khieu Samphan on the day of his arrest, November 2007. Photo by Om Layum
Source: Stuart Isett/Documentation Center of Cambodia Archives

and delay attributable to the conduct of the authorities. No human rights body or international criminal court has set a fixed date after which detention becomes unreasonable. Notably, in one particularly complex case involving multiple accused, the ICTR Trial Chamber found that five years of pre-trial detention had not been unreasonable.[27]

Khieu Samphan has argued that the proceedings "are dogged by delays."[28] Ieng Sary has similarly said that they are not being conducted with due diligence and that little evidence has been placed on the case file relating to him or the other charged persons. In extending the charged persons' detention an additional year, the Co-Investigating Judges determined that the length of detention was not excessive considering the complexity and gravity of the charges and the scope of the investigation. They also highlighted the fact that the charged persons are not cooperating with the investigation, which though their right, "is not conducive to speedy proceedings."[29] These findings have been affirmed by the Pre-Trial Chamber.

On appeal of the CIJs' decision to extend Ieng Sary's detention, the Pre-Trial Chamber considered the CIJs due diligence in the investigation. It likewise highlighted the nature and gravity of the crimes and the necessity of a large-scale investigation and found that the amount of new evidence, witness statements, and pending rogatory letters in the case file indicate that the Co-Investigating Judges have been proceeding with sufficient diligence.

With regard to Duch, the Court has faced an additional question regarding the length of proceedings: the ECCC's responsibility to provide a remedy for the over eight years he was detained without trial by a Cambodian Military Court before being handed over to the ECCC for investigation. Duch has sought not only provisional release and a reduction in sentence for time served, but also a remedy for this human rights violation.

The Trial Chamber, like the Pre-Trial Chamber before it, has found that because of the ECCC's formal and functional independence from domestic Cambodian courts and lack of connection to the Military Court proceedings, it cannot be attributed with prior violations of Duch's rights. Nevertheless, the Trial Chamber has followed international jurisprudence in finding that the Court has "both the authority and the obligation to consider the legality of his prior detention"[30] in determining his sentence. Finding that Duch's prior detention was a violation of applicable Cambodian and international law, the Chamber determined that he was entitled to a remedy for this human rights violation, the nature and extent of which will be determined at sentencing.[31] In addition, the Trial Chamber determined that if convicted he will be entitled to have the full time he has spent in detention since 1999 credited to his eventual sentence.[32] Nevertheless, the Trial Chamber considered his continued detention by the ECCC to be justified under Internal Rule 63(3) and by the requirements of the trial proceedings.[33]

Duch shortly before his arrest by the Cambodian military, 1999. Photo by Stuart Isett.
Source: Stuart Isett/Documentation Center of Cambodia Archives

DETENTION CONDITIONS

In 2007, Ieng Sary and his wife requested that the Co-Investigating Judges grant them permission to meet with each other. The CIJs rejected this request citing the ongoing judicial investigation; although subsequently they allowed once-a-week visits. The Pre-Trial Chamber determined that the initial rejection was a segregation order and heard the appeal, which the Co-Prosecutors did not oppose. The Co-Prosecutors noted that international criminal tribunals rarely separate detainees merely because they are co-defendants in the same case and said that they believed the Iengs' meetings "may have a positive impact on each other's mental and physical health."[34] They further argued that at the ECCC, where all charged persons were co-accused, "any order of non-communication between them may amount, in effect, to solitary confinement."[35]

The Pre-Trial Chamber found that, although the Co-Investigating Judges have the jurisdiction under Internal Rule 55(5) to limit contact between the charged persons in the interest of the investigation, pursuant to Rule 21(2) coercive measures must be "strictly limited to the needs of the proceedings, proportionate to the gravity of the offence charged and fully respect human dignity."[36] The PTC followed international practice in finding that the CIJs had an obligation to "explain how the limitation of contacts is a necessary and proportional measure to protect the interests of the investigation."[37] Noting that the alleged crimes were committed 30 years ago, the PTC found that the Iengs already had time to discuss any matter relating to the investigation and said that it was "not clear" how limiting their contact would protect the investigation.[38] It therefore allowed them to meet in accordance with the applicable detention rules.

Subsequent to this decision, Nuon Chea also appealed to the Pre-Trial Chamber against a CIJ order prohibiting communication among the remaining detainees to curb the "potential for prejudicial collusion."[39] This appeal was supported by the Co-Prosecutors. Both parties argued that the CIJs were bound by the *Ieng* visitation decision and that the Iengs did not form a separate category of detainee because they are married. Citing jurisprudence of the ICC and ECHR, the Pre-Trial Chamber found,

> [L]imitation of contacts can only be ordered to prevent pressure on witnesses or victims when there is evidence reasonably capable of showing that there is a concrete risk that the charged person might collude with the other charged persons to exert such pressure while in detention. With the passage of time, the threshold becomes higher as the investigation progresses and the risk necessarily decreases.[40]

Because the CIJs had not identified any evidence showing a concrete risk of collusion, the PTC determined there were insufficient grounds for segregation.

FITNESS OF CHARGED PERSONS

The ECCC judges, like those at international courts, may order a medical, psychological, or psychiatric examination of persons who are the subject of a criminal investigation "for the purpose of determining whether [they are] physically and mentally fit to stand trial, or for any other reasons[.]"[41] In addition to experts already consulted by the Court, both Ieng Sary and Nuon Chea have requested medical experts to assess their fitness to participate in the judicial investigation. In both cases, the Co-Investigating Judges found it unnecessary to appoint experts to assess their conditions because the question of sending them to trial had not yet arisen.

In response to their appeals from the dismissal of their requests, the Co-Prosecutors did not agree that the facts raised fitness conerns, but did not oppose their requests out of an "abundance of caution." Moreover, they agreed with the Defense that because charged persons participate in proceedings throughout the investigative process, it is not premature to consider the issue of fitness at the pre-trial stage.

In almost identical decisions, the Pre-Trial Chamber noted that neither the ECCC core documents nor Cambodian law defines "fitness to stand trial," and neither states whether or not a charged persons's mental capacity is an issue during the pre-trial phase. As a consequence, the PTC sought guidance from the jurisprudence of international tribunals.

The PTC noted that when faced with a similar lack of statutory guidance, the ICTY Trial Chamber, in the seminal 2004 *Strugar* case, found that the enjoyment of the procedural rights protected by the ICTY Statute "would appear to presuppose that an accused has a level of mental and physical capacity."[42] Moreover, "their effective exercise may be hindered, or even precluded, if an accused's mental and bodily capacities, especially the ability to undertand, *i.e.* to comprehend, is affected by mental or somatic disorder."[43]

The PTC highlighted the fact that *Strugar* was decided at the pre-trial phase and that the rights accorded charged persons by the ECCC core documents are recognized from the beginning of a judicial investigation. Therefore, it found that "the issue of a charged person's capacity to effectively participate in the proceedings is triggered from the very moment an individual is charged with a crime before the ECCC."[44]

In *Strugar,* the ICTY Trial Chamber found that when determining fitness, "[T]he issue is not whether the accused suffers from particular disorders, but…whether he is able to exercise effectively his rights in the proceedings against him."[45] A link must be made between the various medical diagnoses and "the actual affects experienced by th[e] Accused on his relevant capacities."[46] The ICTY identified the relevant capacities as including the ability to plead, understand the nature of the charges, understand the course of proceedings, understand the details of the evidence, instruct counsel, understand the consequences of the proceedings, and testify. The burden is on the Defense to show by "the balance of probabilities" that the accused is not fit to stand trial.[47]

For example, in the *Stanisic* case at the ICTY, the Defense argued that "the medical condition of the Accused and in particular his debilitating intestinal disease ha[d] left him in a declining physical condition and thus significantly impaired in his ability to engage in meaningful preparations for his case."[48] However, in a 2006 decision, the ICTY Trial Chamber found that none of the three medical reports submitted by the defense showed by a balance of probabilities that the accused was unable to participate in his defense and therefore did not "demonstrate an 'adequate reason' to hold an inquiry into the Accused's competence to stand trial."[49]

Comparatively, in a 2004 decision in the *Kovacevic* case, the reports of two medical experts appointed by the ICTY, a psychiatrist appointed by the Defense, and the consulting psychiatrist of the detention unit, all indicated that the accused "suffer[s] from a serious mental disorder which presently renders him unfit to enter a plea and to stand trial"[50] and recommended that he be treated in a health facility where his native language was spoken. The ICTY granted release on this basis.

The ECCC Pre-Trial Chamber recalled that in the 2005 *Nahak* decision by the Special Panels for Serious Crimes in East Timor, the threshold for holding a competency review was found to be a "significant" concern by the court as to an accused's competency. With regard to Ieng Sary, the PTC noted that although he is of advanced age and has medical problems requiring medication, "none of the medical or expert reports indicates that the ailments from which the Charged Person is suffering might have an effect on his mental capacity," and neither was there any such evidence in the case file.[51] It therefore rejected his request to be examined by a psychiatric expert. With regard to Nuon, the PTC noted that none of the reports by numerous medical experts supported the conclusion that his capacities were affected by his heart condition or that his cognitive functions were not normal for a man of his age. In addition, he had made clear relevant statements at hearings. Therefore, the PTC likewise rejected his request.

RIGHT TO CIVIL PARTY PARTICIPATION IN DETENTION APPEALS

In February 2008, the *Nuon Chea* Defense team, joined by all other charged persons except

Duch, objected to the participation of civil parties in appeals against provisional detention. They argued that the Internal Rules do not specifically provide for participation in detention appeals, and that, following ICC practice, civil parties wishing to participate in such appeals have the burden of demonstrating how their interests—which the charged persons defined as the right to reparations—are affected.

ECCC Internal Rule 23(1) provides:

The purpose of Civil Party action before the ECCC is to:

a) Participate in criminal proceedings against those responsible for crimes within the jurisdiction of the ECCC by supporting the prosecution; and

b) Allow Victims to seek collective and moral reparations, as provided in this Rule.

Pursuant to this rule, civil parties' interest in the proceedings is much broader than merely seeking reparations, including also an interest in assisting the prosecution to see justice done. Notably, these dual interests are also emphasized in decisions of the ICC and the ECHR. For example, the ICC Trial Chamber has stressed that victims' interest in participating in ICC proceedings goes beyond receiving reparations and "should encompass their personal interests in an appropriately broad sense."[52] In another decision, an ICC Appeals Chamber judge noted that the Rome Statute recognizes a victim's interest in seeing justice done that "goes beyond the general interest that any member of society may have in seeing offenders held accountable."[53] He found support for this view in *Kiliç v. Turkey*, in which the ECHR found that the right to an effective remedy under the European Convention requires,

[i]n addition to the payment of compensation where appropriate, a thorough and effective investigation capable of leading to the identification and punishment of those responsible for the deprivation of life and including effective access for the complainant to the investigation procedure.[54]

As a consequence of his recognition of this broad view of victims' personal interests, the ICC judge found, against the majority, that victim participants' interest extended even to participating in a proceeding on the narrow question of whether to admit an appeal against the confirmation of charges against the accused.[55] In his view, ultimately "a successful appeal would diminish the prospects of the Victims to receive reparations and to see that justice is done."[56]

Notably, at the ECCC, consistent with Cambodia's civil law system, a person recognized as a civil party "becomes a party to the criminal proceedings."[57] Comparatively, at the ICC—the only international court providing a role for victims to participate as more than witnesses—

victims are not considered "true" parties, but are limited to presenting their "views and concerns...at stages of the proceedings determined to be appropriate by the Court" where their "personal interests are affected."[58] As highlighted by an ICC Appeals Judge:

> The right of victims to participate ... [at the ICC] has no immediate parallel or association with the participation of victims in criminal proceedings in ... the Romano-Germanic system of justice, where victims in the role of civil parties or auxiliary prosecutors have a wide-ranging right to participate in criminal proceedings.[59]

As a consequence, the ICC Appeals Chamber has found that the text of the statute establishing that court "mandates a specific determination by the Appeals Chamber that the participation of victims is appropriate in the particular interlocutory appeal under consideration."[60] Victims must apply for leave to participate in appeals by providing "a statement in relation to how their personal interests are affected by the particular appeal, as well as why it is appropriate for the Appeals Chamber to permit their views and concerns to be presented."[61] At the ICC, unlike at the ECCC, "participation is not a once-and-for-all event but rather [is] decided on the basis of the evidence or issue under consideration at any particular point in time."[62]

It is thus significant that even at the ICC victims have been allowed to participate in the appeal of a detention order. In the *Lubanga* case, the ICC Appeals Chamber found that victims of the case had an interest in "appeals relating to determinations of whether or not a person subject to a warrant of arrest should be granted interim release."[63] The concerns recognized by the Appeals Chamber in that case were nearly identical to those at issue in Nuon Chea's appeal, including the danger that if released the accused might obstruct the investigation.[64]

In its decision on the *Nuon Chea* appeal, the ECCC Pre-Trial Chamber framed the question as whether the scope of a civil party's right to "participate in criminal proceedings...by supporting the prosecution"[65] includes the right to participate in appeals against detention orders. Noting that the language of Rule 23(1)(a) was clear in authorizing civil parties to participate "all criminal proceedings" and that the Internal Rules also explicitly provide active participation rights to civil parties starting from the investigative process,[66] the Pre-Trial Chamber found that they have a right to participate in provisional detention appeals.[67] The Chamber found additional support for this holding by reading Rule 23 in light of the Cambodian Code of Criminal Procedure, which likewise allows civil party participation in detention appeals.

In finding that ECCC civil parties have the right to participate in detention appeals, the ECCC Pre-Trial Chamber highlighted the fact that charged persons may respond to civil party submissions and the requirement that all parties—including civil parties—must file written submissions in advance of the oral detention appeal hearing. Thus, rather than excluding civil parties from certain types of proceedings or adopting the ICC's time-consuming procedures for determining victim "personal interests" at each stage of the proceedings, the ECCC Pre-Trial Chamber determined that the Internal Rules' court management requirements already "preserve a balance between the rights of the parties."[68]

This approach—recognizing broad victim participation rights but limiting their timing and scope—appears to be the most appropriate under the Internal Rules and the most conducive to giving victims a genuine stake in the proceedings. However, there have been serious problems with time management in the *Duch* trial that are being reviewed before the much larger and more contested second case against the four remaining charged persons. Only if the Court carefully manages the interventions of the thousands of civil parties expected to seek to participate in that case will civil party participation in mass crimes trials be seen as viable, and this Court's innovative victim participation scheme be seen as a model for future courts instead of a disaster better avoided. As discussed in Chapter 5, at this time the Court is considering modifying the civil party scheme and appears likely to substantially restrict or eliminate the role of civil parties in future cases.

JURISDICTIONAL CHALLENGES

In 1979 Ieng Sary was convicted of "genocide" *in absentia* by the People's Revolutionary Tribunal, a special court established by the Vietnamese-installed government, and sentenced to death and confiscation of all his property. Unlike the Genocide Convention and the ECCC Law, discussed in Chapter 2, the 1979 tribunal defined genocide as "planned massacres of groups of innocent people; expulsion of inhabitants of cities and villages in order to concentrate them and force them to do hard labor in conditions leading to their physical and mental destruction; wiping out religion; destroying political, cultural and social structures and family and social relations."[69] In 1996, as part of a deal with the government to facilitate Ieng's defection from the Khmers Rouges, King Sihanouk issued a royal decree pardoning Ieng from the 1979 tribunal's sentence and also providing him amnesty from potential prosecution under the 1994 Law to Outlaw the Democratic Kampuchea Group.

In their decision on provisional detention, the Co-Investigating Judges raised the principle of *ne bis in idem* (also known as double jeopardy) and the applicability of the amnesty and pardon to the ECCC and found that (1) Ieng's 1979 conviction did not cover all the acts for which Ieng was currently charged by the ECCC, and (2) neither the pardon nor the amnesty was an obstacle to Ieng's prosecution by the ECCC. On appeal from the CIJ's decision to detain

Ieng Sary, the Pre-Trial Chamber considered what effect, if any, Ieng's conviction, amnesty, and pardon have on the jurisdiction of the Court.

NE BIS IN IDEM

On appeal to the Pre-Trial Chamber, the *Ieng* Defense argued that, in accordance with the principle of *ne bis in idem*, his trial and conviction by the 1979 tribunal bar his prosecution by the ECCC for the same conduct. In support of this view, they cited the Cambodian Code of Criminal Procedure Article 12: "In applying the principle of *res judicata*, any person who has been finally acquitted by a court judgment cannot be prosecuted once again for the same act, even if such act is subject to different legal qualification."

The Co-Prosecutors counter-argued that the *ne bis in idem* principle was not applicable because the 1979 trial was not in accordance with international fair trial norms. Moreover, *ne bis in idem* is intended to protect individuals from the hardship of multiple trials and punishments. Because Ieng was not present at the trial and never served his sentence, he had not suffered from the 1979 conviction. In the alternative, they argued that international law allows cumulative convictions and that any consequent injustice could be addressed at sentencing.

The Pre-Trial Chamber noted that there are different *ne bis in idem* standards under Cambodian and international law. As highlighted by the Defense, under Cambodian law no one may be tried twice for the "same act." However, under the International Covenant on Civil and Political Rights, no one may be tried twice for the "same offense." The Pre-Trial Chamber emphasized that because Ieng was not currently charged with the crime of genocide by the ECCC, the ECCC's prosecution may be for a different offence. Moreover, it found the characterization of the ECCC charges too vague at this point to determine whether or not he was being prosecuted for the same "acts" as those on which the 1979 charges were based. The Pre-Trial Chamber agreed with the CIJs that at this stage of proceedings it was not "manifest or evident" that the 1979 trial and conviction precluded Ieng's prosecution by the ECCC, therefore it left the question for the Trial Chamber to determine after his indictment.[70]

AMNESTY/PARDON

Article 40 of the ECCC Law provides that the scope of any amnesty and pardons granted before its entry into force "is a matter to be decided by the Extraordinary Chambers." Ieng Sary argued the 1994 law outlawing the Khmer Rouge organization, from which he has received amnesty from prosecution, was intended to apply to all criminal acts committed by the Khmers Rouges from 1975-79—the temporal jurisdiction of the ECCC—and that therefore the amnesty deprives the ECCC of jurisdiction over him. The Co-Prosecutors, on the other hand, argued that offenses under the 1994 Law are more limited, explicitly including only succession, destruction against the Royal Government, destruction against organs of public authority, or incitement or forcing the taking up of arms against public authority. Therefore the only question for the Court is the scope of these offenses. In the alternative, they argued that an amnesty for *jus cogens* crimes such as genocide is not recognized under international law.

There is wide, though not universal acceptance, of the assertion that domestic amnesties for serious international crimes are not valid under international law. Nevertheless, there are still some who argue that amnesties and pardons should be respected in order to build support for peace initiatives. Acceptance of their invalidity is at its broadest with regard to crimes for which a state has a treaty obligation to prosecute or extradite. For example, the SCSL Appeals Chamber has said:

> [G]iven the existence of a treaty obligation to prosecute or extradite an offender, the grant of an amnesty in respect of [the international crimes set forth in the SCSL Statute] is not only incompatible with, but is in breach of an obligation of a State towards the international community as a whole.[71]

Cambodia has treaty obligations to prosecute or extradite persons who commit grave breaches under the 1949 Geneva Conventions and genocide under the 1948 Genocide Convention,[72] both of which may be charged by the ECCC.

There is also growing support for the view that domestic amnesties for other serious crimes, such as crimes against humanity, are invalid under customary international law. For example, discussing the effect on the jurisdiction of the SCSL of the amnesty clause in the Lomé Peace Agreement between the warring factions, the UN Secretary General said:

> While recognizing that amnesty is an accepted legal concept and a gesture of peace and reconciliation at the end of a civil war or an internal armed conflict, the United Nations has consistently maintained the position that amnesty cannot be granted in respect of international crimes, such as genocide, crimes against humanity or other serious violations of international humanitarian law.[73]

In its decision, the Pre-Trial Chamber focused narrowly on the appropriateness of holding Ieng Sary in detention and did not reach the question of the amnesty's legal effect on ECCC jurisdiction. It highlighted the fact that there are two inconsistent uses of the term "amnesty" in the royal decree ("amnesty from sentence" and "amnesty from prosecution"), and that neither use is consistent with the amnesty article in the 1993 Constitution. Therefore, it found the meaning of "amnesty" in the decree to be unclear. Moreover, it noted that at the time of the "amnesty from sentence," the death penalty had already been abolished in Cambodia. With regard to the "amnesty from prosecution," it found that the offenses mentioned in the 1994 law are not within the jurisdiction of the ECCC. As a consequence, the Pre-Trial Chamber considered the application of the amnesty uncertain and not manifestly prohibiting prosecution before the ECCC. Therefore, it decided that Ieng's provisional detention would not be inappropriate.[74]

FAIRNESS CHALLENGES

A second main area of dispute before the Pre-Trial Chamber has been challenges to the fairness of proceedings, including the voluntariness of waiver of counsel, the scope of the Court's obligation to translate documents into all three of its official languages, and the effect of the secrecy of the investigatory stage on the rights of the charged persons.

WAIVER OF COUNSEL

One charged person, Nuon Chea, has alleged that his right to a fair trial was impaired by absence of counsel at his initial appearance. Shortly after he was taken into custody, a hearing was held to determine the appropriateness of his provisional detention. At that time, Nuon was not represented by his national counsel due to the latter's unavailability, and Nuon had not yet selected a foreign attorney. He was repeatedly told that the hearing could be postponed until his counsel was available; nevertheless, he agreed to continue without counsel present and made a statement with regard to the charges against him. He subsequently appealed the order of detention, arguing to the Pre-Trial Chamber that he had not voluntarily waived this right.

Under Internal Rule 63(1), after the initial appearance—an adversarial hearing—the Co-Investigating Judges may order provisional detention. If the charged person does not have a lawyer, he or she is to be advised of his or her right to have one provided and a reasonable time to prepare a defense. As noted by the Pre-Trial Chamber, the rule does not mention the possibility of waiver of counsel. Nevertheless, the Pre-Trial Chamber found that the possibility was inferred, if it was voluntary and unequivocal. The Chamber followed ICTY/R jurisprudence to define "voluntary" as informed, knowing, and intelligent, and found that to knowingly and intelligently waive the right to counsel, a charged person "must be able to make a rational appreciation of the effects of proceeding without a lawyer."[75] After examining the case file, including the video-recording of the hearing, the PTC found that there was no indication that Nuon's age or medical condition hampered his decisions, and that therefore he had validly waived his right to counsel.

This decision is consistent with international standards; however, due to the seriousness of the charges and the advanced age of the accused, it may have been more prudent, as was advised by the Co-Prosecutors at the time, to have postponed the hearing until Nuon's counsel was present.

TRANSLATION OBLIGATIONS

A second Defense team has challenged the fairness of the ECCC process due to the failure of the Court to translate all of the documents in the case file into one of the official Court languages. Inadequate translation and interpretation have been and continue to be major problems for the Court, which has three official languages: Khmer, English, and French. For example, during the early months of *Duch* trial, there were complaints that as much as 50% of the meaning of testimony translated from Khmer to English and then from English to French had in some cases been lost during testimony. However, the only jurisprudence on this topic to date relates to the scope of the Court's obligation to translate the case file.

In 2008, the *Khieu Samphan* Defense team requested full translation of all documents in the case file into French—the native language of international counsel Jacques Vergès. During a hearing on appeal of the provisional detention order for Khieu, Vergès suddenly announced to the Pre-Trial Chamber that he could not represent his client until all the documents concerning the case were translated into French. The Chamber granted a motion for adjournment but warned Verges that he faced possible sanctions for his failure to give notice that he would refuse to defend his client. Verges subsequently complained to the press that the proceeding was a "unique scandal" and that Khieu Samphan's detention "is illegal since it was ordered based on documents to which his lawyers did not have access."[76]

The Co-Investigating Judges then issued an order to all parties on the scope of the right to translation. The order recognized that the availability of translation services may impact the rights of a person to a fair trial and attempted to balance those rights against the tribunal's limited resources. Citing international precedent, the CIJs found that charged persons were only entitled to translation of the indictment and the elements of proof on which it relies, the Co-Prosecutors' introductory and final submissions, the footnotes and indexes of factual elements on which those submissions rely, all judicial decisions and orders, and all filings by the Parties. According to the CIJs, "the key requirement is to allow a charged person to have 'knowledge of the case against him and to defend himself, notably by being able to put before the court his version of events.'"[77] Khieu and Ieng Sary appealed from that decision, claiming a violation of their rights. The Pre-Trial Chamber dismissed the appeals on procedural grounds, but nevertheless reviewed and supported the CIJ ruling.

In their appeals, the Defense teams argued that the order limiting the scope of translation violated their clients' rights to effective legal assistance, to participate in the proceedings, to equality of arms, and to have adequate time and facilities to prepare a defense and to be tried within a reasonable time.

The Pre-Trial Chamber decision highlighted the fact that the core ECCC documents do not provide an explicit right to receive all documents in the case file in all three official languages and said that the mere fact that the Court has three official languages "does not amount, in itself, to a right for the Charged Person to have all documents contained in his case file translated into this language."[78] This holding is supported by international jurisprudence, which uniformly has said that a defendants' right to translation into a language they understand is not all encompassing, even if they are representing themselves at trial. An accused's attorney has an even narrower right to have documents translated into his or her language.

The Pre-Trial Chamber also noted that both the Khieu and Ieng Sary legal teams include lawyers and consultants proficient in all three official languages and that the teams had been provided the free full-time assistance of a translator. Moreover, they had been offered the opportunity to identify potentially exculpatory material and request its translation. Altogether, the PTC considered these measures to uphold charged persons' fair trial rights under the Internal Rules and to be in accordance with international standards.

Critics of the CIJ Order argue that it places an unfair burden on national defense counsel to assess and prioritize which of thousands of Khmer-language documents require translation before all team members are capable of reviewing them and assessing their significance. This is a valid concern. Although the Co-Prosecutors face similar translation difficulties, they have bigger teams and more institutional support. At the same time, it is important to recognize that these translation challenges are not unique to the ECCC but have been a major topic of concern at all international tribunals. Moreover, the CIJ Order goes beyond the minimum fairness requirements set by those courts.

Two other criticisms may be more to the point: (1) why does the Court have three official languages when the difficulties of translation and interpretation are known to be so enormous; and (2) is it appropriate or necessary to place thousands of pages of documents in the case files? From trial proceedings in the *Duch* case it appears that neither the Defense, the Co-Prosecutors, nor the judges have fully examined the contents of the S-21 case file and understand their significance. If this is true in a much more focused case against one cooperative accused, it will be an exponentially greater problem in a case against four uncooperative accused. The large number of documents that have survived the DK regime are a great resource to the parties and to history; however, there is a real concern that this Court will bury itself in documents that no one involved in the proceedings has ever read.

TRANSPARENCY OBLIGATIONS

A third challenge to the fairness of the proceedings relates to the confidentiality of the investigation by the Co-Investigating Judges. This topic has been much debated since early in their investigation and became the subject of judicial proceedings when, in March 2009, the Co-Investigating Judges issued an order finding that *Ieng Sary* Defense counsel Michael Karnavas and Ang Udom had "breached ECCC Internal Rule 56(1) by revealing confidential information." Rule 56(1) states:

> In order to preserve the rights and interests of the parties, judicial investigations shall not be conducted in public. All persons participating in the judicial investigation shall maintain confidentiality.

The alleged confidentiality breach by the *Ieng Sary* team was their decision to establish a website providing access to their own "public" filings in the case, which they defined as "[s]ubmissions which are solely the work of the Defence team and which do not relate to the substances of the ongoing judicial investigation but relate solely to legal issues[.]"[79] These included filings on the issues of joint criminal enterprise liability, the health and fitness of the charged person, and potential conflicts of interest within the Office of the Co-Investigating Judges. In contrast, the CIJs defined "public" filings as those that are published on the ECCC website. Moreover, they emphasized that

> the confidentiality of the investigation applies to all documents, including those drafted by the parties and that it is solely for the Judges to decide when and how to disseminate confidential case material, since a decision concerning publicity must take account of objective criteria, such as preservation of the rights and interests of the parties.[80]

The Defense team's decision to establish the website was based on its view that the Co-Investigating Judges were "suppressing Defence filings which may be embarrassing or which call into question the legitimacy and judiciousness of acts and decisions of the judges" under the "fig leaf" of confidentiality.[81] Their arguments included that the level of confidentiality of the judicial investigation was "unnecessary and contradictory" and that documents should only be designated as confidential to protect Ieng Sary's rights—rights that he may waive. They argued further that the failure to post party motions violated the charged person's right to a fair and public trial and Cambodians' opportunity to witness an open and transparent judicial process.⁸²

There have been ongoing complaints from many quarters that the Co-Investigating Judges do not have a consistent and transparent policy for the publication of documents and filings.⁸³ In many cases when orders and decisions are published, the motions on those same issues are not. Notably, in response to the Defense team's appeal of the CIJ order, both a civil party team and the Co-Prosecutors filed briefs supporting the underlying Defense concerns.

Although the Co-Prosecutors argued that the appeal was inadmissible, they agreed that the questions it raised were important. They highlighted the fair trial rights guaranteed in the Framework Agreement and the ECCC Law and the fact that the Pre-Trial Chamber has found that charged persons enjoy these rights "from the beginning of the investigation."⁸⁴ They then identified three fundamental principles in "the spirit" of these rights that are entrenched in Internal Rule 21:

1. the obligation to interpret ECCC documents "to always safeguard the interests of Charged Persons…and Victims and so as to ensure…transparency of proceedings";

2. the "fair and adversarial" nature of the proceedings; and

3. the ECCC's obligation to "ensure that victims are kept informed…throughout the proceedings[.]"

Moreover they emphasized the plain language of Internal Rule 56(1), which clarifies that the purpose of confidentiality during the investigation is "to preserve the rights and interests of the parties."

Citing supporting provisions and practice of the International Criminal Court and French courts, as well as the ECCC's special mandate to bring justice to and set a judicial example for the Cambodian people, the Co-Prosecutors argued that "policies about confidentiality must be balanced against the high value in transparency of public institutions generally and the unique goals and circumstances of this Court."⁸⁵ Moreover, in their view this balance weighs in favor of "greater public access to this Court's proceedings and documents[.]"⁸⁶ They therefore requested the Pre-Trial Chamber to consider issuing guidelines for the Co-Investigating Judges regarding confidentiality during the pre-trial phase.⁸⁷

As the Defense has pointed out, Internal Rule 56(2) allows the Office of the Co-Investigating Judges to "issue such information regarding a case under judicial investigation as they deem essential to keep the public informed of the proceedings, or to rectify any false or misleading information." Nevertheless, the CIJs have shared very little information with the public about their investigation over the past two years. Thus it is notable that on March 3, the same day they issued the order against the *Ieng Sary* team, the CIJs vowed to "communicate more systematically about their activities in the future, and ... [to] publish an increased number of documents with regard to the judicial investigation."[88]

On March 26 and May 19, 2009, they decided to place on the website all the filings related to joint criminal enterprise and also the possible use of confessions obtained under torture during the Democratic Kampuchea period. These decisions were undoubtedly a belated effort to stem the nearly unanimous criticism among parties and outside observers that the CIJs have not followed a clear or consistent policy in determining which documents are confidential and which will be made public. While the CIJs efforts to release more information were welcomed, they also exemplify the arbitrariness of their approach. The first documents they released included a number of those posted by the *Ieng Sary* team. Moreover, to this day neither the parties nor the public has any reasoned guidance as to the CIJs' criteria for "confidentiality" beyond the blunt fact that it is "solely for the Judges to decide."[89]

SUBSTANTIVE CHALLENGES

At this stage of the proceedings there have been very few challenges to the Court's substantive law—the crimes and modes of liability charged. The most significant to date has been sustained efforts by all five suspects to prevent the Co-Prosecutors from charging them with the mode of liability of joint criminal enterprise (JCE). Including the charge of JCE in the *Duch* case would likely have little impact on the number of crimes for which Duch is found guilty, or even the length of his sentence. On the other hand, whether or not it is included in the case against the other four charged persons is expected to have an enormous impact on the number of crimes they can be connected to and for which they can be found responsible. Indeed, with regard to those charged persons against whom there appears to be less evidence of direct involvement in atrocities—Ieng Thirith and Khieu Samphan—it could even mean the difference between a guilty verdict and exoneration on all charges.

JOINT CRIMINAL ENTERPRISE

Joint criminal enterprise (JCE) is a theory of liability first articulated in ICTY jurisprudence and, though not listed in the ICTY/R or SCSL Statutes, is considered to be contained therein as a form of "commission." It is used to connect high-level accused—the planners, organizers, and ideologues who may not be physically connected to criminal acts but were catalysts for them—to the lower-level offenders who executed the crimes at their behest. It is particularly useful in a situation such as that faced by the ECCC, where those who carried out crimes claim they were acting under orders and those at the top claim the crimes were committed by over-enthusiastic lower-level cadre.

There are three JCE categories.[90] All three types involve "a plurality of persons" acting with a common purpose to commit crimes within the jurisdiction of the Court. The accused must contribute to this common plan. Each JCE category has a different mental or *mens rea* requirement. Participants in a type 1 or "basic" JCE must share the intent to commit a crime within the jurisdiction of the court. JCE-2, also known as "systemic" JCE, is a variant of the basic form and is characterized by existence of an organized system of ill-treatment. Thus far it has only been found in cases involving concentration camps. To be held liable for JCE-2, participants must have had personal knowledge of the system of ill-treatment and intended to further that system. An accused who participates in a basic or systematic JCE can also be held responsible for JCE-3, known as "extended" JCE, for crimes falling outside the scope of the plan if it was foreseeable that those crimes would be committed in furtherance of the plan and the accused knowingly took that risk. JCE-3 is the most controversial due to the fact that accused need not intend nor play a role in the "extended" crime with which he or she is charged.

The Co-Prosecutors discussed the existence of a common criminal plan between the charged persons in their initial submission (listing all five charged persons). The cases against the five accused were then split, with the charges against Duch entered into one case file (Case No. 001), and the other four into a second case file (Case No. 002). The Co-Prosecutors again discussed JCE in their final submission in Case No. 001. Nevertheless, the CIJs' closing order indicting Duch for crimes at S-21 does not include JCE. The Co-Prosecutors therefore appealed the closing order, arguing that if Duch were prosecuted only as an aider and abetter or for superior responsibility, it would fail to "reflect[] the totality of his criminal conduct and the central importance of his role in the functioning of S-21."[91]

Prior to deciding the Co-Prosecutor's appeal, the PTC sought a limited group of *amicus curiae* to submit their views on the evolution and applicability of JCE during the temporal jurisdiction of the Court. Ieng Sary also sought to offer submissions on the applicability of JCE at the ECCC, arguing that "[t]he application of JCE liability at the ECCC fundamentally affects Mr. IENG Sary because he is alleged to be part of the same 'common criminal plan' as Duch. In these circumstances, Mr. IENG Sary has a clear interest in the outcome of the appeal[.]"[92]

The Pre-Trial Chamber noted that Ieng was not a party to Case No. 001 and that neither the Internal Rules nor the Cambodian Code of Criminal Procedure provides a right for third party intervention. Ignoring the inevitable impact that a decision on the existence and scope of JCE during the jurisdiction of the Court would have on the charged persons in Case No. 002, the

Pre-Trial Chamber found that its decision on the appeal would "not be directly applicable to Ieng Sary, who will still have the possibility to challenge the application of the theory of joint criminal enterprise in [the case] to which he is a party."[93] A joint intervention by Ieng Thirith, Nuon Chea, and Khieu Samphan was similarly rebuffed. The Pre-Trial Chamber, without considering the ECCC's unique character as a special court tasked with trying very few accused in factually related cases, reasoned,

> it is inherent to courts where several proceedings are pending that a decision in one case on a legal issue will guide the court in future similar cases where no new circumstances or arguments are raised. It does not result from that situation that charged persons have the right to intervene in a case file to which they are not parties to submit their views on an issue.[94]

In its decision on the merits, the Pre-Trial Chamber noted that Internal Rule 67 does not require the Co-Investigating Judges to follow the Co-Prosecutors' submissions in drafting the closing order. It does, however, require that the closing order "state the reasons for the decision." According to the Pre-Trial Chamber, the Co-Investigating Judges "failed to reason why the Co-Prosecutors' proposal to include the allegation of a joint criminal enterprise within S-21 was rejected...[and] did not explain the chosen characterization of the facts in terms of the modes of liability."[95]

The PTC then found that S-21 and Duch had been clearly considered part of a JCE in the Co-Prosecutor's initial submission; however, when Duch's file was separated from the other four charged persons, the JCE involving all five was only related to Case No. 002. Considering whether or not an S-21 JCE formed part of the factual basis for the investigation in Case No. 001, the PTC determined that some JCE elements were, while others were not. Therefore, Duch was not informed of the allegations of his participation in an S-21 JCE prior to the final submission, and the factual basis was not sufficient to allow a characterization of JCE in the closing order.

The Co-Prosecutors have again raised the applicability of JCE in the *Duch* case before the Trial Chamber, but it has yet to issue a ruling. If it also rejects the Prosecutor's request to include JCE on notice grounds, the applicability and scope of JCE at the ECCC will not be decided until charged persons are indicted in Case No. 002.

CO-PROSECUTOR DISPUTE

At the time of publication, the ECCC has charged and detained only five persons as "senior leaders of Democratic Kampuchea" or persons "most responsible" for crimes within the jurisdiction of the ECCC. However, an August 18, 2009 decision by the Pre-Trial Chamber allows the judicial investigation of five more suspects.

On November 18, 2008, former international Co-Prosecutor Robert Petit filed a notice of disagreement among the Co-Prosecutors regarding the appropriateness of opening these new judicial investigations.[96] He sought to file two new introductory submissions and one supplementary submission (since withdrawn) that would include charges against six more persons, one of whom has since died.[97] National Co-Prosecutor Chea Leang, however, did not agree that there should be additional investigations.

Many NGOs and other outside observers have argued that the ECCC will prove its legitimacy and independence from the Cambodian government only if it investigates and prosecutes more than the five persons originally charged. Others have said that whether or not only five or a few more are prosecuted makes no difference, as the numbers of persons tried will be small compared to the number of perpetrators either way. Instead, they prioritized prosecuting the five already charged quickly and well.

Article 20 of the amended ECCC Law provides that, in the event of a disagreement between the Co-Prosecutors, they "shall submit written statements of facts and the reasons for their different positions to the Director of the Office of Administration." The disagreement is then settled by the Pre-Trial Chamber in a decision made by an affirmative vote of at least four judges. If there is no majority decision, "the action or decision done by one Co-Prosecutor shall stand or…the action or decision proposed to be done by one Co-Prosecutor shall be executed."[98]

In the case of the current disagreement, an affirmative vote by four of the Pre-Trial Judges could not be reached: the three Cambodian judges voted against the investigations and the two international judges voted in favor. As a consequence, the international Co-Prosecutor's request for new investigations moves forward by default. There is no opportunity for appeal.

Because the ECCC hybrid international/national structure is unique in having two chief prosecutors, no other court has addressed a similar situation. Prosecutorial discretion in the selection of cases and suspects is extremely broad at internationalized courts set up to prosecute a limited number of offenders for serious crimes. There are no clear limits on their discretion beyond each court's jurisdictional mandate, professional obligations of prosecutorial independence, and the (usually quite limited) opportunities for judicial review of their decisions. As a consequence, there is very little public information about why some suspects have been investigated and prosecuted and others have not. The ECCC

Pre-Trial Chamber thus faced the unprecedented situation of stepping into the shoes of two prosecutors with equally broad discretionary authority to determine which of their views should be supported.

In making its determination, the Pre-Trial Chamber had little textual guidance about how the Co-Prosecutors should exercise their discretion. The primary criterion is contained in ECCC Internal Rule 53(1), governing the filing of introductory submissions. It provides: "If the Co-Prosecutors have reason to believe that crimes within the jurisdiction of the ECCC have been committed, they shall open a judicial investigation[.]"

The international Co-Prosecutor publicly argued that in his view there were reasons to believe that "(1) the crimes described in those submissions were committed, (2) these crimes are within the jurisdiction of this Court, and (3) they should be investigated by the Co-Investigating Judges" in order to have a "more comprehensive accounting" of DK crimes.[99] Moreover, he emphasized that the additional investigations would not endanger Cambodia's peace and stability.

The national Co-Prosecutor initially argued that additional investigations should not be conducted due to "(1) Cambodia's past instability and the continued need for national reconciliation, (2) the spirit of the agreement between the United Nations and the Royal Government of Cambodia ('Agreement') and the spirit of the law that established this Court ('ECCC Law'), and (3) the limited duration and budget of this Court."[100] In her view, these documents envision the prosecution of only a small number of suspects and the Court should use its limited resources to prioritize the five persons currently charged.

In confidential supplementary filings she additionally argued that the new investigations were (4) unnecessary, and (5) preliminarily conducted in violation of ECCC procedures. Although this chapter will discuss her arguments on the merits, it must be noted that there is a widely held perception that the national Co-Prosecutor was making her arguments at the behest of the Cambodian government, which is opposed to additional prosecutions.[101]

In deciding the dispute, the PTC found that "the scope of its review [was] limited to settling the specific issues upon which the Co-Prosecutors disagree."[102] Moreover, it examined only the national Co-Prosecutor's arguments to determine if they prevented the new submissions from being forwarded.

Notably, the Co-Prosecutors did not appear to disagree (at least initially[103]) that they possess both the necessary jurisdiction and sufficient evidence of crimes—the only explicit criteria in the Internal Rules—to request the additional judicial investigations. Instead, they disagreed about what other factors, if any, should be taken into account in deciding whether to move forward with a new investigation.

ILLEGALITY OF THE PRELIMINARY INVESTIGATION

The national Co-Prosecutor argued that the international Co-Prosecutor had conducted the preliminary investigation of the new suspects "without her knowledge or assistance" and that this unilateral act was in violation of the ECCC Law and Internal Rules.[104] The three Cambodian judges agreed that the preliminary investigation had been conducted unilaterally without prior notification in violation of ECCC procedures and that this invalidated the introductory submission. The international judges, however, found that under the Internal Rules the Co-Prosecutors may act unilaterally if neither brings a dispute to the PTC within 30 days. Because the national Co-Prosecutor had not done so, they did not consider this argument to be relevant to the disagreement.

NECESSITY OF THE NEW SUBMISSIONS

The national Co-Prosecutor also argued that the new submissions were not necessary because the facts and crimes they specify were already covered within the first introductory submission, which included crimes that "occurred…all over Cambodia" and resulted in "over 1.7 million…victims."[105] For that reason, in her view the CIJs already have the competency to extend their initial investigation to include unnamed suspects. The three Cambodian judges agreed.

The international judges noted that

> [a]n Introductory Submission so broad that it would include all the legal offences within the jurisdiction of the ECCC committed throughout Cambodia between 17 April 1975 and 6 January 1979, without any reference to precise factual situations, would not be specific enough to meet the requirements of Internal Rule 53(1). [106]

Instead, they determined that the first initial submission had been limited on the facts, and that this was clear from the practice of both Co-Prosecutors as they jointly filed supplemental submissions to it, which would not have been necessary if the national Co-Prosecutor's argument was correct. In their view, she "relie[d] on a confusion between the legal characterization of the alleged criminal acts and the facts concerning alleged criminal acts that are forwarded for investigation."[107] Because new facts were mentioned that could not be investigated without additional submissions by the Co-Prosecutors, the new submissions were necessary.

EXERCISE OF PROSECUTORIAL DISCRETION

The national judges only addressed the two issues above; the international judges also limited their discussion to those topics. However, the national Co-Prosecutor also argued that, in the exercise of prosecutorial discretion, the purpose and spirit of the ECCC Law and Framework Agreement "to promote national unity, reconciliation, stability, security and peace in Cambodia" should "take precedence over Internal Rule 53[.]…[T]hus prosecutions should not be initiated in every case where there is 'reason to believe' crimes have been committed."[118]

As at the ECCC, prosecutors at international courts such as the ICTY, ICTR, and SCSL are only statutorily required to consider objective criteria in deciding whom to prosecute. Only the ICC prosecutor is tasked with considering both if there is a "reasonable basis to proceed" and if the investigation or prosecution would be in the "interests of justice." Nevertheless, it is clear that in practice the prosecutors of all these courts do in fact consider both objective and subjective criteria in exercising their discretion.

Based on the limited case law and the statements of some prosecutors at international courts, the factors that appear to be most widely considered in choosing whom to prosecute include: the gravity of the crimes, the level of responsibility of the alleged perpetrators, political considerations, the need to "tell the whole story" of what happened and why, and national reconciliation.

The national Co-Prosecutor's concerns about national reconciliation therefore may be an appropriate consideration when exercising prosecutorial discretion; however, there is no clear evidence that Cambodian reconciliation would be best achieved by limiting the number of charged persons. Indeed, it is possible to make a strong contrary argument that, as has been suggested by the former international Co-Prosecutor, more prosecutions would positively contribute to national reconciliation by providing more information about what happened during the DK period and who was responsible.

Moreover, while it is clear that only a small number of prosecutions were intended by both the UN and the Cambodian government, it is not obvious that there should be five and not 10. Notably, the report of the Group of Experts set up to advise the UN on the establishment of the Court emphasized that limitations on the number of prosecutions "ignores the principle that criminal culpability should be linked with the degree of personal responsibility of an individual and not partisan political factors[.]"[119] Moreover, they stated, "We do not wish to offer a numerical limit on the number of…persons who could be targets of investigation…. the number of persons to be tried might well be in the range of some 20 to 30[.]"[120] This may be higher than the number of accused the negotiators eventually—if tacitly—agreed to, but there is no information available suggesting that they agreed to a specific number.

Although both the Co-Investigating Judges and the Pre-Trial Chamber have raised public order concerns in determining whether pre-trial detention of the five charged persons is appropriate, their concerns have been supported primarily by reference to a few charged incidents between victims and the accused. The national Co-Prosecutor argued speculatively, "If prosecutions of lower-ranking officials were to be initiated…'ex-members [of the Khmer Rouge] and those who have allegiance to the Khmer Rouge Leaders may commit violent acts'."[121] She also highlighted the fact that new prosecutions could endanger Cambodian national security "given the current border problems near Preah Vihear 'in which former [Khmer Rouge] solders are at the forefront of protecting [Cambodia's] territorial integrity'."[122]

On the other hand, a survey by DC-Cam in March 2009 indicates that at least a slight majority of Cambodians are not concerned about potential public disorder if more suspects are investigated and have confidence in the ability of the government to control any disturbances.[123] As long ago as 1999, the UN Group of Experts noted:

> [M]any of the possible suspects do not now have armed forces at their disposal. As for the possibility that others who have surrendered might remobilize their forces to mount a renewed struggle against the Government, it is our sense that their followers in general do not exhibit the type of loyalty and military discipline necessary for such an outcome, but are rather interested in simply securing a decent life for themselves and their family. Most important, because the targets of investigation will be limited to those in leadership positions from 1975 to 1979 who were responsible for atrocities, and not Khmer Rouge officials who became leaders of the guerrilla army after 1979 and who did not commit atrocities during the period from 1975 to 1979, the risk of troop redefection becomes smaller.[124]

Finally, regarding the national Co-Prosecutor's concern that additional prosecutions would create financial uncertainty for the Court, there is little evidence that finite time and financial resources have played a significant role in decisions of prosecutors at internationalized tribunals, although all have been confronted with these considerations.

There is thus little evidence supporting the national Co-Prosecutor's discretionary arguments against forwarding the new submissions. Moreover, although the PTC did not address this issue in its decision, if it had, it does not appear that the international judges would have supported any consideration of subjective factors. In their view, because Internal Rule 53(1) provides that the Co-Prosecutors "shall" as opposed to "may" open a judicial investigation

(On this spread) The ECCC's detention center for the five individuals in custody. Photo by Dacil Q. Keo.
Source: Documentation Center of Cambodia Archives

The ECCC's detention center for the five individuals in custody. Photo by Dacil Q. Keo.
Source: Documentation Center of Cambodia Archives

if they "have reason to believe that crimes within the jurisdiction of the ECCC have been committed," they have no discretion in the matter. Rather, they are "obliged to open a judicial investigation by sending an Introductory Submission."[125]

As the PTC could not achieve a majority of four judges, the international Co-Prosecutor may now—almost a year after the dispute first arose—forward the two new initial submissions without the support of the national Co-Prosecutor. The Co-Investigating Judges are required to investigate the facts set out in these filings and, if warranted, charge and send additional suspects to trial. However, as with the Co-Prosecutors, the Co-Investigating Judges must conduct their investigations jointly and agree on whether or not the alleged acts in question amount to crimes within the Court's jurisdiction, the perpetrators have been identified, and there is sufficient evidence against any charged persons to issue an order sending them to trial. If the CIJs disagree on how to proceed, their dispute will be settled by the Pre-Trial Chamber, with the same presumption of investigations and orders moving forward if the national and international judges cannot agree. How long this may all take, and whether or not the process can be completed within the Court's budget before more suspects die, are open to question.

CONCLUSION

Although it is formally part of the Cambodian judicial system, as the ECCC grows and evolves through practice, it acts more and more like an international court applying a mixture of both civil and common law. This is likely due to the strong influence of the numerous international staff who have previously worked at mixed tribunals, as well as the absence of statutory guidance or Cambodian legal precedent for many of the novel topics this special Court faces. Court decisions thus far have been soundly based in international law, even if they have not always been as protective of the charged persons' fair trial rights as some might wish.

The Pre-Trial Chamber has issued two important decisions upholding the rights of the charged persons during the pre-trial stage. First, the Pre-Trial Chamber issued a decision overturning the Co-Investigating judges' policy of keeping the charged persons in *de facto* segregation. Second, it recognized that fitness for trial is a requirement not only "at trial," but also during the investigation.

The Pre-Trial Chamber has not been generous in its application of fair trial rights. The charged persons are old and not in the best of health, and the likelihood of their living to judgment may in great part depend on their living conditions over the next few years. Nevertheless, it seems unlikely that the Pre-Trial Chamber will ever decide that the charged persons are entitled to provisional release or home detention. Although its provisional release decisions are defensible, they are not incontrovertible. At some point the Pre-Trial Chamber may be required to rethink the necessity of alternate forms of detention in order to best ensure that the charged persons are mentally and physically fit for trial. In order to make this determination, it may find that receiving the advice of experts on senior care would be prudent as the charged person's health concerns may not be as clear cut as for younger detainees.

The Pre-Trial Chamber has also strictly applied international standards on other questions, such as the charged persons' right to offer their views on the applicability of joint criminal enterprise in the *Duch* case. Although the decision rejecting their requests was soundly based, it ignores the fact that the ECCC, unlike other courts, will only try a few defendants for related crimes. It appears disingenuous for the PTC to ignore that, if the Chambers determine in the Duch case that JCE did in fact exist during the temporal jurisdiction of the Court, this cannot be undone for the second case. There can be no going back; the charged persons' opportunity to challenge the applicability of this mode of liability, if not its scope, would be lost.

One way in which this Court most reflects the civil law tradition is its use of Co-Investigative Judges to conduct the bulk of the investigation. Their decision to carry out their investigations in strict confidentiality, and their failure to issue guidelines governing the scope of confidentiality, have conflicted with the desires of both the parties and the public. Because of the secrecy, there has also been little public information about judicial challenges the Defense and other parties have brought against the practices of the Co-Investigating Judges. For this reason, the decision of the *Ieng Sary* team to flout the CIJ's proscription on publishing their filings, and the other parties' support for their underlying arguments, is notable for bringing to light the depth of the frustration behind the scenes.

Overall, the decisions of all ECCC organs have surpassed many people's expectations. The complexity of Court's structure, the presumptive lack of independence and experience of Cambodia's judges, and the politics ever present in relations between the United Nations and the Cambodian government have led many to write off this Court from the beginning. However, thus far, the Court has acted prudently, if slowly, and its decisions have been generally consistent with international standards.

For many, the real test will be how the Court responds to the first issue that has directly challenged the wishes of the Cambodian government: the international Co-Prosecutor's request to open additional judicial investigations. The fact that the decision was made on national/international lines will reinforce the skepticism of those who believe the Court is inherently political. However, the fact the investigations are now moving forward may also provide a source of some optimism, in that these concerns were anticipated and effectively addressed by the Court's "super majority" requirement (providing that any decision by the judges include at least one international vote). Whether or not the Pre-Trial Chamber's decision—or failure to decide—on this question should be the litmus test of the Court's independence and fairness, for many people it will likely be the only decision that matters.

---

[1] *See, e.g.*, Ilijkov v. Bulgaria, App. No. 33977/96, Eur. Ct. H.R., ¶ 84 (July 26, 2001); Jorge A. Giménez v. Arg., Case No. 11.245, Report 12/96, Inter-Am.C.H.R., OEA/Ser.L/V/II.91, Doc. 7 at 33, ¶ 84 (1996); W.B.E. v. Neth., HRC Comm. No. 432/1990, ¶ 6.3 (1992).

[2] *See, e.g.*, Prosecutor v. Issa Hassan Sesay et al., Case No. SCSL-04-15-AR65, Sesay—Decision on Appeal Against Refusal of Bail, ¶ 36 (Appeals Chamber, Dec. 14, 2004) (noting that "[i]n the particular situation of Sierra Leone, public interest factors such as the ability of the authorities to uphold [bail] conditions may take on a greater relevance" than in situations where greater police enforcement capacity exists); Prosecutor v. Radoslav Brdanin et al., Case No. IT-99-36, Decision on Application for Leave to Appeal (Appeals Chamber Bench, Sept. 7, 2000) (noting that "in applying [international legal standards] account has to be taken of the different circumstances and situations envisaged by those standards which did not visualize the nature and character of the International Tribunal, and that the International Tribunal does not have the same facilities as are available to national courts to enforce appearance").

[3] *See, e.g.*, Prosecutor v. Jean-Pierre Bemba Gombo, Case No. ICC-01/05-01/08, Decision on the Interim Release of Jean-Pierre Bemba Gombo and Convening Hearings with the Kingdom of Belgium, the Republic of Portugal, the Republic of France, the Federal Republic of Germany, the Italian Republic, and the Republic of South Africa, ¶ 38 (Pre-Trial Chamber, Aug. 14, 2009) (noting that "the task is to weigh up and balance the factors presented to [the judge], mindful of the particular circumstances of each individual case"); and Prosecutor v. Issay Hassan Sesay et al., Case No. SCSL-04-15-PT, Decision on Application of Issa Sesay for Provisional Release, ¶ 39 (Trial Chamber, Mar. 31, 2004) (following ICTY jurisprudence in determining that "the focus must be on the particular circumstances of each individual case without considering that the eventual outcome is either the rule or the exception").

[4] *See* Prosecutor v. Vujadin Popović et al., Case No. IT-05-88-AR65.1, Decision on Interlocutory Appeal of Trial Chamber Decision Denying Drago Nikolic's Motion for Provisional Release, at 5 (Appeals Chamber, Jan. 24, 2006) (noting that the Trial Chamber has "considerable discretion when determining the weight to accord…factors [relevant to determining the necessity of pre-trial detention] in light of the specific circumstances of the individual case").

[5] Decision on Appeal Against Provisional Detention Order of Nuon Chea, Case No. 002/19-09-2007-ECCC/OCIJ (PTC01), ¶ 46 (Pre-Trial Chamber, Mar. 20, 2008).

[6] *See* Decision on Ieng Thirith's Appeal Against Order on Extension of Provisional Detention, Case No. 002/19-09-2007-ECCC/OCIJ (PTC 16), ¶ 25 (Pre-Trial Chamber, May 11, 2009); Decision on Khieu Samphan's Appeals Against Order Refusing Request for Release and Extension of Provisional Detention Order, Case No. 002/19-09-2007-ECCC/OCIJ (PTC 14 and 15), ¶ 137 (Pre-Trial Chamber, July 3, 2009).

[7] Decision on Appeal of Ieng Sary Against OCIJ's Order on Extension of Provisional Detention, Case No. 002/19-09-2007-ECCC/OCIJ (PTC17), ¶¶ 19-21 (Pre-Trial Chamber, June 26, 2009).

[8] *See, e.g.*, Prosecutor v. Miodrag Jokić, Case No. IT-01-42-PT, Order on Miodrag Jokić's Motion for Provisional Release, ¶ 26 (Feb. 20, 2002) (finding that the completion of the investigation "may reduce the risk of potential destruction of documentary evidence"); Letellier v. Fr., App. No. 12369/86, Eur. Ct. H.R., ¶ 38 (1991).

[9] *See, e.g.*, Prosecutor v. Issay Hassan Sesay et al., *supra* note 3, ¶ 54 (stating that "the mere ability of the Accused to exert pressure

upon any witness following disclosure of evidence by the Prosecution cannot alone affect his release on bail"); Prosecutor v. Radoslav Brdanin et al., Case No. IT-99-3-T, Decision on Motion by Radoslav Brdanin for Provisional Release, ¶ 19 (Trial Chamber, July 25, 2000) (not accepting that a "heightened *ability* to interfere with victims and witnesses, by itself, suggests that he *will* pose a danger to them…[as] [i]t cannot just be assumed that everyone charged with a crime under the Tribunal's Statute will, if released, pose a danger to victims or witnesses or others.") (emphasis in original, footnotes omitted).

[10] Decision on Appeal against Provisional Detention Order of Kaing Guek Eav alias "Duch," Case No. 001/18-07-2007-ECCC/OCIJ (PTC01), ¶ 32 (Pre-Trial Chamber, Dec. 3, 2007).

[11] *Id.* ¶ 34.

[12] Decision on Appeal against Provisional Detention Order of Ieng Sary, Case No. 002/19-09-2007-ECCC/OCIJ (PTC03), ¶ 99 (Pre-Trial Chamber, Oct. 17, 2008).

[13] *See, e.g.*, Prosecutor v. Sam Hinga Norman et al., Case No. SCSL-04-14-T, Fofana—Decision on Application for Bail Pursuant to Rule 65, ¶¶ 72-73 (Trial Chamber, Aug. 5, 2004).

[14] *Compare* Case of Jan Pawlak v. Poland, Appl. No. 8661/06, Eur. Ct. H.R., ¶ 42 (June 9, 2009) (emphasizing that "while the severity of the sentence faced is a relevant element in the assessment of the risk of absconding or re-offending, the gravity of the charges cannot by itself justify long periods of detention on remand") *with* Decision on Interlocutory Appeal of Trial Chamber Decision Denying Drago Nikolic's Motion for Provisional Release, *supra* note 4, at 6 ("[f]inding that, in the context of the specific circumstances of the case—in particular the gravity of the crimes the Appellant is charged with and the likelihood of a significant prison sentence upon conviction—it was reasonable for the Trial Chamber to find that notwithstanding the Governmental Guarantees and the guarantee provided by the Appellant himself it was not satisfied that the Appellant, if released, would appear for trial") and Prosecutor v. Germain Katanga *et al.*, Case No. ICC-01/04-01/07, Judgment in the Appeal by Mathieu Ngudjolo Chui of Mar. 27, 2008 against the Decision of the Pre-Trial Chamber I on the Application of the Appellant for Interim Release, ¶ 21 (Appeals Chamber, June 9, 2008) ("Evading justice in fear of the consequences that may befall the person becomes a distinct possibility; a possibility rising in proportion to the consequences that conviction may entail").

[15] Fofana—Decision on Application for Bail Pursuant to Rule 65, *supra* note 13, ¶¶ 66-67 (referencing ECHR jurisprudence).

[16] Decision on Khieu Samphan's Appeals Against Order Refusing Request for Release and Extension of Provisional Detention Order, *supra* note 6, ¶¶ 50-58.

[17] *See, e.g.*, Letellier v. Fr., *supra* note 8, ¶ 51; Bronstein et al. v. Argentina, Report No. 2/97, ¶ 36, Inter-Am.C.H.R, OEA/Ser.L/V/II/95, Doc. 7 rev. at 241 (1997).

[18] Decision on Khieu Samphan's Appeals Against Order Refusing Request for Release and Extension of Provisional Detention Order, *supra* note 6, ¶ 55 (quoting press statements by two victims stating "only killing them will make [him] feel calm" and "if she had her way, she would slice the elderly man [Nuon Chea] into ribbons and pour salt into his wounds"). *See also id.* ¶ 56 (noting that at an ECCC press conference one Civil Party "shouted and pointed her finger at the national Co-Lawyer" and another warned that if the Tribunal does not proceed smoothly to deliver justice, he will "call a terrorist from Al Qaida and ask him to perform a terrorist act at the ECCC").

[19] Decision on Appeal Against Provisional Detention Order of Nuon Chea, *supra* note 5, ¶ 77.

[20] Prosecutor v. Kaing Guek Eav alias DUCH, Case No. 001/18-7-2007/ECCC/TC, Decision on Protective Measures for Civil Parties, ¶ 8 (Trial Chamber, June 2, 2009).

[21] *See, e.g.*, Prosecutor v. Jovica Stanšić, Case No. IT-03-68-PT, Decision on Provisional Release, ¶ 39, (Trial Chamber, July 28, 2004)] (need for treatment); Prosecutor v. Simo Drljača et al., Case No. IT-97-24-T, Decision on Defense Motion for Provisional Release, ¶ 12 (Trial Chamber, Jan. 20, 1998) (humanitarian grounds); Prosecutor v. Pavle Strugar, Case No. IT-01, Decision re the Defence Motion to Terminate Proceedings, ¶ 35 (Trial Chamber, May 26, 2004) (fitness).

[22] *See, e.g.*, Prosecutor v. Pavle Strugar, Case No. I-01-42-A, Decision on Defense Request for Provisional Release for Providing Medical

[23] *See, e.g.*, Prosecutor v. Radolav Brdanin et al., Case No. IT-99-36-T, Decision on the Motion for Provisional Release of the Accused Momir Talic, ¶ 35 (Trial Chamber, Sept. 20, 2002).

[24] Decision on Appeal Against Provisional Detention Order of Ieng Sary, *supra* note 12, ¶ 123.

[25] Decision on Appeal of Ieng Sary Against OCIJ's Order on Extension of Provisional Detention, *supra* note 7, ¶ 38.

[26] *See, e.g.*, Prosecutor v. Thomas Lubanga Dyilo, Case No. ICC-01/04-01/06, Decision on the Application for the Interim Release of Thomas Lubanga Dyilo, at 7 (Pre-Trial Chamber, Oct. 18, 2006); Toth v. Austria, App. No. 11894, Eur. Ct. H.R., ¶ 67 (Dec. 12, 1991).

[27] Prosecutor v. Joseph Kanyabashi, Case No. ICTR-96-15-T, Decision on the Defence Motion for Provisional Release of the Accused, ¶ 12 (Trial Chamber, Feb. 21, 2001).

[28] Decision on Khieu Samphan's Supplemental Application for Release, Case No. 002/19-09-2007-ECCC/OCIJ (PTC15), ¶ 5 (Pre-Trial Chamber, Dec. 24, 2008).

[29] *See, e.g.*, Ieng Sary Order on Extension of Provisional Detention, Case No. 002/19-09-2007-ECCC/OCIJ, ¶ 41 (Office of the Co-Investigating Judges, Nov. 10, 2008).

[30] Prosecutor v. Kaing Guek Eav alias DUCH, Case No. 001/18-07-2007/ECCC/TC, Decision on Request for Release, ¶ 16 (Trial Chamber, June 15, 2009).

[31] *See id.* ¶¶ 35, 36.

[32] *Id.* ¶ 29.

[33] *Id.* ¶¶ 23-26.

[34] Co-Prosecutors' Response to the Charged Person Ieng Sary's Appeal on Visitation Rights, Case No. 02/19-09-2007-ECCC/OCIJ (PTC 05), ¶ 1 (Pre-Trial Chamber, Apr. 1, 2008).

[35] *Id.* ¶ 2.

[36] Decision on Appeal Concerning Contact Between the Charged Person and His Wife, Case No. 002/19-09-2007-ECCC/OCIJ (PTC05), ¶ 15 (Pre-Trial Chamber, Apr. 30, 2008) (citing Internal Rules of the Extraordinary Chambers in the Courts of Cambodia [hereinafter ECCC Internal Rules], R. 21(2))

[37] *Id.* ¶ 18.

[38] *Id.* ¶ 20.

[39] Order Concerning Provisional Detention Conditions, Case No. 002/19-09-2007-ECCC/OCIJ, ¶ 5 (Office of the Co-Investigating Judges, May 21, 2008).

[40] Decision on Nuon Chea's Appeal Concerning Provisional Detention Conditions, Case No. 002/19-09-2007-ECCC/OCIJ (PTC09), ¶ 21 (Pre-Trial Chamber, Sept. 26, 2008).

[41] ECCC Internal Rules, *supra* note 36, R. 32.

[42] Decision on Nuon Chea's Appeal Regarding Appointment of an Expert, Case No. 002/19-09-2007-ECCC/OCIJ (PTC07), ¶ 21 (Pre-TrialChamber, Oct. 22, 2008) (citing Decision Re the Defence Motion to Terminate Proceedings, *supra* note 21, ¶ 21.

[43] *Id.* (citing Decision Re the Defence Motion to Terminate Proceedings, *supra* note 21, ¶ 23).

[44] *Id.* ¶ 26.

[45] Decision Re the Defence Motion to Terminate Proceedings, *supra* note 21, ¶ 35.

[46] *Id.* ¶ 47.

[47] *Id.* ¶ 38.

[48] Prosecutor v. Jovica Stänsić et al., Case No. IT-03-69-T, Decision on Stansic Defence's Motion on the Fitness of the Accused to Stand Trial with Confidential Annexes (Trial Chamber, Apr. 27, 2006).

[49] *Id.* (citation omitted).

[50] *See* Prosecutor v. Vladimir Kovacević, Case No. IT-01-42/2/I, Decision on Provisional Release, at 1 (Trial Chamber, June 2, 2004).

[51] Decision on Ieng Sary's Appeal Regarding the Appointment of a Psychiatric Expert, Case No. 002/19-09-2007-ECCC/OCIJ (PTC10), ¶ 43 (Oct. 21, 2008). *See also id.* ¶¶ 42-46.

[52] Prosecutor v. Thomas Lubanga Dyilo, Case No. 01/04-01/06, Decision on Victims' Participation, ¶ 98 (Trial Chamber, Jan. 18, 2008) [hereinafter January 2008 ICC Trial Decision].

[53] Prosecutor v. Thomas Lubanga Dyilo, Case No. 01/04-01/06(OA 8), Decision of the Appeals Chamber on the Joint Application of Victims a/0001/06 to a/0003/06 and a/0105/06 concerning the "Directions and Decision of the Appeals Chamber of 2 February 2007" (Appeals Chamber, June 13, 2007) [hereinafter June 2007 ICC Appeals Decision], Separate Opinion of Judge Sang-Hyun Song ¶ 13.

[54] ECHR App. No. 22492/92, ¶ 91 (Mar. 28, 2000). *See also* Case of the Caracazo v. Venezuela, Inter-Am. Ct. H.R. (ser. C) No. 95, ¶ 115 (Aug. 29, 2002) ("any person who considers himself or herself to be a victim of [human rights] violations has the right to resort to the system of justice to attain compliance with … [States' duty to investigate and punish such violations], for his or her benefit and that of society as a whole").

[55] *See* June 2007 ICC Appeals Decision, Separate Opinion of Judge Sang-Hyun Song, *supra* note 53, ¶ 18.

[56] *Id.*

[57] ECCC Internal Rules, *supra* note 36, R. 23(6)(a).

[58] Rome Statute of the International Criminal Court, U.N. Doc. A/CONF.183/9 (1998), art. 68(3).

[59] June 2007 ICC Appeals Decision, *supra* note 53, Separate Opinion of Judge Georghios M. Pikis, ¶ 11 (footnotes omitted).

[60] Prosecutor v. Thomas Lubanga Dyilo, Case No. 01/04-01/06(OA 7), Judgment on the Appeal of Mr. Thomas Lubanga Dyilo against the Decision of Pre-Trial Chamber I entitled "Décision sur la demande de mis en liberte provisoire de Thomas Lubanga Dyilo, ¶ 40 (Appeals Chamber, Feb. 13, 2007) [hereinafter February 2007 ICC Appeals Judgment].

[61] *Id.* ¶¶ 2, 38.

[62] January 2008 ICC Trial Decision, *supra* note 52, ¶ 101.

[63] February 2007 ICC Appeals Judgment, *supra* note 60, ¶ 54.

[64] *See* Prosecutor v. Thomas Lubanga Dyilo, Case No. 01/04-01/06, Observations of victims a/0001/05, a/0002/06 and a/0003/06 in respect of the application for release filed by the Defense, ¶¶ 11-15 (Pre-Trial Chamber, Oct. 9, 2006).

[65] Decision on Civil Party Participation in Provisional Detention Appeals, Case No. 002/19-09-2007-ECCC/OCIJ (PTC01), ¶ 35 (Pre-Trial Chamber, Mar. 20, 2009).

[66] *See, e.g.,* ECCC Internal Rules, *supra* note 36, R.55(10),(11) (authorizing Civil Parties to request the CIJs to make orders and undertake investigative actions and to consult the case file); R.59(5) (authorizing Civil Parties to request the CIJs to "interview him or her, question witnesses, go to a site, order expertise or collect other evidence on his or her behalf"); R.74(4) (authorizing Civil Parties to appeal against certain orders of Co-Investigating judges, including primarily those relating to investigative actions and Civil Party application). *See also* Cambodian Code of Criminal Procedure, art. 134.

[67] Decision on Civil Party Participation in Provisional Detention Appeals, *supra* note 65, ¶ 36.

[68] *Id.* ¶ 43 (referencing Internal Rule 21(1)(a)). *See also id.* ¶ 44.

[69] *See* Decision on Appeal against Provisional Detention Order of Ieng Sary, *supra* note 12, ¶ 24 (*citing* Decree Law No. 1: Establishment

of People's Revolutionary Tribunal at Phnom Penh to Try the Pol Pot-Ieng Sary Clique for the Crime of Genocide (July 15, 1979)).

[70] *Id.* ¶¶ 43, 51-54.

[71] Prosecutor v. Morris Kallon, Case No. SCSL-04-15-AR72(E) & Prosecutor v. Ibrahim Bazzy Kamara, Case No. SCSL-04-16-AR72(E), Decision on Challenge to Jurisdiction: Lomé Accord Amnesty, ¶ 73 (Appeals Chamber, Mar. 13, 2004).

[72] *See* Convention for the Amelioration of the Condition of the Wounded and Sick in Armed Forces in the Field (Geneva Convention No. I), Aug. 12, 1949, art. 49, 75 UNTS 31; Convention for the Amelioration of the Condition of the Wounded, Sick, and Shipwrecked Members of Armed Forces at Sea (Geneva Convention No. II), Aug. 12, 1949, art. 50, 75 UNTS 85; Geneva Convention Relative to the Treatment of Prisoners of War (Geneva Convention No. III), Aug. 12, 1949, art. 129, 75 UNTS 135; Convention Relative to the Protection of Civilian Persons in Time of War (Geneva Convention No. IV), Aug. 12, 1949, art. 146, 75 UNTS 287; 1948 Convention on the Prevention and Punishment of the Crime of Genocide, arts. I, IV, 78 U.N.T.S. 277, entered into force Jan. 12, 1951.

[73] Report of the Secretary-General on the Establishment of a Special Court for Sierra Leone, UN Doc. S/2000/915, ¶ 22 (2000) (footnote omitted).

[74] *See* Decision on Appeal against Provisional Detention Order of Ieng Sary, *supra* note 12, ¶¶ 57-63.

[75] Decision on Appeal Against Provisional Detention Order of Nuon Chea, *supra* note 5, ¶ 31.

[76] Douglas Gillison, *Translation Row Stalls Khieu Samphan Hearing*, Cambodia Daily, Apr. 24, 2008.

[77] Order on Translation Rights and Obligations of the Parties, Case No. 002/19-09-2007-ECCC/OCIJ, at B.2. (Office of the Co-Investigating Judges, June 19, 2008) (citing ECHR jurisprudence).

[78] Decision on Khieu Samphan's Appeal Against the Order on Translation Rights and Obligations of the Parties, Case No. 002/19-09-2007-ECCC/OCIJ (PTC11), ¶ 40 (Pre-Trial Chamber, Feb. 20, 2009).

[79] Letter from the Ieng Sary defense team to Deputy Director Rosandhaug and the Co-Investigative Judges (Dec. 18, 2008) [hereinafter Ieng Sary Letter], *quoted in* Order on Breach of Confidentiality of the Judicial Investigation, Case No. 002/14-08-2006, ¶ 2 (Office of the Co-Investigating Judges, Mar. 3, 2009).

[80] Order on Breach of Confidentiality of the Judicial Investigation, *supra* note 79, ¶ 12.

[81] Ieng Sary Letter, *supra* note 79, ¶ 2.

[82] *Id.*

[83] *See, e.g.,* Open Society Justice Initiative, Recent Developments at the Extraordinary Chambers in the Courts of Cambodia: May 2008 Update 24-25 (2008), *available at* www.justiceinitiative.org/activities/ij/krt.

[84] Co-Prosecutors' Observations on Ieng Sary's Appeal Against the Co-Investigating Judges' Confidentiality Order, Case No. 002/19-09-2007-ECCC/OCIJ (PTC 18), ¶ 17 (Pre-Trial Chamber, Mar. 27, 2009) (citing Decision on Nuon Chea's Appeal Regarding Appointment of an Expert, ¶ 26).

[85] *Id.* ¶ 25.

[86] *Id.* ¶ 26.

[87] *Id.* ¶ 51(iv).

[88] Co-Investigating Judges of the ECCC, press release dated Mar. 3, 2009, *available at* www.eccc.gov.kh/english/cabinet/press/100/

OCIJ_press_statement_EN.pdf.

[89] Order on Breach of Confidentiality of the Judicial Investigation, *supra* note 79, ¶ 12.

[90] *See generally* Prosecutor v. Dusko Tadic, Case No. IT-94-1-A, Judgment, ¶¶ 226-28 (Appeals Chamber, July 15, 1999).

[91] Co-Prosecutors' Appeal of the Closing Order Against Kaing Guek Eav "Duch" Dated Aug. 8, 2008, Case No. 001/18-07-2007-ECCC/OCIJ (PTC 02), ¶ 63 (Pre-Trial Chamber, Sept. 5, 2008).

[92] Ieng Sary's Expedited Request to Make Submissions on the Application of Joint Criminal Enterprise Liability in the Co-Prosecutors' Appeal of the Closing Order Against Kaing Guek Eav "Duch," Case No. 001/18-07-2007-ECCC/OCIJ (PTC02), at I.1. (Pre-Trial Chamber, Sept. 15, 2008).

[93] Decision on Ieng Sary's Request to Make Submissions on the Application of the Theory of Joint Criminal Enterprise in the Co-Prosecutors' Appeal of the Closing Order Against Kaing Guek Eav "Duch," Case No. 001/18/-07-2007-ECCC/OCIJ (PTC 2), ¶ 12 (Pre-Trial Chamber, Oct. 6, 2008).

[94] Decision on Urgent Joint Defence Request to Intervene on the Issue of Joint Criminal Enterprise in the OCP Appeal Against the Duch Closing Order, Case No. 001/18/-07-2007-ECCC/OCIJ (PTC 2), ¶ 8 (Pre-Trial Chamber, Nov. 5, 2008).

[95] Decision on Appeal Against Closing Order Indicting Kaing Guek Eav *alias* Duch, Case No. 001-18-07-2007-ECCC/OCIJ (PTC 02), ¶ 115 (Pre-Trial Chamber, Dec. 5, 2008).

[96] ECCC International Co-Prosecutor Robert Petit, press statement dated Apr. 24, 2009, *available at* www.eccc.gov.kh/english/press_release.list.aspx.

[97] Considerations of the Pre-Trial Chamber Regarding the Disagreement Between the Co-Prosecutors Pursuant to Internal Rule 71 (Annex I: Public Redacted Version), Case No. 001/18-11-2008-ECCC/PTC, ¶ 6 (Pre-Trial Chamber, Aug. 18, 2009) (noting that the international Co-Prosecutor withdrew the supplementary submission after confirming evidence of the suspect's death).

[98] ECCC Internal Rules, *supra* note 36, R. 71(4)(c).

[99] Co-Prosecutors of the ECCC, press statement dated Jan. 5, 2009, *available at* www.eccc.gov.kh/english/press_release.list.aspx.

[100] *Id.*

[101] *See, e.g.,* Seth Mydans, *Efforts to Limit Khmer Rouge Trials Decried*, NY Times, Jan. 31, 2009; EK Madra, *Cambodian PM Rejects Wider Khmer Rouge Trials*, Reuters, Mar. 31, 2009.

[102] Considerations of the Pre-Trial Chamber Regarding the Disagreement Between the Co-Prosecutors, *supra* note 97, ¶ 24.

[103] Six months after the disagreement first arose, the national Co-Prosecutor for the first time argued in written submissions that "the suspects identified in the new Introductory Submissions are not senior leaders or those most responsible because of their comparably lower rank in the Democratic Kampuchea regime[.]" *Id.* ¶ 32. However, the Co-Prosecutor argued that this argument was an "afterthought" and the PTC did not address it in its decision.

[104] *Id.* ¶ 38.

[105] *Id.* ¶ 29.

[106] *Id.*, Opinion of Judges Lahuis and Downing, ¶ 8.

[107] *Id.*, Opinion of Judges Lahuis and Downing, ¶ 14.

[108] Considerations of the Pre-Trial Chamber Regarding the Disagreement Between the Co-Prosecutors, *supra* note 97, ¶ 31.

[109] Report of the Group of Experts for Cambodia established pursuant to General Assembly resolution 52/135, ¶ 107 (Feb. 18, 1999).

[110] *Id.* ¶ 110.

[111] Considerations of the Pre-Trial Chamber Regarding the Disagreement Between the Co-Prosecutors, *supra* note 97, ¶ 34.

[112] *Id.* ¶ 38.

[113] *See* Terith Chy, *A Thousand Voices*, Mar. 5, 2009, *available at* www.dccam.org/Tribunal/Analysis/pdf/A_Thousand_Voices.pdf.

[114] Report of the Group of Experts for Cambodia, *supra* note 109, ¶ 109.

[115] Considerations of the Pre-Trial Chamber Regarding the Disagreement Between the Co-Prosecutors, *supra* note 97, Opinion of Judges Lahuis and Downing, ¶ 23.

4.

JOHN A. HALL

The Extraordinary Chambers in the Courts of Cambodia (ECCC, "Court," or "tribunal") have achieved noteworthy judicial success since they began operating three years ago, including the filing of introductory submissions by the Co-Prosecutors, the charging of the first five accused, and the beginning of the trial of Kaing Guek Eav in February 2009. It is hard to overestimate the profound significance and symbolism for Cambodia in what is now unfolding in the courtroom of the ECCC. Unfortunately, this progress is set against a backdrop of administrative and operational scandals, ranging from systemic human resource (HR) and management shortcomings, to allegations of widespread corruption within the tribunal. Significant improvements have taken place in HR management and administration at the tribunal. However, the corruption allegations remain unresolved and have been the cause of conflict both inside and outside the Court. These allegations have garnered negative media coverage, led to legal challenges from the Defense teams, and have the potential to taint the legal proceedings. Amnesty International has noted that the allegations "have cast significant doubts on the [ECCC's] competence, independence, and impartiality" and that the "failure of the government and the United Nations to respond to the allegations in a transparent way further threatens to undermine the institution's credibility."[1]

In this chapter, I discuss some of the major administrative challenges facing the ECCC since its inception, including the related issues of HR practices and procedures, allegations of corruption, the dynamics of a funding scheme based on voluntary contributions from donor nations, and, briefly, discrete issues such as translation and transcription services and the Court's outreach efforts.

SPLIT ADMINISTRATIVE STRUCTURE OF THE ECCC

Under the agreement between the Royal Government of Cambodia (RGC) and the United Nations (UN) that established the ECCC, the Court has a "hybrid" structure and operates with a mixture of Cambodian and international staff, law and judges. Responsibility for the

The ECCC Courtroom, 2006. *Source: Documentation Center of Cambodia Archives*

Court's administration likewise includes a mixture of national and international staff. General administrative functions at the ECCC are the responsibility of the Office of Administration (OA).[2] The OA is charged with overall responsibility for providing administrative support to all arms of the Court.[3] In addition to hiring and supervising tribunal personnel, the OA supports the tribunal's legal organs by serving as the official channel for ECCC communications, maintaining a database containing copies of all case files, preserving and storing evidence, providing security, monitoring detention conditions for the accused, training staff, and providing a wide variety of other administrative requirements including supplies, equipment, facilities management, information technology, and transportation.[4] The Director of the Office of Administration—the most senior administrator at the ECCC—is a Cambodian national appointed by the RGC, while the Deputy Director is appointed by the UN. The agreement establishing the ECCC states that "The Director and Deputy Director shall cooperate in order to ensure an effective and efficient functioning of the administration."[5] Deputy Prime Minister Sok An selected Sean Visoth, a trusted political appointee with little practical managerial experience, to be Director of the Office of Administration. In that capacity, Sean Visoth had overall responsibility for all administrative and support functions at the Court, and for developing and implementing HR policies and procedures.

In keeping with the overall structure of the Court, the administrative functions at the ECCC are divided between national and international "sides," each with their own distinct budgets and lines of accountability. Court administration at the ECCC consists of a number of integrated sections of both national and international staff (see chart on p. 175).[6] Four of these sections are headed by international staff (Security and Safety, General Services, Information and Communication Technology, and Defense Support), while three others are headed by national staff (Court Management, Public Affairs and the Victims Unit). The personnel and budget sections have both Cambodian and international heads to manage their respective sides.[7]

UN Legal Counsel Hans Corell and Cambodian Deputy Prime Minister Sok An signing the Framework Agreement, June 6, 2003. Photo by Heng Sinith.
Source: Documentation Center of Cambodia Archives

ON TRIAL: THE KHMER ROUGE ACCOUNTABILITY PROCESS

COURT ADMINISTRATION AT THE ECCC

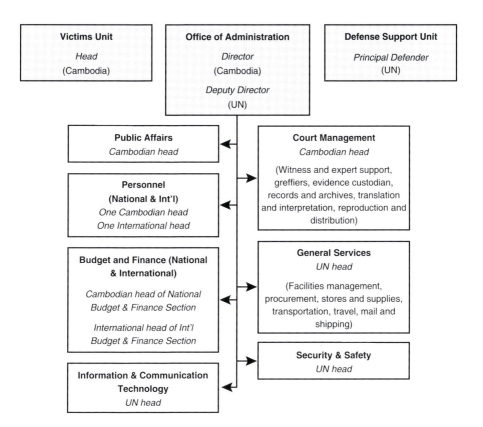

Hans Corell and his team at Phnom Penh International Airport, 2003. Photo by Heng Sinith.
Source: Documentation Center of Cambodia Archives

Co-Prosecutors Chea Leang and Robert Petit meeting with Tuons and Hakems (Cham-Muslim religious leaders) at the ECCC, 2006.
Photo by Dacil Q. Keo.
Source: Documentation Center of Cambodia Archives

Victims at the Killing Fields of Choeung Ek, 2006. *Source: Documentation Center of Cambodia Archives*

Victims at the Killing Fields of Choeung Ek, 2006. *Source: Documentation Center of Cambodia Archives*

Portraits of former S-21 prisoners at the Tuol Sleng Genocide Museum, 2006.
Source: Documentation Center of Cambodia Archives

Survivors at the Tuol Sleng Genocide Museum. *Source: Documentation Center of Cambodia Archives*

It became the norm that Cambodian personnel in the various administrative sections were formally supervised by the Director of the Office of Administration, while the international staff answered to the Deputy Director of the Office of Administration.[8] The result was that international supervisors were almost entirely excluded from exercising fundamental managerial responsibilities regarding recruitment, appointment, retention and professional review of the Cambodian staff within their sections. This split managerial structure, with national staff answering to the RGC-appointed Director of Administration rather than to their immediate international supervisors, has contributed to dysfunctional and inefficient administrative practices.

SHORTCOMINGS IN HUMAN RESOURCE POLICIES AND PRACTICES

The recent history of Cambodia has had an impact directly and indirectly on human resources practices in that nation. Emerging from years of war, social and economic dislocation, and one-party control, Cambodia has found itself ill-positioned to meet globally accepted HR management standards.[9] Employment practices in Cambodia are heavily influenced by nepotism and corruption, with employers often making hiring decisions favorable to applicants willing to provide gifts or bribes to decision-makers. Jobs are used to reward allies, create networks of loyalty, and favor friends and family. Qualifications, experience and the ability of applicants are often less important than political connections and a willingness to kick back a portion of salaries to supervisors. An assessment prepared for the U.S. Agency for International Development concluded that corruption has reached "pandemic" proportions: "Patronage and mutual obligations are the center of an all-embracing system. Appointment to public office hinges on political connections or payment of surprisingly large sums, and these payments are recouped through a widely accepted 'right' to collect bribes."[10] It was in this context that HR practices and policies at the ECCC were expected, as auditors from Deloitte and Touche noted, to rapidly meet international standards, especially with regard to transparency and accountability measures, and ensure an appropriate level of ECCC operational capacity.[11] This was probably an unrealistic expectation in the Cambodian context.

On October 4, 2006, Open Society Justice Initiative (OSJI)—a leading non-governmental program focused on promoting legal reform and international human rights norms—addressed a memorandum to donors and states interested in the ECCC, raising concerns regarding the transparency of the hiring practices on the Cambodian side of the ECCC.[12] On October 31, 2006, the UN Development Program's representative office in Cambodia ("UNDP-Cambodia")

(TOP) Michelle Lee, former Deputy Director of the ECCC Office of Administration. (Bottom, left to right) Youk Chhang, Michelle Lee, Giovanni Bassu (legal officer), Reach Sambath (ECCC Public Affairs Officer), and Sean Visoth (Director of Office of Administration of ECCC).Photos by Heng Sinith. *Source: Documentation Center of Cambodia Archives*

requested the UN's Office of Audit and Performance Review (OAPR) to initiate a special audit ("Special Audit") as a result of concerns regarding the human resources practices of the ECCC.[13] The Special Audit was conducted in two phases by auditors from the audit firm Candide Consulting and from the Regional Audit Services Centre in Malaysia. The first phase was carried out between January 29 and February 8, 2007, and the second phase took place between March 27 and 30, 2007. The Special Audit covered the overall human resources management at the ECCC and covered the period from June 2006 to February 2007.[14]

Completed in June 2007, the Special Audit was not made public—in keeping with general UNDP policy—despite frequent requests from the media and watchdog groups. Peter Foster, then spokesperson for the UN team assisting the Khmer Rouge Tribunal (UNAKRT), had argued for the release of the Special Audit's findings, concerned that failure to do so would be interpreted as an attempt by the tribunal and the UN to suppress potentially embarrassing information.[15] His warnings proved prescient when, on September 21, 2007, a *Wall Street Journal* opinion piece by this author quoted sections of a leaked draft of the Special Audit, and called for the entire document to be made public.[16] The disclosure of some of the Special Audit's worrying conclusions and recommendations stung the UN and the tribunal. On September 25, UNDP published its own summary of the Special Audit on its website, followed on October 1 by the ECCC posting the entire audit along with Cambodian responses on the tribunal's website. Director of Administration Sean Visoth asserted that he was releasing the findings "in the interests of transparency and fairness" and to counter "a distorted and negative view of the ECCC" caused by the selective leaking of the audit. He stated that the Cambodian side of the tribunal had previously desired the public release of the audit, and that UNDP had refused.[17]

The Special Audit painted a bleak picture of the human resources practices of the ECCC. The auditors noted that the Project Board established to support the ECCC ("Project Board"), provided for in the June 2006 project document—which was chaired by the ECCC and comprised representatives of UNDP, the UN Department of Economic and Social Affairs, the European Commission and other contributing donors—had not been effective in fulfilling its role in overseeing and monitoring the activities of the ECCC. The auditors also noted that allowing the ECCC representative to chair the Project Board potentially created a conflict of interest.[18] The Project Board, the auditors noted, had not met since the start of the project in June 2006.

The Special Audit criticized what was seen as the high salary scale for the ECCC national professional staff[19]; an unjustified excess in Cambodian staffing; weaknesses in the performance evaluation process; and the fact that in three ECCC units headed by international staff, the international unit heads are "kept away from normal managerial functions" relating to the Cambodian staff in their unit, such as participating in their recruitment, conducting performance assessments, and verifying and signing attendance sheets.

The Special Audit also found serious problems with the selection and interview procedures for national personnel: Cambodians were hired without meeting the minimum requirements specified in vacancy announcements in terms of academic qualifications or professional working experience; job vacancies were not widely advertised and the number of responses was rather low; documentation was poor, and it was impossible to ascertain exactly how many applications were received; the process by which applicants were short-listed was not properly recorded; and there were "a number of discrepancies in the selection and interview processes suggesting that the recruitment was not performed in a transparent, competitive and objective manner that ensures the selection of the most suitable candidate for the job."[20] The auditors also noted that they were denied access to the records of 28 Cambodian staff members appointed by the RGC in the start-up phase of the ECCC, and so could not verify whether there were appropriate job descriptions for these positions, or whether the individuals had the necessary qualifications, though the auditors uncovered salary increases of up to 338% for some.[21]

The Special Audit made a number of specific recommendations for action by both UNDP-Cambodia and the ECCC to address each of the various problems uncovered by the auditors in their investigation of the human resources practices of the ECCC. In one extraordinary recommendation, OAPR appeared to recommend the wholesale firing of all Cambodian staff at the ECCC: "taking into account the serious lapses in the recruitment process to-date, all recruitments of staff made by ECCC to-date should be nullified and a new recruitment exercise launched with clearly established procedures under the close supervision of UNDP to ensure that the most suitable and competent candidates are recruited for every position and therefore, increase the project's chances of success."[22] "If the Cambodian side does not agree to the essential measures that are, from UNDP perspective, necessary to ensure the integrity and success of the project," OAPR concluded, "then serious considerations should be given to withdrawing from participation in the project altogether."[23]

The Special Audit was not the only review that found serious administrative problems at the tribunal. An assessment team hired by the international side of the Court to assess the Court's readiness to begin trials criticized the significant leadership and administrative problems stemming from the division of the tribunal into distinct national and international "sides."[24] In their confidential June 2007 report—which has never been made public but was leaked to Erika Kinetz of *The Cambodia Daily*—two U.N. experts—Robin Vincent, the former registrar for the Special Court for Sierra Leone, and Kevin St. Louis, the Chief of Administration for the

International Criminal Tribunal for the Former Yugoslavia—called the split structure "divisive and unhelpful." They said they could see no good reason why the Court had been set up as such "save for possibly a sense that the division was in place to protect the 'sovereignty' of the National Staff side." They cited "considerable frustration" with the Court's leadership among international staff, which they feared had so corroded morale that key staffers—several of whom had already quit the tribunal—would continue to leave. After more than a year, the UN experts said, renovation work on the main courtroom had not even begun, and they pointed to serious problems with crucial court functions like translation, witness protection and public affairs.[25] The administrative division "serves only to constantly hinder, frequently confuse and certainly frustrate the efforts of a number of staff on both sides of the operations."[26] This split authority between the national and international sides of the Office of Administration with regard to budget, hiring, and staff reporting, "appears to be undermining [the Director and Co-Director's] best efforts to meet the daunting challenges of running a complex new tribunal."[27]

INSTITUTIONAL RESPONSES TO THE HR SHORTCOMINGS

The Project Board and the ECCC initiated a number of significant managerial improvements in response to the disturbing findings of the Special Audit and the Vincent/St.Louis assessment team, including the implementation of a personnel handbook and the implementation of enhanced HR procedures.[28] In early 2008, the Project Board, based on a recommendation by the European Commission, decided to conduct a special review to assess "whether or not the agreed actions designed to convincingly solve the management problems of the operations of ECCC have been implemented and have been effective."[29] The Indian branch of the international auditing and consulting firm of Deloitte Touche Tohmatsu India Pvt. Limited ("Deloitte and Touche") was retained for that purpose. A Human Resource and Management Review Team from Deloitte and Touche submitted its Report on the Special HRM Review ("HRM Review") to the Project Board in April 2008. The HRM Review's conclusions were very positive and reflected significant improvements in HR policies and practices at the ECCC since June 2007: "In its current state, the HRM practices of ECCC national side are ready to take on the challenges of the next phase of operations. Robust HR systems have been developed and implemented to address previous shortcomings, provide effective support to the judicial process and minimize the risk of questionable HR practices occurring in the future."[30]

The HRM Review praised the Personnel Handbook, adopted in August 2007 following review and revision with assistance from independent HR consultant Daniel Conway, the purpose of which was to set out policy and procedure guidelines for key HR processes. The HRM Review found that the Personnel Handbook provides guidelines "that are comprehensive, clear and has become the standard reference document for key HR processes." The HRM Review concluded that the Personnel Handbook was "being adhered to" by the ECCC in a wide range of HR processes related to recruitment, selection and appointment, performance evaluation, position classification, attendance and leave management and compensation. The HRM Review Team confirmed that international staff now had an opportunity as part of an *ad hoc* selection committee to provide meaningful contributions to recruitment of national staff. The Review Team noted the "meticulous documentation" that was now being maintained regarding these HR processes and decisions.[31] The review also concluded that salary rates for Cambodian staff were not inappropriately high despite the concerns raised by the Special Audit, finding them at the top of the market without being above the market.[32]

Implementing all of the recommendations contained in the Special Audit and the report of Vincent/St.Louis Assessment Team—such as the firing of all the Cambodian staff, and the restructuring of the Court's administrative structure—were largely impractical and would require renegotiating the agreements that established the tribunal, a move that would endanger the whole process. Peter Foster, UNAKRT spokesperson, noted that "Renegotiation would take some time... We have to remember that it took 13 years to get to the agreement that we have in place now, and we certainly don't want to reopen that and spend another 13 years." Nevertheless, Foster suggested that the UN could take more of a "leadership role" without making major changes to the existing agreements: "We can certainly make adjustments within the current system to provide greater advice to our Cambodian colleagues."[33]

The UN did indeed become more effective in taking the leadership role in addressing the administrative weaknesses at the Court. Just one week after portions of the Special Audit were leaked to *The Wall Street Journal*, the ECCC's international Deputy Director of Administration, Michelle Lee, announced that she would resign the following summer upon reaching the UN's mandatory retirement age.[34] She was replaced by Knut Rosandhaug, who took a somewhat more determined position when dealing with Cambodian officials. Another key development was the selection by Secretary-General Ban Ki-moon of David Tolbert, the highly experienced and principled former deputy prosecutor for the ICTY, to act as a short-term expert advisor on issues related to the ECCC. Tolbert took up the post in New York on March 16, 2008, and arrived in Phnom Penh on April 27.[35] Tolbert's mandate included working closely with the ECCC to develop a realistic budget; streamlining the administrative operations of the UN side of the Court; and instituting anti-corruption efforts.[36] OSJI noted that his breadth of experience "provides the UNAKRT with expertise urgently needed to deal with the leadership, administrative, and budgetary challenges the international side of the ECCC faces and will benefit the court as a whole."[37] He quickly earned a strong reputation, and was instrumental in streamlining a budget that would see the Court through 2011; raising more money in the wake of a funding crisis; and hiring experienced international staff to provide expertise in areas including court management, victim participation and witness protection and support. Tolbert and Rosandhaug together played a significant role in encouraging Cambodian staff to come forward with allegations of corrupt practices on the national side of the Court.

CORRUPTION ALLEGATIONS

Public allegations of corruption have dogged the ECCC since early 2007. *The Voice of Khmer Youth*, a Khmer-language newspaper, reported that ECCC judges, prosecutors and other officials were required to "contribute thirty-percent of their salar[ies] to the [Cambodian People's Party]" in exchange for their positions at the Court.[38] These allegations were subsequently repeated in the English-language media.[39] In February 2007, OSJI issued a press release referencing "serious allegations that Cambodian court personnel, including judges, must kick back a significant percentage of their wages to Cambodian government officials in exchange for their positions on the court."[40]

James A. Goldston, executive director of OSJI, noted that: "Donors, the international community, and the Cambodian people have the right to know that money entrusted to the ECCC is being spent transparently and honestly. If these allegations of corruption are confirmed, it would strip the ECCC of its integrity and undermine its ability to provide accountability for mass crimes."[41]

In September 2007, *The Cambodia Daily* reported that an anonymous Cambodian employee of the ECCC "claimed that he had to hand over 25 percent of his salary for his job" and "that three other employees at the Court had told him directly that they too had to make payments."[42] In June 2008, ECCC Director of Administration Sean Visoth circulated a notice within the tribunal regarding what were apparently new allegations of corruption.[43] In late summer 2008, several Cambodian staff directly approached senior UN officials at the tribunal with allegations concerning on-going corrupt practices at the Court. The allegations implicated Cambodian officials within the Court. Through a process set up by the ECCC's Special Expert David Tolbert, these allegations were referred to the UN's Office of Internal Oversight Services (OIOS) in New York, which began a confidential review in early August 2008.[44]

In late 2008, a former ECCC employee speaking anonymously to *The Phnom Penh Post* described an alleged graft scheme operating at the Court: "The employee's monthly salary is paid in full, but when you [collect] it, you put it in an envelope and give it to the collector.... In front of people, you're told to say, 'No one is taking away my money', [and] the money transferred into your account is the full amount, but then you have to…give over the percentage." This interview was not published by the *Post* until late February 2009, at which time the newspaper also quoted another anonymous "court staffer": "For the first four months [of my contract], I paid 70 percent [of my salary in kickbacks], then it went down to 10 percent…. Let's say you are the supervisor. You have 3 people under you, so the people under you know to give their envelope [containing the kickback] to you, and you hand it to Sean Visoth…. In all sections it is the same thing."[45]

In early April 2009, an op-ed in *The Wall Street Journal Asia* suggested that Cambodian judges at the tribunal were implicated in the corrupt scheme: "At the heart of the corruption charges is a single allegation: Cambodian employees, including some judges, were given lucrative positions at the court on the basis they would then pay a portion of their salaries every month to the government officials who secured them their jobs."[46] In April 2009, *The Economist* reported that three anonymous court staffers had "accuse[d] Sean Visoth…of collecting money from every Cambodian in his department, including court employees and Cambodian legal assistants in the office of the [OCIJ and OCP]…Some of the cash, they were told, was intended for Sok An, a deputy prime minister." *The Economist*, however, noted that "there is no indication that the minister took the money."[47] Also in April 2009, CNN International aired a documentary including an interview with an anonymous ECCC staffer who asserted that Sean Visoth had collected kickbacks from tribunal staff in the amount of "thirty or forty thousand dollars a month."[48]

OFFICIAL RESPONSE TO THE CORRUPTION ALLEGATIONS

Response to the corruption allegations has been mixed. Writing in *Foreign Affairs* in April 2009, Joel Brinkley noted that the allegations "have enraged UN officials but have evoked little surprise among Cambodians. After all they learn about corruption firsthand—starting at first grade."[49] In August 2009, an agreement was reached between the UN and RGC to establish a new post of "Independent Counsellor," staffed by a Cambodian national. However the agreement fails to specify the scope of his authority or the process by which allegations will be reviewed and acted upon. To date, the corruption allegations remain unresolved; the existing anti-corruption mechanisms at the ECCC appear inadequate and flawed; and no effective system exists to protect Cambodian personnel who come forward with information about corrupt practices.

At the time of the initial January 2007 allegations that ECCC national personnel were forced to kick back a portion of their wages to RGC officials, auditors from Candide Consulting and the Regional Audit Services Centre in Malaysia were already in the middle of conducting the Special Audit for OAPR stemming from assorted concerns raised by UNDP-Cambodia regarding human resources practices at the ECCC (see discussion of the Special Audit above). Based on a preliminary assessment of the corruption allegations, OAPR concluded that "[the kickback allegations] do not pertain to holders of UNDP letters of appointment but personnel of the Government of Cambodia and therefore fall outside UNDP's jurisdiction which precludes OAPR from conducting an investigation of personnel of the Government of Cambodia."[50]

Despite an arguable lack of jurisdiction to investigate RGC officials, the auditors retained by OAPR decided to carry out some self-described "special audit work" regarding the kickback allegations. During the second phase of the OAPR audit which took place in Phnom Penh between March 27 and 30, 2007, the auditors "took into account the above [kickback] allegations and encompassed a number of steps including the interview of individuals who volunteered to share information with OAPR."[51] It is unclear how many such interviews took place, what criteria were used in selecting the interviewees, who made the selection decision, under what circumstances the interviews took place, or whether Cambodian staff were assured that whistleblowers would be protected and their identities kept confidential. Nevertheless, the Special Audit subsequently stated that the auditors "found no evidence that would conclusively support the above [kickback] allegations." It concluded that "it is OAPR's opinion that additional efforts to establish [the allegations'] validity are unlikely to provide more material that would warrant further actions in this respect."[52]

While multiple independent reviews have been conducted into the ECCC's management and human-resources practices, none of the audits have to-date included a mandate to review allegations of corruption involving Cambodian staff and RGC officials. The terms of reference for the human resource and management review conducted by Deloitte and Touche (HRM Review—see discussion in the text above) in early 2008, for example, which was commissioned by UNDP and the Project Board, clearly indicated that such an investigation was not within the scope of the HRM Review.[53] The RGC has steadfastly rejected calls for any such investigation, and has refused international offers of help in this regard. In January 2008, the RGC declined an offer by the UNDP to secure international assistance for an investigation into the allegations as "a way to ensure the continued public and donor confidence in the tribunal."[54] Director of administration Sean Visoth dismissed the allegations as "unspecific, unsourced and unsubstantiated.... There is no government policy to take kickbacks from staff."[55]

In July 2008, David Tolbert, the UN's new special expert to the ECCC, outlined to senior tribunal staff his new anti-corruption program, which would apply to the international side of the

Court and consisted of three parts: a reporting system in which complaints from either UN or Cambodian staff would be initially reviewed by the UN's OIOS in New York; the appointment of a high level staff person within the Office of Administration as an "ethics officer" with responsibility to receive confidential complaints, counsel staff and officials, and provide training on ethics issues and standards; and proposed revisions to the Code of Conduct for staff and Code of Ethics for judges to expressly forbid corrupt practices including giving or requesting kickbacks.[56]

The Cambodian court administration also took steps to create a more formal anti-corruption system for the national side of the ECCC. In August 2007, for example, the ECCC adopted a Code of Conduct and all staff members had to acknowledge receipt of a copy, and a committee was set up to deal with complaints and alleged Code of Conduct violations.[57] A suggestion box was also placed in the tribunal to receive staff comments. While progress of a sort, these steps were inadequate. Most importantly, there were no guarantees that Cambodian personnel filing complaints could do so and be assured that their identities would remain confidential from Cambodian officials, or that they and their families would be protected from retaliation and retribution. It was simply naïve to believe that in the absence of such demonstrable and credible protections, Cambodian staff would be willing to report senior government officials for wrongdoing. The anti-corruption mechanism in place at the ECCC by mid-2008, therefore, was deeply flawed, and likely to send a chilling message to prospective whistleblowers.

OSJI and other observers repeatedly called for a thorough, professional and independent investigation into the corruption allegations.[58] These calls were rejected by the RGC, which maintained a position that it alone has the jurisdiction to investigate allegations involving Cambodian officials or staff at the ECCC. In June 2008, Deputy Prime Minister Sok An informed the UN's Office of Legal Affairs that Cambodia had both the means and the exclusive right to deal with allegations involving Cambodian officials without international interference.[59] The RGC's vigorous assertion of exclusive jurisdiction on this issue was problematic for observers who saw senior officials within the RGC as fundamentally disinclined to permit any credible investigation of corrupt practices implicating government appointees at the Court.

In the summer of 2008, new kickback allegations "by more than one Cambodian court staffer" were brought directly to senior international officials at the tribunal, including Tolbert and Rosandhaug. These allegations were—in accord with the UN's new anti-corruption policies introduced by Tolbert—referred to the UN's OIOS in New York, which began a confidential review in August 2008.[60] The allegations reportedly named several senior Cambodian officials. Given the RGC's assertion that it alone had jurisdiction to undertake investigations of such individuals, this move by the UN was significant. Tolbert justified the referral of the allegations to OIOS by focusing on specific language: while the RGC may claim sole jurisdiction to undertake an "investigation," OIOS was merely conducting a "review" intended to assess whether a *prima facie* case was made justifying a Cambodian investigation. Seen in this light, OIOS was conducting a benign "review" that did not implicate Cambodian claims of sole jurisdiction. Perhaps, however, the OIOS review was part of a new UN strategy intended to pressure the RGC into finally responding in a positive way to the corruption allegations. It would certainly become more difficult for the RGC to simply dismiss allegations as unfounded if the UN concluded that they were credible and worthy of further investigation.

In the face of the new allegations and the OIOS review, UNDP-administered funding for the tribunal's Cambodian side was indefinitely frozen while donor countries considered their response.[61] This added to the growing pressure on the RGC to respond in a meaningful way. In late August 2008, the Office of Administration announced the establishment of a new anti-corruption committee to hear and resolve any graft claims involving Cambodians.[62] The national side also designated two "Ethics Monitors"—the president of the Cambodian Supreme Chamber, Kong Srim, and the controversial RGC-appointed head of the Public Affairs Office, Helen Jarvis (who will be discussed later in this chapter)—to receive complaints of corruption, and established a program whereby alleged wrongdoing would be reported directly to Deputy Prime Minister Sok An.[63] The national side also made public statements that it would not tolerate corruption.[64] These initiatives were intended to reassure donors that the Cambodian government was fully competent to deal with any allegations of corruption, without international interference or independent UN review of the allegations.

The new Cambodian mechanism was flawed in several ways, most significantly in its continued lack of articulated and credible protections for Cambodian staff who brought forward complaints. National staff with information about corruption must feel able to report it freely, confidentially, and without fear of retaliation or intimidation. The new Cambodian mechanism—just like that which was in place before—lacked those core guarantees. Further, by claiming that all allegations involving Cambodians must now be reported only to the Cambodian Ethics Monitors, the RGC was explicitly attempting to block the very mechanism which whistleblowers actually trusted and which the UN had encouraged: the direct reporting of complaints to UN officials who would guarantee confidentiality.

In September 2008, OIOS sent a report to the RGC regarding its confidential review.[65] The report has not been made public, but is believed to have found that the corruption allegations were credible and deserved further investigation.[66] The Cambodian government acknowledged receipt of the OIOS report, but took no public action and expressed hostility towards the UN efforts.[67]

Nevertheless the OIOS report may have had some impact within the ECCC, by increasing pressure on the RGC to do something to defuse growing frustration within the donor community. Two senior Cambodian administrators, Keo Thyvuth and Sean Visoth, who were reportedly implicated in the corruption allegations, left the Court. In August 2008, Keo Thyvuth, the Court's Cambodian chief of personnel, was transferred to a position at the RGC's Council of Ministers.[68] More significantly, Sean Visoth, the embattled Director of the Office of Court Administration, also departed. He had initially responded to speculation in the media about his role in the alleged kickback scheme by promising to resign if he were found to have participated in corrupt practices.[69] In late October 2008, Knut Rosendhaug allegedly told a visiting delegation from the German parliament that Sean Visoth had been investigated by the UN and found "guilty of corruption."[70] Sean Visoth left the ECCC on medical leave citing unspecified health-related issues.[71] He was apparently removed from the Court's payroll after his sick leave of three months expired, though court spokesperson Reach Sambath stated in mid-May 2009 that Sean Visoth was "still the director."[72] Tony Kranh was appointed acting director of administration in Mr. Sean's absence. Mr. Sean continues to maintain his innocence.

With funding for the national side of the Court frozen by UNDP, the RGC and the UN's Office of Legal Affairs continued to meet periodically with the goal of agreeing on an anti-corruption mechanism acceptable to each. Successive proposals were presented by both sides and the parties noted "important progress made by the joint sessions in their meetings during January and February 2009 toward strengthening the ECCC's human resources management, including anti-corruption measures."[73]

On February 23, 2009, Deputy Prime Minister Sok An met with Peter Taksoe-Jensen, UN Assistant Secretary-General for Legal Affairs. A joint statement issued by the RGC and the UN suggested that a breakthrough in the negotiations had occurred: "It was important that agreement be reached rapidly on a mechanism so that the judicial process could continue to move forward without interruption…H.E. Sok An and Mr. Taksoe-Jensen agreed the essential elements of a structure devoted to strengthening the ECCC's entire administration."[74] This structure, it was announced, "would ensure the requirements of due process of law, including full protection of staff against any possible retaliation for good faith reporting of wrongdoing."[75] The new structure would be "based on existing mechanisms" with parallel national and international mechanisms to receive complaints and suggestions. On the national side this mechanism consists of the existing Ethics Monitors and Review Committee, while on the international side UNAKRT will establish a parallel mechanism consisting of one Ethics Monitor. "These mechanisms," the Joint Statement noted, "shall carry out their functions autonomously, ensure the confidentiality of any complaints received, copy to their counterpart mechanism in a manner that respects confidentiality and transmit the complaints forthwith to the Joint Session with a recommendation for any necessary action." The Joint Session, with an equal number of votes assigned to the national and international members, shall make decisions according to the formula of super-majority.[76] The parties agreed that the Joint Sessions should conclude the negotiation of the details of this agreement, and report to the Royal Government Task Force and to the Steering Committee by March 23, 2009.[77]

Some observers expressed skepticism about the proposed system. In particular, it was noted that the Joint Statement envisaged parallel mechanisms that kept in place the existing Cambodian model of RGC-appointed Ethics Monitors. It was of concern that the language of the Joint Statement was ambiguous regarding whether ECCC staff would have the right to report their concerns to their choice of either the international or national Ethics Monitors, and whether adequate whistleblower protections would be guaranteed.[78] Donors had hoped that the proposed new mechanism would offer an opportunity to finally put the corruption issue aside, and were distressed when civil society groups voiced skepticism about the ambiguous language of the proposed mechanism.

Unfortunately that skepticism was justified. No report was forthcoming by the March 23 deadline and it soon became evident that the UN and RGC remained far apart on a number of significant issues. Taksoe-Jensen met Sok An in a series of one-on-one meetings in Phnom Penh on April 6, 7 and 8, 2009, but they failed to reach agreement. In a statement issued on April 8, Taksoe-Jensen noted:

> I met with H.E. Sok An with an ambition to work together to put the issue of corruption behind us by concluding an agreement, which would establish a credible mechanism addressing allegations of corruption...We did not manage to reach final agreement today...[T]he United Nations continues to believe that for the ethics monitoring system to be credible the staff should have the freedom to approach the Ethics Monitor of their own choice and put forward complaints without fear of retaliation. Such freedom of choice is an imperative element of a trustworthy ethics monitoring system.[79]

On April 24, 2009, James A. Goldston applauded the UN's position: "The United Nations has made the right decision in refusing to sign on to a sub-standard anti-corruption proposal."[80]

Representatives of the donor nations had met with both Taksoe-Jensen and Sok An during the negotiations in Phnom Penh in an effort to encourage a quick resolution of the corruption issue that would facilitate the release of the frozen donor funds and enable them to again visibly support the ECCC's efforts. Some observers have seen the efforts of some donors as undermining the UN's negotiating position regarding the anti-corruption mechanism. Despite Taksoe-Jensen's clear warning that the current mechanism did not provide ECCC staff with the right to report to the Ethics Monitor of their choice —"an imperative element of a trustworthy ethics monitoring system"—the donors clearly wished to proceed regardless. The Australian government requested the release of the frozen Australian funds held by UNDP despite the failure to reach a UN-sanctioned anticorruption agreement. UNDP refused the Australian request, indicating that it "was not in a position to release the funds at this time" pending "a resolution of the [corruption] allegations.[81]

Other donor nations began to increase pressure on the UN, signaling their support for the ECCC and their desire to move forward. In a Statement of the Co-Chairs of Friends of the Court issued on April 30, 2009, the Ambassadors of France and Japan noted that the donors welcomed the continued momentum in the work of the ECCC, and in particular the ongoing trial of Kaing Guek Eav; supported the tribunal proceeding in a "fair, efficient and expeditious manner"; and welcomed "the progress achieved in the Joint Sessions" between the RGC and the UN to strengthen the ECCC's human resources management, "including anti-corruption measures." They also noted that the RGC and the UN "have made broad progress to set up anti-corruption measures within the ECCC." While the donors did "urge" the RGC and UN to agree on an ethics monitoring structure that "would ensure the requirements of due process of law, including full protection against any possible retaliation for good faith reporting of wrongdoing," the donors unambiguously stated that they "stand ready to assist the ECCC in reaching its important goal."[82] This could arguably be interpreted as a capitulation of elements of the donor community to the RGC on the corruption issue.

In August 2009, the long awaited UN-RGC agreement on a new anti-corruption mechanism was announced. In addition to the national and international Ethics Monitors and the Joint Sessions already in place, the position of "Independent Counsellor" was established "to be available to all staff to bring their concerns confidentially."[83] Unfortunately, however, this is the extent of the information yet made public about the Independent Counsellor's authority, responsibilities, or the procedures he must follow.

As part of the agreement, RGC Auditor-General Uth Chhorn was selected for the position of Independent Counselor. As Auditor-General, Mr. Chhorn runs the National Audit Authority, "an independent body created in 2000 to review the finances and operations of government bodies."[84] However this body's reports to lawmakers are reportedly behind schedule, and though legally public information, are "frequently marked confidential and...closely held from the public[.]"[85]

Despite the apparent lack of teeth of this new mechanism, a joint statement by negotiators Deputy Prime Minister Sok An and Assistant Secretary-General for Legal Affairs Peter Taksoe-Jensen predicted that it will "enable staff in the entire administration of the ECCC to raise concerns confidentially without fear of retaliation...[and] be capable of effectively addressing any allegations of misconduct."[86] Likewise, the two largest court donors immediately issued a statement calling the mechanism "credible and effective."[87]

The Nuon Chea Defense Team summarized the situation facing the Court in early May 2009: "In short, 'cumuli of corruption' continue to hover ominously over the tribunal, and there is no indication that the RGC, the UN, or the donors are willing and/or able to take the necessary steps to clear the air."[88] Former International Co-Prosecutor Robert Petit has expressed the frustration undoubtedly felt by many at the ECCC as the corruption allegations have dragged on without resolution for years, at times overshadowing the significant legal successes at the Court: "This has got to go away so it no longer shares the headlines with the more important work of the Court. Half the headlines are about the problem they refuse to deal with. It threatens the continuation of the Court. It's a very real problem."[89]

LEGAL CHALLENGES TO THE CORRUPTION ALLEGATIONS

Unresolved allegations of corruption within the ECCC are especially serious. As James Goldston has noted, "any forthcoming judgments [in the Court] will be potentially vulnerable to crippling legal challenges."[90] International law is clear in requiring that "everyone shall be entitled to a fair and public hearing by a competent, independent and impartial tribunal established by law."[91] The corruption allegations at the ECCC, however, suggest an "entanglement of money, political favors, government officials, and judicial officers" that raises concerns that the national staff is subject to government interference and may not be able to act independently.[92]

The Cambodian Center for Human Rights and the Asian Human Rights Commission noted in April 2009 that "[c]orruption introduces an element of external control that effects both the tribunal's independence and the fairness of the trials—a person paying kickbacks is not truly independent and impartial."[93] This must be particularly true when the corruption implicates individuals involved in legal decision-making. The original allegations from early 2007 had suggested that Cambodian judges at the tribunal were required to kickback part of their salaries in return for their appointment.[94] Despite vehement denials from the judges and others, these allegations persisted. In April 2009, *The Wall Street Journal Asia* carried an op-ed piece that once again asserted that Cambodian judges may be involved in the kickback scheme, paying portions of their salaries to the government officials who secured them their jobs.[95]

In early January 2009, the Nuon Chea Defense team filed a complaint with the Municipal Court of Phnom Penh, requesting a criminal investigation of the alleged administrative corruption within the tribunal.[96] The municipal court dismissed the complaint.[97] In response to the complaint, the Cambodian judges at the ECCC issued a public statement in which they angrily denied any implication that judges were involved in any alleged misconduct. Further, they announced that "if the above accusation stems from bad faith in putting the blame on the judges, we reserve the right to legal recourse against any individuals who have provoked such a problem."[98] The international defense counsel who filed the complaint objected to these statements as a form of intimidation that could have a chilling effect on persons with information about possible corrupt practices at the ECCC.[99]

On March 27, 2009, the Nuon Chea Defense Team filed a request with the OCIJ (the "Request"), asking the Co-Investigating Judges to obtain from the UN, the RGC, or any other organization or individual, "a. the results of the OIOS inquiry; b. any correspondence between the UN and RGC related to the OIOS inquiry; and c. any other information suggesting an organized regime of institutional corruption at the ECCC."[100] The Request also asked "the OCIJ to request an administrative inquiry into the outstanding allegation of corruption at the tribunal."[101] Counsel for Ieng Sary, Ieng Thirith, and Khieu Samphan filed separate motions in support of the Request. On April 3, 2009, the OCIJ denied the defense request, concluding that it has no jurisdiction to provide the relief sought because the requested information was "totally foreign to the facts covered by the current judicial investigations"[102]; that the "negative effects" of corruption are speculative; and that "a request by the [OCIJ] for an administrative inquiry into this issue would be superfluous, since the Cambodian and United Nations authorities are already seized of the issue and already have all the information contained in the Request at their disposal."[103] Notably, only five days later the negotiations between the UN and the RGC over the proposed joint investigative mechanism ended in failure.

On May 4, 2009, the Nuon Chea Defense Team filed an Appeal against the OCIJ's Order. Again, counsel for Ieng Sary, Ieng Thirith, and Khieu Samphan filed separate motions in support of the Appeal. The Appeal was able to focus on the collapse in the negotiations between the UN and the RGC and the continued media coverage of the corruption allegations. The Appeal argued that the OCIJ has the inherent power to provide the requested relief and ensure the integrity of their own proceedings, that the Request was sufficiently factually motivated given the relief sought, and that the evidentiary approach embraced by OCIJ in its Order was too strict and too passive:

> The Defense has presented sufficient evidence to suggest that the threat posed by corruption is real, the risk great, and—if left untreated—the consequences potentially harsh. There is no principled reason why the OCIJ should impede the Defense in uncovering acts of wrongdoing which threaten to undermine the proceedings by imposing an unnecessarily high burden of proof on what is essentially a straightforward request for disclosure.[104]

As to OCIJ's argument that an administrative investigation is superfluous, the Appeal argued,

> the behavior of the UN and the RGC over the last several months…should make it abundantly clear to any reasonable observer that neither body has the intention of providing the Defense with the desired (and necessary) material. Moreover, because exposure of the alleged scheme would likely discredit senior CPP officials and embarrass the UN, neither institution possesses the requisite impartiality to deal with the matter.[105]

Nevertheless, the PTC rejected the Defense appeal on the basis that the issue does not fall within the Court's jurisdiction.

Lawyers for all 93 civil parties in the trial of Kaing Guek Eav have also sought the disclosure of the UN report, arguing that the potential disclosure of the report after the trial could jeopardize the legitimacy of its outcome.[106] The Co-Prosecutors, in their responses to both the defense appeal and the civil party request, while vigorously opposing the defense team's legal arguments for a judicial investigation of the corruption allegations, concluded that they supported the release of the OIOS report: "Despite lack of jurisdiction, there are indeed 'compelling motives' to address, transparently and forcefully, this issue which may severely endanger this Court's reputation. To this end, the Co-Prosecutors observe that the credibility of this Court's process would be enhanced by a release of the OIOS Report and a timely and credible resolution of this issue."[107]

FUNDING ISSUES

Problems surrounding corruption relate closely to one of the other key administrative challenges for the ECCC: the question of funding. Indeed, before the start of the first trial, the unaddressed corruption allegations gave donors pause about committing money to the Court. Funding for the ECCC is solely based on a voluntary contributions model and has no other regular form of financial support like, for example the ICTY and ICTR. Voluntary funding is unpredictable and makes it hard to plan for the long-term, especially when budgets for these hybrid models tend to underestimate how much funds will be needed to, in fact, support the courts' operations for a number of years.

Funding for the ECCC is divided into two distinct components: an international trust fund managed by the UN under the UNAKRT; and a national program, consisting of government funds, direct bi-lateral assistance and international funds that are administered by UNDP.[108] The national program is intended to administer the national personnel and affairs of the ECCC, and covers other specified items, including costs for renovating the courtroom and the office buildings of the tribunal. The international trust fund administers the international personnel and affairs of the ECCC, and had an initial budget of $43 million, while the national program had a three-year budget of $13.3 million.[109] A portion of the funds pledged by donor nations to the Cambodian side is administered and distributed by UNDP, including funds from the European Commission and the United Nations Trust Fund consisting of a balance of funds from the UN Transitional Authority in Cambodia (UNTAC), which administered the country briefly in 1992-93 (see Chapter 1).[110] Though UNDP does not implement or manage the national side of the tribunal, it is responsible "to ensure the correct utilization of donor funds."[111]

By September 2007, it had become apparent that the ECCC's original three-year budget of $56.3 million was inadequate for completion of the Court's mandate. The original budget omitted funding for many core functions of the Court and underestimated the cost of other functions. It was also becoming clear that the Court, facing delays in adopting Internal Rules, could not be expected to complete the trials by mid-2009 as originally envisaged.[112] The Office of Administration indicated that it planned to begin additional fundraising efforts with donors. A revised budget was released to donors in New York in January 2008, seeking approximately $113.7 million through the first quarter of 2011 in addition to the original budget of $56.3 million.[113] The Court also reported that the funds for the Cambodian side of the budget, including salaries for national staff, would be exhausted in March or April 2008 without the new funding.[114]

Unfortunately, these fundraising efforts came on the heels of audits that had uncovered serious shortcomings and inefficiencies within the tribunal, and with a backdrop of public allegations of kickback schemes and corruption implicating Cambodian court officials including Director of Administration Sean Visoth. This was to become a familiar pattern in subsequent fundraising efforts: the ECCC—particularly the national side—facing fiscal crises and serious budget shortfalls, reliant on convincing increasingly skeptical donors to contribute desperately needed funds while fending off damaging allegations of managerial inefficiency and corruption. What developed was a tense balance of interests between donors, the RGC, UN and ECCC.

Civil society groups took the opportunity to try to educate donor nations as to the utility of using their financial leverage to demand positive changes at the tribunal. The heavy reliance on donor funding meant that the ECCC, and by implication the RGC, were theoretically more vulnerable to outside pressure than they would have been otherwise. OSJI noted that "[d]onors contributing additional funding may be able to place conditions on their donations which, while respecting the independence of the ECCC, could help remedy some of the problems that have hindered the Court since its inception."[115] OSJI recommended such "reasonable preconditions" as requiring the tribunal to adopt procedures to prevent corruption and encourage its reporting; remedying problems with human resource practices; and appointing a high-level monitor to advise the UN Secretary General.[116] Implicitly, unless the donor nations could be satisfied on a wide range of issues including HR shortcomings, corruption, and political interference, funding would be withheld and, theoretically, the tribunal could collapse.

The possibility of collapse became more likely after July 2008 when, in response to new allegations of corruption on the national side of the tribunal, UNDP indefinitely froze the donor funds it was responsible for distributing to the national side.[117] Cambodian staff faced the real possibility of not being paid at the end of each month, and the national side of the tribunal expressed concern that it would run out of money in a matter of weeks. Morale on both sides of the ECCC fell. The Japanese government averted an immediate crisis by offering financial assistance directly to the RGC to enable the national side to pay its staff and temporarily continue to function. Nevertheless the crisis was real and the future of the ECCC was in jeopardy. The future of funding and therefore of the ECCC itself, appeared to have become inextricably linked to the resolution of the corruption allegations.

Financial pressure exerted by UNDP helped push the RGC to the negotiating table regarding an overhaul of the anti-corruption efforts at the Court. However, as mentioned earlier, in early April 2009 the Australian government requested that UNDP release frozen Australian funds to the national side of the Court. This request was made in the middle of negotiations between the UN and RGC over details of a proposed anti-corruption mechanism. The Australian request was described as "inexplicable" by Heather Ryan, a trial monitor for OSJI.[118] Clearly something had changed in the analysis of some donors, and the Australian move signaled an apparent willingness to proceed with funding even in the absence of an anti-corruption mechanism considered credible by the UN. One explanation is that between July 2008 and April 2009, the dynamics and calculations of donors shifted to reflect the fact that the first trial had started and seemed to be going well. Indeed, a spokesperson for the Department of Foreign Affairs in Canberra said the decision to request the release of Australian funds held by UNDP was based on general satisfaction with the tribunal, including the "broad progress" in the Cambodian efforts to address corruption concerns. UNDP refused the request to release the funds. Joe Scheuer, UNDP's country manager, explained: "We are the ones accountable for the proper use of what at the end of the day is taxpayers' money…We have said for the last nine months that we need to see allegations resolved and mechanisms put up before we can resume our role, and that today is still the same position."[119]

The continued UNDP funding freeze prompted the Japanese government to once again provide enough money to enable the national side to meet its monthly payroll for April 2009. At the end of that month, however, the Japanese government decided to donate a lump sum of over $4 million directly to the national side of the tribunal.[120] This was an amount considered adequate to fund the Cambodian side through the end of 2009. Such a large direct donation was significant in that it immediately took pressure off the Cambodian government to come to an agreement with the UN about establishing a credible anti-corruption mechanism at the Court. A joint statement issued by the French and Japanese ambassadors on behalf of the donor nations further reinforced the impression that the donors had decided to proceed with funding the national side even in the absence of a UN-approved anti-corruption mechanism.[121] In one stroke, the donors had undercut much of the financial leverage the UN had taken into the negotiations with the RGC.

One result of the funding uncertainties at the ECCC has been that Court officials, including judges, felt that they were constantly going "cap in hand" to donor nations simply so that the tribunal could survive from one month to the next. At times this was felt to have been a distraction from the important legal work at hand. Cambodian staff members were often unsure whether they would be paid at the end of the month, and on several occasions their salary was delayed. Morale inevitably suffered among both Cambodian and international staffers in an atmosphere of financial uncertainty, rumor and allegation.

OTHER ADMINISTRATIVE ISSUES

Lack of an adequate budget, continued financial uncertainty, and initially profoundly flawed HR management practices and procedures, have impacted several other administrative responsibilities within the tribunal, such as translation and transcription services and outreach.

ON TRIAL: THE KHMER ROUGE ACCOUNTABILITY PROCESS

Swearing-in ceremony at the Royal Palace, July 3, 2006. Photo by Heng Sinith.
Source: Documentation Center of Cambodia Archives

Co-Investigating Judges You Bunleng and Marcel Lemonde meeting with victims at DC-Cam, 2006.
Source: Documentation Center of Cambodia Archives

CHALLENGES OF TRANSLATION

The ECCC has three official working languages: Khmer, English and French. The Court has struggled to recruit an adequate number of qualified translators and interpreters, and independent auditors concluded that individuals were hired as translators who lacked the required qualifications and experience. A Special Audit requested by UNDP in 2007 noted that Cambodians hired by the Office of Administration to work as translators at the tribunal "did not meet the minimum requirements." While a job posting required candidates to hold a degree in the English language and at least three years' professional experience in interpreting, the Special Audit found "the selected candidate had only some part-time translating experience and was pursuing a degree in education. The position pays a monthly salary of US$3,500."[122]

The failure of the Office of Administration to hire an adequate number of capable translators has had a significant impact on court proceedings. By September 2007, major backlogs and delays in the translation of documents reportedly hindered the progress of work in the Office of the Co-Prosecutor and the Office of the Co-Investigating Judges.[123] The Office of Administration, and experts Robin Vincent and Kevin St. Louis hired by the international side to assess the Court's preparedness for trial, identified inadequate translation and interpretation capacity as a critical issue.[124] Not only would the Court have to have in place adequate interpretation and transcription services when the hearings began, but there was a need to translate documents needed for counsel to prepare for the trials. The daunting scale of this undertaking became clear when in April 2008, the Court translation unit chief, Kong Sophy, indicated that while the Co-Prosecutors' introductory submission had been translated into the three official languages of the ECCC, most of the estimated 16,000 pages of documents attached in support had not been translated.[125]

As discussed in Chapter 3, the defense teams of Khieu Samphan and Ieng Sary have argued that inadequate translation services at the ECCC compromise the fairness of the trials. Those challenges are likely to continue, as defense teams contend that it is unreasonable to expect Cambodian defense lawyers to in effect become responsible for reviewing tens of thousands of pages of Khmer-language documents and then translating them for their foreign colleagues. This situation raises due process concerns that almost all internationalized criminal tribunals have had to face.[126]

The ongoing inadequacy of translation and transcription services is related to administrative failures at the ECCC, which resulted in the hiring of ill-qualified Cambodian translators, inadequate supervision of national staff, and inefficient lines of administrative responsibility. These problems were exacerbated by an inadequate and ill-considered initial budget which underestimated the crucial role that translation and transcription services would be required to play at a tribunal conducted in three languages, where international judges and lawyers lack familiarity with spoken or written Khmer and indeed often have only a limited knowledge of the language of their international colleagues.

DIFFICULTIES IN OUTREACH

The Court's outreach efforts have also been hampered by the tribunal's inadequate budget, uncertain financing, and flawed HR procedures and policies. It is recognized that the ECCC needs to engage in effective public outreach in order to keep the Cambodian public advised of its work, and to ensure that the Court receives cooperation with essential witnesses.[127] This is all the more important given that one key justification for holding the trials is to provide an opportunity for closure for victims and an avenue for reconciliation and healing for the nation. Outreach and transparency, then, are necessary for the ECCC to succeed in this important non-legal capacity. The tribunal—facing a wide range of competing demands for limited resources—has insufficiently prioritized its outreach efforts. The Court has instead relied heavily on the free services offered by the NGO community to educate the Cambodian population. Though this was described as a "partnership," some NGO's have expressed concern about the lack of leadership and proactive action from the ECCC.

The need for broader and more effective outreach efforts was highlighted in 2007 when Court investigators found potential witnesses uncooperative after having been misinformed about the ECCC and their potential role in any proceedings.[128] Many former members of the Khmer Rouge incorrectly fear that they may face prosecution if they cooperate with the tribunal, while other potential witnesses and civil parties distrust and typically try to avoid the notoriously corrupt Cambodian court system.

There was reason to be concerned that many Cambodians—including victims who may be eligible to participate as civil parties—lacked sufficient knowledge about the work of the ECCC. A late 2008 survey conducted by the Human Rights Center, University of California, found that 39 percent of the respondents had no knowledge of the ECCC, and another 46 percent had only limited knowledge.[129]

The tribunal has become somewhat more active within the confines of the limited committed resources: several thousand informative posters in Khmer and English have been distributed around the country as visual aids; a website has been established; radio and television programs have been created; and a community outreach meeting was held in the former Khmer Rouge stronghold of Pailin.[130] Most noteworthy, Public Affairs has begun providing free busing for groups of 30 or more who wish to attend Court proceedings for the day.[131] As a consequence of these and NGO efforts, the courtroom has been near its 500-seat capacity many days of the *Duch* trial—with reportedly 20,000 attendees from the start of full trial on March 30 through the end of August 2009.[132] Outreach efforts have benefitted from the appointment of the energetic Reach Sambath as head of the Public Affairs Office in June 2009. Since he took over, the hearings have gone from being often sparsely attended by Cambodians to being often overflowing. Mr. Reach has consistently and persuasively articulated to Cambodians that "[T]he court is yours."[133]

Reach replaced Helen Jarvis, an Australian national with Cambodian citizenship who had served as the tribunal's Cambodian-side spokesperson as head of the ECCC's Public Affairs office. Jarvis was "redeployed" by the Cambodian government to serve as Director of the Victims' Unit (VU) in what became a controversial adjustment in the Court's outreach responsibilities. That redeployment was made without following the new HR procedure requirement of advertising the open position publicly beforehand. Youk Chhang, Director of DC-Cam, expressed concern "that after allegations of hiring improprieties aimed at the Office of Administration and commendable efforts to resolve them, the OA appears not to have followed its newly adopted guidelines."[134]

It was announced at the same time that the aspects of the Court's outreach efforts supposed to be conducted by the VU—namely those related to participation issues—would now be consolidated under Jarvis' direction. This amalgamation of the VU with the Court's outreach efforts raised concerns of an "inescapable conflict of interest": Ieng Sary's co-lawyer, Ang Udom, suggested that Director of the VU Jarvis would play a "very active" role as a party in the Court which would make it impossible for her to impartially perform outreach duties.[135]

Critics were concerned that Jarvis lacked credibility in her new role both because of her lack of relevant experience and her close association with the RGC—including her work as an advisor for Deputy Prime Minister Sok An and her history of outspoken support for the Hun Sen regime. Youk Chhang, among others, questioned appointing someone to head the VU who was not of Cambodian ethnicity:

> In my view, the appointment of a non-Cambodian does not live up to the spirit of the agreement establishing the Court and its promotion of strong Cambodian ownership of the process. Regarding the Head of Victims Unit in particular, in designating this as a Cambodian national position, the Court has recognized both the symbolic and practical importance of having it filled by a native Khmer speaker who can empathize with victims from a Cambodian perspective.[136]

Defense counsel for Nuon Chea and Ieng Sary, amongst others, also attacked her selection based on her membership of the Leninist Party Faction (LPF) in Australia, and her signing a controversial LPF letter in 2006 which stated: "We too are Marxists and believe that 'the ends justify the means'...In time of revolution and civil war, the most extreme measures will sometimes become necessary and justified. Against the bourgeoisie and their state agencies we don't respect their laws and their fake moral principles."[137]

Civil parties questioned whether a Leninist was an appropriate choice to represent victims of a Leninist regime at the tribunal.[138] For further discussion of the Court's outreach efforts related to victim participation, see Chapter 5.

CONCLUSIONS

There is a real danger in allowing a judicial process to become hostage to administrative deficiencies. Unfortunately, the administrative problems facing the ECCC have risen to such a level that they threaten to damage the legitimacy and viability of the legal process. One lesson to be learned, of course, is that the fine details of a tribunal's administrative functions are vital components in the success and legitimacy of a judicial undertaking. Ensuring that a hybrid tribunal's administrative responsibilities are properly and honestly administered is not a matter that can rest upon a reliance of the good intentions of the host nation, particularly when that country has a weak and suspect legal structure.

Cambodia posed significant challenges for those seeking to establish a hybrid tribunal there: a regime that routinely asserts its control over the judiciary; little history of judicial independence; and a culture of corruption and political control permeating all levels of the legal system. Yet it was in this context that the international community agreed to Cambodian demands that Cambodian officials should have significant autonomy and responsibility within the administrative structure of the Court. The resultant problems were, unfortunately, predictable.

What key steps are required—whether at the ECCC or at other hybrid tribunals—to make the process a success from an administrative standpoint? Fundamentally, the divided international-national administrative structure of the ECCC has been unsatisfactory on several levels. While it is important for practical as well as symbolic reasons to meaningfully incorporate nationals into any hybrid administrative function, the ECCC highlights the potentially negative consequences of a naïve reliance on local government officials to efficiently administer a complex tribunal involving millions of dollars in a country where courts lack independence and where corruption is deeply ingrained. In such a situation, certain safeguards can perhaps mitigate the worst harm: donors, for example, can take an active stance, providing funding piecemeal and only on condition that certain changes are made and benchmarks met. Areas of particular concern must include a requirement that the Court effectively resolve any administrative divisions, address in a transparent and thorough manner any corruption allegations while ensuring whistleblower protections, minimize translation backlogs, institute best practices in HR management, and adequately prepare the courtroom and other facilities while increasing transparency through the timely release of documents and information. An active management oversight group can ensure that all donor funds are administered effectively and efficiently, while a UN-appointed special advisor to the Court can assist with administrative and management reforms and monitor their effectiveness. In other words, the donor community, the UN, civil society groups, and the international community must remain vigilant in ensuring that inefficient or corrupt local practices are not allowed to become the norm at the tribunal.

In certain administrative areas, as I have shown, the ECCC has indeed successfully implemented changes that have addressed many of the worst abuses and flaws within the Court's administration. This is important, and suggests that a degree of positive change is possible within the tribunal's current structure. On the other hand, the serious allegations of corruption remain stubbornly unresolved. This may reflect the political reality of the ECCC: a public investigation of corrupt officials is unacceptable to the Cambodian government, while for the UN and the donors this matter is ultimately not considered fatal to the ability of the tribunal to continue with its mandate. It remains unclear how—or indeed whether—the corruption allegations will be addressed. It is, surely, of great concern that this issue has persisted for so long and still remains with the potential to undermine the reputation and work of the Court.

---

[1] Amnesty International, *Cambodia: After 30 Years Khmer Rouge Crimes on Trial*, report number ASA 23/003/2009 (2009), at 3, available at www.amnesty.org/en/library/asset/ASA23/003/2009/en/072d0502-d596-4a47-b441-30fb1a6c952b/asa230032009en.pdf.

[2] Agreement between the United Nations and the Royal Government of Cambodia Concerning the Prosecution under Cambodian Law of Crimes Committed During the Period of Democratic Kampuchea (June 6, 2003), art. 8(1); Internal Rules of the Extraordinary Chambers in the Courts of Cambodia, as revised on Mar. 6, 2009 [hereinafter ECCC Internal Rules], R. 9(1).

[3] OPEN SOCIETY JUSTICE INITIATIVE, RECENT DEVELOPMENTS AT THE EXTRAORDINARY CHAMBERS IN THE COURTS OF CAMBODIA: SEPT. 24, 2007 UPDATE 10 [hereinafter OSJI Sept. 2007 Update].

[4] Law on the Establishment of Extraordinary Chambers in the Courts of Cambodia for the Prosecution of Crimes Committed During the Period of Democratic Kampuchea, with inclusion of amendments as promulgated on Oct. 27, 2004, NS/RKM/1004/006 [hereinafter

ECCC Law], art. 30; ECCC Internal Rules, R. 9(2)-(7) and R. 10(3); Anne Heindel with John D. Ciorciari, *Why the ECCC Office of Administration Would Benefit from Being Structured More Like a 'Registry,'* SEARCHING FOR THE TRUTH, Oct. 2007.

[5] ECCC Law, *supra*, art. 8(4).

[6] Deloitte Touche Tohmatsu India Pvt. Ltd., HRM Review Team, Report on the Special HRM Review Apr. 25, 2008 [hereinafter Deloitte Touche HRM Review], at 9.

[7] *Id.* at 9-10.

[8] *Id.* at 10.

[9] *Id.* at 5.

[10] Michael M. Calavan, Sergio Diaz Briquets, and Gerald O'Brien, *Cambodian Corruption Assessment*, report prepared for USAID/Cambodia (Aug. 19, 2004), at 2-3, *available at* www.usaid.gov/kh/democracy_and_governance/documents/Cambodian_Corruption_Assessment.pdf.

[11] Deloitte Touche HRM Review, *supra* note 6, at 2. *See also* ECCC Law, *supra* note 4, art. 8(4), which states: "The Director and Deputy Director shall cooperate in order to ensure an effective and efficient functioning of the administration."

[12] UN Development Program, Audit of Human Resources Management at the Extraordinary Chambers in the Courts of Cambodia (ECCC), Report No. RCM0172 (June 4, 2007) [hereinafter UNDP Audit], at 8.

[13] Sallappan Kandasamy, UN Office of Audit and Performance Review, Confidential Interoffice Memorandum June 4, 2007, This memo was the cover letter for the UNDP audit and is publicly available at www.unakrt-online.org/Docs/Other/2007-06-04%20UNDP%20Special%20Audit%20of%20ECCC%20HR.pdf.

[14] *Id.*

[15] When the Director of the Office of Administration, Sean Visoth, threatened to ban OSJI—a key watchdog NGO—from the tribunal following that group's raising corruption allegations involving Cambodian officials, Peter Foster acted quickly to publicly support OSJI's role and point out that Mr. Sean lacked the authority to unilaterally exclude NGOs.

[16] John A. Hall, *Yet Another U.N. Scandal*, WALL ST. J., Sept. 21, 2007; also as John A. Hall, *Courting Disaster*, WALL ST. J. ASIA, Sept. 21, 2007.

[17] Extraordinary Chambers in the Courts of Cambodia, press release dated Oct. 2, 2007, *available at* www.eccc.gov.kh/english/cabinet/press/42/audit_report_comment.pdf.

[18] UNDP Audit, *supra* note 12, at 3, § I.1.S.

[19] *Id.*

[20] *Id.* at 4, § I.1.S.

[21] *Id.* at 4-5, § I.1.S.

[22] *Id.* at 5, § I.1.S.

[23] *Id.*

[24] UNAKRT Summary of Recommendations of the Assessment Team (Vincent/St.Louis), [n.d], *available at* www.unakrt-online.org/Docs/Other/2007-06-13%20UNAKRT-Summary%20of%20Expert%20 Recommendation.pdf (last viewed July 5, 2009); OPEN SOCIETY JUSTICE INITIATIVE, RECENT DEVELOPMENTS AT THE EXTRAORDINARY CHAMBERS IN THE COURTS OF CAMBODIA: FEBRUARY 2008 UPDATE 16, n. 43 [hereinafter OSJI Feb. 2008 Update].

[25] Erika Kinetz, *Another Delay for Justice?* NEWSWEEK, Oct. 6, 2007.

[26] Erika Kinetz, *Report Finds Flaws in ECCC Administration*, CAMBODIA DAILY, Sept. 25, 2007.

[27] Heindel with Ciorciari, *supra* note 4, at 35.

[28] Deloitte Touche HRM Review, *supra* note 6, at 2.

[29] *Id.* at 5.

[30] *Id.* at 4.

[31] *Id.* at 2.

[32] OPEN SOCIETY JUSTICE INITIATIVE, RECENT DEVELOPMENTS AT THE EXTRAORDINARY CHAMBERS IN THE COURTS OF CAMBODIA: MAY 2008 UPDATE 21 [hereinafter OSJI May 2008 Update].

[33] Rory Byrne, *UN Reports Call for Changes in Structure of Khmer Rouge Tribunal*, VOICE OF AMERICA, Oct. 5, 2007.

[34] *Michelle Lee Resigns*, DEVELOPMENT WEEKLY, Oct. 1, 2007.

[35] OSJI May 2008 Update, *supra* note 32, at 20.

[36] *Id.* at 4.

[37] *Id.* at 20.

[38] So Phal, *CPP-Appointed Judges, Prosecutors in KR Court See 30% of Their Wages Deducted*, VOICE OF KHMER YOUTH, Jan. 31, 2007.

[39] Cat Barton, *Kickback Claims Stain the KRT*, PHNOM PENH POST, Feb. 23-Mar. 8, 2007.

[40] Open Society Justice Initiative, "Corruption Allegations at Khmer Rouge Court Must Be Investigated," press release dated Feb. 24, 2007.

[41] *Id.*

[42] Erika Kinetz, *Report Finds Flaws in ECCC Administration*, CAMBODIA DAILY, Sept. 25, 2007.

[43] Douglas Gillison, *ECCC Reviews New Graft Allegations on Eve of Funds Drive*, CAMBODIA DAILY, July 29, 2008.

[44] Douglas Gillison, *UN 'Reviews' Claims of Graft: ECCC Official*, CAMBODIA DAILY, Aug. 5, 2008.

[45] Cat Barton, *Tribunal Graft Charges Spread: German Delegation Exposes Results of Secret UN Probe; Staff Concur*, PHNOM PENH POST, Feb. 27, 2009.

[46] Cat Barton, *Disorder in the Court*, WALL ST. J. ASIA, Apr. 1, 2009.

[47] *The Khmers Rouges and Justice: The Court on Trial*, ECONOMIST, Apr. 2, 2009.

[48] *Cambodia's Long Road to Justice*, CNN INTERNATIONAL, Apr. 30, 2009, *available at* edition.cnn.com/2009/WORLD/asiapcf/04/29/wus.cambodia.genocide/#cnnSTCVideo; full documentary *available at* KI Media, ki-media.blogspot.com/2009/05/killing-fields-long-road-to-justice.html. *See also* Elena Lesley, *CNN Spotlights Corruption at Tribunal*, PHNOM PENH POST TRIBUNAL BLOG, May 3, 2009, *available at* www.phnompenhpost.com.

[49] Joel Brinkley, *Cambodia's Curse: Struggling to Shed the Khmer Rouge's Legacy*, FOREIGN AFF. (Apr. 2009), at 115.

[50] Kandasamy, *supra* note 13.

[51] *Id.*

[52] *Id.*

[53] OSJI May 2008 Update, *supra* note 32, at 21.

⁵⁴ Erika Kinetz, *Gov't Rejects UN Call to Probe ECCC*, Cambodia Daily, Feb. 20, 2008.

⁵⁵ *Cambodian Genocide Tribunal Denies Financial Mismanagement*, Agence France Presse, Apr. 25, 2008.

⁵⁶ John A. Hall, *New Corruption Allegations Pose Test for Future of KR Tribunal*, Cambodia Daily, Aug. 15, 2008.

⁵⁷ OSJI May 2008 Update, *supra* note 32, at 21.

⁵⁸ *Id.* at 22.

⁵⁹ Douglas Gillison, *Government Asserts Jurisdiction Over KR Tribunal Graft Claims*, Cambodia Daily, Aug. 9-10, 2008.

⁶⁰ Gillison, *supra* note 44.

⁶¹ Douglas Gillison, *ECCC Funding Delayed Over Graft Claims*, Cambodia Daily, Aug. 6, 2008; Douglas Gillison, *KR Tribunal Donors Extend Funding Delay*, Cambodia Daily, Aug. 12, 2008.

⁶² Neth Pheaktra, *KRT Forms New Anti-Corruption Committee*, Mekong Times, Aug. 18, 2008.

⁶³ Pheaktra, *supra*; Georgia Wilkins and Vong Sokheng, *Govt to Review Future KRT Graft Complaints in Secret*, Phnom Penh Post, Sept. 16, 2008.

⁶⁴ Douglas Gillison, *KRT Chief, Khmer Judges in Anti-Graft Pledge*, Cambodia Daily, Aug. 16-17, 2008.

⁶⁵ Douglas Gillison, *Gov't Receives UN Findings on KR Tribunal Graft Review*, Cambodia Daily, Sept. 18, 2008; Douglas Gillison, *Government: UN Review of KRT Wrong to Name Names*, Cambodia Daily, Sept. 20-21, 2008; Georgia Wilkins, *KR Court Graft Unfairly Names and Shames, Govt Says*, Phnom Penh Post, Sept. 22, 2008.

⁶⁶ Barton, *supra* note 45.

⁶⁷ Open Society Justice Initiative, Recent Developments at the Extraordinary Chambers in the courts of Cambodia: October 2008 Update 2 [hereinafter OSJI Oct. 2008 Update].

⁶⁸ Craig Guthrie, *KRT Appoints New Chief of Troubled Personnel Department*, Mekong Times, Aug. 12, 2008; Prak Chan Thul and Douglas Gillison, *ECCC Gets New Cambodian Chief of Personnel*, Cambodia Daily, Aug. 12, 2008; Douglas Gillison, *Court: Staff Rotation Unrelated to Allegations*, Cambodia Daily, Aug. 13, 2008.

⁶⁹ Pheaktra, *supra* note 62.

⁷⁰ Bundestag Delegation, "[Draft] report on the trip to Cambodia and Indonesia by a delegation of the Committee for Human Rights and Humanitarian Aid," Oct. 25-Nov. 3, 2008, *available at* www.bundestag.de.ausschuesse/a17/reisen/ASEAN2008.pdf; Douglas Gillison, *UN Officer Cites Gov't Meddling in Tribunal: Panel*, Cambodia Daily, Feb. 26, 2009; Barton, *supra* note 45.

⁷¹ Douglas Gillison, *Official: Rumors About ECCC Chief's Exit False*, Cambodia Daily, Nov. 27, 2008; Prak Chan Thui and Douglas Gillison, *KR Tribunal Chief Sole Witness in Closed Probe*, Cambodia Daily, Feb. 11, 2009; Michiel Pestman, Victor Koppe, and Andrew Ianuzzi, Letter to the Editor, Phnom Penh Post, Feb. 27, 2009.

⁷² Cheang Sokha and Georgia Wilkins, *Testimony Halted Over Document Row at KRT*, Phnom Penh Post, May 21, 2009.

⁷³ Joint Statement by the Royal Government of Cambodia and United Nations, Phnom Penh, Feb. 23, 2009 [hereinafter Feb. 2009 RGC-UN Joint Statement], *available at* www.eccc.gov.kh/english/cabinet/fileUpload/108/Joint_Statement_EN.pdf.

⁷⁴ *Id.*

⁷⁵ *Id.*

⁷⁶ *Id.*

⁷⁷ *Id.*

[78] John A. Hall, *Judging the Khmer Rouge Tribunal*, Far Eastern Econ. Rev., Mar. 2, 2009.

[79] Feb. 2009 RGC-UN Joint Statement, *supra* note 73.

[80] James A. Goldston, comment for Voa Khmer, Apr. 24, 2009.

[81] Chun Sakada, *Calls Mount for Release of Tribunal Funding*, Voa Khmer, Apr. 21, 2009.

[82] Jean-Francois Desmazieres, Ambassador of France in Cambodia, and Katsuhiro Shinohara, Ambassador of Japan in Cambodia, Statement of the Co-Chairs of Friends of the Court, Phnom Penh (Apr. 30, 2009) [hereinafter French-Japanese Statement], *available at* www.ambafrance-kh.org/KH/spip.php?article1163.

[83] Agreement to Establish an Independent Counsellor at the Extraordinary Chambers in the Courts of Cambodia, Aug. 11, 2009, at 1.

[84] Douglas Gillison and Neou Vannarin, *Government Auditor Named New ECCC Graft Monitor*, Cambodia Daily, Aug. 13, 2009, at 26.

[85] *Id.*

[86] Joint Statement by the Royal Government of Cambodia and the United Nations, Phnom Penh (Aug. 11, 2009), *available at* www.un.org/News/Press/docs/2009/I3146.doc.htm.

[87] Laurent Lemarchand, Chargé d' Affaires, French Embassy in Cambodia, and Katsuhiro Shinohara, Ambassador of Japan in Cambodia, Statement from the Co-Chairs of the Friends of the ECCC on the Agreement to Establish an Independent Counsellor (Aug. 12, 2009).

[88] Nuon Chea Defense Team, Appeal Against Order on Eleventh Request for Investigative Action, filed May 4, 2009, D158/5/1/1, at 6.

[89] Susan Postlewaite, *Khmer Rouge Trial Threatened*, Asia Sentinel, Apr. 24, 2009.

[90] James Goldston, *Justice Interrupted: Cambodia's Khmer Rouge Tribunal Risks Becoming a Sham*, Wall St. J., Dec. 14, 2008.

[91] International Covenant on Civil and Political Rights, art 14. Cambodia is a party to the ICCPR.

[92] Open Society Justice Initiative, "Corruption Allegations at Khmer Rouge Court Must Be Investigated," press release dated Feb. 24, 2007.

[93] Joint Statement by the Cambodian Center for Human Rights and the Asian Human Rights Commission, "Cambodia: Tolerance of corruption at the Khmer Rouge Tribunal Is Unacceptable," Apr. 17, 2009.

[94] So Phal, *CPP-Appointed Judges, Prosecutors in KR Court See 30% of Their Wages Deducted*, The Voice of Khmer Youth, Jan. 31, 2007; Barton, *supra* note 39; Open Society Justice Initiative, *supra* note 92.

[95] Barton, *supra* note 46.

[96] Phorn Bopha and Katie Nelson, *Nuon Chea Defense Submits Graft Complaint*, Cambodia Daily, Jan. 9, 2009; Joint Statement by the Cambodian Center for Human Rights and the Asian Human Rights Commission (Apr. 17, 2009).

[97] Douglas Gillison and Prak Chan Thul, *Phnom Penh Court Halts ECCC Investigation*, Cambodia Daily, Feb. 7-8, 2009.

[98] National Judges of the ECCC, press release dated Jan. 9, 2009, *available at* www.eccc.gov.kh/english/cabinet/press/85/National_Judges_Press_Release_En.pdf.

[99] Douglas Gillison and Prak Chan Thul, *KR Defense Chief: Judges Put Fairness at Risk*, Cambodia Daily, Jan. 17-18, 2009; Open Society Justice Initiative, Recent Developments at the Extraordinary Chambers in the Courts of Cambodia, February 2009 Update 7-8 [hereinafter OSJI Feb. 2009 Update].

[100] Eleventh Request for Investigative Action, Case No. 002/19-09-2007-ECCC/OCIJ, ¶ 22 (Office of the Co-Investigating Judges, Mar. 27, 2009).

[101] *Id.*

[102] Order on Request for Investigative Action, Case No. 002/19-09-2007-ECCC/OCIJ, ¶ 10 (Office of the Co-Investigating Judges, April 3, 2009).

[103] *Id.* ¶ 13.

[104] Appeal Against Order on Eleventh Request for Investigative Action, Case No. 002/19-09-2007-ECCC/OCIJ (PTC 21), ¶ 30 (Pre-Trial Chamber, May 4, 2009).

[105] *Id.* ¶ 31.

[106] Douglas Gillison, *S-21 Civil Parties Say They Are United on Graft Review Dispute*, CAMBODIA DAILY, June 20-21, 2009.

[107] Co-Prosecutors' Joint Response to Defense Appeals Against the Co-Investigating Judges' Order Denying Request for Investigative Action Regarding Allegations of Administrative Corruption, Case No. 002/19-09-2007-ECCC/OCIJ (PTC 19, 20, 21 & 22), ¶¶ 77-78 (Pre-Trial Chamber, May 29, 2009) (footnote omitted); Co-Prosecutors' Response to Certain Civil Parties' Request for Disclosure of the UN-OIOS Report, Case No. 001/18-07-2007-ECCC/TC, ¶¶ 19-20 (Trial Chamber, June 2, 2009). *See also* John A. Hall, *In the Cambodian Judges' Court,* WALL ST. J. ASIA, May 28, 2009.

[108] UNDP Audit, *supra* note 12, at 8.

[109] UNDP Statement on the HR Management Audit in ECCC, May 8, 2007; UNDP Audit, *supra* note 12, at 8.

[110] Deloitte Touche HRM Review, *supra* note 6, at 5; UNDP Audit, *supra* note 12, at 8.

[111] Update on UNDP audit of the ECCC, May 25, 2007.

[112] OSJI Feb. 2008 Update, *supra* note 24, at 16; *Cambodia Requests More Funds for Genocide Tribunal*, ASSOCIATED PRESS, Oct. 25, 2007.

[113] OSJI Feb. 2008 Update, *supra* note 24, at 4.

[114] *Id.*

[115] OSJI Sept. 24, 2007 Update, *supra* note 3, at 10.

[116] *Id. See also* OSJI, Critical Issues Surrounding the Fundraising Drive of the Extraordinary Chambers in the Courts of Cambodia, Nov. 16, 2007.

[117] Gillison, articles on "ECCC Funding," and "KR Tribunal," *supra* note 61.

[118] Robert Carmichael, *Australia in Controversy over Khmer Rouge Trials,* RADIO AUSTRALIA, Apr. 27, 2009, *available at* www.abc.net.au/news/stories/2009/04/27/2553753.htm?section=world.

[119] *Id.*

[120] Sopheng Cheang, *Japan Donates $4 Million to Khmer Rouge Tribunal,* ASSOCIATED PRESS, May 1, 2009; Elena Lesley, *Once Again, Japan Comes to the Court's Rescue*, PHNOM PENH POST TRIBUNAL BLOG, May 1, 2009, *available at* www.phnompenhpost.com.

[121] French-Japanese Statement, *supra* note 82.

[122] *UN Auditors Slam Cambodia Over Alleged Malpractice in Hiring Staff for Genocide Tribunal*, ASSOCIATED PRESS, Oct. 2, 2007.

[123] OSJI Sept. 24, 2007 Update, *supra* note 3, at 11.

[124] ECCC Yearly Financial and Activity Progress Report, § 7.1 "Court Management Issues—Translation and Interpretation Services," (Dec. 31, 2007) at 19; Robin Vincent and Kevin St. Louis, "Summary of United Nations Expert Report on ECCC," July 13, 2007; OSJI May 2008 Update, *supra* note 32, at 8-9.

[125] Douglas Gillison, *Translation Row Stalls Khieu Samphan Hearing*, CAMBODIA DAILY, Apr. 24, 2008; Statement of Kong Sophy at press conference at ECCC, Apr. 24, 2008, *quoted in* OSJI May 2008 Update, *supra* note 32, at 8.

[126] OSJI Oct. 2008 Update, *supra* note 67, at 4.

[127] OSJI Feb. 2008 Update, *supra* note 24, at 14.

[128] *Id.*

[129] OSJI Feb. 2009 Update, *supra* note 99, at 9.

[130] OSJI Feb. 2008 Update, *supra* note 24, at 3.

[131] Extraordinary Chambers in the Courts of Cambodia, *Court Report*, Issue 15 (July 2009), at 7, *available at* www.eccc.gov.kh/english/publications.courtReport.aspx.

[132] Extraordinary Chambers in the Courts of Cambodia, "More Than 20,000 Visitors Have Attended the Duch Trial," *press release dated* Aug. 26, 2009.

[133] Elena Lesley, *"The Court Is Yours," Public Affairs Head Tells Cambodians*, Phnom Penh Post Tribunal Blog, Aug. 6, 2009, *available at* www.phnompenhpost.com.

[134] E-mail from Youk Chhang to Tony Kranh, Acting Director of the ECCC Office of Administration and Knut Rosandhaug, Deputy Director of the OA (July 15, 2009), on file at the Documentation Center of Cambodia.

[135] Robbie Corey-Boulet, *Attacks on Jarvis Multiply*, Phnom Penh Post, June 8, 2009.

[136] E-mail from Youk Chhang, *supra* note 134. *See also* Robbie Corey-Boulet, *Nationality and the Jarvis Debate*, Phnom Penh Post, June 12, 2009.

[137] Douglas Gillison, *Nuon Chea Team Pursue Inquiry, Victims Chief*, Cambodia Daily, June 3, 2009; Elena Lesley, *Jarvis's Leninist Ties Under Fire*, Phnom Penh Post Tribunal Blog, June 4, 2009, *available at* www.phnompenhpost.com; Sophal Ear, *Cambodian 'Justice,'* Wall St. J. Asia, Aug. 31, 2009.

[138] Georgia Wilkins, *KR Victims Question Jarvis' Politics*, Phnom Penh Post, June 19, 2009.

5.

SARAH THOMAS AND TERITH CHY

Throughout the 20th century, the international community—first, through the victors of World War II and, more recently, the United Nations (UN) Security Council—has made considerable efforts to bring perpetrators of international crimes to justice through criminal prosecutions. This legacy of prosecutions reaches from Nuremburg, to Tokyo, to The Hague and Arusha. By concentrating narrowly on prosecutions, however, the international community has omitted the survivors of the atrocities from those accountability processes, causing many survivors to feel alienation and disillusionment. At the turn of the 21st century, the international community has begun to compensate for these shortcomings by providing in the Rome Statute for limited victim participation in International Criminal Court (ICC) proceedings and in the Internal Rules of the Extraordinary Chambers in the Courts of Cambodia (ECCC or "the Court") for broader survivor participation.

With a groundbreaking scheme for survivor participation—stretching far beyond that of the International Criminal Court—the Extraordinary Chambers have the potential to succeed where other tribunals have failed. The Court's Internal Rules accord a role to all survivors—not only victims—and conceive of certain recognized victims as full parties to the proceedings, analogous to the prosecution or defense. Due to inadequate planning, funding and commitment from key stakeholders, however, this initiative is currently being reconsidered and may be eliminated after use in only one trial. There are consequently real concerns that the Court's survivor participation initiative may fail to live up to survivors' expectations, causing many Cambodian survivors frustration and disappointment. Its failure also threatens to set a discouraging precedent for future internationalized tribunals.

In this Chapter, the Authors evaluate the ability of the ECCC's survivor participation initiative to meaningfully involve survivors. First, we explain survivor participation in domestic systems and summarize its genesis at the international level. With this background, the reader may better understand the importance of survivor participation. Second, we provide an overview of the framework for survivor participation at the Extraordinary Chambers as of late August 2009. Drawing on our professional experience, we identify obstacles to its success engendered by both its implementation and the Cambodian situation. Third, we focus upon the most ambitious form of survivor participation—the civil party action—and report upon its incorporation into the *Duch* trial. Fourth, we briefly analyze the initiative's achievements and failures to date and offer our recommendations for ensuring its future success.

THE BACKGROUND TO SURVIVOR PARTICIPATION IN CRIMINAL PROCEEDINGS

Schemes for victim (or, more broadly, survivor) participation vary considerably across legal systems. Most schemes limit participation to victims (i.e., direct or indirect victims of crime), whereas other schemes open participation to survivors more generally. Survivors are individuals who have survived a criminal situation, though they may not have been victims themselves. Survivors may include eyewitnesses and individuals who have heard of crimes. Survivors may even include perpetrators! In this Chapter, the Authors have chosen to use the term "survivor participation," as the Extraordinary Chambers allow for the participation of *all* survivors of the Democratic Kampuchea regime, not only the direct victims of crimes.

THE LIMITED VALUE OF RETRIBUTIVE JUSTICE TO SURVIVORS

Criminal prosecutions provide an important—arguably, the most important—means of achieving justice for wrongdoing, for both survivors and society at large. Many survivors derive considerable satisfaction and some measure of closure from seeing their abusers publicly held to account and punished. Society may also derive additional benefits from prosecutions. First, trials may generate a historical record of the crimes, albeit a limited one. Second, punishment may prevent future crimes by deterring potential offenders and by incapacitating or rehabilitating potential repeat offenders. Third, following a period of societal transition, trials may offer an important means for the establishment of the rule of law by marking an end to impunity.[1]

Generally speaking, in both the domestic and international context, legal systems appoint prosecutors to conduct prosecutions of wrongdoers on behalf of society at large. Most legal systems fail to accord survivors an active role within the proceedings, casting them as "witnesses." Despite sharing a common goal (the conviction of the perpetrator), the interests of the prosecution do not necessarily reflect those of survivors. Punishment following a successful prosecution commonly results in imprisonment or payment of a fine but fails to redress the consequences of crime suffered by victims. This exclusionary understanding of survivors' role may cause survivors to feel marginalized and disempowered.

As they seek only to establish guilt and to punish wrongdoers, prosecutions offer a limited, one-dimensional form of justice called *retributive justice*. The needs of survivors are, however, multifaceted and may not be satisfied by prosecutions alone. In addition to ensuring that wrongdoers receive their "just deserts," survivors commonly seek: (a) redress for injuries suffered as a result of crimes (through reparations); (b) the promotion of an accurate historical understanding of the crimes (through mechanisms of inquiry); and (c) remembrance of crimes and memorialization for the victims. In order to achieve such multifaceted justice, survivors require multiple legal mechanisms.

Unfortunately, in many contexts, implementation of complementary justice mechanisms, such as truth commissions and reparations schemes, proves impossible for a variety of reasons, including insufficient resources and the lack of political will. In such cases, the participation of victims (or, more broadly, survivors) in proceedings can be an important means of remedying the shortcomings of prosecutions alone. Survivors can bring important knowledge and insights into the courtroom and trial process, and their participation provides an important voice to the victims who suffered from the alleged criminal abuses. Encouragingly, studies have shown that victims enjoy improved mental health and welfare if accorded a voice in judicial proceedings.[2]

FRAMEWORKS FOR SURVIVOR PARTICIPATION IN DOMESTIC SYSTEMS

Survivors' participation rights include the right to participate in the criminal proceedings and/or the right to request reparation for injury caused by the crime. Examples of participation in domestic systems vary from the mere presentation of a victim impact statement to participation as a full party to the proceedings. In all systems, victims commonly act as witnesses in criminal proceedings. Victims' rights advocates do not, however, consider the provision of witness testimony to constitute participation, as witnesses have only a passive role. Proponents of this view argue that the provision of witness testimony fails to empower victims, as witness-victims act merely as "puppets" of the prosecution.

Provision for survivor participation differs considerably across legal systems, with the greatest difference found between the common-law and civil-law traditions. Common law systems, as found in most English-speaking countries and as based upon the Anglo-American model, adopt a restrictive approach and conceive of victims as having a very limited role in criminal proceedings, typically limited to the provision of witness testimony. In certain jurisdictions, victims may be permitted to make impact statements at sentencing. While victims may seek compensation for injury through a separate civil suit, such actions commonly prove unsuccessful as most criminals are indigent and, therefore, practically judgment-proof.

Generally, civil law systems, as found in most countries and as based upon the continental European model, permit victims to play a very active role in the proceedings. Most legal systems based on the French (rather than Germanic) civil-law model allow victims to intervene directly in criminal proceedings to request reparation from the wrongdoer, obviating the need for a separate civil suit. Civil law systems treat such victims—so-called *parties civiles* ("civil parties")—as full parties to the proceedings with rights analogous to those of the prosecution or defense. The French Code of Criminal Procedure, for example, accords civil parties various rights, such as the rights to request investigatory action and to question witnesses.[3]

As a result of colonialism, most countries have legal systems based upon either the common- or civil-law traditions. Having been a French protectorate from 1863 to 1953, Cambodia's civil-law system is heavily influenced by French law. With French experts providing ongoing assistance, Cambodian drafters have adopted many French provisions directly into domestic law with little amendment. The new Cambodian Code of Criminal Procedure (Criminal Procedure Code), for example, mirrors French law in allowing victims to participate as civil parties and to request reparation.[4] Interestingly, at the 1979 People's Revolutionary Tribunal, three victims—Mr. Abdul Koyom, Mrs. Denise Alfonso and Miss Chhay Ny—participated in the proceedings as civil parties.[5]

EVOLUTION OF VICTIMS' RIGHTS AT THE INTERNATIONAL LEVEL

Although international and regional human rights treaties have long spoken of a general right to a remedy, victims have only recently received specific recognition of their rights at the international level. Only in 1985 did a UN General Assembly Resolution—the Declaration of Basic Principles of Justice for Victims of Crimes and Abuse of Power—specifically establish minimum standards (principles) for the treatment of victims of crime.[6] Although not a legally binding instrument, the Victims Declaration proved an important milestone in the advancement of victims' rights. It specifically proclaimed for the first time that victims of crime should have "access to the mechanisms of justice" and should receive "fair restitution."[7]

The Victims Declaration did not, however, speak of victims having "rights" and failed to place a duty on states. Instead, it spoke of principles that states "should" adhere to. It did, however, initiate a discussion of victims' rights at the international level. In 1989, the UN Commission on Human Rights began to consider victims' rights, resulting in the drafting and revision of a set of "basic principles" throughout the 1990s. In December 2005, the General Assembly passed resolution adopting these Basic Principles and Guidelines on the Right to a Remedy

ON TRIAL: THE KHMER ROUGE ACCOUNTABILITY PROCESS

(THIS SPREAD) Victims at the Killing Fields of Choeung Ek, 2006. Photos by Dacil Q. Keo.
Source: Documentation Center of Cambodia Archives

Cham Muslims pray at Choeung Ek during DC-Cam's Genocide and Justice Tour, 2007. Photo by Dacil Q. Keo. *Source: Documentation Center of Cambodia Archives*

The ceremony Bang Skaul preformed at Cheung Ek Killing Fields Memorial, Feb 1, 2007. Photo by Dacil Q. Keo.
Source: Documentation Center of Cambodia Archives

(This spread and following pages) DC-Cam Peace and Justice Walk towards the ECCC courtroom, led by nuns, monks, touns and mi-touns (Cham Muslim leaders) from across Cambodia, 2008. Photos by Piseth Phat and Heng Sinith.
Source: *Documentation Center of Cambodia Archives*

and Reparation for Victims of Gross Violations of International Human Rights Law and Serious Violations of International Humanitarian Law.[8]

Enacted through a resolution of the General Assembly, the Basic Principles bind states only insofar as they reflect existing treaty obligations and customary international law. The drafters have used the words "shall" to denote binding obligations and "should" to denote non-binding guidelines. In contrast to the Victims' Declaration, the Basic Principles adopt a rights-based discourse. They proclaim the right of victims to a remedy (Principle VII), including the rights to: "[e]qual and effective access to justice"; "[a]dequate, effective and prompt reparation for harm suffered"; and "[a]ccess to relevant information concerning violations and reparation mechanisms."[9]

The Basic Principles are widely regarded to reflect international standards of justice, which require that victims of crime have access to justice and receive "adequate, effective and prompt" reparation. Specifically, the Basic Principles codify the existing, binding obligations on states to provide victims of crime with an effective judicial remedy through accessible procedures and to provide reparation if their actors caused the harm. In addition, the Basic Principles proclaim a number of non-binding duties incumbent upon states, including: to afford victims legal standing in criminal proceedings; to allow victims to present their views and concerns; to afford victims proper assistance; and to provide reparation if a responsible third party proves unable to do so.

FAILURE OF THE *AD HOC* TRIBUNALS TO INCLUDE SURVIVORS

Developments in victims' rights have, however, failed to keep pace with the re-emergence and expansion of prosecutions for violations of international human rights and humanitarian law. In 1993, by Resolution 827, the UN Security Council established the International Criminal Tribunal for the former Yugoslavia (ICTY) to prosecute crimes committed during the wars in the former Yugoslavia. Then, in 1994, by Resolution 955, the Security Council established a similar tribunal for Rwanda (ICTR).[10] These *ad hoc* tribunals marked the international community's first attempt since Nuremburg and Tokyo to prosecute individuals at the international level for the most serious international crimes.

Resolutions 827 and 955 proclaimed the "sole purpose" of the *ad hoc* tribunals to be the prosecution of individuals responsible for crimes within their jurisdiction.[11] In doing so, the drafters placed a clear emphasis on retributive justice. Despite the adoption of the Victims Declaration ten years earlier, neither the resolutions nor the *ad hoc* tribunals' statutes attempted to meaningfully include survivors of the atrocities. Being heavily influenced by the common-law adversarial model, the *ad hoc* tribunals fail to provide for the participation of survivors in any capacity other than as witnesses. This contrasts with international recognition that victims should have legal standing and should be able to present their views and concerns.

Although Resolution 827 emphasized that the proceedings would not "prejudice…the right of victims to seek, through appropriate means, compensation…,"[12] neither resolution created a means for victims to claim reparations through the tribunals themselves. Therefore, as in common-law systems, victims must initiate a separate civil action in domestic courts to claim compensation. This places an onerous burden upon the victims of international crimes and effectively frustrates their right to reparation. The drafters likely feared the immense administrative burden imposed by a reparations initiative. In September 2000, the ICTY judges considered these problems and published a report. Speaking of reparation, the judges concluded, "[I]t [was] difficult to envisage steps that could be taken within current resources limitation [sic] to expand the assistance provided…"[13]

Commentators have long criticized the *ad hoc* tribunals for failing to address the needs of survivors. The tribunals have failed to reach out and involve survivors, in part due to poor outreach and in part due to their location far from the scene of the crimes. Survivors have only participated as witnesses and have not been afforded an opportunity to claim reparations. As such, these first, modern-day attempts at international criminal justice have been limited to offering retributive justice alone. Despite recognition of the *ad hoc* tribunals' shortcomings, similar mistakes were repeated in Sierra Leone, where survivors too have been excluded from active participation in the proceedings and from requesting reparations.

ROME STATUTE HERALDS NEW DAWN FOR VICTIM PARTICIPATION

The Rome Statute marked a significant step towards the realization of victims' rights on the international stage. In contrast to the statutes of the *ad hoc* tribunals, the Rome Statute allows victims to participate in proceedings before the ICC by according them rights to be represented, to present their observations at stages of the proceedings where their interests are implicated, and to obtain reparations. The International Criminal Court's model for victim participation draws on the schemes adopted by civil law systems and the principles laid down in the Victims Declaration and the Basic Principles. The scheme responds to the widespread support of non-governmental organizations (NGOs) and certain governments for victims' rights, which proved critical during the drafting of the Rome Statute and the ICC Rules of Procedure and Evidence.

The Rome Statute permits victims to participate in proceedings by presenting their views and concerns to the ICC, but only "at stages of the proceedings determined to be appropriate by the ICC and in a manner which is not prejudicial to or inconsistent with the rights of the accused and a fair and impartial trial."¹⁴ This was a very important development, as victims' rights had only previously been recognized in principle rather than in practice at the international level. This provision for victim participation should help victims—participants and non-participants alike—to feel more involved in the process. This proves especially important due to the ICC's location in The Hague, far from the scene of the crimes.

Although a significant milestone, victims' rights remain limited before the International Criminal Court. Victims are not full parties to the proceedings and do not have the same rights as the prosecution and defense. Victims cannot, for example, participate in the Prosecutor's investigation, access the evidence gathered by the parties, or call witnesses to testify. Undoubtedly, these limitations proved necessary to garner the support of tribunal-weary donors in the face of mounting expenses and fear of the difficulties inherent in administering the participation of potentially large numbers of victims. Despite these limitations, the ICC Prosecutor has openly opposed victim participation.

The Rome Statute empowers the ICC to award reparations to victims. The ICC has great discretion as to the appropriate beneficiaries and forms of awards.[15] The judges may, if they wish, make individual or collective awards and may stipulate the appropriate form of reparation, including (but not limited to) "restitution, compensation and rehabilitation." Funds for reparations may be derived from two sources: (1) from an order for reparations from the accused; and (2) from the ICC Trust Fund for Victims.[16] Therefore, the Rome Statute provides for the establishment of a Trust Fund "for the benefit of victims of crimes within the ICC's jurisdiction, and of the families of such victims."[17]

THE IMPORTANCE OF SURVIVOR PARTICIPATION IN TRIALS FOR INTERNATIONAL CRIMES

Internationalized criminal tribunals have as their primary objectives the establishment of guilt and the punishment of perpetrators. Many commentators have criticized such tribunals for offering only a limited form of retributive justice which fails to meet the multifaceted needs of victims. Through victim (or, more broadly, survivor) participation initiatives, internationalized criminal tribunals have the potential to satisfy other needs of victims and survivors, including national reconciliation, remembrance and memorialization, and historical justice. Unfortunately, in setting objectives and budgetary plans, the Extraordinary Chambers—like other internationalized criminal tribunals—have focused upon the achievement of objectives other than meeting the needs of victims.

As societies plagued by mass atrocities often suffer from sharp divisions, appropriate justice mechanisms must be capable of promoting national reconciliation. By allowing victims to have their day in court and to claim reparations, participation initiatives promote restoration and closure on a personal level. Widespread dissemination of the powerful and evocative image of victims confronting the perpetrators of atrocities may, in turn, promote both retributive and *restorative justice*, which relates to the need to make victims whole for the abuses they suffered. This may help to heal divisions within society, allowing its members to move forward and to achieve national reconciliation.

Ideally, justice mechanisms should ensure the remembrance and memorialization of past abuses. The involvement of survivors in the justice-seeking process promotes memorialization by ensuring that their accounts are recorded and are not forgotten. In Cambodia, the Authors have found that survivors are eager that their experiences be documented for future generations. Where survivor participation schemes have the ability to offer reparations, such initiatives have the ability to heighten remembrance and ensure memorialization through the award of symbolic reparations. These may take the form of, for example, statues, commemorative banknotes, days of remembrance and genocide education.

In addition, an appropriate mechanism for the achievement of justice following mass atrocities should promote discovery and recognition of the truth. Inevitably, following mass crimes, there may be confusion about the correct historical account. Survivor participation initiatives promote the creation of a comprehensive historical record by soliciting and recording survivors' accounts. By opening involvement in criminal proceedings to a broad selection of survivors, survivor participation initiatives promote the generation of broad historical records and thus offer *historical justice*. As such, by including survivors in the proceedings, criminal trials may assume the character of "informal truth commissions."

SURVIVOR PARTICIPATION AT THE EXTRAORDINARY CHAMBERS

In accordance with the growing trend in international criminal law for the inclusion of victims and in keeping with Cambodian criminal procedure, the Extraordinary Chambers allow victims and other survivors to participate in the proceedings. Both of the Court's constituting documents—the 2003 framework agreement between the United Nations and Cambodian government (the "Framework Agreement") and the revised 2004 law establishing the Court (the "ECCC Law")—failed to provide expressly for such participation.[18] However, the Court has through its Internal Rules, practice directions and jurisprudence evolved to offer the most progressive survivor participation scheme of all the internationalized criminal tribunals. Being situated where the crimes were committed, the Court has excellent potential to offer survivors the opportunity to participate meaningfully in the proceedings.

BUILDING THE FRAMEWORK FOR SURVIVOR PARTICIPATION

From April 1975 to January 1979, the Khmers Rouges committed some of the worst human rights abuses of the 20th century. The total number of deaths during the Democratic Kampuchea period is thought to be around 1.7 million. Some scholars suggest that the number exceeded two million—almost one-third of the population. The regime's atrocities affected the whole of Cambodian society and the period's impact upon the population has been immeasurable. Despite the horrific nature of these atrocities, Cambodians have been waiting for justice for over 30 years. As described in Chapter 1, negotiations for a tribunal to try senior Khmer Rouge leaders lasted many years.

Throughout the negotiations, very little consideration was given to the survivors' place within the process. Neither the Framework Agreement nor the ECCC Law provided expressly for survivor participation or for reparations. While an argument may be made that the parties envisaged and provided for survivor participation in the ECCC Law,[19] the parties likely chose to avoid these thorny issues due to difficulties experienced in concluding an agreement. The Agreement and Law did, however, contain some indication as to the appropriate resolution of these questions. Both provide that Cambodian criminal procedure law—which allows for the participation of victims as civil parties—is to apply unless it fails to deal with a particular matter or is inconsistent with international standards.[20]

Despite the omission of provision for survivor participation or reparations in the ECCC Law or the Framework Agreement, the drafters of the Court's internal procedural rules read the Court's constituting documents in conjunction with applicable Cambodian criminal procedures to provide for survivor participation in the proceedings. The provisions on survivor participation contained in the Draft Internal Rules issued by the Rules and Procedure Committee on November 3, 2006, resembled those found in Cambodian law with several modifications appropriate for the context of mass human rights abuses. Despite some ambiguity, these draft provisions met with warm praise from civil society.[21] The draft Internal Rules were adopted, with amendments, on June 12, 2007.[22]

DEFINING THE MODES OF SURVIVOR PARTICIPATION

The drafters of the Internal Rules provided for various modes of participation for victims and other survivors. First, "any person, organisation or other source who witnessed or was a victim of such alleged crimes, or who has knowledge of such alleged crimes" may file a *complaint* with the Co-Prosecutors.[23] Second, victims of crimes within the Court's jurisdiction may apply to participate as *civil parties* in order to support the prosecution and to claim "collective and moral" reparations.[24] Third, victims and other survivors may volunteer to participate in the proceedings as *witnesses*. The ECCC's Practice Direction on Victim Participation (Practice Direction), issued in October 2007, confirmed this tri-partite participation structure.[25]

COMPLAINANTS

Complainants submit information in written form regarding crimes within the Court's jurisdiction in order to initiate or assist prosecutions. In contrast to other internationalized criminal tribunals, the Extraordinary Chambers provide a procedure for individuals, organizations and other entities to submit information directly to the Co-Prosecutors.[26] This non-exclusionary approach is most desirable; in fact, the Authors have found that perpetrators are often best placed to provide useful information (though rarely choose to do so). The Co-Prosecutors are required to decide—at their discretion—whether to initiate an investigation based on information provided or incorporate it into an ongoing investigation and to inform complainants of their decision within 60 days of submission.[27]

CIVIL PARTIES

Civil parties are victims who act as full parties to the proceedings with rights similar to those of the prosecution and defense. The Internal Rules open the possibility of civil party participation only to those survivors defined as "victims." As discussed fully below, in order to qualify as a "victim," the survivor must have suffered a "physical, material or psychological" injury and this injury must be "the direct consequence of the offence, personal and have actually come into being."[28] During the pre-trial stage, the Co-Investigating Judges are responsible for reviewing applications and recognizing civil parties; during the trial stage, the Trial Chamber has this responsibility. If recognized as a civil party, a victim is entitled to play a direct role as a full party to the proceedings and to claim collective or moral reparations.

"VOLUNTEER" WITNESSES

Witnesses provide live testimony about crimes that they suffered or witnessed. The Practice Direction provides that survivors may volunteer to become witnesses at the Extraordinary Chambers. The characterization of "being called as a witness" as a form of participation surprises the Authors. Victims' rights advocates do not consider witness testimony to be a form of participation, as courts typically have the power to coerce individuals to testify against their will. This is the case at Extraordinary Chambers. In the Authors' opinion, survivor participation should be an empowering experience and must always be voluntary. Fortunately, recent practice has shown that the Victims Unit treats all applications to become witnesses as complaints.

ESTABLISHING A MECHANISM TO FACILITATE PARTICIPATION: THE VICTIMS UNIT

In order to facilitate survivor participation, the drafters of the Internal Rules provided for the creation of a Victims Unit under the auspices of the Office of Administration. As neither the ECCC Law nor the Framework Agreement provided for such an entity, the Victims Unit was an afterthought in the establishment of the Court and is the "youngest" of the Court's organs. Although victims and survivors began to submit complaints and civil party applications in October 2007, the Unit was not established until a few months later. In the interim, the Offices of the Co-Prosecutors and the Co-Investigating Judges accepted submissions. The Unit became operational as a bare-bones venture in early 2008, following the appointment of an international Deputy Head in December 2007.

In the absence of a Court registry, the Victims Unit proves vital to ensuring the success of the survivor participation initiative. The Internal Rules task the Unit with various responsibilities, such as maintaining a list of lawyers willing to represent civil parties, assisting victims and other survivors in filing complaints or civil party applications, assisting civil parties in engaging lawyers, facilitating participation and common representation of civil parties, and assisting in victim-related outreach.[29] The amended Practice Direction expressly provides that survivors must make their submissions through the Victims Unit, rather than directly to the Co-Prosecutors or Co-Investigating Judges.[30]

The Victims Unit has suffered greatly as a result of its late creation and the halfhearted support of donors. Until early 2009, the Unit was severely understaffed and relied heavily on interns and volunteers. The Victims Unit is to have a Cambodian Head of Unit and an international Deputy Head of Unit. As of late August 2009, the international post has stood vacant for nearly nine months. Slow creation of and recruitment for posts in the Unit have severely hampered its capabilities. At the time of writing, the Unit has a growing number of Cambodian staff and is in the process of recruiting a handful of international consultants and lawyers to represent civil parties. Although the situation has improved significantly in recent months, staffing remains inadequate.

Due to its small budget and lack of staff, the Unit has struggled to fulfill its mandated tasks.[31] Recently, the Unit's primary focus has been to process complaints and civil party applications and file them with the relevant organs of the Court. With the recruitment of a number of Khmer data entry clerks, the Unit has finally begun to tackle the considerable backlog of complaints and civil party applications received since October 2007. Despite their best efforts, over 1,500 remained unfiled as of late July 2009. The Victims Unit delegates all other responsibilities— including outreach and the provision of assistance in securing legal representation—to a small number of NGOs operating in Phnom Penh, including the Documentation Center of Cambodia (DC-Cam).

THE PROCEDURE FOR PARTICIPATION

The drafters of the Internal Rules left many important questions relating to survivor participation unanswered and placed considerable discretion in the hands of those responsible for the initiative's implementation. The Rules do not, for example, describe how victims and survivors may submit complaints or apply to become civil parties. In October 2007, the Rules and Procedure Committee closed this lacuna by issuing the aforementioned Practice Direction. In addition to outlining the modalities of participation, the Practice Direction provided a "Victim Information Form" (referred to below as the "Form") for survivors to complete. Unfortunately, the Form has proven to be far too complex for almost all survivors—Cambodian and international alike—to complete.

The Victims Unit processes all Forms received and submits them with a summary to the relevant organ of the Court. As of late July 2009, the Victims Unit had received 4,072 Forms and had processed 2,493. Throughout 2008, the Unit prioritized the processing of Forms related to Case No. 001 against Kaing Guek Eav ("Duch"). As a result, Forms unrelated to that case had remained unprocessed until recently, despite having been submitted as far back as October 2007. Following the aforementioned recruitment of new Khmer data entry clerks, the Unit has now become more efficient in its processing of Forms.

Once processing is complete, the Unit forwards complaints to the Office of the Co-Prosecutors and civil party applications to the Office of the Co-Investigating Judges or Trial Chamber as appropriate. Thereafter, the Co-Prosecutors decide whether to use the information contained in the complaints and the Co-Investigating Judges or Trial Chamber Judges decide whether to admit the applications. In order for a civil party application to be admissible, the civil party applicant must be a "victim" within the meaning of the Internal Rules. This definition includes relatives of individuals who died as a result of crimes.[32] If recognized as a civil party by the Judges, the applicant's Form is placed on the case file and he or she may exercise his or her participation rights.

Survivors have the right to request protective measures if their participation "is liable to place their life or health or that of their family members or close relatives in serious danger" (Internal Rule 29). Most commonly, successful requests for protective measures would result in non-disclosure of the survivor's identity. Survivors request such measures in a rider to the Form. The Witnesses & Experts Support Unit (WESU) conducts risk assessments of requests and forwards their assessments to the relevant judicial organ for a decision. In order for their requests to be successful, survivors must articulate a concrete reason for their fear (e.g., past threats), rather than a general or baseless fear.

IDENTIFYING OBSTACLES TO PARTICIPATION

While the Internal Rules make provision for an ambitious survivor participation scheme, the ability of victims and survivors to participate is, as a practical matter, limited by the dedication of donors and other organs of the Court to the scheme's implementation. The support of donor nations for survivor participation has been decidedly lackluster. This is perhaps unsurprising for three reasons. First, the Court's budget is already far greater than originally anticipated. Second, the Court's constituting documents did not expressly provide for the initiative, which was only added as an afterthought by the Internal Rules' drafters. Third, allegations of corruption on the Cambodian side have likely discouraged donors from further donations.

The Victims Unit has suffered greatly as a result of weak donor support. Due to inadequate funding, the Victims Unit has delegated responsibility for one of its core mandated tasks— outreach—almost entirely to NGOs operating in Phnom Penh. Crippled by a tiny budget throughout 2008 and into the first half of 2009, the Victims Unit has been unable to conduct outreach to inform survivors of their participation rights. In fact, the Unit has not even produced materials explaining the complex process and the cumbersome Victim Information Form. Promisingly, following receipt of a USD $1.9 million donation from the Deutsche Gesellschaft für Technische Zusammenarbeit (GTZ) in November 2008, the Unit is recruiting numerous outreach personnel and expects to hold a small number of victims' meetings.

Despite its superior resources and critical role, the Office of the Co-Prosecutors (OCP) has done little to ensure the success of the initiative. Although required to respond to complaints within 60 days of submission, the Co-Prosecutors made no attempt until recently to comply with this obligation. This failure has caused many survivors to lose faith in the process. For instance, in January 2008, a Cham Muslim religious leader told staff from the Documentation Center of Cambodia that he felt "uneasy" about not having heard from the Court for four months following submission. This is unfortunate, as survivors would attach great meaning to any official response. In mid 2009, couriers began delivering notifications to complainants on behalf of the OCP.

Finally, the survivor participation initiative faces obstacles particular to the Cambodian context. Most survivors have poor access to information and are, therefore, unaware of the initiative. Even if survivors do learn of the initiative, most lack the means to contact the Victims Unit and the requisite literacy and education to complete the complex Victim

Information Form. Even if offered the assistance required to complete and submit the Form, some survivors fear for their own safety. As survivors lack a concrete reason for their fear, WESU typically does not recommend grants of protective measures. The Authors are aware of only one grant of protective measures made to civil parties at the pre-trial stage and of none made to complainants.[33] At the trial stage, the Trial Chamber denied the requests of five civil parties who had requested protective measures, finding that they had "furnish[ed] insufficient particulars regarding the specific circumstances warranting such orders."

INTERMEDIARY ORGANIZATIONS CRITICAL IN ASSISTING SURVIVORS TO OVERCOME OBSTACLES

In the Cambodian context, effective outreach proves critical to the success of the survivor participation initiative due to poor access to information, poor education and illiteracy. As noted above, the Authors have found that the Victim Information Form is far too complex for the average Cambodian to complete without assistance. As such, survivors require direct assistance in order to exercise their participation rights. As the Victims Unit lacks the funding to conduct such resource-intensive outreach, responsibility for outreach has fallen on the shoulders of Cambodian civil society. In late 2007, a small number of NGOs operating in Phnom Penh assumed the role of intermediary organizations.

The Unit's reliance on local NGOs is necessary and understandable given these groups' established relationships with survivors. Some organizations, such as DC-Cam, have worked with survivors for many years. Since late 2007, several intermediary organizations—primarily DC-Cam, the Cambodian Human Rights and Development Association (ADHOC), the Center for Social Development, and the Khmer Institute for Democracy—have worked tirelessly to inform survivors throughout Cambodia (and, to a lesser extent, overseas) of their participation rights and to assist them in completing and submitting the Form. As mentioned above, as of late July 2009, the Victims Unit had received 4,072 Forms, almost exclusively with intermediary assistance. However, by delegating outreach to intermediary organizations, the Court misses an important opportunity to win support for its work.

Unfortunately, the Unit's reliance on intermediary organizations has been so extensive as to be overwhelming. In addition to victims' rights education, the Unit has relied on intermediary organizations to assume a number of its responsibilities, including the delivery of official notifications and the provision of assistance in drafting requests for protective measures and in selecting lawyers. The Court does not avoid donor fatigue by delegating its responsibilities to intermediary organizations, as international donors ultimately consider donations to intermediary organizations tantamount to donations to the Court.[34]

(On this spread) Terith Chy, leader of DC-Cam's Victim Participation Project helps victims fill out ECCC complaint forms to report atrocities committed during the Khmer Rouge regime.
Source: Documentation Center of Cambodia Archives

ON TRIAL: THE KHMER ROUGE ACCOUNTABILITY PROCESS

Pichet Men of the Victim Participation Project (far right), assisting villagers fill out complaint forms.
Source: Documentation Center of Cambodia Archives

Terith Chy describing to villagers the process of filing ECCC complaint forms.
Source: Documentation Center of Cambodia Archives

Sokvisal Kimsroy of the Victim Participation Project helping an elderly man fill out a complaint form.
Source: Documentation Center of Cambodia Archives

ON TRIAL: THE KHMER ROUGE ACCOUNTABILITY PROCESS

(Top) Terith Chy describing to villagers the ECCC process of filing complaint forms. (Bottom) Sarah Thomas, a legal associate of DC-Cam, passing out ECCC complaint forms in Pursat province. *Source: Documentation Center of Cambodia Archives*

The various intermediary organizations have adopted very different outreach strategies and policies on ongoing assistance. DC-Cam has adopted a policy of reaching out primarily to those survivors who signed *Renakse* Petitions in the early 1980s[35] and collects primarily complaints. ADHOC has adopted a policy of reaching out primarily to victims of situations under investigation and collects civil party applications only. The Center for Social Development, on the other hand, focuses upon the creation of an "orphan class" of civil parties and collects primarily civil party applications from survivors orphaned by the regime. All intermediary organizations have expressed concern at the prospect of having to provide ongoing assistance, particularly delivering notifications and arranging update meetings.

CIVIL PARTIES AT THE EXTRAORDINARY CHAMBERS: A FAILURE OR A MODEL FOR SURVIVOR PARTICIPATION?

Undoubtedly, the civil party action has been the most visible mode of survivor participation before the Extraordinary Chambers as civil parties participate directly in the proceedings as full parties, sitting in the courtroom (if space permits) and being permitted (on occasion) to address the Chamber. While other modes of participation prove just as important, the civil party action deserves special consideration because of its complexity and the implications—both positive and negative—of efforts to limit or eliminate it ahead of future trials before the Extraordinary Chambers. Furthermore, as these are the first internationalized proceedings including victims as full parties, the continued use or elimination of the civil party action may have ramifications for the conduct of future internationalized criminal trials.

BECOMING A CIVIL PARTY

Under the current procedure as described above and in operation as of late August 2009, victims apply to become civil parties by submitting applications to the Victims Unit. In contrast to the Criminal Procedure Code,[36] the Internal Rules require victims to submit their applications at least 10 days prior to the Initial Hearing.[37] Although the President of the Trial Chamber has the power to consider applications received after the deadline, he has indicated that he intends only to exercise this power where "exceptional circumstances" have prevented the applicant from filing before the deadline. In light of the Court's inadequate outreach capabilities, the Authors disapprove of the Trial Chamber's inflexibility. Its formalistic approach has, unfortunately, already resulted in the denial of civil party status to one victim, a child survivor of S-21, who missed the deadline by just two days.[38]

After processing, the Victims Unit forwards all timely applications to the relevant organ of the Court. During the pre-trial stage, the Co-Investigating Judges receive applications and decide on their admissibility with the possibility of appeal to the Pre-Trial Chamber. Following completion of the pre-trial stage and pending the commencement of trial, the Trial Chamber receives applications. Recent amendments to the Internal Rules clarify that applicants may appeal orders rejecting their applications to the Supreme Court Chamber.[39]

Only those survivors who qualify as "victims" within the meaning of the Internal Rules are eligible to become civil parties. This narrow definition unfortunately excludes many survivors who legitimately consider themselves victims. In order to be eligible, a survivor must have suffered "physical, material or psychological" injuries and these injuries must have been "the direct consequence of the offence, personal and have actually come into being."[40] The Practice Direction clarifies that "[p]sychological injury may include the death of a kin who were the victim of such crimes" and provides that any "victims" may become civil parties, regardless of current residence or nationality.[41] In fact, DC-Cam has assisted a number of non-Khmer victims to become civil parties.

The admissibility criteria laid down in the Practice Direction lack clarity. First, the Practice Direction does not clarify whether members of the extended family may be considered "kin."[42] In the Authors' opinion, an expansive interpretation is appropriate, as families in Cambodia tend to have an extended (rather than nuclear) arrangement. Second, and most importantly, the Practice Direction fails to state whether applicants must introduce evidence of their injury (e.g., confessions, execution orders or medical records). Such a requirement would set an impossibly high standard for most applicants, as the Khmers Rouges did not keep such records (other than at S-21). In the Authors' opinion, the Judges should issue clearer directions to avoid disappointment and disillusionment with the process.

Problematically, in Case No. 001, neither the Co-Investigating Judges nor the Trial Chamber judges have provided guidance on these admissibility criteria. Nor have they proactively applied these criteria to applicants. Instead, at the Initial Hearing, the Trial Chamber indicated that it had applied "a *prima facie* standard of proof for the existence of criteria" and emphasized that it had not conducted "an examination on substance or merit."[43] The Judges ultimately recognized all applicants except one as civil parties. The Chamber indicated, however, that it intended to "examine each of the applications to be perfectly certain that the alleged harm did in fact occur" during the substantive proceedings.[44] This two-step approach is very problematic, as it may result in the participation of ineligible victims in part of the proceedings and their later disqualification. Recognition of their ineligibility at a late stage in the proceedings may cause prejudice to the accused person and considerable disappointment to the disqualified victim.[45]

THE RIGHT TO PARTICIPATE IN PROCEEDINGS

The Internal Rules bestow upon civil parties an extensive list of procedural rights, almost—though not quite—identical to those of the charged person or the accused. Key rights include: to be represented by a lawyer;[46] to request investigative action by the Co-Investigating Judges;[47] to summon witnesses;[48] to question the accused and witnesses;[49] to make closing and rebuttal statements;[50] and to have a decision made on their reparations claims.[51] Civil parties may testify during the proceedings and are not required to take an oath. These rights largely accord with Cambodian criminal procedure.[52] In contrast to the Criminal Procedure Code,[53] however, civil parties do not have the right to appeal the Trial Chamber's judgment on the merits to the Supreme Court Chamber.[54]

Inevitably, there has been considerable debate as to the appropriate application of these rights in practice. Civil parties have, of course, argued for an expansive interpretation of their rights, while the defense has argued for a restrictive interpretation. In stark contrast to the ICC Prosecutor, the Co-Prosecutors have largely supported civil parties' calls for robust civil party participation in the proceedings. Particularly at the start of the proceedings, the Judges tended to adopt expansive interpretations favorable to civil parties unless textual interpretation required otherwise. For example, on March 20, 2008, the Pre-Trial Chamber interpreted civil parties' right to participate in the "proceedings" under Internal Rule 21(3)(a) to pertain from the investigative stage onwards. As the proceedings have developed, however, the Judges have adopted increasingly restrictive interpretations.

The Judges have shown themselves to be less than favorably disposed to civil party participation where it threatens the expediency of the proceedings. The Pre-Trial Chamber has, for example, taken a dim view of civil parties addressing the bench directly. In an early pre-trial hearing, a civil party sought to do so. The Chamber exploited a textual ambiguity within the Internal Rules to deny her request, finding that she must address the bench through her lawyer. When she dismissed her lawyer, the Chamber denied her request once again.[55] Following a submission by several genuinely unrepresented civil parties, the Chamber was forced to issue directions permitting unrepresented civil parties to submit requests to address the bench ten days before a pre-trial hearing.[56]

The Judges have also shown themselves willing to limit civil party participation where, in their opinion, it threatens the fairness of the proceedings. In the Initial Hearing in Case No. 001, held on February 17, 2009, lawyers for one group of civil parties announced their intention to call an expert witness to provide an opinion on sentencing. Defense counsel for the accused strongly opposed this, on the grounds that, in the French system, civil parties may not make statements pertaining to sentencing and that it would be unfair to the accused. Ultimately, the Trial Chamber rejected the request. On June 9, 2009, lawyers for two groups of civil parties filed a joint request that the Trial Chamber announce whether it intends to hear civil parties' submissions on sentencing. On August 27, 2009, the Trial Chamber ruled definitively that civil parties may not make submissions related to sentencing. Evidencing their disdain for civil party submissions in the latter stages of the trial, the Chamber also ruled that civil parties may not question character witnesses, effectively ending substantive participation by civil parties until closing arguments.[57]

THE RIGHT TO REQUEST REPARATIONS

Neither the Framework Agreement nor the ECCC Law provides victims with a right to claim reparations before the Extraordinary Chambers. In fact, while Article 39 of the ECCC Law permits the Trial Chamber to "order.the confiscation of personal property, money, and real property acquired unlawfully or by criminal conduct," it appears to simultaneously preclude the award of reparations to victims by providing that "[t]he confiscated property shall be returned to the State." Despite this, and in accordance with French-inspired Cambodian law,[58] the drafters of the Internal Rules describe one of the purposes of the civil party action to be to seek reparations.[59]

Internal Rule 23(1) provides that the Chambers may award "collective and moral reparation" and that such awards are to "be borne by convicted persons." The Authors have found that survivors respond very positively to this provision, considering it appropriate that convicted persons should be required to make reparation. Certain survivors do, however, consider it inappropriate or unnecessary, as they believe that no reparation can be made for their suffering. Buon Phon, 49, from Kampong Thom explained, "I don't care about reparation; what is crucial to me is that I can lodge my complaint against the Khmer Rouge [leaders]…I hope the United Nations can help bring justice for the Cambodian people."

Despite overwhelming survivor support, it remains to be seen whether the reparations referred to in the Internal Rules may be realized. The provision in Internal Rule 23(11) that awards "shall…be borne by convicted persons" is subject to Article 39 of the ECCC Law, which provides that any property confiscated from convicted persons is to be returned to the State. Even if the government chooses to waive this right, it is unlikely that confiscated property would be adequate to fund meaningful awards, as senior leaders have likely anticipated prosecution and hidden or transferred their assets accordingly. As convicted persons may have assets in foreign countries, seizure may depend upon the cooperation of third parties. In spite of these obvious difficulties, the Internal Rules fail to identify alternative sources.

The Internal Rules appear to limit the right to request reparations to civil parties only. In light of the immense number of victims, the Authors consider it inappropriate that only those victims recognized by the Court should benefit. Due to the Court's poor outreach efforts, most victims have not been afforded an opportunity to become civil parties. Certain civil parties—in particular, survivors of S-21—have, however, argued that their suffering proved particularly great and have expressed their belief that they in particular should receive reparations. It is thought that Court officials trained in the French system support the limitation of reparations to civil parties only, as this practice reflects French (and, thus, Cambodian) practice.

POTENTIAL FORMS OF REPARATION AVAILABLE TO CIVIL PARTIES

The Internal Rules do not provide for the same right to individual, financial compensation as found in domestic law. Instead, the Internal Rules modify the provision for reparations to fit the context of mass human rights violations. As such, only "collective and moral reparations" may be awarded to civil parties.[60] Given these statutory limitations, the difficulties inherent in administering any reparations initiative, and the Court's budgetary restraints, it is clear that the Judges will not award individual, financial compensation to victims. In light of the widespread and horrific nature of the atrocities perpetrated by the Khmers Rouges, collective and moral reparations prove entirely appropriate.

It remains to be seen what falls within the parameters of "collective and moral." Given that Internal Rule 100(1) permits the Judges to deliver their judgment on reparations *after* their judgment on the merits, the Judges may choose to postpone this difficult decision until resources are in place to fund awards. Clearly, "collective" reparation refers to awards made to a group (such as, for example, a village, an organization or perhaps all victims). The Internal Rules specifically suggest that awards may fund non-profit activities benefiting victims.[61] The appropriate interpretation of "moral" is considerably less clear. "Moral" reparation may refer to awards of a symbolic, non-monetary nature (such as a statue or publication of the judgment in the media).

There is a danger that public support for the Court as a whole may be undermined if reparations are promised and later denied. The Authors have found clear, unequivocal explanation of the unavailability of individual, financial compensation to be crucial in conducting outreach. Given that most Cambodians are very poor,[62] most survivors' hopes are raised at the very mention of reparations (in Khmer, *somnong* ("compensation")). With clear explanation of the obstacles to individual financial compensation, survivors soon appreciate the difficulties and the vast majority express satisfaction knowing that, at least, certain Khmer Rouge leaders will be brought before a court and have any discovered stolen assets confiscated if convicted.

The Authors have found that most survivors wish to play a role in dictating the reparations to be made by the Court. Most survivors completing the Victim Information Form choose to provide suggestions for potential reparations. With their permission, DC-Cam has compiled statistics on survivors' desired forms of reparations. These statistics demonstrate that survivors commonly request schools, roads, hospitals, wells, bridges and housing. In light of the poverty plaguing most survivors, their focus on developmental needs is unsurprising. Many do, however, suggest victim-centered forms of reparations, including ceremony halls, memorials and statues, genocide education, mental health clinics, and the construction of temples, pagodas and stupas.

LEGAL REPRESENTATIVES AS GATEWAYS TO THE PROCEEDINGS

Civil parties have a right to legal representation before the Extraordinary Chambers under Internal Rule 23(7). Legal representatives play an extremely important role in assisting victims to realize their right to participate by explaining the Court's procedures, advising them of their rights, and acting as their advocates. Without legal representatives, civil parties would simply be unable to access the proceedings. The Authors have found that, in practice, civil parties rely entirely upon their lawyers to marshal their participation, as most lack the ability, means and/or time to follow the proceedings closely. Without legal representation, the vast majority of civil parties would not be able to participate meaningfully in the proceedings.[63]

Legal representation of civil parties before the Extraordinary Chambers is, however, a right and not a requirement. Internal Rule 23(7) does not require civil parties to appoint a lawyer. The drafters clearly assumed that civil parties would necessarily engage legal representatives, however, as Internal Rule 86 provides that only "the Co-Prosecutors and the lawyers for the other parties shall have the right to examine and obtain copies of the case file…" and not civil parties. The Authors understand that the Judges oppose self-representation by civil parties and have toyed with the idea of amending the Internal Rules to require legal representation. Following a barrage of criticism by civil society,[64] however, the Judges did not adopt the proposed amendment.

Unfortunately, given that the right to legal representation is not a requirement, the drafters of the Internal Rules did not provide for the establishment of an ECCC-funded legal aid scheme (as exists for charged persons) to fund civil parties' legal representation. As most civil parties are indigent and uneducated, the Authors consider it entirely inappropriate that the Court place responsibility for securing legal representation upon their shoulders. Fortunately, intermediary organizations have assisted civil parties to secure *pro bono* legal representation. Despite their best efforts, *pro bono* representatives inevitably cannot match the superior resources of the prosecution and defense and the quality of representation suffers as a result.

Given the large number of civil parties, the effective management of legal representation is critical. Ineffectively managed civil party submissions—particularly, oral—undermine the expeditious conduct of the proceedings. Ideally, civil parties should group together (preferably, in as few groups as possible) and choose common legal representatives.[65] Where civil parties are unable or unwilling to do so and "[t]he interests of Justice so require," the Judges may have the power to forcibly group civil parties and designate a common legal representative.[66] In Case No. 002—the case against Nuon Chea and possibly others—thousands of civil parties may be recognized. Thus, if some form of civil party participation is retained in future trials, the designation of a single pair of representatives (Cambodian and international) may prove critical in ensuring the success of the proceedings.

CIVIL PARTY PARTICIPATION IN THE PROCEEDINGS—FROM PRINCIPLE TO PRACTICE

Due to the late inception of the survivor participation initiative, civil parties did not have the opportunity to participate in the earliest pre-trial hearings. Civil parties first participated in the proceedings on February 4, 2008, when a small number of civil parties and their lawyers participated in a pre-trial hearing on an appeal on the pre-trial detention of Nuon Chea in Case No. 002. In a statement, the Victims Unit rightly described this as an "[h]istoric achievement in international criminal law."[67] Since then, civil parties have participated in all proceedings before the Court. Twenty-two civil parties have testified before the Trial Chamber in Case No. 001, giving moving testimony of their experiences.

Ninety-three victims have been recognized as civil parties in the proceedings before the Trial Chamber in Case No. 001.[68] These civil parties have formed into four groups based upon their affiliations with intermediary organizations. For example, the largest civil party group—Civil Party Group 1—consists of thirty-eight civil parties assisted exclusively by DC-Cam. The reasoning behind intermediary-based grouping has been entirely pragmatic: intermediary organizations are better placed to provide ongoing assistance to civil parties if they all share legal representation. If civil party participation is retained in Case No. 002, grouping based upon personal interests or characteristics—e.g., ethnicity or religion—is more far likely due to the wide variety of crimes under investigation and the differing interests of victims. In Case No. 001, however, civil parties had very similar interests regardless of ethnicity, religion or other factors, as they were all victims of the same criminal situation: S-21.

Each of the four groups is represented by a team of *pro bono* lawyers. The teams possess varying levels of experience in national—and, in some cases, international—systems. Given their very different backgrounds and varying levels of fluency in the Court's official

(Top) Hun Sen Ang Snoul High School students at the Tuol Sleng Genocide Museum, December 2006. (Bottom) Hun Sen Ang Snoul High School students with ECCC Public Affairs Officer Reach Sambath behind the ECCC courtroom, December 2006. Photos by Dacil Q. Keo. *Source: Documentation Center of Cambodia Archives*

languages, the quality of representation has varied considerably. Unsurprisingly given their scarce resources, civil party lawyers have reportedly often been unprepared and have been chastised by the Judges on more than one occasion. Several of the teams have failed to adequately prep their clients before taking the stand.[69] Unfortunately, this has aggravated the difficulties victims already face in taking the stand, such as their advanced age, trauma and poor recollection.[70] Civil parties have appeared uncomfortable and have given confused and often inconsistent testimony. Worryingly, this will likely have a negative impact upon the weight that the Judges accord to their testimonies.

As of late August 2009, twenty-two civil parties—both survivors of S-21 and relatives of S-21 prisoners who were killed—have testified against Duch. Civil party lawyers have sought to have their clients corroborate and elaborate upon facts and practices at S-21 that have emerged during the course of the proceedings. Worryingly, civil party lawyers' submissions have been extremely repetitive and often mirrored those of the Co-Prosecutors. In addition, international commentators have noted that the Trial Chamber initially appeared ill prepared to treat civil parties with the required sensitivity. It is reported that the Chamber's President, Nil Nonn, at first treated civil parties rather insensitively, ordering traumatized victims to compose themselves when they broke down on the stand and refusing them breaks.[71] Commendably, the Chamber appears to have been sensitive to these criticisms and has treated witnesses and civil parties more sympathetically over the course of the trial.

The Court's failure to apply the admissibility criteria proactively to civil party applicants has resulted in a very undesirable situation: the consideration of defense challenges to the eligibility of twenty-four recognized civil parties at the very end of the *Duch* trial. Consideration of these challenges is ongoing as of late August 2009. Despite indicating at the Initial Hearing that they would consider challenges to the admission of civil parties during the substantive proceedings, only on August 17, 2009—one month before conclusion of the substantive proceedings—did the Judges enquire as to whether the defense intended to raise such challenges.[72] By failing to require that such challenges be made at an earlier juncture, the Trial Chamber has permitted the participation of possibly ineligible victims. In addition to prejudice caused to the accused, the disqualification of recognized civil parties at this late stage in the proceedings is likely to cause significant anguish to the individuals concerned.

REFLECTIONS ON THE SURVIVOR PARTICIPATION INITIATIVE

SURVIVOR PARTICIPATION—A (QUALIFIED) SUCCESS STORY

In establishing the Extraordinary Chambers and trying senior Khmer Rouge leaders, the

ON TRIAL: THE KHMER ROUGE ACCOUNTABILITY PROCESS

(Top) Farina So, leader of DC-Cam's Cham Muslim Oral History Project, discuss an essay writing contest with Cham high school students, March 2007. (Bottom) Hun Sen Ang Snoul High School students copy down the "Security of Regulations" display board at the Toul Sleng Genocide Museum. They would be tested on their visit to the museum later in class. December 2006.
Photos by Dacil Q. Keo. *Source: Documentation Center of Cambodia Archives*

Cambodian government and the United Nations sought to deliver to survivors of the regime a measure of justice and closure on this difficult chapter. By permitting survivors to play a role in the justice-seeking process, the survivor participation initiative has maximized the Court's ability to do so. Though the initiative has unfortunately reached only a small fraction of survivors to date, many survivors offered the opportunity to participate have jumped at the chance and have found it to be an empowering experience. For example, in expressing his appreciation, Mr. Een Ann, 56, a survivor and complainant from Kampong Thom, told the Authors that he was "delighted to pursue justice for all the Khmer people."

Survivors particularly appreciate the opportunity to speak of their experiences under the regime. The Authors have observed that meetings with DC-Cam staff have provided many survivors with their first organized forum in which to speak of their experiences under the regime and to have their tales of suffering recognized and recorded. It matters little to them that their information may not be used by the Co-Prosecutors. Many survivors express a sense of relief after completing Victim Information Forms. For example, the Authors overheard one survivor tell his neighbor, "I am relieved now that I've finally spoken about my miserable experiences under the regime." Another victim and civil party told one of the Authors that the Court has already largely lived up to his expectations. "[The Court] has fulfilled 70 percent of my expectations of it," said Mr. Neth Phally, 52, from Kampong Cham, after observing a few days of trial.[73]

Of course, not all survivors choose to participate. Some survivors consider themselves to be too uneducated or too old to get involved with the Court's work. On occasion, the Authors have encountered survivors who chose not to participate due to mistrust of the Cambodian government's involvement. A survivor from Kampong Thom, for example, explained that he did not want to participate because "the tribunal seems to be delayed all the time and is allowing the leaders to die peacefully before they can be brought to justice..." He further explained that he believed that the Court "could not deliver a fair judgment because, if it were to do so, it would implicate incumbent government officials." Nevertheless, the Authors have found that even skeptical survivors are very interested in learning about the Extraordinary Chambers and opportunities for survivors to participate.

The Authors consider the survivor participation initiative's greatest achievement to have been the opportunity it has provided to survivors in villages across Cambodia to speak of their suffering under the regime, often for the first time. This success is, however, qualified by the initiative's ability to date to reach out to only a very small portion of Cambodia's population of 14 million. Furthermore, the delays in the commencement of the trials have denied some survivors the opportunity to see the fruits of their participation. To provide an example, Mrs.

Suos Sarin—the sister of an executed S-21 prisoner and a DC-Cam-assisted civil party—sadly died on December 27, 2008, less than two months before the Initial Hearing. It had been her greatest wish to see her sister's murderer convicted before she died.[74]

EFFECT OF SURVIVOR PARTICIPATION UPON THE PROCEEDINGS

While considering its greatest achievement to date to have been the creation of a forum for survivors at the grassroots level, the Authors believe that the survivor participation initiative has made valuable, if limited, contributions to the trial proceedings. A leading trial monitor has noted that the moving oral testimonies of civil parties in Case No. 001 "[properly injected] the passion and anger of [victims] into the trial."[75] In fact, the same monitor described the testimony of Mr. Chum Mey—a civil party and S-21 survivor—as "the most powerful day of trial to date." Observers at the proceedings have been particularly interested in observing survivors' oral testimony. In the Authors' opinion, the participation of survivors has the ability to pique the interest of the public in the proceedings, which can otherwise become dry and technical, and thus maximize the social impact of the trials.

Unfortunately, civil parties' contributions to the proceedings have largely been overshadowed by difficulties engendered by the implementation of their participation. One criticism of the civil party process is that it is inefficient. Due to the Court's awkward mix of inquisitorial and adversarial elements, civil parties have been afforded a far greater role than normal in proceedings in civil-law systems. Until recently, the Judges had permitted civil parties to make oral and written submissions on almost all matters. In the Authors' opinion, its ambitious incorporation into the proceedings has complicated the proceedings and undermined their expeditious conduct to some extent.

Challenges by the defense to the eligibility of victims recognized as civil parties during the course of the trial proceedings have also undermined the efficiency of the proceedings. If civil party participation is retained, this would likely be cause for even greater concern in Case No. 002 due to the far larger number of applicants expected. Currently, there are nearly 2,000 civil party applicants, and at least 2,500 are anticipated. At an August 21, 2009 meeting with NGOs to discuss the Trial Chamber's concerns about civil party participation in future trials, the Austrian Reserve Trial Judge, Ms. Claudia Fenz, estimated that vetting this number of applications would take a dedicated legal officer one year and that judicial consideration of defense challenges to 1,000 such applications would take eight months.[76]

A third set of concerns relates to fairness. Defense teams have asserted repeatedly that civil party participation endangers the equality of arms among the parties and have warned that this may be a subject of future appeal. This principle requires that no party be placed at a

(Top) At DC-Cam, UN Co-Investigating Judge Marcel Lemonde meets with victims who have filed complaints regarding Khmer Rouge atrocities to the ECCC. (Bottom) At DC-Cam, Cambodian Co-Investigating Judge You Bunleng meets with victims who have filed complaints regarding Khmer Rouge atrocities to the ECCC. *Source: Documentation Center of Cambodia Archives*

ON TRIAL: THE KHMER ROUGE ACCOUNTABILITY PROCESS

(Top) Smoat Master Prom Uth and his student Srey Peou at Choeung Ek, February 2007. (Bottom) Hun Sen Ang Snoul High School student taking a picture at the Tuol Sleng Genocide Museum, December 2006. Photos by Dacil Q. Keo.
Source: Documentation Center of Cambodia Archives

ON TRIAL: THE KHMER ROUGE ACCOUNTABILITY PROCESS

(Top) Farina So, leader of the Cham Muslim Oral History Project, interviewing a survivor at the Tuol Sleng Genocide Museum. (Bottom) Youk Chhang with Cham leaders from Kampong Chhang province. Photos by Dacil Q. Keo.
Source: Documentation Center of Cambodia Archives

The DC-Cam exhibition entitled "Gunnar Bergstrom in the Living Hell" in a village in Kampong Cham province, 2008. Bergstrom was part of a delegation from the communist Sweden-Kampuchea Friendship Association that visited Democratic Kampuchea in 1978 for a 14-day guided tour, which included lunch with Pol Pot and Ieng Sary. At the time, Bergstrom supported the revolution in Democratic Kampuchea, despite having some reservations. In 2008, he returned to Cambodia with a photo exhibition to apologize for what he calls his part in the "propaganda machine for murder." *Source: Documentation Center of Cambodia Archives*

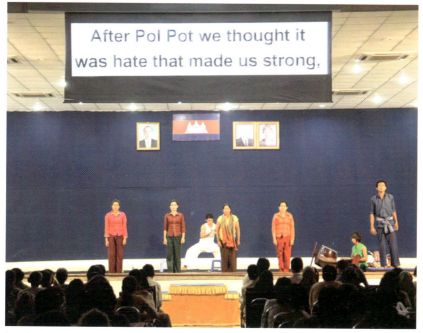

Scene from the play, Breaking the Silence. *Source: Documentation Center of Cambodia Archives*

Breaking the Silence, directed by Annemarie Prins and produced by Amrita Performing Arts. This play carefully explores the psyches of seven survivors of the Khmer Rouge regime. Local teachers from the Royal University of Fine Arts dramatize the emotions of both victims and perpetrators through modern dance and traditional Cambodian music. The theatrical expressions of suffering, anger, and confusion on stage resonate well with audience members who are all survivors of the regime. The honest interpretations contained in the play have even prompted past audiences to informally name the play "stories from Pol Pot's time." In many ways, the actors are vicariously emoting for survivors who have for too long kept silent about their pain and anguish. The onstage display of distressed sentiments and verbalized heartache also indicates to audiences that it okay to have such thoughts and feelings and make them known. "Breaking the Silence" is thus able to tap into survivors' emotions from the Khmer Rouge era, making them more at ease- and at times even eager, to reflect upon their tragic stories and share their opinions. Accordingly, DC-Cam has used the play as part of its outreach effort to promote community dialogue and healing. After each play, village forums are held. These forums offer a venue for survivors who cannot attend the ECCC hearings in Phnom Penh to communicate their thoughts and concerns about the justice process and tribunal developments right in their own neighborhood. Having such localized discussions take place across Cambodia is a vital step towards national healing.
Source: Documentation Center of Cambodia Archives

substantial disadvantage vis-à-vis another with respect to its ability to present its case. Defense teams have labeled the prosecution and civil parties collectively as the "super-prosecution."[77] On March 6, 2008, defense counsel for Ieng Sary called upon the Pre-Trial Chamber to "scrupulously...uphold" the equality of arms, alleging that civil party participation enabled the Co-Prosecutors to "gain more than twice the amount of time allocated to the Defence." Visually, the Authors agree that the sight of five legal teams facing off against the defense in Case No. 001 has been shocking and lends support to the argument for a single pair of civil party representatives.

Finally, there is a danger that civil party participation may undermine the presumption of innocence guaranteed to accused persons by Internal Rule 21(1)(d). Indeed, one of the most basic principles of criminal law is that an accused person must be presumed innocent until proven guilty by the prosecution. In making their submissions, victims may appeal to emotion by recounting their harrowing experiences. During the pre-trial hearing on February 8, 2008, for example, a civil party stated: "If Nuon Chea claimed he was not responsible, then who was for the loss of my parents and other victims' loved ones?" Such emotional arguments may compel agreement. However, the danger of such emotional arguments influencing the outcome of trials is mitigated to a great extent by the use of professional judges.

JUDICIAL *LAISSEZ-FAIRE* AND THE FUTURE OF CIVIL PARTY PARTICIPATION

Although the survivor participation initiative has enjoyed the support of survivors, NGOs and even the Co-Prosecutors, the Judges have taken an exceedingly hands-off approach at most stages of the proceedings. The Judges—even those schooled in the French legal tradition—have largely declined to attempt meaningful management of civil party participation. In the Authors' opinion, many of the problems identified in this Chapter could easily have been avoided through timely and robust judicial intervention. These problems include the existence of numerous civil party groups, ineffective though well-intentioned representation by *pro bono* lawyers, and the participation of possibly ineligible civil parties. Unfortunately, the Judges made no such intervention, allowing the process to evolve largely as intermediary organizations and civil party lawyers have seen fit.

The ramifications of this poor judicial management have quickly become apparent. Clearly, the expediency of the proceedings in Case No. 001 has been compromised by the participation of multiple civil party groups and their representation by unfunded and/or inexperienced lawyers. Of even greater concern to the Judges have been vigorous defense challenges to the alleged imprisonment of a number of civil parties and/or their relatives.[78] As described above, on August 17, 2009, the defense announced its intention to challenge the recognition of twenty-four of the ninety-three civil parties. If it is recognized at this late stage in the proceedings that ineligible applicants have participated, the Judges' failure to review each applicant individually may give rise to defense arguments that prejudice has resulted to the accused person, particularly if ineligible applicants have testified.

These difficulties have caused the Judges to conclude that civil party participation in Case No. 001 "has failed to achieve the core goals of victim participation before the ECCC...."[79] Unfortunately, rather than seeking to remedy the problems in the existing model, the Judges issued a statement in August 2009 informing intermediary organizations and other stakeholders that they are considering alternatives to civil party participation. Recent discussions by the Judges have emphasized that, while "[v]ictim participation remains fundamental to the success of the ECCC," civil party participation "is not the only form of Victim Participation."[80] In advance of the September 2009 plenary, it appears clear that the Judges are poised to significantly restrict or, more likely, eliminate civil party participation.

As of late August 2009, the future of survivor participation before the Extraordinary Chambers remains uncertain. While the complaint procedure will likely remain largely unmodified, dramatic changes are expected to civil party participation at the next plenary. Commendably, the Authors understand that the Judges are considering alternative models for representation of victims' interests in the proceedings. The foremost proposal appears to be the creation of a so-called "Victims' Advocate." It appears that the Victims' Advocate would not have individual clients and would instead represent the collective interests of victims. He or she would be able to call representative victims to speak of their suffering. In relation to this proposal, Youk Chhang, Director of the Documentation Center of Cambodia, has recommended that the input of existing civil parties and applicants should be considered in the selection of such representative victims.[81]

The Authors do not dispute that the challenges to civil party participation in Case No. 002 are formidable and far greater than exist in Case No. 001. As noted above, several thousand civil party applications are expected to be submitted before the start of Case No. 002 and it is highly unlikely that victims possess evidence of their suffering. The Authors believe that these difficulties may, however, be overcome with careful planning and put forward a number of proposals below. The Authors strongly discourage the Judges from completely eliminating the involvement of victims in trial proceedings before making a meaningful attempt to reform the existing model. Such drastic reforms would signal the failure of the Court's survivor participation initiative and would have significant ramifications for the individual victims concerned and for survivor participation in future internationalized criminal tribunals.

RECOMMENDATIONS TO ENSURE THE SUCCESS OF THE SURVIVOR PARTICIPATION INITIATIVE

The success of the survivor participation initiative is crucial to the legacy of the Extraordinary Chambers and the achievement of multifaceted justice for victims, but it currently stands in great jeopardy. Without significant reform, the initiative will fail. Based on the analysis above, the Authors recommend that the Court take a number of specific measures to make the initiative a success:

1. ALLOCATE ADEQUATE RESOURCES TO THE INITIATIVE

Looking forward, if the Court is to remedy the problems identified in this Chapter, it must allocate adequate resources to the survivor participation initiative. With the recent (and, as noted in Chapter 4, controversial) transfer of Dr. Helen Jarvis from the Public Affairs Section and her appointment as Head of the Victims Unit, the Authors hope that support—both financial and political—for the initiative may increase, particularly on the Cambodian side. Soon after her appointment on May 18, 2009, Dr. Jarvis expressed her intention to "empower" the Unit and indicated that its planned renaming as the "Victims Support Section" would appropriately recognize its importance within the Court's structure. Under her leadership, the Unit has already commenced recruitment of additional outreach personnel.

In allocating its scarce resources, however, the Authors counsel the Unit against significant investment in outreach initiatives at this late stage in the tribunal process. Having conducted outreach for almost two years, intermediary organizations possess far greater experience in the provision of victims' rights education than the Unit and have already secured the involvement of more survivors than the Court may be able to handle. While recognizing Dr. Jarvis' extensive experience in public outreach, the Authors suggest that the Unit should not duplicate the successful efforts of intermediary organizations and should instead focus upon the processing of Forms channeled though such organizations and the provision of support to existing complainants and civil parties.

First, the Authors recommend that the Unit focus its efforts upon the processing of Forms. If survivor-provided information is to prove useful, the Co-Prosecutors must receive Forms in a timely manner in order that they may incorporate the information into their investigations. Unfortunately, this did not occur in Case No. 001, as the Unit did not begin filing complaints related to S-21 until only a few months before the Initial Hearing. Slow processing and filing by the Unit threatens the initiative's ability to contribute to the justice-seeking process. Happily, the situation in relation to Case No. 002 is much improved, as the Unit has been prioritizing the processing and filing of Forms related to situations under investigation.

Second, and perhaps more importantly, the Authors recommend that the Unit focus its efforts upon supporting existing complainants and civil parties. Complainants and civil parties desperately require prompt notification of all documents from the Court; assistance in selecting legal representatives; funding for legal representation; and regular updates on developments in the proceedings. As the Unit lacks the ability to provide ongoing support to existing complianants and civil parties, the Authors believe that it would be irresponsible to encourage the involvement of even more survivors through outreach. Similarly, intermediary organizations should re-evaluate their activities and shift their focus to the provision of ongoing support to existing civil parties, applicants and complainants.

2. PROVIDE APPROPRIATELY QUALIFIED LEGAL COUNSEL

If the Court is to ensure the expeditious conduct of the proceedings and the equality of arms in future trials, it must provide funding for civil parties' legal representation. By forcing civil parties to rely on *pro bono* lawyers in Case No. 001, the Court compromised their ability to put forward their best case. To their credit, all lawyers made their best efforts on behalf of their clients. However, most—though not all—of the *pro bono* lawyers lacked qualifications and experience comparable to those of the prosecution and defense. Some even experienced difficulties expressing themselves in one of the official languages. All lacked the resources necessary to match the other parties, including the necessary administrative, investigative and technological capabilities.

Following this experience in Case No. 001, key officials at the Court have clearly recognized that it is infeasible to expect civil parties to provide their own legal representation. As of late August 2009, the Victims Unit is in the process of recruiting three legal teams to represent civil parties in future cases (though this may, of course, change depending on the Court's reassessment of civil party participation at the plenary in September 2009). If recruited, it is anticipated that these teams will be funded by the Unit but operate independently. In the Authors' opinion, the recruitment of legal teams is a praiseworthy alternative to an ECCC-funded legal aid scheme for civil parties. Given the large number of civil parties, a legal aid scheme permitting civil parties to select lawyers of their choice would prove immensely costly and impracticable. The Authors anticipate that most civil parties would happily choose to appoint Court-recruited legal representatives.

Despite this promising development, the details of the recruitment for these positions bring into question the Court's commitment to the initiative. The International Co-Lawyers for civil parties are not being recruited by the United Nations with funds from the UN budget, as would be the case for comparable prosecution and defense positions. Instead, the International Co-Lawyers are being recruited by the Cambodian administration and the remuneration offered is considerably less than would be offered by the United Nations. Furthermore, the recruitment notice fails to specify that applicants must have qualifications commensurate with P-5 Level on the UN scale and does not require experience in international criminal proceedings, as would be the case for comparable prosecution and defense positions.

Certainly, the conduct of a Cambodian-administered recruitment offers certain benefits. First, it avoids the delay inherent in the lengthy UN recruitment process, ensuring that civil party lawyers are in place as early as possible to begin preparation for Case No. 002. Second, it offers the possibility of reducing the cost of the survivor participation initiative by denying these lawyers the almost overgenerous benefits of UN positions. On balance, however, the Authors fear that this recruitment will attract significantly less qualified candidates, placing civil parties on an unequal—albeit slightly improved—footing in future trials. The Authors counsel that the UN should conduct the recruitment for such positions in the future. If a Victims' Advocate position is to be created, the Authors recommend that any such recruitment be conducted in accordance with UN standards.

3. ENGAGE IN CAREFUL MANAGEMENT OF CIVIL PARTIES

The difficulties caused by the participation of four civil party groups in the proceedings in Case No. 001 have shown that there is a pressing need for the Court to play an active role in managing the involvement of victims in future trials. This need is likely to be particularly great in Case No. 002, in which thousands of civil parties are seeking to be recognized. The Authors consider grouping—i.e., the association and common representation of similarly-placed civil parties—to be one of the most important means by which the Court may manage civil party participation. Through careful grouping, the Court may minimize repetitive submissions and ensure expediency and the equal treatment of like victims.

In addition to addressing practical concerns such as delay and repetition, grouping has the potential to improve the moral force of victims. If victims do not group, the Authors believe that there is a danger that they may appear petty and divided. However, if victims present a unified voice, they are more likely to gain respect and support from the Court and from the public. Furthermore, grouping enables victims to present a stronger voice. A recent report prepared by Human Rights Now, a Japanese non-governmental organization, suggests that requests for non-monetary reparations prove more successful when presented by a group, rather than individuals.[82]

Although the Internal Rules permit the Chambers to play an active role in encouraging—and,

Cambodians rejoicing, signs read (from left to right): "Hooray, Cambodia has been completely liberated" and "Hooray, the People's Advisory Council, Revolutionary Kampuchea." January 17, 1979.
Source: Documentation Center of Cambodia and Vietnamese News Agency.

Villagers gather for meeting to discuss the *Renakse* petitions cataloguing the crimes of Pol Pot, 1982.
Source: Documentation Center of Cambodia and Vietnamese News Agency.

Villagers gather for meeting to discuss the *Renakse* petitions cataloguing the crimes of Pol Pot, 1982. The banner reads, "Congratulations on Victory, Renakse for Solidarity and Saving the New Cambodian Nation".
Source: Documentation Center of Cambodia and Vietnamese News Agency.

DC-Cam outreach activities in Kampot province.
Source: Documentation Center of Cambodia Archives.

DC-Cam outreach activities in Kampong Chhang province.
Source: Documentation Center of Cambodia Archives.

(Top) DC-Cam outreach activities in Takeo province. (Below) Aun Long of DC-Cam assisting an elderly villager fill out an ECCC complaint form. *Source: Documentation Center of Cambodia Archives.*

A map of mass graves drawn by Sok San, a survivor from Takeo province.
Source: Documentation Center of Cambodia Archives.

An elderly woman at one of DC-Cam's outreach activities in Prey Veng.
Source: Documentation Center of Cambodia Archives.

DC-Cam outreach activities in Pursat province.
Source: Documentation Center of Cambodia Archives.

(In this spread) DC-Cam outreach activities in Kampong Thom province.
Source: Documentation Center of Cambodia Archives.

{In this spread} DC-Cam outreach activities in Svay Rieng province.
Source: Documentation Center of Cambodia Archives.

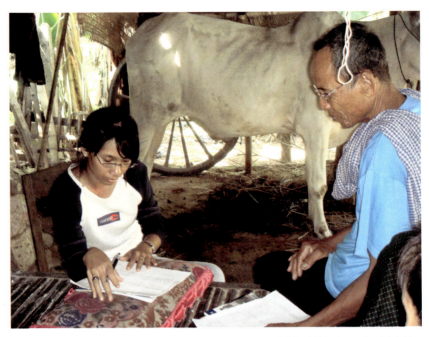

DC-Cam outreach activities in Prey Veng province. (Above) Savina Sirik, co-leader of DC-Cam's Living Document project, helping a villager fill out an ECCC complaint form. *Source: Documentation Center of Cambodia Archives.*

DC-Cam outreach meeting, 2006. Photo by Phat Piseth and Heng Sinith.
Source: Documentation Center of Cambodia Archives.

Village meeting of DC-Cam Victim Participation Project, 2009. Photo by Men Pichet and Sa Fatily.
Source: Documentation Center of Cambodia Archives

if necessary, compelling—grouping, the Trial Chamber unfortunately did not do so in Case No. 001. Despite the best efforts of the Victims Unit to informally encourage grouping, four groups of civil parties emerged in Case No. 001, as described above. In the Authors' opinion, these civil party groups do not have discernibly different interests in the proceedings and should ideally have been represented by the same legal team. The existence of multiple legal teams has undermined the impact of civil parties' submissions, as the teams have been forced to divide the time allocated to civil parties between them. This has resulted in short, repetitive submissions.

If civil party participation is retained in some form for Case No. 002, the Authors recommend that the Judges invoke the apparent authority in Internal Rule 23(8) to group and impose common legal representation upon civil parties. Given the compromised legal representation in Case No. 001, the Authors suggest that "the interests of Justice" clearly favor forced grouping, even if this undermines the civil parties' right to select lawyers of their own choosing. In their professional experience, the Authors have seen that civil parties generally have little to no interest in the selection of lawyers, caring only whether they are appropriately qualified. Being mostly uneducated and inexperienced in legal matters, the vast majority of civil parties would likely be very happy to accept the Chambers' guidance in this regard.

4. INSTITUTE REALISTIC AND EFFECTIVE REPARATIONS SCHEME

In order to avoid frustrating survivors' expectations, the Authors believe that there is a pressing need for the Court to address the availability of reparations and to begin planning for awards immediately. Having raised survivors' hopes by providing for a right to request reparations in the Internal Rules, it is imperative that the Court put plans in place to provide meaningful reparations awards in the event of convictions. If it fails to do so, the Authors anticipate frustration of survivors' expectations (particularly those of civil parties), undermining the Court's legitimacy and legacy. The Authors have found that the reparations initiative enjoys widespread survivor support; this is true despite the Court's ability to make only collective and moral awards.

In the Authors' opinion, the Court should make clear that any reparations awards will be made for the benefit of victims generally, as opposed to for the benefit of civil parties only. While recognizing that one of the purposes of the civil party action is to "[a]llow Victims to seek collective and moral reparations," the Authors recommend that the Court interpret this as a quest for reparations on behalf of all victims. Given the widespread nature of the atrocities and the inability of the initiative to include any more than a fraction of victims, the Authors submit that such interpretation is entirely appropriate. Furthermore, such interpretation would be in line with civil parties' expectations, as most do not expect or even hope for any personal benefit other than the satisfaction of being involved in the proceedings.

In the Authors' opinion, given the Court's budgetary constraints and donors' lackluster support for survivor participation, it is—unfortunately—unrealistic to speak of a comprehensive reparations scheme for victims of Democratic Kampuchea. Instead, the Authors recommend commencement of planning at this time for a small number of significant reparative measures benefiting victims on the national level. Youk Chhang, DC-Cam Director, has proposed, for example, special nationwide commemorations at existing memorials and a commemorative ceremony at Udong, the old capital, at the conclusion of the trials.[83] These commemorative ceremonies could, of course, be televised and broadcast over the radio for all. Alternative proposals benefiting victims at the national level include: the creation of a commemorative directory of victims' names; a commemorative national statue located in Phnom Penh; and commemorative banknotes and stamps.[84]

Less resource-intensive reparative measures are desirable, as such measures would prove feasible for the cash-strapped Court and avoid many of the administrative difficulties engendered by more costly proposals. If the Court were to attempt to implement resource-intensive reparative measures, it would likely have to establish a mechanism similar to the ICC Trust Fund for Victims to administer and implement awards. As Youk Chhang has argued, the creation of any such mechanism should be avoided in corruption-rife Cambodian given the impossibility of "establish[ing] a fund of money involving the Government or local NGOs that would be transparently administered and reach its intended beneficiaries: the victims."[85] The implementation of a small number of less resource-intensive reparative measures may, on the other hand, be implemented by the Court with assistance of the Cambodian government and donors.

5. ACCORD RESPECT TO VICTIMS IN REFORMING OR ELIMINATING CIVIL PARTY PARTICIPATION

As of late August 2009, the Judges are reassessing the Internal Rules' provision for civil party participation and appear poised to eliminate it at the plenary in September without any attempt at reform. Its elimination after just one trial threatens to relegate the survivor participation initiative to a failed experiment in international criminal justice and to discourage future internationalized criminal tribunals from adopting similar initiatives. This is unfortunate, given its many achievements, particularly at the grassroots level. Worryingly, if eliminated, this "experiment" will have been conducted at the expense of the 2,000 civil party applicants who have already become invested in the process and legitimately expect to participate in future trials.

If the Judges do decide at the Plenary to eliminate civil party participation, the Authors recommend that the Judges make every effort to remedy the harm caused to the 2,000 existing civil party applicants stripped of their participation rights. At a very minimum, as proposed by Youk Chhang, the Judges should write to each and every applicant to acknowledge their application and inform them of the change in procedure.[86] In order to reflect their importance, these notifications should be delivered by Court officials, rather than intermediary organizations. The Authors further recommend that the Judges invite all affected applicants to Phnom Penh to learn of these changes in person from Court officials.

Even if the Judges were to adopt appropriate notification procedures, the elimination of civil party participation would inevitably cause disappoint many victims. The Authors recommend that, in revising the Internal Rules at the plenary in September, the Rules and Procedure Committee should at very least provide for continued victim involvement in a lesser capacity in future trials. The proposed appointment of a "Victims' Advocate" to represent victims' interests may meet many victims' needs. The Authors have found that victims have little interest in their specific legal rights; rather, they typically desire to be involved and to have their interests represented. If civil party participation is replaced by representation of victims' collective interests, however, the Court must explain to applicants that their participation rights have been eliminated.

The Authors consider particularly promising the proposal made by Reserve Trial Judge Fenz that the proposed Advocate would be empowered to call representative victims to testify. If so, the Authors recommend, as Youk Chhang has proposed, that the Advocate involve existing applicants in the selection of these representative "victim-witnesses." The Advocate should pre-select a small number of "victim-witnesses" and then permit victims to decide among themselves which of the pre-selected "victim-witnesses" would best represent their interests. Although only a token form of involvement in the proceedings, applicants' disappointment would likely be lessened somewhat if they know that they have had a say in the representation of their interests.

CONCLUSION

Irrespective of the difficulties identified in this Chapter, the Extraordinary Chambers' achievements in the area of survivor participation have been groundbreaking. For the first time in the history of internationalized criminal tribunals, victims of mass human rights violations have been accorded a highly visible role as 'civil parties' in the criminal proceedings against their oppressors. In this capacity, twenty-two victims have testified before the Court's Trial Chamber, providing moving testimony as they tell the world of their suffering. On an individual level, the Authors have seen firsthand that this participation has been very meaningful for civil parties. Many feel empowered knowing that they have stood up to Duch; most simply feel proud to have been involved in the historic proceedings.

As of late August 2009, around 4,000 survivors from across Cambodia and overseas have become involved in the initiative and have filed Victim Information Forms with the Victims Unit. Most survivors assisted by DC-Cam consider themselves too old, unwell or uneducated to play an active role in the proceedings; instead, they choose to become complainants, appreciating the opportunity to speak of their suffering and to have their accounts recorded for future generations. In this way, the initiative really does operate as an informal truth commission. Interestingly, most survivors have never heard of many of the charged persons and have only a limited interest in retribution. Most are far more interested in remembrance and accurate historical understanding of their suffering under the regime.

Of course, the impact of the initiative has been limited due to the Victims Unit's limited resources and consequent inability to conduct outreach. The 4,000 survivors currently involved represent only a tiny fraction of all survivors. Civil society in Phnom Penh has risen to the challenge imposed by the Unit's delegation of its outreach responsibilities and has successfully reached out to a significant number of survivors. Worryingly, the Unit is now focusing its efforts upon the creation of an outreach capacity. Given the inability of the Unit and intermediary organizations to provide comprehensive ongoing assistance to existing complainants and civil parties, the Authors counsel against this, as the involvement of further survivors would force the Unit and intermediaries to spread their limited resources even more thinly. Responsibility for further outreach should lie with intermediary organizations, which already possess significant experience in this area.

The survivor participation initiative's contribution to the proceedings to date has, as a matter of law, been limited. Inefficient processing of Forms by the Victims Unit has meant that information collected from survivors in form of complaints has not contributed to the Co-Prosecutors' and Co-Investigating Judges' investigations in Case No. 001. The absence of funding for legal representation in Case No. 001 has forced civil parties to rely upon overburdened *pro bono* lawyers lacking the resources to put their best case forward. This has significantly hampered their ability to make legally meaningful contributions to the proceedings. As noted above, it is quite possible that the Judges may give little weight to civil parties' testimonies.

Fortunately, the Court's administration and the donor community appear to be learning from their mistakes in Case No. 001. First, following receipt of a generous grant from the GTZ, the Victims Unit has recruited a number of Khmer data entry clerks and is now processing Forms submitted by survivors swiftly. The Co-Prosecutors will hopefully give full consideration to this information and include it in their investigations. Second, the Court—at least until recently—was in the process of recruiting ECCC-funded legal representatives for civil parties in Case No. 002. Although not recruited to UN standards, these legal representatives should have resources far superior to the current *pro bono* lawyers, increasing the likelihood that civil parties may make legally valuable contributions in future if civil party participation is retained.

Despite these promising recent developments, the future of the most visible form of survivor participation—the civil party action—stands in jeopardy as of late August 2009. Frustrated by inexpediency and defense challenges to the eligibility of certain civil parties, the Judges appear poised to eliminate civil party participation at the plenary in September without any attempt at reform. This is most unfortunate given that the Court has raised the hopes of some 2,000 civil party applicants. The elimination of civil party participation after only one trial would be particularly disappointing in light of the Judges' *laissez-faire* attitude. Had the Judges made timely and robust interventions to manage civil party participation at an earlier juncture, many of the problems witnessed in Case No. 001 could have been avoided.

Looking forward, any reforms to the survivor participation initiative must be sensitive to the needs of the victims whose involvement the Court has solicited over the past two years. If applicants' rights are to be eliminated, the Court must inform victims of this in a prompt and respectful manner. Insofar as possible, the Court should strive to provide for the involvement of victims in the proceedings, albeit it in a lesser capacity than as civil parties. Although seemingly toothless, the appointment of a so-called "Victims' Advocate" may be the best means of ensuring the continued representation of victims' interests in the face of refusal by the Judges to attempt to reform the civil party procedure.

---

[1] *See* Ruti G. Teitel, Transitional Justice 28 (2001).

[2] Erin Ann O'Hara, *Victim Participation in the Criminal Process*, 13 J.L. & Pol'y 229, 244 (2005).

[3] C. pr. pén. arts. 85-91, 418-26, R15-40, D49-64 (Fr.).

[4] Cambodian Code of Criminal Procedure, art. 2 [hereinafter Criminal Procedure Code].

[5] A GROUP OF CAMBODIAN JURISTS, DOCUMENTS OF PEOPLE'S REVOLUTIONARY TRIBUNAL HELD IN PHNOM PENH OF THE TRIAL OF THE GENOCIDE CRIME OF THE POL POT-IENG SARY CLIQUE, JUDGMENT 271-311 (1979) (Eng. version) (reporting that three civil parties participated in the proceedings and were represented by Mr. Mohammed Hikmet Turkmanee, a Syrian lawyer).

[6] Declaration of Basic Principles of Justice for Victims of Crime and Abuse of Power, G.A. Res. 40/34, annex, 40 U.N. GAOR Supp. (No. 53) at 214, U.N. Doc. A/40/53 (1985).

[7] *Id.* arts. 4, 8.

[8] Basic Principles and Guidelines on the Right to a Remedy and Reparation for Victims of Gross Violations of International Human Rights Law and Serious Violations of International Humanitarian Law, G.A. Res. 60/147, U.N. Doc. A/60/147 (2005).

[9] *See id.*

[10] *See* U.N. Security Council Resolution 827, U.N. SCOR, Annex, U.N. Doc. S/RES/827 (1993) [hereinafter ICTY Resolution]; U.N. Security Council Resolution 955, U.N. SCOR, Annex, U.N. Doc. S/RES/955 (1994) [hereinafter ICTR Resolution].

[11] ICTY Resolution, *supra* note 10, art. 2; ICTR Resolution, *supra* note 10, art. 1.

[12] ICTY Resolution, *supra* note 10, art. 7.

[13] INT'L CRIM. TRIBUNAL FOR THE FORMER YUGOSLAVIA, JUDGES' REPORT ON VICTIMS' COMPENSATION AND PARTICIPATION (Sept. 2000), *available at* www.un.org/icty/pressreal/tolb-e.htm [hereinafter ICTY Judges' Report].

[14] Rome Statute of the International Criminal Court, U.N. Doc. A/CONF.183/9 (1998) [hereinafter Rome Statute], art. 68(3).

[15] *Id.* art. 75(1).

[16] *Id.* art. 75(2).

[17] *Id.* art. 79.

[18] *See generally* Law on the Establishment of Extraordinary Chambers in the Courts of Cambodia for the Prosecution of Crimes Committed During the Period of Democratic Kampuchea, as amended and promulgated on Oct. 27, 2004, NS/RKM/1004/006 [hereinafter ECCC Law]; Agreement between the United Nations and the Royal Government of Cambodia Concerning the Prosecution under Cambodian Law of Crimes Committed During the Period of Democratic Kampuchea (June 6, 2003) [hereinafter Framework Agreement].

[19] Article 36 new of the ECCC Law reads: "The Extraordinary Chamber of the Supreme Court shall decide appeals made by the accused, the victims, or the Co-Prosecutors against the decision of the Extraordinary Chamber of the trial court."

[20] Framework Agreement, *supra* note 18, art. 12; ECCC Law, *supra* note 18, arts. 20, 23, 33.

[21] *See, e.g.,* INTERNATIONAL CENTER FOR TRANSITIONAL JUSTICE, COMMENTS ON DRAFT INTERNAL RULES FOR THE EXTRAORDINARY CHAMBERS IN THE COURTS OF CAMBODIA 4 (Nov. 17, 2006), *available at* www.ictj.org/images/content/6/0/601.pdf ("[T]he Internal Rules demonstrate a commitment to protecting the rights and interests of victims of the crimes within the ECCC jurisdiction through allowing for their participation in the process and right to seek reparation. . . .").

[22] Internal Rules of the Extraordinary Chambers in the Courts of Cambodia, as revised on Mar. 6, 2009 [hereinafter ECCC Internal Rules], R. 49.

[23] *Id.* R. 49.

[24] *Id.* R. 23.

[25] Practice Direction on Victim Participation of the Extraordinary Chambers in the Courts of Cambodia, ECCC Doc. No. Practice Direction/02/2007/Rev.1, art. 1.1, as revised on Oct. 27, 2008 [hereinafter Practice Direction].

[26] ECCC Internal Rules, *supra* note 22, R. 49(2). The Rome Statute of the International Criminal Court permits the Prosecutor to "initiate investigations *proprio motu*" and to "seek additional information from States, organs of the United Nations, intergovernmental or non-governmental organizations, or other reliable sources." In contrast to the Internal Rules, however, the Rome Statute does not provide a mechanism for such entities or individuals to submit such information on their own initiative. *See* Rome Statute, *supra* note 14, art. 15(1)-(2).

[27] ECCC Internal Rules, *supra* note 22, R. 49(4).

[28] *Id*. R. 23(2).

[29] *Id*, R. 12(2).

[30] The Rules and Procedure Committee made this amendment following repeated attempts by lawyers for a civil party group to circumvent the overstretched Victims Unit by making submissions directly to the relevant organs of the Court.

[31] ECCC Revised Budget Estimates From 2005 to 2009, at 24-45 (July 2008) (on file with authors) (allocating a total of only USD $670,622 under the UN and Cambodian sides of the budget to fund a mere 14 posts in the Victims Unit, including legal representatives).

[32] It remains to be seen whether a relative of a direct victim of another crime (e.g., rape) may be considered a "victim."

[33] *See* Decision on Civil Party Request for Protective Measures Related to Appeal Against Provisional Detention Order, Case File No. 002/19-09-2007-ECCC/OCIJ (PTC03), ECCC Doc. No. C22/I/57 (Pre-Trial Chamber, July 8, 2008).

[34] As evidence of this, the Authors point to the significant decline in donor interest in funding intermediary organizations since the announcement of a USD $1.9 million donation to the Victims Unit from the GTZ.

[35] On the *Renakse* petitions, *see generally*, Chapter 1; William J. Schulte, *The History of the Renakse Petitions and Their Value for ECCC Proceedings*, paper published online by the Documentation Center of Cambodia, *available at* www.dccam.org/Projects/Tribunal_Response_Team/Victim_Participation/PDF/Renakse_by_BJ.pdf.

[36] The Criminal Procedure Code provides that victims may apply to become civil parties at any time prior to the Prosecutor's final submission. Criminal Procedure Code, *supra* note 4, art. 311.

[37] ECCC Internal Rules, *supra* note 22, R. 23(4).

[38] Despite denying his civil party application, the Trial Chamber permitted the victim in question—Mr. Norng Chan Phal, a DC-Cam-assisted applicant—to testify as a witness on July 2, 2009. Chan Phal testified to his imprisonment at S-21 as an 8-year-old boy, along with his mother and younger brother. His father had previously been arrested and imprisoned there. Chan Phal described in detail their arrival at the prison and his subsequent forced separation from his mother. He testified that, even as the Khmers Rouges escaped, he refused to leave and searched the compound for his mother. He and other children hid in a workshop and were found by the Vietnamese troops. Chan Phal never saw his parents again. Laura MacDonald, After Heartbreaking Testimony from a Child Survivor of S-21, Duch Denies He Was a Prisoner There, Cambodia Tribunal Monitor Blog, July 2, 2009, *available at* cambodiatribunal.org/images/CTM/ctm_blog_7-2-2009.pdf. On the story of Norng Chan Phal, *see generally*, Spencer Cryder, Investigative Inertia During the ECCC Trial Phase, The 1979 "S-21 Video" & Child Survivor Norng Chanphal, Searching for the Truth (forthcoming Third Quarter 2009).

[39] ECCC Internal Rules, *supra* note 22, R. 23(4), 105(1).

[40] *Id*. R. 23(2).

[41] Practice Direction, *supra* note 25, art. 3.2.c-d.

[42] *Id*. art. 3.2.c. The Khmer version of the Practice Direction uses *nheat san da-an* (in English, "relatives") for "kin." In the Cambodian Co-Author's opinion, this wording permits a broad interpretation extending beyond the nuclear family. To the Authors' knowledge, the Co-Investigating Judges have recognized at least one cousin of a deceased victim as a civil party in Case No. 001.

[43] Transcript of Initial Hearing of Feb. 17, 2009, Case File No. 001/18-07-2007-ECCC/TC, ECCC Doc. No. E1/3.1 at 47 (Trial Chamber,

Feb. 17, 2009).

[44] *Id.* at 42.

[45] For an excellent analysis of this issue before the ECCC and ICC, *see* Brianne McGonigle, *Apples and Oranges: Victim Participation Approaches at the ICC and ECCC*, in The Effectiveness of International Criminal Justice, International Law Vol. 3, at 91 (Cedric Ryngaert ed., Aug. 2009).

[46] ECCC Internal Rules, *supra* note 22, R. 23(7), 83(1).

[47] *Id.* R. 59(5).

[48] *Id.* R. 80(2).

[49] *Id.* R. 90(2), 91(2).

[50] *Id.* R. 94.

[51] *Id.* R. 100.

[52] The Criminal Procedure Code provides civil parties with a set of rights, including the rights: to be represented by a lawyer (Article 150); to request investigative action by the investigating judge (Article 134); participate during the investigation (Article 137-138); to summon witnesses (Article 298); to object to hearing testimony of a particular witness (if such testimony is not helpful in ascertaining the truth) (Article 327); to question the accused and witnesses (Article 153 and 325); to introduce evidence (Article 334); and to make a closing statement (Article 335).

[53] The Criminal Procedure Code provides civil parties with the right to appeal to the Court of Appeal or the Supreme Court (Articles 402, 418).

[54] ECCC Internal Rules, *supra* note 22, R. 105.

[55] It is worth noting that the civil party in question was Ms. Theary Seng, the prominent Khmer-American Executive Director of the Center for Social Development. She had previously addressed the Chamber on several occasions and had made inflammatory statements towards the accused. It is further worth noting that she had fired her lawyer in dramatic fashion during the course of the hearing precisely in order that she may address the Chamber directly.

[56] Directions on Unrepresented Civil Parties' Right to Address the Pre-Trial Chamber in Person, Case File No. 002/19-09-2007-ECCC/OCIJ (PTC03) (Pre-Trial Chamber, Mar. 13, 2009). *See also* Response of Three Unrepresented Civil Parties to the Application for Reconsideration of Civil Party's Right to Address the Chamber, Case File No. 002/19-09-2007-ECCC/OCIJ (PTC03) (Pre-Trial Chamber, July 20, 2008) (arguing for the right of unrepresented civil parties to make oral submissions during pre-trial hearings).

[57] Decision on Protective Measures for Civil Parties, Case File No. 001/18-07-2007/ECCC/TC, ECCC Doc. No. E71, ¶¶ 12-13 (Trial Chamber, June 2, 2009).

[58] The Criminal Procedure Code accords civil parties the right to claim reparations from the convicted person or, in the event of his or her death during the proceedings, from the convicted person's successor (Article 24).

[59] ECCC Internal Rules, *supra* note 22, R. 23(1).

[60] *Id.* R. 23(11).

[61] *Id.* R. 23(12).

[62] Int'l Monetary Fund, Cambodia: Statistical Appendix, IMF Country Report 09/48 (Dec. 23, 2008), *available at* www.imf.org/external/pubs/ft/scr/2009/cr0948.pdf (reporting that in 2007 the average annual income for a Cambodian was at US$649 in 2007 and that in 2005 35% of the population was living under the poverty line).

[63] The Authors recognize that rare exceptions do exist. To provide an example, Ms. Theary Seng, the aforementioned civil party and

Executive Director of the Center for Social Development, is a capable U.S.-educated lawyer.

[64] *See, e.g.*, Terith Chy and Sarah Thomas, *Letter to the Editor, Civil Party Participation*, PHNOM PENH POST, Sept. 2, 2008; Cambodian Human Rights Action Committee, Press Release: Seven Months of Active Participation by Civil Parties: Safeguarding Rights and Moving Forward, Aug. 29, 2008 (on file with the authors).

[65] ICC Trial Chamber II has already noted the importance of grouping of victim participants. *See* Situation in the Democratic Republic of the Congo in the Case of the Prosecutor v. Germain Katanga & Mathieu Ngudjolo Chui, Order on the Organisation of Common Legal Representation of Victims, Case No. 01/04-01/07, Decision on Victims' Participation, ¶ 11 (Trial Chamber II, July 22, 2009).

[66] ECCC Internal Rules, *supra* note 22, R. 23(8)(c).

[67] ECCC Victims Unit, "Historic Achievement in International Criminal Law: Victims of Khmer Rouge Crimes Fully Involved in Proceedings of the ECCC," press release dated Feb. 4, 2008, *available at* www.eccc.gov.kh/english/cabinet/press/58/Victim_Unit_Press_Release.pdf.

[68] As of late August 2009, ninety-one civil parties are participating in the proceedings in Case No. 001. Ninety-four victims applied to become civil parties and all were recognized by the Trial Chamber with the exception of one who lacked documentation "[]sufficient to establish his identity." Two recognized civil parties subsequently withdrew their applications. For the declaration of inadmissibility, *see* Decision on the Civil Party Status of Applicants E2/36, E2/51 and E2/69, Case File No. 001/18-07-2007/ECCC/TC, ECCC Doc. No. E2/94/2 (Trial Chamber, Mar. 4, 2009).

[69] *See* U.C. Berkeley War Crimes Studies Center, The KRT Trial Monitor, Report No. 13 (July 16, 2009), *available at* socrates.berkeley.edu/~warcrime/documents/KRT%20Monitor%20Week%2013%20Final.pdf.

[70] *See id.* At least one civil party has been determined to be unable to testify due to the effects of severe trauma.

[71] *See* U.C. Berkeley War Crimes Studies Center, The KRT Trial Monitor, Report No. 11 (July 5, 2009), *available at* socrates.berkeley.edu/~warcrime/documents/KRT%20TRIAL%20MONITOR%20WEEK%2011.pdf. *See also* Laura MacDonald, *Traumatized Survivor Painted Pol Pot Amidst Screams for Help*, CAMBODIA TRIBUNAL MONITOR BLOG, July 1, 2009, *available at* www.cambodiatribunal.org/images/CTM/ctm_blog_7-6-2009.pdf.

[72] Transcript of Trial Day 59 of Aug. 17, 2009, Case File No. 001/18-07-2007-ECCC/TC, ECCC Doc. No. E1/63.1 at 1 (Trial Chamber, Aug. 17, 2009).

[73] Terith Chy, *Victim Reactions to Duch's Apology: Is Forgiveness Possible?*, *available at* www.dccam.org/Projects/Tribunal_Response_Team/Victim_Participation/PDF/Victims'_Reactions_to_Duch_apology.pdf.

[74] Decision on Motion Regarding Deceased Civil Party, Case File No. 001/18-07-2007/ECCC/TC, ¶ 13 (Trial Chamber, Mar. 13, 2009). The Internal Rules do not address whether a civil party's successor may succeed to the decedent's civil action. Upon application by her lawyers, the Trial Chamber recognized Suos Sarin's husband, Um Piseth, as successor to her civil action. This decision accords with Article 16 of the Criminal Procedure Code, which provides: "In case of death of the victim, a civil action can be started or continued by his successor."

[75] Laura MacDonald, *Thirty Years Ago, Duch Took His Toenails; Today He Took It to Duch*, CAMBODIA TRIBUNAL MONITOR BLOG, June 30, 2009, *available at* www.dccam.org/Projects/Tribunal_Response_Team/Victim_Participation/PDF/Victims'_Reactions_to_Duch_apology.pdf.

[76] PowerPoint Presentation of Reserve Trial Judge Claudia Fenz, Sunway Hotel, Phnom Penh (Aug. 21, 2009) [hereinafter Fenz Presentation] (on file with the authors).

[77] Laura MacDonald, *Details About Duch's Role at S-21 Explored, While Details About Civil Parties' Role in Trial Avoided*, CAMBODIA TRIBUNAL MONITOR BLOG, June 22, 2009, *available at* cambodiatribunal.org/images/CTM/ctm_blog_6-22-2009.pdf.

[78] In fact, Duch first contested the imprisonment of Norng Chan Phal, a child survivor of S-21 assisted by DC-Cam. As described above, the Trial Chamber denied his civil party application due to late filing. On July 2, 2009, Chan Phal gave moving testimony as a fact

witness for the prosecution. Duch stated that he did not accept the imprisonment of Chan Phal or his mother at S-21.

[79] Pending Review of Victims' Participation Before the ECCC (Draft) (on file with the authors).

[80] Fenz Presentation, *supra* note 76.

[81] Letter from Youk Chhang to Susan Lamb, Senior Judicial Coordinator for the Extraordinary Chambers in the Courts of Cambodia, on behalf of the Rules and Procedure Committee (Aug. 26, 2009) [hereinafter Chhang Letter to Susan Lamb] (on file with the authors) (proposing that representative victims "should be voted for by current civil party applicants from among a group pre-selected by the Victims' Advocate"). The Authors emphasize that, if adopted, any such procedure should provide for appropriate representation of the interests of minority groups (e.g., Cham Muslims, foreigners).

[82] HUMAN RIGHTS NOW (JAPAN), MASS VICTIMS LITIGATION PRACTICES: SUGGESTIONS FOR VICTIMS' PARTICIPATION AT THE ECCC FROM JAPANESE EXPERIENCES IN MASS PLAINTIFF CASES 7 (July 9, 2008) ("In Japan, mass victims are often successful in obtaining non-monetary reparations from settlements if the requests are based on coordinated or unified requests among multiple groups of plaintiffs.").

[83] Letter from Youk Chhang to Judge Silvia Cartwright, Extraordinary Chambers in the Courts of Cambodia (Aug. 20, 2009) [hereinafter Chhang Letter to Judge Cartwright] (on file with the authors).

[84] Sarah Thomas, Responding to the Cambodian Genocide: DC-Cam's Present and Future Reparations Initiatives, paper delivered at CHRAC & ECCC Victims' Unit Conference on Reparation for Victims of the Khmer Rouge Regime (Sunway Hotel, Phnom Penh, Nov. 26, 2008). In August 2009, the Victims Unit made a similar proposal for a "Victims' Register."

[85] Chhang Letter to Judge Cartwright, *supra* note 83.

[86] Chhang Letter to Susan Lamb, *supra* note 81.

6. THE ECCC'S ROLE IN RECONCILIATION

JOHN D. CIORCIARI AND SOK-KHEANG LY

Although the tragedy of Democratic Kampuchea (DK) occurred three decades ago, Khmer Rouge atrocities left deep scars on individual victims and Cambodian society as a whole. Millions of Cambodians endure physical and psychological pain from the Pol Pot period. The children of DK survivors, who now make up a majority of the population, are also affected. Many suffer from poverty and other disadvantages that flow in part from the utter demolition of Cambodia's economy, governance structures, and educational system during the late 1970s. At both local and national levels, Cambodians have taken important steps to restore peace and a degree of social harmony, but that process is not complete. Although revenge killings are now rare, many survivors of Democratic Kampuchea have found it difficult to put the pieces of their shattered lives back together, and many harbor deep resentment and distrust of former adversaries.

In this concluding chapter, we discuss ways that the Extraordinary Chambers in the Courts of Cambodia (ECCC) can help to advance reconciliation with respect to the crimes of the DK era. First, we define what we mean by "reconciliation." We describe it as a multi-faceted process, rooted in personal healing, that involves rebuilding relations at both local and national levels. We then review some of the ways to promote reconciliation. We argue that efforts by governments and international organizations can be useful, but processes need to take root at personal and community levels to be effective.

Second, we examine some ways in which Cambodians pursued reconciliation—both at personal and societal levels—long before the ECCC was created. We argue that Cambodians have achieved significant progress toward reconciliation since the Pol Pot era. However, for many the journey remains incomplete. We contend that reconciliation efforts to date have fallen short largely because they have not produced a widely shared sense of justice and because they have not involved sufficient emphasis on public education.

Third, we explore the role that the ECCC has to play in the reconciliation process given all that has come before it. Despite the tribunal's significant limits and shortcomings, we retain optimism that the trials can have a positive effect on reconciliation by providing a definitive legal judgment for the Cambodian people. Criminal trials are not always conducive to reconciliation, but we believe that they are at this stage in Cambodia's evolution. In addition to issuing credible verdicts, the ECCC's contribution to reconciliation depends on conducting effective outreach and cooperating with supporting non-governmental organizations (NGOs) and other entities that can pass along the lessons of the trials to survivors and their children. We review the tribunal's progress in these areas to date.

Finally, we examine some reactions from survivors to provide a preliminary indication of the ECCC's effects on reconciliation during its first three years of operation. Public responses to the Khmer Rouge trials have been far from uniform. The trials are reopening old wounds, and some survivors do not believe that they will ever feel "reconciled" with the Khmers Rouges. However, the trials have not led to violence, and many Cambodians believe that credible verdicts and truth-telling can ultimately help them and their loved ones achieve a more definitive sense of closure. These reactions suggest that the ECCC can make a meaningful contribution to many survivors, particularly on a personal level.

DEFINING AND PURSUING RECONCILIATION

In Cambodia and elsewhere, it is difficult to define "reconciliation" neatly. Most definitions of the term focus on the healing of relationships between former adversaries to build a sustainable peace. Some also focus on the need for a degree of personal healing or closure. The Khmer translation of the term, *phsas phsa*, implies both. It literally means "reconnecting the broken pieces." For a shattered society to rebuild, reconciliation usually needs to occur at multiple levels: between individuals, between communities, and between nations. That need is clear in Cambodia, where victims of Khmer Rouge atrocities often live side by side with their former tormentors and where political divisions run deep.

WHAT DOES IT MEAN TO RECONCILE?

There is a large and growing body of scholarly literature on reconciliation, and the concept is subject to much debate. To most analysts, it implies a complex process leading to a number of different (and often contested) moral, social, and political objectives. Reconciliation is not just a descriptive term; speakers usually invoke the concept to suggest developments that *ought* to occur.

As a process, reconciliation generally signifies an accommodation among former adversaries and repair of fractures in societies that have been subject to war or widespread atrocities. It means moving beyond mere coexistence; simply putting away the guns or trying to forget the past are not enough. At both personal and societal levels, reconciliation requires a

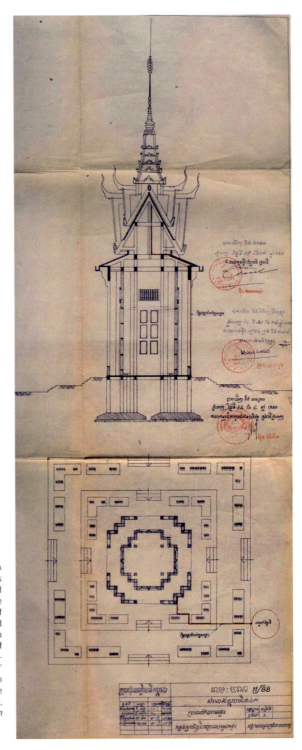

Building plan of the Choeung Ek memorial. The text at right reads (from top to bottom): "Witnessed and Agreed, Phnom Penh 17 June 1988, President of the Ministry of Culture, Chum Kanal;" "Witnessed and Properly Investigated, Phnom Penh 20 June 1988, President of Construction and Building, Permanent Vice-President, Kry Beng Hong;" and "Witnessed and Agreed, Phnom Penh 24 June 1988, Committee of the People's Revolution, Phnom Penh, Mok Mareth." *Source: Documentation Center of Cambodia Archives.*

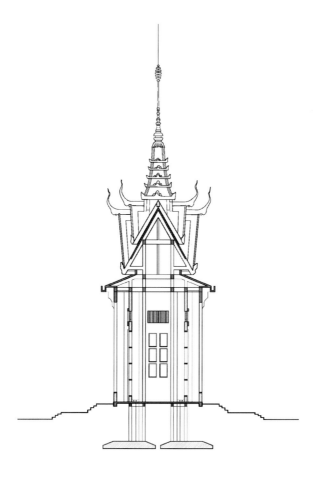

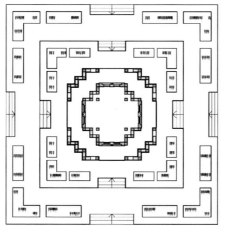

Building plan of the Choeung Ek memorial by David Salazar of StudioMDA in New York. *Source: David Salazar.*

degree of healing. Reconciling means acknowledging and grappling with the past, coming to understand it, and changing attitudes to make more positive relationships possible.[1] Even if they do not forgive or forget past wrongs, former adversaries mutually acknowledge past suffering and develop the ability to re-establish productive relationships and live peacefully with one another. The desire for vengeance and redress gradually gives way to a greater priority on building a shared future and a more stable society.[2]

South African's Archbishop Desmond Tutu has described reconciliation as involving:

> …a very long and painful journey, addressing the pain and suffering of the victims, understanding the motivations of offenders, bringing together estranged communities, trying to find a path to justice, truth and, ultimately, peace.[3]

John Paul Lederach argues similarly that reconciliation is "a journey to a place where truth, justice, peace and mercy meet."[4] These are relatively ambitious concepts of reconciliation, because they envision a process whereby former adversaries achieve a degree of mutual understanding and agreement about how to deal with the past.

The various goals of the reconciliation process—such as truth, justice, and peace—seldom come neatly bundled together. Some scholars and practitioners have cast doubt on the extent to which truth begets reconciliation. Others have expressed doubt about the contribution of justice—at least retributive criminal justice—to reconciliation. As Lederach argues, the process of reconciliation often involves dealing with profound paradoxes: trying to build a shared future while seeking truths about a divided past and promoting mercy and mutual acceptance while insisting on justice and accountability for past offenses.[5]

There is also ample disagreement on the end-state that qualifies a society and its citizens as "reconciled." The concept is loaded with moral, ideological, cultural, political, and often religious content. Is the principal goal of a reconciliation process to achieve a farewell to arms and non-violent co-existence, or is it aimed at a high degree of harmony and mutual acceptance among former foes? Does it simply imply the establishment of a workable social order or the creation of a robust democracy? These debates are not merely academic: they affect real policy choices and have played themselves out in Cambodia for the past thirty years.

AVENUES TO RECONCILIATION

Whether one simply seeks peace and stability or broader objectives, achieving "reconciliation" after conflict or mass atrocities is a long and challenging process. Governments, non-state organizations, and ordinary people can attempt to rebuild and reconcile in a number of ways.

These include amnesty programs, coercive reintegration measures, truth commissions, criminal trials, civil remedies (such as awards of reparations), and a variety of other measures such as public ceremonies, memorials, and individual or community-level counselling.

Not all of these approaches work synergistically all of the time, however. Each approach tends to prioritize some goals above others. For example, a government amnesty plan may retard justice but advance peace, while criminal trials may have an opposite effect, at least in the short run. Cultural context, timing, and other factors also complicate the business of reconciliation. An approach—such as the establishment of a tribunal—might be highly conducive to reconciliation in some times and places but not others. The section below introduces some of the major approaches to reconciliation that are most germane to Cambodia.

POLITICAL COMPROMISES OR COERCION

In post-conflict societies, the term "reconciliation" almost always refers in part to a political process whereby various factions try to put away their arms and reconstitute a functioning state. It requires active engagement of former adversaries—such as opposing political parties, rival ethnic groups, or other constituencies. In Cambodia, the term "reconciliation" has often been used to stress the need to terminate decades of civil and international armed conflict. In the 1990s, "reconciliation" usually referred to the goal of ending the Khmer Rouge insurgency and reintegrating guerillas into the society. The term has sometimes also been used to imply a coming together of rival political parties—namely the Cambodian People's Party (CPP) and its principal rivals, such as the royalist party FUNCINPEC and the Sam Rainsy Party.

The political aspects of reconciliation are almost always contentious. Even when feuding parties can agree on the need to reconcile, they seldom agree on the terms. Political transitions almost inevitably have winners and losers, and the losers are often loath to put down their guns. In Cambodia, the political aspects of reconciliation have been highly controversial and closely related to naked power politics. Each political party has a very different conception of how a "reconciled" Cambodia would look. In many ways, "reconciliation" has been a buzzword that politicians have used to serve their partisan objectives. The challenge, in Cambodia and other conflict-torn countries, is to establish a new order that is flexible enough to accommodate the legitimate concerns of diverse parties but strong and durable enough to ensure security and basic human rights.

Forming a new government after a period of conflict often requires bitter compromises among warring factions. Even after a government takes shape, some "unreconciled" opponents of the new order almost always exist, for good reasons or bad. Governments sometimes try to welcome those opponents into the fold with amnesty policies, co-opting their adversaries with promises of criminal immunity and sometimes desirable official posts.

Alternatively, governments can try to impose a form of "reconciliation" by subjecting adversaries to re-education and demanding shows of loyalty. As scholar and current ECCC official Craig Etcheson argues, coercive approaches to reconciliation are often ignored in the literature, because they are morally disfavored.[5] Nevertheless, forceful reintegration programs are common, and power relations are unavoidably relevant to reconciliation processes. Whether governments use carrots or sticks, their efforts to deal with adversaries are usually controversial. As discussed later in this chapter, both of these approaches have been taken in Cambodia, where political reconciliation has been difficult to achieve.

TRUTH & RECONCILIATION COMMISSIONS

Political compromises are seldom sufficient to deliver deep, broad-based reconciliation. Some societies have thus adopted "truth-telling" mechanisms that lay out the history of past abuses for public discussion. Truth commissions have often been set up with the explicit goal of fostering reconciliation by airing the full history of odious regimes or armed conflicts. The best-known example was the Truth and Reconciliation Commission (TRC) in South Africa to reveal the abuses of the Apartheid regime, but numerous other TRCs have been organized in countries including Chile, Liberia, Peru, Sierra Leone, the Solomon Islands, and South Korea. Other variants of truth commissions have also been established throughout the world.

Advocates of truth commissions argue that they contribute to reconciliation by building a greater degree of mutual understanding between estranged communities. The claim that truth begets reconciliation is difficult to test empirically. James Gibson has examined the South African case and does find some empirical linkage between truth-telling and reconciliation in that country.[7] Nevertheless, governments are sometimes fearful—or at least profess to be fearful—that truth commissions will backfire in terms of reconciliation, exposing painful facts that incite renewed violence.

Still, truth commissions enjoy relatively broad support as useful facilitators of reconciliation in many contexts. Revealing the truth is not a panacea, but most analysts believe that at a minimum, TRCs provide useful functions by acknowledging past offenses and helping survivors better understand the past. Returns to violence have been rare, diminishing fears that TRCs will spark renewed hostilities.

Some analysts have argued that a truth commission would be more appropriate for Cambodia than a limited set of criminal trials to deal with the Khmer Rouge legacy and promote reconciliation. For example, Jaya Ramji has argued that a TRC could be preferable in a Cambodian context, because "national reconciliation is an overriding goal for many Cambodians and is arguably more consistent with Buddhist philosophy than a trial."[8]

THE PURSUIT OF JUSTICE

Ultimately, the Cambodian government and United Nations decided to organize a tribunal rather than a TRC. As emphasized by many scholars and statesmen, criminal tribunals are often in tension with the goals of peace and reconciliation.[9] They provide a salient reminder of past injustices that has the potential to reopen old wounds or reinforce divisions between former adversaries. As discussed in Chapter 5, they tend to focus particular attention on retributive justice and do less well at providing restoration. They are also designed to focus on narrow sets of facts relevant to a handful of specific defendants. Thus, they are not ideally suited to provide a full statement of historical truth surrounding episodes of mass human rights abuses.

Still, a number of transitional societies have prioritized delivering justice to victims, viewing justice both as an end in itself and a means for facilitating reconciliation. Domestic or international trials are the most obvious way to pursue justice. The Nuremberg court, Tokyo Trials, *ad hoc* tribunals in Rwanda and Yugoslavia, and International Criminal Court are the best known international examples. The trials of Adolf Eichmann in Israel and Augusto Pinochet in Chile are examples of domestic proceedings conducted in domestic courts. The ECCC and other hybrid courts in Sierra Leone, East Timor, and Kosovo lie in between, mixing domestic and international elements.

Such trials generally are not designed with reconciliation foremost in mind, but advocates suggest that they facilitate reconciliation by putting selected defendants on trial, assigning culpability, acknowledging victims' suffering, and expunging impunity. In some cases, criminal trials may even elicit explanations, confessions, and apologies. Supporters of criminal trials argue that after those considered most responsible for mass atrocities are prosecuted, victims are less likely to harbor vindictive feelings and are more apt to look forward toward building a shared future. Advocates of the ECCC generally hold this position, though opinions on the tribunal's potential impact on reconciliation vary.

Trials are not the only ways to deliver a sense of justice. In some states, such as post-communist countries in Eastern Europe, lustration laws bar certain members of abusive past regimes from holding public office. Lustration is often seen as a way to "purify" the new regime while exacting some retribution for their offenses. However, it is problematic because it involves a presumption of guilt and sometimes excludes some of the most technically competent people from serving in the new government. Cambodia implemented a partial lustration policy in the 1990s by banning the Khmer Rouge organization, but that policy was blended with an amnesty plan that allowed certain rebels to gain government posts.

A different approach to justice is "restorative." Restorative mechanisms focus not on punishment but on compensating victims for abuse, usually through economic means. Civil remedies can be provided to victims—either in the form of financial compensation or more symbolic measures—to recognize and help address their suffering. The theory is again that people are less likely to be resentful and vindictive if they perceive some of their losses to be redressed. In Cambodia, it would be impossible to offer millions of survivors adequate financial compensation for all of the damage wreaked by Khmer Rouge rule. Thus, as discussed in Chapter 5, the ECCC created a new mechanism for civil party participation—a mechanism that is now in some jeopardy—and is considering "collective or moral" reparations as a complementary path to restorative justice.

CEREMONIES AND MEMORIALS

Moral or collective reparations point to a further way to promote reconciliation. Public ceremonies, memorials, or artistic performances may help survivors express their pain, honor lost loved ones, and achieve a greater degree of healing. Such ceremonies and memorials do not always promote reconciliation—they can easily have an opposite impact if used to stoke resentment or deepen divides. (As we will discuss below, that has sometimes been the case in Cambodia.) Nevertheless, ceremonies and memorials offer at least the potential for healing and reconciliation, especially when both sides of a former conflict participate as a show of unity. A notable example occurred in May 2005, when Germany's political leaders presided with Jewish delegates over the opening of a new Holocaust memorial in Berlin.

PSYCHOLOGICAL AND SPIRITUAL COUNSELLING

Grave human rights abuses leave deep psychological scars on their victims. Untold numbers of survivors suffer from post-traumatic stress disorder (PTSD) and related ailments. They may experience a range of symptoms including insomnia, depression, nightmares, headaches, vertigo, intestinal ailments, occasional blackouts, and a heightened propensity to violence. PTSD and related illnesses are also correlated to drug and alcohol addiction, suicide, spousal and child abuse, and many other social ills. These psychological ailments help explain the lamentably high rates of substance abuse, domestic violence, and other destructive behavior in many post-conflict societies. Most developing countries that emerge from war are poorly equipped to offer the types of mental health services required by their populations due to poverty, poor health care infrastructure, and frequent biases against mental illness.

Contemporary Cambodian society exhibits all of these problems.

Mental health professionals may find some of their most valued allies in wats, churches, mosques, and other places of worship and reflection. To many people, in Cambodia and other societies, the concept of reconciliation has a strong spiritual or religious connotation. People "reconcile" as they achieve a sense of spiritual peace and either accept or forgive the wrongs committed against them. In Cambodia, where over 90 percent of the population is Buddhist, reconciliation by individuals and among former victims and perpetrators is related to Buddhist principles of tolerance and forgiveness. The Khmer religious tradition of prioritizing forgiveness is one of the possible keys to healing past wounds, both at individual and societal levels.

Individual and community-level reconciliation are closely related, especially in countries like Cambodia where former adversaries—and the victims and perpetrators of serious past crimes—often live side by side. As individuals achieve a degree of personal healing, societal problems become easier to address, and vice versa. Daniel Bar-Tal argues that psychological reconciliation must be coupled with a "societal-cultural process" aimed at engaging people from all walks of life and creating the conditions for "psychological changes in society members' beliefs, attitudes, and motivations for the reconciliation process."[10]

THE NEED FOR A MULTI-FACETED APPROACH

Advancing reconciliation at the individual, community, and national levels almost always requires a variety of processes. As Johan Galtung wrote candidly, "nobody really knows how to successfully achieve it."[11] The effectiveness of each individual measure depends on timing, cultural context, and other factors. Louis Kreisberg warns that reconciliation efforts can sometimes work at cross-purposes, and their effects are normally complex, affecting people in many different ways.[12] Desmond Tutu adds that: "There is no handy roadmap for reconciliation…each society must discover its own route."[13] He thus provides a reminder that mechanisms need to be carefully designed and sequenced with an eye toward local culture and political conditions to be effective.[14] Reconciliation is not a process that can be easily imposed "from above." National governments and international agencies can certainly play facilitating roles, but to be effective, reconciliation needs to take hold locally and work from the "bottom up" as well. In a leading study on reconciliation in Khmer society, Suzannah Linton has emphasized the importance of grassroots-level processes.[15] The next section of this chapter reviews some past approaches to reconciliation in Cambodia, leading up to the establishment of the ECCC.

Scene from the play, Breaking the Silence. Photo by Ritch Martens.
Source: Documentation Center of Cambodia Archives.

Living Documents leader Sok-Kheang Ly leading a DC-Cam outreach activity in Kampong Speu province.
Source: Documentation Center of Cambodia Archives.

DC-Cam film team member Bunthy Chey working at a DC-Cam outreach activity in Stung Treng province.
Source: Documentation Center of Cambodia Archives.

CAMBODIA'S PATH TOWARD RECONCILIATION

The ECCC is certainly not the first effort to promote reconciliation in Cambodia. By 1979, when the DK regime collapsed, Cambodian society had been torn asunder by years of civil war and the Killing Fields. In the three decades since the fall of the Khmer Rouge regime, Cambodians have sought in various ways to move on with their lives and seek a degree of closure. The Cambodian government and non-state actors have undertaken numerous efforts to deal with the disaster of the 1970s and to foster various types of "reconciliation." A number of governmental initiatives, faith-based or community efforts, and personal journeys have helped Cambodians survive and begin to rebuild. Indeed, the ECCC might not have been possible if a quarter century of such efforts had not provided enabling social and political conditions for the Khmer Rouge trials.

Nevertheless, Cambodia's journey toward reconciliation has not been straightforward or entirely successful. Not all of the efforts to deal with the legacy of Democratic Kampuchea have been conducive to restoring hope and mutual trust among former adversaries. In the sections below, we review progress toward reconciliation to date, cite a number of key shortcomings, and discuss what remains to be done if Cambodians are to enjoy a more genuine or complete form of reconciliation in the future.

EARLY REPRISALS AND THE PEOPLE'S REVOLUTIONARY TRIBUNAL

Reconciliation does not happen automatically, and many Cambodians initially found it difficult to forgive the atrocities they had suffered. In the years following the DK regime, much (and perhaps most) of the population harbored vindictive feelings against former Khmer Rouge cadres. Some survivors turned to violence to release their anger. Revenge killings took place in various parts of the country, as survivors took reprisal for the deaths of their loved ones and other members of their communities. Violence was not the response of most survivors; many victims decided to leave Khmer Rouge cadres to face their *Karmic* consequences. The killings were largely spontaneous and were not conducted in a systematic, widespread or organized fashion. Nevertheless, some survivors of the Killing Fields felt that only revenge could give them a sense of justice and a degree of closure with the past. As blood spilled in villages across the country, reconciliation seemed a distant dream.

The new People's Republic of Kampuchea (PRK) regime—the successor government to Democratic Kampuchea—faced a dilemma. Many of its own officials and troops sought revenge against the Khmer Rouge, and demonizing Pol Pot's forces helped legitimize PRK rule. However, violent reprisals against some former Khmer Rouge cadres threatened to exacerbate Cambodia's civil war and push greater numbers of former DK rank and file into the jungles, where they would fight alongside Pol Pot's forces instead of defecting to the new government or dropping their arms. Thus, the PRK had powerful incentives to stop the revenge killings, even if it had little sympathy for former Khmer Rouge cadres. As the PRK beefed up security and strengthened law and order, most parts of the country gradually became more peaceful.

Partly to reduce the continuing cycle of violence, the PRK government arranged the People's Revolutionary Tribunal in August 1979. That brief trial—discussed in Chapter 1—resulted in condemnation of the Khmer Rouge regime and death sentences for Pol Pot and Ieng Sary. There were several reasons for holding the trial, but one was evidently to foster a degree of societal reconciliation by identifying senior DK chieftains and their "hegemonic" Chinese sponsors as the primary sources of Khmer Rouge terror. The 1979 tribunal did not target low-level DK cadres or even mid-level officers.

The 1979 tribunal was an important part of the PRK government's policy to bring about a form of national political reconciliation on politically favorable terms. By assigning primary responsibility for the atrocities of Democratic Kampuchea to the "Pol Pot clique" and its sponsors, and by avoiding an all-out effort to prosecute lower-level Communist Party of Kampuchea (CPK) cadres, the PRK sought to leave the door open to defectors.

It is difficult to measure the effects of the 1979 tribunal on Cambodian society; credible studies are lacking. The tribunal may have had some positive effects on the margins. It provided public recognition of the suffering of millions of people under DK rule. Without the trials, survivors might have felt that their suffering was simply ignored, and the cycle of the revenge killings might have been more difficult to stop. Indeed, revenge killings subsided. Nevertheless, the tribunal was no panacea. Many observers—especially abroad—saw the process as a show trial aimed at justifying the Vietnamese occupation of Cambodia. The convicted defendants eluded capture, the Khmer Rouge movement survived, and guerilla war continued. Many survivors found the trials inadequate to make them forgive and reconcile with low-level Khmer Rouge cadres. Societal tension remained very close to the surface.

There were also other judicial processes in Cambodia to deal with the crimes of Democratic Kampuchea. Numerous former Khmer Rouge cadres faced punishment, particularly those captured in battle after the fall of the Pol Pot regime. Some were reportedly executed by Vietnamese troops after summary proceedings. Others were sent to prison or subject to other penalties by Cambodian courts or administrative agencies.[16] Nevertheless, the primary thrust of PRK policy was to lure Khmer Rouge insurgents out of the jungle and reintegrate them into society. The PRK government even dispatched a circular to Khmer Rouge rebels in April 1979 explaining that they would be welcomed back into the fold if they ceased their rebellion, apologized, underwent re-education, and pledged allegiance to the new government.[17]

A TYPE OF TRUTH COMMISSION

From 1980 to 1983, the PRK government carried out additional measures to supplement criminal trials. The PRK National Assembly passed a resolution condemning the crimes of the "Pol Pot-Ieng Sary-Khieu Samphan clique," and an organization within the government called the *Renakse* (Salvation Front) also organized a systematic review and condemnation of past Khmer Rouge atrocities. In 1983, the *Renakse* organized a "Conference of Intellectuals and Monks" to shed light on the DK regime's abuses. The *Renakse* then undertook a major program around the country to gather local communities to discuss the DK experience.

The series of community meetings organized by the PRK government in 1983 were much like a truth commission, although they were not labeled as such. The *Renakse* committee in charge of the process interviewed DK survivors around Cambodia, amassed evidence of damage done by the Khmer Rouge to people and property, dug up mass graves, examined documents, and wrote a report to the government. The *Renakse* commission also invited victims to sign petitions enumerating Khmer Rouge atrocities in particular parts of the country. According to PRK authorities, nearly 9,000 petitions were drafted. Well over 1,000 survive today in the Documentation Center of Cambodia (DC-Cam) archives, containing the signatures or thumbprints of 1,166,307 victims.[18] The petitions were designed partly to recognize the victims of DK terror, acknowledge their suffering, and make their voices heard. The petitions indeed became a meaningful tool among the survivors to condemn the despicable and inhumane acts of the Khmer Rouge.

Nevertheless, the truth commission-type process organized by the PRK government was not nearly as effective as it could have been. Like the 1979 trials, it suffered from both procedural flaws and overt politicization. As Etcheson has argued, the process failed to disseminate its findings widely to the public, limiting its ability to inform the public about the past.[19] The process was also one-sided in the sense that it did not seek to provide a voice to former Khmer Rouge officials and cadres. It thus lacked dialogue among adversaries, which is often crucial in the quest for truth and reconciliation.

The *Renakse* process also had limited effects due to the same political factors that undermined the 1979 tribunal's legitimacy. It was undeniable that the petitions were initiated to serve the political interests of the new regime. The petitions were signed during a period when the PRK government was seeking domestic and international legitimacy and lobbying to occupy Cambodia's seat at the United Nations. As discussed in Chapter 1, at that time most of the world recognized a "coalition government" including royalist and Khmer Rouge members as the rightful sovereigns of the country.

Most of the *Renakse* petitions were drafted by PRK officials, and many included arguments about the legitimacy of the PRK government and its entitlement to Cambodia's UN seat. In fact, the government intended to submit the petitions to the United Nations in furtherance of its claim to the General Assembly seat. The *Renakse* report also estimated the death toll in Democratic Kampuchea at almost 3.5 million—much higher than other estimates. All of these facts contributed to a sense in many quarters that the PRK's fact-finding inquiry was more about politics than truth and reconciliation.

MEMORIALS AND CEREMONIES

In addition to the 1979 tribunal and the *Renakse* process, the PRK government attempted to address the Khmer Rouge legacy by erecting national or local memorials and organizing ceremonies to honor the deceased. A stupa at the infamous "Killing Fields" of Choeung Ek near Phnom Penh was one prominent example; a museum at the former Tuol Sleng Secondary School, site of the infamous S-21 prison, was another.

Many Cambodians believed that victims who died violent deaths and received improper burials would not be able to be reborn. Thus, during the *Renakse* investigation, PRK officials and ordinary people excavated the remains from nearly 20,000 mass graves around the country and consecrated those remains in religious ceremonies honoring the dead. In 1983 and 1984, approximately 89 memorials were constructed around the country to serve as public spaces for both individual and public mourning and as educational sites for visitors.

The government also played a key role in developing ceremonies around the memorials. Beginning on May 20, 1983, Cambodians began to celebrate a "Day of Anger" to recall the abuses of the Khmer Rouge regime. The ceremony has been used partly to provide Cambodians with an opportunity to acknowledge past suffering, come together as a community, and remember the dead. However, as with the other PRK initiatives described above, it has also served a clear political purpose. The ceremony has directed public venom at the Khmer Rouge and built support for the PRK leadership and successive governments. A speech by President of the PRK National Assembly Chea Sim on the 1986 Day of Anger reflected this dynamic:

> Beloved comrades and friends…those who died are reminding us to be vigilant, to strengthen our solidarity and practice revolutionary activities. We must be on the alert against the cruelties and poisonous tricks of the enemy…[20]

In the context of a continuing guerilla war, the Day of Anger functioned more as a rallying cry against the surviving Khmer Rouge movement than as a call to lay down arms and reconcile.

Even after the dissolution of the Khmer Rouge insurgency, Cambodian leaders have too often used the Day of Anger to stir vitriol for the sake of partisan advantage, reducing the ceremony's possible contribution to reconciliation. Going forward, Cambodians need a national day of remembrance that focuses on all of the deceased and brings together survivors to commemorate their lost loved ones in a neutral, non-political spirit.

Not all of the social responses to the Khmer Rouge tragedy after 1979 were organized by the government. Cambodians also took steps toward reconciliation on personal or community levels. Many built small private stupas and engaged in individual prayer to cope with their grief. Families and communities also developed numerous ways of remembering their lost loved ones and attempting to reconcile. Many such efforts have taken place around the annual *phchum ben* festival, in which Khmer Buddhists honor their ancestors.

Phchum ben and other religious festivals—including those of other faiths such as Christianity and Islam—have provided sacred public spaces where survivors can preserve their memories and support one another. After suffering relentless attack from the atheistic DK regime, religious organizations have rebuilt in Cambodia, and they again form a crucial part of the fabric of most of the country's local communities. In the absence of robust medical and social services, religious structures and gatherings will continue to serve as some of the most important places where survivors go to talk about their experiences and to heal.

The outpouring of anguish and resentment on the Day of Anger, *phchum ben*, and other occasions are reminders that for many Cambodians, the process of healing is by no means complete. These local reconciliation processes must continue and be strengthened to achieve genuine reconciliation in Cambodia at individual and societal levels in harmony with Cambodia's traditions and culture.

WAR AND DEFERRED RECONCILIATION

During the early and mid-1980s, Cambodia's warring factions were anything but reconciled. In fact, the PRK government was taking active and controversial measures under the so-called "K-5" plan to build walls between Khmer Rouge guerillas and the rest of the population. The PRK government created wooden fences, pursued deforestation, and laid down a belt of landmines along the Thai-Cambodian border to prevent the infiltration of Khmer Rouge into the country. Hundreds of thousands of Cambodians were recruited or compelled to participate in the K-5 scheme.[21] It resulted in thousands of deaths and injuries on both sides of the conflict and contributed to lasting resentment in some communities against the PRK regime and the Cambodian People's Party (CPP).

One goal of the policy was to compel Khmer Rouge cadres to lay down their guns and defect to the government. The PRK government established an effective "Battlefield Radio Program" designed to entice defectors. Broadcasts emphasized the strength and nationalistic credentials of the new regime by playing powerful renditions of traditional Khmer music on buffalo horns. Radio and other media were also used to announce that defecting Khmer Rouge cadres would be welcome to return to their communities. Radio programs included the voices of wives of Khmer Rouge guerillas, asking their husbands to come home.[22]

Instead of putting defectors on trial, the PRK said that they would be accepted back into the fold after a period of re-education. Normal soldiers were required to undertake only five days of re-education and had to ask for forgiveness from the community. Defectors with serious debts of blood had to endure longer periods of re-education from three to five years.[23] The re-education program was run at the commune level and was designed "to explain the policy of compassion endowed with humanitarianism for all those who come back to the people and the genuine revolution."[24] Defectors who showed fealty to the PRK regime were eventually accepted; those identified as disloyal to the PRK were punished.[25]

The K-5 plan proved highly unpopular—at home and abroad—due to the heavy loss of life that resulted from its aggressive counter-insurgency measures. It was also difficult to reconcile in any meaningful way while the war continued. Nevertheless, the conciliatory aspects of PRK policy in the late 1980s contained the seeds of a fruitful approach to reconciliation. Opening the door to social reintegration has been an essential part of healing Cambodia's wounds after decades of conflict. Seeking forgiveness is also crucial. The PRK requirement that former Khmer Rouge cadres apologize for wrongdoing was particularly resonant with Cambodian cultural norms and conducive to social healing.

PEACE AND THE CHALLENGES OF POLITICAL RECONCILIATION

The efforts to hammer out a peace settlement in Cambodia—described in Chapter 1—were to be a turning point toward political reconciliation. On October 23, 1991, a comprehensive political settlement to Cambodia's civil war was a major step toward ending the long suffering of the Cambodian people and opening the space for longer-term peace-building. The Paris Peace Agreement was reached and designed, among other things, to "restore and maintain peace in Cambodia [and] to promote national reconciliation."[26] The Agreement paved the path for disarmament, demobilization and reintegration endorsed by the United Nations Transitional Authority in Cambodia (UNTAC).

UNTAC provided an important contribution to Cambodia's political reconstitution. UN officials administered many aspects of the country's affairs for 18 months, helping to dampen conflict and organizing national elections. The UNTAC-overseen elections led to the formation of a new government in 1993 and were the first democratic elections in the country after decades of war and mass atrocities.

Nevertheless, UNTAC's effort to bring peace and reconciliation to the Cambodian people was not entirely successful. Although the Khmers Rouges were signatories to the Paris Peace Accords, they refused to disarm and demobilize. Instead, they boycotted the election and continued waging guerrilla warfare. Cambodia would enjoy neither peace nor genuine reconciliation as long as the insurgency continued.[27]

AMNESTY AND PARDONS IN THE 1990S

The Cambodian government's drive to dismember the Khmer Rouge movement and pacify the countryside continued in the mid-1990s. The government implemented a "reconciliation policy" that it considered the most promising way to deal with the Khmer Rouge problem and wipe out the still-festering insurgency. It essentially gave Khmer Rouge guerillas the same choice they had in the 1980s: they could face a hard-nosed counterinsurgency or seek to re-integrate peacefully. The difference was that the insurgents had dwindling support and a weaker bargaining position after the UNTAC period.

The government's "reconciliation" program was quite successful in securing defections. In 1996, Ieng Sary, former DK foreign minister, led a large fraction of the guerilla forces to defect. In September of the same year, King Norodom Sihanouk granted him a royal amnesty and pardon. The mass defections almost brought the Khmer Rouge armed resistance to a halt. Two years later, former DK Head of State Khieu Samphan and former Deputy Chairman of the Communist Party of Kampuchea Nuon Chea followed in Ieng Sary's footsteps. Those former DK leaders were welcomed into the national fold by Prime Minister Hun Sen, who lauded their roles in fostering reconciliation. King Sihanouk also congratulated Hun Sen for his policy of national reconciliation.

For a time, the government's reconciliation plan put the question of justice on the back burner. It was only in late 1990s, after the Khmer Rouge movement essentially imploded—and Hun Sen had announced that reconciliation had been achieved in Cambodia—that the negotiations for a criminal tribunal began in earnest. The Cambodian government's approach to reconciliation and justice was thus sequential in nature, with the goal of justice subordinated to the interest in stabilizing the country politically.

THE LIMITS OF PAST APPROACHES

Critics of the Cambodian government argue that the "reconciliation" obtained through its amnesty policy is illusory. Indeed, the reconciliation processes pursued to date have been limited in a few important respects. They have not provided justice; they have not contributed to a full and impartial history of the period; and they have not involved sufficient grassroots public participation. Deals cut among rival elites have helped pacify the country—which is an achievement not to be overlooked—but those deals have not adequately addressed the needs of ordinary survivors.

THE ABSENCE OF JUSTICE

The first problem with reconciliation efforts to date has been the continuing existence of impunity. Criminal trials cannot guarantee individual and societal healing, and they are not always conducive to peace and reconciliation. However, we argue that at this stage in the process, justice can help to advance Cambodians' quest for personal and societal reconciliation. Assigning responsibility helps meet victims' needs, challenges impunity, and reduces the tendency of victims to act out revenge or impute collective guilt to an entire community of perceived abusers.[28] Youk Chhang argues that:

> Peace requires more than the absence of armies in open combat. A peaceful society is a just society, and the Cambodian people have not yet found justice. Peace will not truly come to Cambodia until there is real justice for the crimes of the Khmer Rouge regime.[29]

Impunity has made it difficult for most Cambodians to cope with past injustices. Without genuine apologies or explanations from the architects of Khmer Rouge terror, many have also been unable to begin trusting (or even forgiving) the low-level former Khmer Rouge cadres living in their midst.

The idea that justice will facilitate reconciliation is subject to legitimate debate. Until the late 1990s, the Cambodian government said little about prosecuting Khmer Rouge defectors, concerned that trials would discourage others from laying down their arms and coming out of the jungle.[30] The government instead focused on enticing defectors and promoting "national reconciliation." Some observers criticized the policy, but in the midst of a simmering guerilla war, it was not an outlandish path to follow. Even after the Khmer Rouge insurgency ceased to be a credible military threat, critics of the tribunal argued that putting DK officials on trial poses a major risk to the reconciliation wrought by the government's amnesty program. In 1999, Ieng Sary issued a thinly veiled public warning against the trials, arguing that: "anything that leads to the division of national reconciliation should be avoided."[31]

Since the negotiations for the tribunal began, the Cambodian government has often warned of possible conflict if the trials were to expand beyond a handful of key defendants. Hun Sen has echoed that argument in recent months as part of his opposition to charging additional suspects, saying that he "would prefer to see this tribunal fail rather than seeing war return to my country."[32] This again emphasizes the frequent tension between concepts of justice and national reconciliation. CPP leaders are not the only political figures to argue that trials could reopen old political and societal wounds. The King's brother, Prince Norodom Yuvaneath—warned in 2006 of the potential destabilizing effect of trials. This risk has also been cited by some analysts as a reason why King-Father Norodom Sihanouk should not be directly involved in the proceedings.[33]

The possibility that the Khmer Rouge trials could trigger violence should not be dismissed lightly in Cambodia, which has suffered many bouts of conflict in recent decades. The argument that amnesty programs need to be credible to be effective also cannot be easily brushed aside. The more often international tribunals override pardons, the more likely it is that combatants will view amnesty schemes with caution in the future. The concepts of reconciliation and justice do not always fit as neatly together in the real world as one would like.

Still, pursuing justice in Cambodia is more likely to enhance reconciliation (in all of its forms) than to jeopardize it. The first three years of the ECCC's operations have not prompted outbreaks of violence, and upheaval appears unlikely in the near future. The passage of time is one reason, but another appears to be broad-based public acceptance of the basic legitimacy of the process. It is worth noting that even in societies with more recent conflicts—such as East Timor, Sierra Leone, and Kosovo—mixed tribunals have not provoked widespread violence. Whether the trials have caused the restoration of relative peace and stability in those countries is difficult to establish, but mixed tribunals have not generated a resumption of hostilities. The same is true for the international tribunals established for the former Yugoslavia and Rwanda.

INSUFFICIENT TRUTH-TELLING AND PUBLIC EDUCATION

A second problem with past reconciliation efforts has been their limited contribution to the truth and their failure to provide sufficient education to the general population. As noted above, even the process of collecting the *Renakse* petitions—which involved well over one million Cambodians—did not result in publicly disseminated findings. The Cambodian government has generally shied away from grassroots programs that would encourage more robust discussion of Khmer Rouge atrocities and contribute to a fuller historical account of the period. The government has consistently expressed concern that reopening dialogue could provoke revenge killings and civil unrest. Those concerns had to be taken seriously until the Khmer Rouge movement fell apart in the late 1990s but appear less well-founded today.

A somewhat seamier reason for the reluctance to examine the past by the Cambodian government—and at least some key international actors—may be that a broad public discussion of the Khmer Rouge problem would expose dirty laundry. Domestically, it could draw attention to deals that both the CPP and FUNCINPEC made with Khmer Rouge villains during the amnesty process. Even more problematically, public discussion could unearth details about the activities of numerous current officials during the early stages of the DK era. A truth commission could also unearth (or focus attention on) embarrassing and damaging facts about foreign involvement in the country during the DK era and in surrounding periods.

The government's amnesty plan certainly did have profound consequences for ordinary Cambodians by helping to pacify the country, but it was primarily conducted between rival political elites. The major turning points involved deals struck between major political parties and members of the Khmer Rouge leadership. Far from including a broad spectrum of Cambodians, these deals were often done quietly to avoid inviting public indignation. Amnesty deals that seemed to reward Khmer Rouge thugs for their conduct would certainly have been unwelcome to many survivors of the DK period.

The government's plan did not include broad public participation, and it did not produce apologies sufficient to generate significant public forgiveness. In late December 1998, Hun Sen required two former Khmer Rouge heavyweights—Khieu Samphan and Nuon Chea—to hold a press conference at the start of a "national reconciliation tour" around the country. Their meager apologies did little to ease the suffering of victims. Khieu Samphan said that he was sorry but added that Cambodians should "forget the past" and "let bygones be bygones." Nuon Chea expressed vague sorrow for the "lives of the people" and "animals that suffered because of the war."[34] Hun Sen announced that the two key defectors should be greeted not with handcuffs but with a "bouquet of flowers."[35] This approach facilitated peace, which was no mean feat, but it did not provide the public with a sense of justice or offer any explanation for the atrocities of the late 1970s.

FAILURE TO ADDRESS INDIVIDUAL NEEDS

A third shortcoming of past reconciliation approaches has been their limited treatment of individual needs. Those needs are partly economic, as the destruction of the economy and educational system by the CPK and ensuing warfare contributed to widespread poverty in Cambodia today. The Cambodian government has had neither the resources nor the apparent political will to make a serious effort at reparations. Indeed, many DK survivors have suffered continuing economic injustice due to high levels of official corruption and mismanagement in the post-1979 period.

Individual needs are also emotional and psychological. Research by DC-Cam, the Transcultural

Psychosocial Organization, and international experts suggests that a tremendous number of DK survivors—perhaps into the millions—suffer from PTSD and related disorders.[36] Accurate clinical statistics are difficult to find in a country with such a limited mental health care apparatus, but mass human rights abuses during the 1970s and surrounding periods clearly inflicted deep psychological wounds on many (and probably most) survivors.

Treating psychological wounds is not easy in any society, and Cambodia lacks the health care infrastructure needed to do so effectively. One terrible legacy of Democratic Kampuchea is that it decimated the country's corps of medical professionals. Doctors and psychologists were among the many intellectuals that *Angkar* sought to wipe out in the population. During the 1980s, the PRK government labored under international sanctions, and the country's few medical students learned much of their craft from second-rate Soviet and Vietnamese textbooks.

Even after the UNTAC period, the country has been slow to rebuild its health care system, particularly in the area of mental health. A lack of resources, "brain drain" to Western countries, and a degree of societal discomfort with mental health issues—common in many developing countries—have all conspired against the development of robust mental health capacity. Today, only about three dozen trained psychiatrists operate in a country of almost 15 million.[37] The woeful inadequacy of trained mental health professionals places severe limits on Cambodia's ability to address reconciliation on an individual level.

THE ECCC'S ROLE IN RECONCILIATION

The preceding section points to important unfinished business in Cambodia's effort to achieve reconciliation. One is the need for a greater sense of justice. Another is the need for a broader public discussion of the history surrounding Khmer Rouge abuses. Supporters of the tribunal argue that by delivering justice and providing a more official historical account of the period, the ECCC will help Cambodians reconcile. Critics respond that trying a handful of Khmer Rouge defendants ensures that justice will be limited in nature and that the history revealed in the trials will be far from complete. They express scepticism about the capacity of the tribunal to help Cambodians heal old wounds and divides.

In this section, we contend that the ECCC can contribute meaningfully to societal healing in Cambodia, though its effects on reconciliation will almost certainly be diffuse and difficult to measure. We argue that the Khmer Rouge trials are occurring at a time when a limited set of trials is unlikely to precipitate renewed hostilities. Cambodians have achieved a level of peaceful co-existence, and many are prepared to go further down the road of reconciliation to achieve a better historical understanding and begin to close long-standing societal cleavages. Impunity stands as a roadblock, and we believe the ECCC can facilitate reconciliation in large part by removing that barrier and providing at least a partial sense of justice. It can also help Cambodia take the next step by exposing truths about Democratic Kampuchea. To achieve these outcomes, the ECCC will need to redouble its efforts on public outreach, participation, and education and work synergistically with other relevant organizations.

DELIVERING CREDIBLE JUSTICE

By creating the ECCC instead of a truth commission or alternative mechanism, the United Nations and Cambodian government put justice at the center of their effort to deal with the Khmer Rouge legacy. Justice can be considered an end in itself, but as discussed above, it can also promote reconciliation at both societal and individual levels. By putting an end to the unfettered impunity that Khmer Rouge officials have enjoyed since their reign of terror, the ECCC can ease at least some of the frustration that makes it difficult for DK survivors to achieve closure.

TACKLING IMPUNITY

For individuals who suffered under Khmer Rouge rule, seeing key perpetrators brought to justice is likely to be important in healing deep emotional and psychological wounds. In Cambodia as elsewhere, many victims will not perceive justice to be done unless they see that people most responsible for their suffering are held accountable and punished. Public participation in the ECCC process gives victims a chance to air their grievances formally and enables at least some to participate directly in the trials. Victims are likely to feel a sense of vindication when they see former CPK leaders standing in the dock, confronted for their alleged crimes, and punished if found guilty.

The ECCC proceedings may also produce a number of apologies or explanations by Khmer Rouge defendants or lower-level witnesses. One Khmer Rouge defendant, Duch, has already confessed to crimes, apologized, and sought forgiveness at the ECCC. Others currently in custody, including Nuon Chea and Khieu Samphan, have issued relatively vague apologies in the past but have not yet apologized during the ECCC proceedings. As we discuss below, most survivors have rejected past apologies by senior Khmer Rouge figures and continue to demand criminal justice. By apologizing, however, defendants assume a certain responsibility for Khmer Rouge terror. Implicit or explicit admissions by senior CPK officials could help some Cambodians proceed toward reconciliation with former low-level Khmer Rouge cadres, many of whom can also be considered victims of the DK regime.

As critics of the tribunal emphasize, criminal trials are not without dangers. Any trials after a period of conflict run at least a small risk of reopening old wounds—one reason why the Cambodian government has sometimes expressed ambivalence about the trials. If that were to happen, the ECCC could frustrate national reconciliation rather than advancing it. Like other tribunals, the ECCC has tried to reduce that possibility (and conserve scarce resources) by focusing only on former senior leaders of the CPK and others deemed "most responsible" for the crimes of Democratic Kampuchea. This approach implicitly recognizes the distinction between key policymakers and lower-level foot soldiers who were, in some cases, swept up in the machinery. One reason for making such a distinction is to help alleviate tensions between ordinary Cambodians and contribute to the reintegration of former Khmer Rouge cadres into mainstream Cambodian society.

If the ECCC is able to deliver credible verdicts, it can help regenerate Cambodians' faith in societal norms and the legal and institutional system designed to enforce them. Indeed, one of the arguments in favor of mixed tribunals like the ECCC is that they can facilitate knowledge transfer and set a powerful local example of justice. There is limited evidence to date that mixed tribunals markedly strengthen domestic judiciaries, and the ECCC certainly will not revolutionize Cambodia's legal and political systems overnight. Still, the ECCC represents an important step in developing a stronger "rule of law" in Cambodia—a system that protects basic individual rights and holds no people or entities above the law. One of the end-goals of the reconciliation process in a troubled society is to establish precisely such a system that reduces the likelihood of future crimes and enables people to redress wrongs in courtrooms rather than the battlefield.

RESTORATIVE JUSTICE AND RECONCILIATION

In addition to delivering retributive justice, the ECCC is designed to provide a modest measure of restorative justice. As emphasized in Chapter 5, the creation of a civil party mechanism and the possibility of collective moral reparations were major advances by the ECCC and offer the possibility of a lasting contribution to reconciliation (though the civil party mechanism is now in doubt). Reparations in the form of monuments, parks, or community service centers will never amount to full compensation for past atrocities, and it is important to manage expectations among survivors about the extent of resources that the tribunal can realistically devote to such projects. Still, collective reparations can provide a meaningful sense of recognition of survivors' suffering. They can also help survivors reconcile by creating public spaces for dialogue, reflection, and possibly even certain forms of treatment or counseling.

REVEALING THE TRUTH

If Cambodians are to cope effectively with the Khmer Rouge tragedy, they must understand more about how and why such staggering abuses occurred during the late 1970s. A better understanding of what happened in Democratic Kampuchea, why it happened, and who was most responsible for that era's atrocities can help people achieve a sense of closure and move on. For this reason, some analysts continue to advocate a formal TRC in Cambodia.[38]

The establishment of a formal TRC in Cambodia in the future is unlikely for a few reasons. First, the government and key international actors have dedicated considerable resources to the ECCC, and neither is likely to be eager to fund a TRC after paying the final bill for the Khmer Rouge trials. Second, the Cambodian government has long been wary of a TRC for fear of reopening old wounds at local levels or unearthing politically inconvenient facts about some former Khmers Rouges who are now in positions of power. For reasons explained elsewhere in this book, both the CPP and key international actors have preferred to focus financial resources and attention on assigning responsibility to a limited universe of former Khmer Rouge leaders. When the ECCC completes its work, there will likely be little political momentum, at home or abroad, for a TRC. The key question is therefore how the ECCC can best contribute to truth in addition to its "core mission" of providing criminal justice.

Knowing more about the history of Democratic Kampuchea is exceedingly important to survivors and other members of the public. In a 2002 survey conducted by DC-Cam, 73% of Cambodian interviewees indicated that they wanted additional information about the history of the Khmer Rouge organization and the DK regime. In a 2008 survey of 1,000 adult Cambodians by the Human Rights Center at the University of California-Berkeley, 85% of respondents said that they wanted to know more about the Khmer Rouge period. Cambodians have a right to learn the truth about their country's troubled history so that they can take appropriate steps to reconcile and prevent future abuses.

The current state of Cambodians' knowledge about the Khmer Rouge regime is dire. Most Cambodians know little about the suspects now in custody or about the overall workings of Democratic Kampuchea. In the Berkeley survey, 81% of respondents who did not live under the Pol Pot period indicated that their knowledge of that period was poor or very poor. 84% said that their main source of information about the Khmer Rouge period was friends and family; only 6% said that their main source was school.[39] Somewhat shockingly, an educational curriculum on the Pol Pot era is only now being established in Cambodia.[40] The Extraordinary Chambers' findings can help to establish an accepted history that can be disseminated to Cambodians, now and for future generations.

DEVELOPING AN IMPROVED HISTORICAL RECORD

Expectations about the ECCC's ability to serve a "truth-telling" function should be realistic.

The ECCC is not set up as a truth commission. A truth commission would be staffed and organized quite differently, with a much greater focus on arranging for local dialogues and disseminating information for widespread public consumption. Even such a truth commission would be unable to reveal all of the facts about Democratic Kampuchea. One should not expect the ECCC to do so. Its mandate as a criminal tribunal requires that its lawyers and judges focus on the facts relevant to particular charges against specific defendants. One danger of criminal tribunals like the ECCC is that by focusing on the misdeeds of relatively senior officials, they may suggest that only those individuals bore responsibility for the crimes of Democratic Kampuchea.[41] A related problem is that the trials will likely shed light on the high-level operations of the DK regime, but they will not tell most ordinary people what happened in their own communities or to their lost loved ones.

The limited temporal jurisdiction of the tribunal—discussed in Chapter 1—is another reason why the Extraordinary Chambers almost certainly will not provide an exhaustive account of the complex domestic and international forces that helped bring the Khmers Rouges to power or prolonged conflict in the country after 1979. When Cambodians attend public forums about the period, inside and outside of the country, they often ask questions that extend beyond the subjects likely to be featured at the tribunal. Schools and NGOs will need to expand upon the ECCC's findings and provide more information about the many uncomfortable truths of modern Cambodian history.

The complex nature of judicial proceedings will limit the tribunal's truth-telling capability as well. To respect due process and uphold the law, the ECCC needs to deal with a large number of technical legal principles, such as those discussed in Chapters 2 and 3 of this book. Court documents and debates dealing with those principles will be difficult for many non-experts to understand. This is a particularly important point in a country like Cambodia, where many survivors of the DK era have limited literacy and education. That does not mean that the ECCC should avoid the finer points of law, but it does mean that many aspects of the trials will need to be "translated" to maximize their educational value for the public.

The ECCC's form and focus present real challenges; truth and justice do not necessarily come together. Nevertheless, the tribunal can contribute to Cambodians' search for the truth. Numerous histories of the period have been written, but certain aspects of the DK period remain obscure. Key questions still need to be answered. For example, further information is required to show how broad policies established by the Communist Party of Kampuchea translated into concrete abuses. To what extent were atrocities centrally orchestrated, and to what extent did crimes depend on the initiative of local commanders? The motives for Khmer Rouge terror must also be further illuminated. How important was their "ultra-Maoist" ideology? How important were ethnic animosities? The role of foreign powers is a further issue to be clarified. How involved were DK allies from China and elsewhere? Did other states or international organizations contribute to the Khmer Rouge tragedy?

Historians have debated the answers to these and other questions fiercely. The ECCC should not be expected to settle all historical debates, but it has potential to shed light on the workings of the DK regime and its motives. Its legal mandate to collect a wide range of evidence, its accumulated institutional manpower and expertise, and its ability to demand answers from defendants under oath all give it the capacity to add crucial information to the historical record. The suspects in custody occupied important positions in the Khmer Rouge hierarchy, and all except Duch had relatively broad policy responsibility. Adjudicating their cases should therefore require reference to a broad array of facts about Khmer Rouge policies and the workings of the DK organization. Some aspects of the Khmer Rouge regime will remain shrouded without further historical study, but the tribunal can clarify some key points and draw attention to the need for further work outside of the judicial arena.

COMMUNICATING THE TRUTH TO THE PUBLIC

The historical record developed by the ECCC must be communicated effectively to the public if the tribunal is to be a success. The ECCC trials will certainly include some punchy statements or speeches by lawyers, witnesses, and defendants that can be transmitted widely to educate the public. However, as noted above, many of the tribunal's findings will be buried in complex legal documents and long courtroom exchanges that cannot be easily understood by the general population without substantial grooming. The tribunal staff and supporting actors from governments, international organizations, and civil society need mechanisms to share information clearly, accurately, and responsibly.

Communicating complex information to millions of survivors is no easy task, and as argued in Chapter 5, public outreach has been a relative weakness of the tribunal to date. Part of the problem relates to resource allocation. The ECCC Office of Public Affairs was not given enough people or money at the start and remains under-funded. That decision probably reflects an assumption (or hope) that NGOs will pick up much of the slack, but it also sends a worrying signal that informing the general Cambodian public is not a sufficiently high priority. The ECCC organized a "town hall" style gathering in the former Khmer Rouge stronghold of Pailin in January 2008, where court officials explained their work to local communities. The ECCC has also enabled NGOs to bring ordinary Cambodians to the court proceedings.[42] Those efforts are entirely welcome, but they are not nearly enough.

The ECCC has done better at keeping donors and international visitors apprised of progress.

It has produced sophisticated printed materials about the tribunal, organized a very helpful website, welcomed scores of interns, and held routine meetings with diplomats, journalists, and scholars. These are notable successes, but they have steered resources and attention away from the more difficult—and more important—job of helping survivors understand the process.

This is hardly a new challenge for an internationalized tribunal. Almost all other tribunals have been more successful in educating sophisticated observers than the general public. Visiting diplomats, journalists, and scholars generally "speak the same language" as court officials, frequent the same circles, and enjoy personal or professional relationships. Sophisticated observers are also the ones who finance or advertise the tribunals' operations, giving court officials a concrete incentive to keep them informed. Reaching out to the general public is tougher. It requires a different set of communication skills, including local language familiarity, and the time and willingness to spend long hours on dusty rural roads.

Even though the ECCC is not a truth commission, it needs a more sizeable staff with the specific mission of taking the court's findings into the provinces. They need to be armed with simple talking points and very short, accessible printed information that can be disseminated cheaply to hundreds of thousands of readers. That type of outreach effort will likely cost millions of dollars, but it will be only a small part of the tribunal's total outlays and will be money well spent. NGOs can certainly help, especially in areas of the country where citizens have limited access to media outlets, but there is no substitute for sending ECCC officials frequently into the field.

The ECCC also needs to work with newspapers, magazines, and other media outlets to broadcast its message in a clear, digestible manner. It has already made considerable progress on the Internet. The ECCC has developed a site that includes major court documents—a very welcome resource that is conducive both to organizational transparency and public education if it continues to be updated consistently. Although relatively few Cambodians have access to the web, many overseas Khmers and international observers rely on Internet sites to follow the process.[43]

Television is a further key to public outreach. Although most Cambodians do not have easy access to television, those who do have access often prefer TV as a medium for learning about the trials. In the fall 2008 Berkeley survey, about 28% of Cambodian respondents reported seeing some TV news reports about the trials. An overwhelming majority (98%) said that they would be interested in watching live broadcasts of the trials.[44] There are indeed some live broadcasts of the proceedings, as well as weekly digests, and these appear to be generating

A memorial in Siem Reap province. Source: *Documentation Center of Cambodia Archives.*

A memorial in Kampot province. *Source: Documentation Center of Cambodia Archives.*

A memorial in Kandal province. *Source: Documentation Center of Cambodia Archives.*

A memorial in Pursat province. *Source: Documentation Center of Cambodia Archives.*

A memorial at Tuol Sleng. *Source: Documentation Center of Cambodia Archives.*

A memorial in Takeo province. *Source: Documentation Center of Cambodia Archives.*

A memorial in Svay Rieng province. Source: *Documentation Center of Cambodia Archives.*

A memorial in the city of Sihanoukville. *Source: Documentation Center of Cambodia Archives.*

A memorial in Banteay Meanchey province. *Source: Documentation Center of Cambodia Archives.*

significant followings. Although many of the day-to-day proceedings at the ECCC involve technical legal and procedural issues and would hardly make for exciting TV drama, regular news digests of ECCC proceedings are an essential part of the public education process.

MEETING THE NEEDS OF VICTIMS

Last but not least, the ECCC needs to address a crucial factor in the reconciliation process: taking care of victims. Although most Cambodians support the Khmer Rouge trials as a way to challenge impunity and shed light on the reasons for DK atrocities, stirring up those painful memories entails risks. The process could "re-traumatize" many survivors of the Pol Pot era and contribute to added pain before helping them deal with the past and achieve closure. In a psychiatric study conducted in 2006-07, a team of international experts found that 87% of Cambodians surveyed who were over the age of 35 expected the Khmer Rouge trials to bring back painful memories.[45] The trials also have the potential to generate fears of retribution. The road to reconciliation may not be a straight one, and strong protective measures need to be in place.

Direct participants in the trials could be the most vulnerable to re-traumatization.[46] A well-staffed psychological support unit is essential during and after the completion of the trials. This has represented a challenge for the ECCC given budgetary limits and the small number of trained Cambodian counselors. The ECCC has established a psychological support unit through a contract with the Transcultural Psychosocial Organization, which works with both the Victims Unit and Witness and Expert Support Unit. However, that function needs to be expanded, even if resources need to be increased or pulled from other court activities. As the trials proceed, more and more victims and witnesses will need psychological support. The government and civil society will need to be ready to play a much larger role in this area as well, since the trials may generate powerful psychological reactions among many members of the general public.

Public participation—as witnesses, complainants, or civil parties—also presents risks to societal reconciliation. In a study by Geerteke Jansen in Takeo province, many interviewees were asked about the possibility of being called as witnesses at the ECCC. Some said that serving as witnesses would put them in a good position to condemn former Khmer Rouge leaders and release their anger, thus advancing their personal reconciliation. Many said that they no longer feared retribution if they participate in the trials.

Nevertheless, some expressed fear that they would receive threats if called to be witnesses. Many survivors underlined that their safety and that of their families would be in danger when they returned to their home villages. They feared revenge attacks from former low-level cadres or relatives of the Khmer Rouge leaders.[46] These survivors' fears and concerns should be taken into serious consideration, as many now live in close proximity to former Khmer Rouge cadres in their communities. Witness protection mechanisms and confidentiality safeguards are now in place. In implementing those safeguards, the ECCC should err on the side of caution to reduce the possibility of vendettas, which could undermine the social reconciliation that has taken hold in many Cambodian communities where former DK cadres and their families reside. Respecting requests for confidentiality is a cheap way to deal with that problem and will go a long way toward protecting participants. Bolstering witness protection is therefore essential and will require added attention.

IMPACT OF THE ECCC TO DATE

With the trials of former Khmer Rouge officials just underway, it remains to be seen how effective the ECCC and its supporting organizations will be in promoting reconciliation through justice and truth-telling. This section briefly discusses the apparent effects of the ECCC to date, drawing on surveys and studies done by scholars and the NGO community.

AWARENESS OF THE PROCEEDINGS

The Khmer Rouge trials can only foster reconciliation if the public is able to follow and understand them. The Berkeley survey found that most Cambodians do not possess detailed knowledge about the tribunal. 39% of respondents were unaware of its existence, and 46% described their knowledge as limited. Fewer than 1% had participated in an outreach activity in 2007-08.[48] A survey conducted by DC-Cam in 2009, roughly six months later and after the start of the highly publicized *Duch* trial, suggests that some progress is being made. Respondents to that survey indicated that only 17% were unaware of the ECCC; 44% had heard a little; and 39% had been exposed to a significant amount of information about the tribunal.[49] Still, these survey results suggest that the ECCC and supporting organizations have a significant way to go.

PUBLIC EXPECTATIONS OF THE TRIBUNAL

To the extent that Cambodians do know about the tribunal, they generally see it as an important step to achieving a measure of justice. Surveys consistently show that the public supports criminal accountability for at least some former Khmer Rouge officials. In the 2009 DC-Cam survey, 93% of respondents expressed support for the Khmer Rouge trials. Prior surveys by DC-Cam, the International Republican Institute, and Center for Social Development produced similar findings.[50] Moreover, Cambodians who are aware of the ECCC generally approve of its work to date. Their views tend to be considerably more favourable than the views of international observers and human rights groups. In the Berkeley survey, 87% believed that the ECCC should be involved in addressing the Khmer Rouge legacy, and 67% of interviewees perceived the court as fair and impartial.[51] In response to a survey, 74% agreed with the statement that the ECCC would contribute to justice for Khmer Rouge victims and their families, and 67% agreed that the trials would contribute to national reconciliation.[52]

The most common refrain from Cambodians who support the ECCC is that the trials will contribute to justice. Even a modest number of verdicts will end the impunity that senior Khmer Rouge leaders have enjoyed for three decades. Many Cambodians also express the hope that the trials will help them understand why the killing happened—they seek explanations, and perhaps even apologies or confessions.

Not all Cambodians are optimistic about the trials' potential outcome. In the Berkeley survey, 33% of respondents with some knowledge of the court said that they did not expect the ECCC judges to be entirely fair. When asked why they doubted the Court's fairness, this subset of interviewees voiced concerns about the lack of judicial results to date, alleged corruption, and the tribunal's ties to the government. The speed of the trials appears to be a particular concern to the tribunal's Cambodian skeptics.[53] Although these interviewees comprise only a small fraction of the surveyed population, some of the same issues likely concern other Cambodians as well. Moreover, such public concerns could grow if administrative challenges at the ECCC are not adequately addressed. As discussed in Chapter 4, dealing with public perceptions of mismanagement is imperative if the tribunal is to deliver credible justice and contribute to reconciliation.

Overall, the bulk of public opinion appears to rest clearly in favor of the proceedings, even after three years of sometimes bumpy ECCC operations. Most people interviewed by DC-Cam as part of the Living Documents Project—which seeks to educate people about the ECCC and takes survivors to the tribunal to watch selected proceedings—believe that the proceedings are contributing something to justice and the search for the truth.

IS THE ECCC CONDUCIVE TO RECONCILIATION?

It is slightly more difficult to determine whether the ECCC proceedings are contributing to a sense of reconciliation. That challenge stems largely from the difficulty of defining the term "reconciliation" precisely—a challenge emphasized throughout this chapter. The Cambodian government has tended to treat political stability and security as the principal elements of reconciliation, and many Cambodians agree.

In surveys conducted by DC-Cam, most Cambodians associate reconciliation with an end to war, a greater sense of national unity, and a state of working together with former enemies to develop the country for everyone's benefit.[54] For example, one respondent argued that the concept of reconciliation could help Cambodians refrain from shedding blood, raising a well-known adage that: "united, we survive; divided, we die" and "blood needs to be washed by water, if blood is washed by blood, it will remain tainted."[55] The vast majority of Cambodian interviewees approve of this form of reconciliation.

VIEWS AT THE OUTSET OF THE ECCC

At the outset of the ECCC proceedings, most Cambodians interviewees expressed cautious optimism about the potential of the trials to foster reconciliation. DC-Cam conducted extensive interviews with hundreds of survivors around the country in late 2006 and early 2007 and asked them about the trials' possible contribution to reconciliation. Most respondents saw justice and reconciliation as closely related and mutually reinforcing. They considered justice to be essential in getting rid of malice and revenge, deterring future crimes, and thus promoting peace and reconciliation. Two responses from Kampong Cham were indicative:

- "Cambodia was a broken society with protracted internal conflict for many years. The main causal factor was injustice in the society. Therefore, justice at ECCC must be done for the victims if longer-term reconciliation is to be achieved."

- "The idea of reconciliation is good, but to get there legal punishment of the wrongdoers must be meted out severely. In so doing, the tribunal would help prevent future reoccurrence of crimes."[56]

The trials also had support from many key religious figures in the Theravada Buddhist, Cham Muslim, and other communities. Scholar Ian Harris found that Cambodia's senior Buddhist monks broadly agreed that a legal accountability process could be beneficial to reconciliation if it was conducted in accordance with Cambodia's distinct cultural and religious traditions. This, they suggested, would require focusing on truth and reconciliation, not just enforcing the letter of the law and exacting punishment. The very notion of a trial in Buddhist philosophy implies reconciliation through a cathartic revelation of the truth, a calming of anger, and a degree of harmony between estranged parties.[57]

Not everyone shared the view that criminal trials would lead to reconciliation, however. Some Cambodians feared that criminal proceedings will jeopardize a fragile peace among former enemies. For example, one respondent wrote: "I love the ideas of national unity and reconciliation. Justice must not put reconciliation in jeopardy, because we have suffered many generations of hardships and disunity."[58] While most Cambodians were supportive of the trials, a significant minority remained cautious, fearful that old divisions would be redrawn and that national security and stability would be compromised.

VIEWS OF THE ECCC AND RECONCILIATION TODAY

In May 2009, Sok-Kheang Ly conducted a number of additional interviews with Cambodians from Kampong Chhnang province to assess changing attitudes during the first few years of the ECCC's operations. In general, views appear consistent with those expressed at the outset of the trials. The interviews results suggest that most Cambodians believe that the ECCC can deliver justice, contribute to the truth, and foster reconciliation.

Some Cambodians clearly view the Khmer Rouge trials as a way to ease suffering and thus facilitate the reconciliation process. For example, 75-year-old Kai Tit, a representative from the Cham Muslim community, argued that the court proceedings would be beneficial and that "seeing justice done will help us feel relieved. It is like dressing a wound that needs medicine, although it does not provide complete relief." He also argued that collective reparations—in the form of schools or other compensation—had the potential to heal old wounds. Salim, a man whose family members were killed during the DK era, expressed a similar view, arguing that only by using legal means could Cambodia stop the cycle of violence and revenge.[59]

That view appears to be held by many Cambodians, giving hope that the ECCC proceedings can contribute meaningfully to reconciliation. For example, in a series of interviews conducted by Sok-Kheang Ly in August 2009, respondents in the Bakan district of Pursat province said the following:

- "I think that legal justice will bring me some peace of mind. Although I lost five siblings and parents, continuing anger will provide me with no constructive outcome. My vindictiveness will not end. Let the wrong-doers face the consequences, and reconciliation will be easier for me." – *Ngao Ly*, age 43.

- "Justice could bring me a certain degree of reconciliation. However, the losses make it hard for me to reconcile with the losses of my three brothers. Anger at the Khmer Rouge regime will never vanish from my mind." – *Tak Pes*, age 45.

- "I feel so angry about the Khmers Rouges, who caused the death of my parents and two siblings. I wish to see those responsible for the crimes tried and imprisoned. In so doing, reconciliation could be brought to me. I could reduce my tense feeling, but not entirely." – *Slem Sok*, age 54.

- "I lost my father and two siblings. Before the trial, I was overcome with anger at the Khmers Rouges. With the tribunal, I can take a breath of relief now." – *Tort Chea*, age 45.[60]

A significant number of Cambodians remain skeptical of the contribution of the trials to reconciliation, however. They retain deep-seated anger toward both Khmer Rouge leaders and the lower-level cadres who inflicted abuse on their families. During Ly's May 2009 interviews, a woman named Ran—who lost her children during the Pol Pot years—said that she would kill the Khmer Rouge defendants if she could and that peace would not come to her until she passed away. Her fellow villager Sim, who lost her husband to the Killing Fields, also voiced feelings of revenge, favoring the death penalty for defendants—a penalty prohibited by the Cambodian constitution.[61]

These sentiments are understandable; revenge is a normal human impulse in response to grave harm and suffering. The depth of vindictive feelings harbored by many DK survivors will doubtlessly limit the ECCC's contribution to reconciliation, which is a long-term process after a period of mass atrocities. Expectations of the tribunal's impact should be realistic.

PRELIMINARY REACTIONS TO THE DUCH CASE

Public reactions to the case against Duch also provide an indication that the ECCC can help contribute to reconciliation by delivering credible justice, but it cannot produce a deep sense of reconciliation for everyone overnight. Duch's case is particularly interesting in this regard, because he has admitted to wrongdoing and issued an apology. On the second day of his trial, Duch said:

> I would like to express my regretfulness and heartfelt sorrow and loss for all the crimes committed by the [Communist Party of Kampuchea] from 1975 to 1979....I would like to emphasize that I am responsible for the crimes committed at S-21 especially the torture and execution of the people there....May I be permitted to apologize to the survivors of the regime and also the families of the victims whose loved ones died brutally in the regime at S-21...I would like you to please leave an open window for me to seek forgiveness.[62]

Apologies by former perpetrators are often advanced as one possible avenue toward reconciliation. Though no survey or systematic study has been undertaken to gauge the impact of Duch's public confession and apology, recent interviews by DC-Cam with selected civil parties suggest the limits of apologies in facilitating reconciliation and reinforce the importance of justice in the eyes of many survivors.

In May 2009, Terith Chy of DC-Cam interviewed a number of people who survived S-21 or lost relatives there. In general, survivors were loath to accept Duch's apology or request for forgiveness. Indicative quotes include the following:

- "I cannot forgive him in light of what victims suffered. He has to be tried and deserves the punishment imposed by the court."- *Sophan,* Kampong Cham province, who lost her sister at Tuol Sleng.

- "I believe people in general, including me, cannot forgive him. He will have to be judged and punished for the crimes he has committed."- *Piseth*, Svay Rieng province, whose sister-in-law perished at S-21.

- "With the anger I have, I want Duch to be sentenced to life. I want him to live and see the development of the country he once made poor…Although we cannot physically beat him the way he did to us, I do not want him to enjoy freedom as we do." - *Khon*, Kampong Thom province, whose brother was an S-21 victim.

- "It has been 30 years and I cannot lift myself out of poverty because I do not have a father…[Duch's] cooperation is simply to avoid a longer sentence…I cannot reconcile with him." - *Sophea*, Kampong Thom province, who lost her father at S-21 shortly before her birth and discovered his ultimate fate in 2006.[63]

Many Cambodians share the view that bringing former Khmer Rouge officials to justice is a key to reconciliation. Apologies alone will be insufficient, if a large number of survivors accept them at all.

LOOKING AHEAD

As the ECCC proceeds, most Cambodians expect it to facilitate reconciliation, particularly on a personal level. The testimony of S-21 survivor Chum Mey in late July offered a powerful reminder of the tribunal's importance to survivors. He said to the Trial Chamber: "I could never forget the suffering that I received at S-21, until the day that I die…. [but if] justice can be done by Your Honors, then I would feel better." Speaking of Duch's apology, he said that "a few teardrops" from the former S-21 chief "could not wash away the suffering of the more than two million Cambodian people who perished during the regime…only the Court can help to wash away those sufferings."[64]

Still, some continue to fear that the trials could backfire. This latter possibility has been raised more frequently of late, as the Co-Prosecutors consider the possibility of charging additional suspects (an issue discussed in Chapter 3). In the 2009 DC-Cam survey, 37% of respondents expressed concern that expanding the Khmer Rouge trials beyond the existing five defendants could lead to public disorder or violence.[65] The ECCC, like all tribunals of its kind, is grappling with the difficult question of what type of justice can be most conducive to reconciliation.

CONCLUSION

Cambodia faces both special challenges and special opportunities with respect to reconciliation. The challenges are momentous, even long after the demise of the Pol Pot regime. At the level of individuals, the Khmer Rouge reign of terror was particularly destructive due to its relentless attack on victims' most sacred beliefs and relationships. DK ideology targeted family structures, religious creeds, cultural practices, traditional senses of identity, education, and other core parts of the human experience. From a societal standpoint, one particularly painful aspect of the DK experience is that it was not simply a result of malignant external interference. Most atrocities were Khmer-on-Khmer, and throughout the country, survivors continue to live next door to the people who tortured or killed their family members.

The brutalities inflicted by the Khmers Rouges between 1975 and 1979 are not the only sources of Cambodia's contemporary ills. The war and strife that came before and after the Pol Pot era also contributed to poverty, political divisions, and other problems and have made reconciliation more difficult to achieve.

REASONS FOR CAUTIOUS OPTIMISM

Nevertheless, some factors in Cambodia appear to favor reconciliation at individual and societal levels. First, as emphasized in this chapter, past reconciliation efforts and the passage of time make Cambodia more "ripe" for genuine reconciliation than some other societies dealing with past atrocities. Second, the country's religious tradition is broadly conducive to a healing process that does not involve violence or extralegal retribution. Theravada Buddhism is the primary religion in Cambodia, and its basic teachings emphasize forgiveness. Buddhism is not inconsistent with the concept of criminal trials, but Buddhist principles of justice stress that vindictiveness is ended not by inflicting injury to others but by achieving self-control, attempting to forgive past injustices, and ceasing to be vengeful. Other religious traditions in Cambodia—such as Christianity and Islam—have also evolved in a manner that appears broadly consistent with a peaceful resolution to past injustices. One rarely hears a religious or community leader in Cambodia exhorting violence to deal with the past.

KEYS FOR THE ECCC

The ECCC has been entrusted with a prodigious set of tasks, and it is sometimes burdened with unrealistic expectations of what it can achieve. The Khmer Rouge trials certainly cannot cure all of the problems that flow from the cataclysm of Democratic Kampuchea and the many other wrongs committed in Cambodia over the past half century. They are also not enough to foster "total" reconciliation. Still, the ECCC has the potential in its remaining years of operation to advance reconciliation in Cambodia by providing a sense of justice and

A scene from a carving on a memorial in Battambang province. *Source: Documentation Center of Cambodia Archives.*

A scene from a carving on a memorial in Battambang province. *Source: Documentation Center of Cambodia Archives.*
(Right) A memorial in Battambang province. *Source: Documentation Center of Cambodia Archives.*

performing an important truth-telling function.

One key to the tribunal's success in advancing reconciliation—emphasized throughout this book—will be its ability to hold trials that respect due process and exude judicial and administrative integrity. The ECCC has also encountered some significant bumps in the road during its first three years of operations. It has proceeded at a higher cost and lower speed than originally anticipated, and it has been plagued by a variety of administrative deficiencies and irregularities.

Both the verdicts and the "truth" delivered by the tribunal will only be accepted to the extent that the ECCC is seen as a legitimate, well-run institution. Cambodians will not be an easy audience to satisfy in this regard. They are all too accustomed to a court system that frequently places money, power, and patronage above truth and justice. Surveys show that Cambodians have a dismal view of their judiciary. If the ECCC appears unfair or corrupt, the record it develops will carry little weight, and its verdicts will ring hollow. Corruption in particular has the potential to undermine the credibility of the court and its capacity to contribute meaningfully to the historical record. It needs to conduct itself in an exemplary fashion to fulfill its potential.

Another key to the ECCC's success, also stressed throughout this volume, will be to connect with ordinary people. Normal courts do not provide extensive public education or outreach functions, but the ECCC is not an ordinary court. Its activities need to be seen and understood by survivors to be effective. The ECCC cannot possibly inform and engage the public alone. It will need to continue partnering with NGOs and other supporting organizations to bring people to the court, hear their stories, and help address their grievances. By redoubling its commitment to the needs and interests of survivors and their children, the ECCC has the best chance to contribute to the personal and societal reconciliation that have been so long coveted in Cambodia.

---

[1] Many such definitions of reconciliation exist. See, e.g., SUZANNAH LINTON, RECONCILIATION IN CAMBODIA 106 (2004); Brandon Hamber and Gráinne Kelly, *Beyond Coexistence: Towards a Working Definition of Reconciliation*, in JOANNA R. QUINN, RECONCILIATION(S): TRANSITIONAL JUSTICE IN POST CONFLICT SOCIETIES 287-95 (Joanna R. Quinn, ed., 2009).

[2] See Karen Brouneus, *Reconciliation and Development*, FRIEDRICH-ELBERT-STIFTUNG DIALOGUE ON GLOBALIZATION, Nov. 2007, at 6.

[3] Desmond Tutu, *Foreword* to RECONCILIATION AFTER VIOLENT CONFLICT: A HANDBOOK 4 (David Bloomfield, Teresa Barnes, and Luc Huyse, eds., 2003).

[4] John Paul Lederach, Building Peace: Sustainable Reconciliation in Divided Societies 9 (1997).

[5] Lederach, *supra*, at 31.

[6] Craig Etcheson, Reconciliation in Cambodia: Theory and Practice 26-27 (2004).

[7] James L. Gibson, *Overcoming Apartheid: Can Truth Reconcile a Divided Nation?* 603 Annals Am. Acad. Pol. and Soc. Sci. 82-110 (2006).

[8] *See, e.g.*, Jaya Ramji, *Reclaiming Cambodian History: The Case for a Truth Commission*, 24 Fletcher Forum of World Aff 137 (2000).

[9] *See, e.g.*, Andrew Rigby, Justice and Reconciliation After the Violence 1-15 (2001); Martha Minow, Between Vengeance and Forgiveness: Facing History After Genocide and Mass Violence 1-23 (1998); Michelle Parlevliet, *Telling the Truth in the Wake of Mass Violence, in* People Building Peace 46-47 (European Centre for Conflict Prevention ed., 1999).

[10] Daniel Bar-Tal, *From Intractable Conflict Through Conflict Resolution to Reconciliation: Psychological Analysis*, 21 Pol. Psychology 356-362 (2000).

[11] Johan Galtung, *After Violence, Reconstruction, Reconciliation, and Resolution: Coping with Visible and Invisible Effects of War and Violence, in* Reconciliation, Justice, and Coexistence: Theory and Practice 3-4 (Mohammed Abu-Nimer, ed., 2001).

[12] *See* Louis Kriesberg, *Changing Forms of Coexistence, in* Reconciliation, Justice, and Coexistence, *supra*, at 47-64.

[13] Tutu, *supra* note 3, at 4.

[14] Etcheson, *supra* note 6, at 29.

[15] Linton, *supra* note 1, at 225-26.

[16] Etcheson, *supra* note 6, at 40-42.

[17] Evan Gottesman, Cambodia After the Khmer Rouge: Inside the Politics of Nation-Building 61-62 (2002).

[18] For further discussion of the PRK petitions, *see* William J. Schulte, *The History of the Renakse Petitions and their Significance to the ECCC Proceedings*, Searching for the Truth, Dec. 2007.

[19] Etcheson, *supra* note 6, at 43.

[20] A copy of the speech transcript is available at the Documentation Center of Cambodia. Translated by Sour Bunsou and quoted in Rachel Hughes, *Memory and Sovereignty in Post-1979 Cambodia: Choeung Ek and Local Genocide Memorials, in* Genocide in Cambodia and Rwanda: New Perspectives 267 (Susan E. Cook, ed., 2006).

[21] For a description of the K-5 program, *see* Gottesman, *supra* note 17, at 231-37.

[22] Sok-Kheang Ly, *State and Individual efforts to Bring about Reconciliation*, unpublished paper on file with the Documentation Center of Cambodia (Aug. 11, 2009).

[23] Craig Etcheson, After the Killing Fields: Lessons from the Cambodian Genocide 18 (2005).

[24] Margaret Slocomb, The People's Republic of Kampuchea 1979-1989: The Revolution After Pol Pot 242 (2003).

[25] *Id.*

[26] *See* Introduction to the Agreement on a Comprehensive Political Settlement of the Cambodia Conflict, Oct. 23, 1991.

[27] *See* Michael W. Doyle, *Authority and Elections in Cambodia, in* Keeping the Peace: Multidimentional UN Operations in Cambodia and El Salvador 156-58 (Michael W. Doyle et al., eds., 1997). Interestingly, Ieng Sary later claimed that in a 1999 meeting, Boutros Boutros-Ghali, the UN Secretary-General during the UNTAC years, acknowledged to him that the Paris Peace Agreement was "not thoroughly implemented" and that "national healing and reconciliation remained uncompleted." *See* Ieng Sary, Statement of the General Assembly, Session 2 of the Democratic National United Movement, Jan. 25, 1999, *available at* www.dccam.org/Tribunal/Documents/Ieng_Sary_Declaration_1999.htm.

[28] MENG-TRY EA, RECONCILIATION! IN CAMBODIA 4-6, 21-24 (2007). *See also* Héleyn Uñac, *The Tribunal's Broader Roles: Fostering Reconciliation, Peace, and Security*, in THE KHMER ROUGE TRIBUNAL 157-64 (John D. Ciorciari, ed., 2006).

[29] Youk Chhang, Speech for the Truman-Reagan Freedom Award, Washington, DC (Nov. 4, 2000), *available at* www.wccpd.org/news/news70.html.

[30] One notable exception was the Cambodian government's decision to try three former Khmer Rouge commanders for their roles in the 1994 abduction and murder of a trio of Western tourists. John Hall, *In the Shadow of the Khmer Rouge Tribunal: The Domestic Trials of Nuon Paet, Chhouk Rin and Sam Bith, and the Search for Judicial Legitimacy in Cambodia*, 20 COLUM. J. OF ASIAN L. 236-95 (2006).

[31] Kay Johnson and Ham Samnang, *Ieng Sary Warns of New Unrest Over KR Trial*, CAMBODIA DAILY, Feb. 5, 1999.

[32] Ek Madra, *Cambodia PM Rejects Wider Khmer Rouge Trials*, REUTERS, Mar. 31, 2009.

[33] Sok Khemara, *Sihonauk "Will Not Go" to Tribunal: Aid*, VOA KHMER, July 20, 2009; *Khmer King's Brother Opposes Trial*, KHEMERA TIMES, June 3, 2006, at 1.

[34] Seth Mydans, *Under Prodding, 2 Apologize for Cambodian Anguish*, N.Y. TIMES, Dec. 30, 1998.

[35] John Gittings, *Pol Pot Men Say Sorry for Killing Fieds*, GUARDIAN, Dec. 30, 1998.

[36] A 2001 study by international experts found a 28% prevalence of PTSD among over 600 Cambodians randomly surveyed in different parts of the country. Joop T.V. M. DeJong et al., *Lifetime Events and Posttraumatic Stress Disorder in 4 Postconflict Settings*, 286 J. AM. MED. ASS'N 555-562 (2001). A more recent study found an incidence of roughly 11%. Jeffrey Sonis et al., *Probable Posttraumatic Stress Disorder and Disability in Cambodia: Associations with Perceived Justice, Desire for Revenge, and Attitudes Toward the Khmer Rouge Trials*, 302 J. AM. MED. ASS'N 527-36 (2009). The Transcultural Psychosocial Organization has also reported a high incidence of PTSD in its studies of Khmer Rouge survivors and victims of torture. Some of its findings are reproduced in Documentation Center of Cambodia, VOT Project Final Report (2005), *available at* www.dccam.org/Projects/VOT/Fianl_Report_2005.pdf [sic].

[37] Mon Kunthear and Christopher Shay, *Few Resources for the Mentally Ill*, PHNOM PENH POST, July 23, 2009, *quoting* Kim Savoun, head of the mental health department at Cambodia's Ministry of Health.

[38] *See, e.g.*, Sopheap Chak, *Khmer Rouge Trials Will Not Bring Justice*, UPI ASIA, Apr. 15, 2009.

[39] PHUONG PHAM ET AL., SO WE WILL NEVER FORGET 3 (2009). Patrick Vinck, Mychelle Balthazard, Sokhom Hean, and Eric Stover co-authored this report by the Berkeley Human Rights Center.

[40] The introduction of a new genocide studies curriculum organized by the Ministry of Education and DC-Cam is a promising start. That curriculum will include a textbook published by DC-Cam. *See* KHAMBOLY DY, A HISTORY OF DEMOCRATIC KAMPUCHEA (1975-1979) (2007).

[41] Tara Urs, *Imagining Locally-Motivated Accountability for Mass Atrocities: Voices from Cambodia*, 7 SUR—INTERNATIONAL JOURNAL FOR HUMAN RIGHTS 62 (2007).

[42] DC-Cam has helped approximately 7,000 villagers from 24 provinces and cities revisit execution sites and observe court hearings at the ECCC. For more information on the Center's Living Documents Project, *see* www.dccam.org/Projects/Living_Doc/Living_Documents.htm.

[43] Outside reports, commentary, and live proceedings are widely available online. The Cambodia Tribunal Monitor website, developed by Northwestern University and DC-Cam, is one prominent example and contains footage of ECCC hearings. *See* www.cambodiatribunal.org.

[44] PHAM ET AL, *supra* note 39, at 38.

[45] Sonis et al., *supra* note 36, at 527.

[46] One example comes from a Rwandan woman named Anges, who testified against Clement Kayishema at the International Criminal Tribunal for Rwanda. She explained the intimidation she felt when confronting Kayishema, who was accused of orchestrating the

murder of her family members, and facing hostile questions from his defense lawyers. She recalled: "The moment I entered the court...I quickly noticed that something I hadn't thought about: there wasn't going to be anyone from Kibuye other than Kayishema in the courtroom, listening to what I was saying—they were all strangers...Once it came to Kayishema's lawyer's turn to question me, he was deliberately working on humiliating me and injuring my feelings. He asked me questions like 'how come you survived if Tutsis were being killed?'—as if the fact that I was alive meant that my testimony on the massacres of Tutsis was false." HELENA COBBAN, AMNESTY AFTER ATROCITY: HEALING NATIONS AFTER GENOCIDE AND WAR CRIMES 2 (2007).

[47] Geerteke Jansen, *Voices of Takéo: A Pilot Fear Assessment with Respect to Possible Witnesses of the Extraordinary Chambers in the Courts of Cambodia* 45 (Oct. 2006), report published online by the Documentation Center of Cambodia, *available at* www.dccam.org.

[48] PHAM ET AL., *supra* note 39, at 2.

[49] Terith Chy, *A Thousand Voices* 13 (Mar. 2009), report published online by the Documentation Center of Cambodia, *available at* www.dccam.org.

[50] *See* INTERNATIONAL REPUBLICAN INSTITUTE, SURVEY OF CAMBODIAN PUBLIC OPINION: JANUARY 25-FEBRUARY 26 (2008); CENTER FOR SOCIAL DEVELOPMENT, THE KHMER ROUGE AND NATIONAL RECONCILIATION: OPINIONS FROM THE CAMBODIANS (2002).

[51] PHAM ET AL., *supra* note 39, at 39.

[52] *Id.*

[53] *Id.* at 39-42.

[54] For a number of examples, *see* Sok-Kheang Ly, *Follow-Up Survey on National Reconciliation* (2007) (on file with the Documentation Center of Cambodia).

[55] *Id.*

[56] *See* Ly, *supra* note 54.

[57] Ian Harris, *'Onslaught on Beings': A Theravada Buddhist Perspective on Accountability for Crimes Committed in the Democratic Kampuchea, in* BRINGING THE KHMER ROUGE TO JUSTICE: PROSECUTING MASS VIOLENCE BEFORE THE CAMBODIAN COURTS 85-86 (Jaya Ramji and Beth Van Schaack, eds., 2005).

[58] *See* Ly, *supra* note 54.

[59] *See* Sok-Kheang Ly, *DC-Cam Field Report: Justice Under Surveillance* (May 2009), report published online by the Documentation Center of Cambodia, *available at* www.dccam.org.

[60] Sok-Kheang Ly, interviews with Ngao Ly, Tak Pes, Slem Sok, and Tort Chea in Bakan district, Pursat province (Aug. 2, 2009).

[61] Ly, *supra* note 59.

[62] Transcript of Trial Proceedings for Kaing Guek Eav, Case File No. 001/18-07-2007-ECCC/TC (July 30, 2009), at 69, 90.

[63] Chy, *supra* note 49, at 16.

ABOUT

YOUK CHHANG is the Executive Director of DC-Cam and has led the Center since its inception as an independent Cambodian NGO in January 1997. He is a survivor of the killing fields and received the Truman-Reagan Freedom Award from the Victims of Communism Memorial Foundation in Washington, DC in 2000. He was also named one of *Time* magazine's "60 Asian heroes" in 2006 and one of the "Time 100" most influential people in the world in 2007 for his stand against impunity in Cambodia and elsewhere.

TERITH CHY heads DC-Cam's Victim Participation Project, which seeks to enfranchise survivors of the Khmer Rouge regime in the tribunal process and to educate the public about the proceedings. In 2007-08, he was a Sohmen Fellow at the Office of the United Nations High Commissioner for Human Rights regional office for Southeast Asia in Bangkok. He holds an LL.M. in human rights law from Hong Kong University and a Certificate in International Humanitarian Law and International Justice from American University's Washington College of Law.

JOHN D. CIORCIARI is an Assistant Professor at the Gerald R. Ford School of Public Policy, University of Michigan, and Senior Legal Advisor to DC-Cam, which he has advised since 1999. He was a 2007-08 Shorenstein Fellow at the Asia-Pacific Research Center and 2008-09 National Fellow at the Hoover Institution, both at Stanford University. He has a J.D. from Harvard Law School and a D.Phil. in International Relations from Oxford University.

JOHN A. HALL is an Associate Professor of Law at the Chapman University School of Law. His research focuses on international law and human rights, particularly in Southeast Asia. Before becoming a human rights attorney, he taught history for ten years at Albion College. He holds a B.A. (Hons.) in American Studies from Sussex University, a D.Phil. in Modern History from Oxford University, and a J.D. from Stanford Law School, where he became the first student twice awarded the Carl Mason Franklin Prize in International Law.

ANNE HEINDEL is a Legal Advisor to DC-Cam. Before joining the Center in 2007, she served as assistant director of the War Crimes Research Office at American University's Washington College of Law. She has also worked as deputy convenor of a coalition of American NGOs supporting the International Criminal Court. She holds a J.D. from the University of California—San Francisco, Hastings College of Law, and an LL.M. in International Law from New York University School of Law.

SOK-KHEANG LY is co-head of the Living Documents Project at DC-Cam, which helps survivors of Democratic Kampuchea and other Cambodian citizens observe court proceedings and otherwise learn about the ECCC. He is also the manager of DC-Cam's Public Information Room, which facilitates research by students, scholars, and the general public about Khmer Rouge history. He holds an M.A. in Peace and Reconciliation Studies from Coventry University in the United Kingdom and is currently a Ph.D. candidate in that department. He has also received training from the Institute for International Criminal Investigations.

SARAH THOMAS is an Associate at a law firm in New York City. She was the 2008-09 David W. Leebron International Human Rights Fellow at DC-Cam, where she provided legal counsel to DC-Cam's Victim Participation Project. She continues to advise the Project. She has previously interned at the UN Office of the Legal Counsel, the International Justice Program at Human Rights Watch and the International Criminal Tribunal for the former Yugoslavia. She holds a J.D. from the Columbia University School of Law and an LL.B. from the London School of Economics.

(This page) Choeung Ek memorial. Photo by Piseth Phat. *Source: Documentation Center of Cambodia Archives.*
(Right) Construction of the Choeung Ek memorial. Source: Documentation Center of Cambodia Archives.

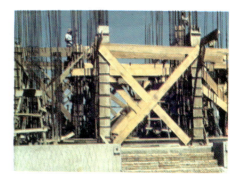

Construction of the Choeung Ek memorial. *Source: Documentation Center of Cambodia Archives.*